More Than Atonement

A Study in

GENETIC THEOLOGY

By

JOHN B. CHAMPION, M. A.
Professor of Christian Doctrine
Eastern Baptist Theological Seminary
Author of "The Living Atonement"; "The Virgin's Son"

"I came not to destroy but to fulfil."
"Till it be fulfilled in the Kingdom of God."
"On the third day I am perfected."
"For by one offering hath he perfected
for ever them that are sanctified."

"*The old order changeth, giving place to new,
And God fulfils Himself in many ways.*"
—*Tennyson*

WIPF & STOCK · Eugene, Oregon

Wipf and Stock Publishers
199 W 8th Ave, Suite 3
Eugene, OR 97401

More Than Atonement
A Study in Genetic Theology
By Champion, John B.
Softcover ISBN-13: 978-1-6667-4417-0
Hardcover ISBN-13: 978-1-6667-4418-7
eBook ISBN-13: 978-1-6667-4419-4
Publication date 4/1/2022
Previously published by The Evangelical Press, 1927

This edition is a scanned facsimile of the original edition published in 1927.

TO MY STUDENTS

PREFACE

THIS book contains the lectures which are being used in the study of Genetic Theology. They represent an attempt to set forth the Redemptive Work of Christ as the fontal doctrine of Christianity. Because the work is constructive rather than critical, it deals with that which makes Christianity the power of God unto salvation, rather than something else. Unless we have a theology of redemption from sin, it is worse than useless, a liability instead of an asset.

In setting forth Christ's Redemption from a new point of view—that of the fulfilment of the divine nature—I have tried to keep in mind some of the things in this connection recommended by Prof. Franklin Johnson. With some addition and considerable adaptation they are:

1. A fair and natural reproduction of the Scriptural teaching on this subject.

2. Avoiding iconoclasm toward time-honored interpretations which have helped in days gone by.

3. Shunning fragmentary treatment of Divine Personality that ignores one part and favors another.

4. Endeavoring to use the terms of experience and personality with a view to interpreting the fulfilment of personality.

5. Correlating genetically and generically the other great truths of Christianity which form the body of Christian doctrine.

6. Presenting the Godward and the manward aspects of Redemption as complementary, and that it makes a difference for both God and man.

7. The whole structure of Redemption founded and built upon the sacrifice of God in Christ's death, with an open view to all related divine sacrifice.

It has been many years since an interpretation of the Work of Christ has commanded general assent. I cherish the hope that the Fulfilment Interpretation may be of help to those seeking one that equally grips heart and head. It is surely wise to look for a view of the redeeming sacrifice of Christ in the light of its soul-satisfying and personality-making power.

Though some fifteen years of work have gone into this presentation, the author feels that it can be improved and strengthened at several points. Anything however imperfect that in any measure clears the way to a fuller appreciation of Christ as Redeemer is surely of value to those "in the Way."

I am indebted specially to three of my colleagues, Professor William W. Adams, Th.D., and Professor David Lee Jamison, LL.B., Professor Arthur Emerson Harris, D.D., for corrections in the text, and to one of the students, Rev. George Thomson, who has assisted also in the reading of the proof.

J. B. C.

Philadelphia, Pennsylvania.

CONTENTS

CHAPTER   PAGE

PART ONE — THE GENESIS OF CHRISTIAN THEOLOGY
- I. Genetic Theology 11
- II. Philosophy and Theology 23
- III. Thought and Spirit 34

PART TWO — DIVINE FULFILMENT
- IV. The Term Atonement 49
- V. A More Excellent Sacrifice 62
- VI. The Meaning of Fulfilment 77
- VII. Triune Divine Fulfilment 89
- VIII. Source and Substance 99
- IX. The Sacrificial Source 110
- X. The Spirit of Love 120
- XI. The Spirit of Fulfilment 129
- XII. Means and Method 141
- XIII. The Process of Fulfilment 151
- XIV. Sacrificial Self-Realization 165
- XV. The Cross of Christ 177
- XVI. The Extent of Fulfilment 190
- XVII. The Godward Effect 202
- XVIII. The Enablement of Fulfilment 214
- XIX. Sacrificial Enablement 223
- XX. The Fulfilment of Enablement 232
- XXI. Able Unto the Uttermost 239

PART THREE — THE NEED OF REDEMPTION
- XXII. The Fact of Sin 253
- XXIII. Varying Views of Sin 261
- XXIV. The Meaning of Sin 267
- XXV. The Godward Effect of Sin 274

CHAPTER		PAGE
XXVI.	Sin from Modern Viewpoints	282
XXVII.	Sin and Experience	289
XXVIII.	Sin's Treatment of Christ	296
XXIX.	Self-Realization in Sin	303
XXX.	Sin and Penalty	308

PART FOUR — REDEMPTION OF SELF-REALIZATION

XXXI.	Christian Personality	319
XXXII.	Christian Consciousness	331
XXXIII.	From Guilt to Justification	342
XXXIV.	Faith's Genesis and Exodus	352
XXXV.	The Sonship of Love	362
XXXVI.	The Riches of Sacrifice	372
XXXVII.	Neighborly Christianity	383
XXXVIII.	Education	394
XXXIX.	Freedom	403
XL.	Authority	415
XLI.	The Blood-Bought Church	428
XLII.	The Success of the Cross	442

Part One
The Genesis of Christian Theology

CHAPTER I

GENETIC THEOLOGY

THEOLOGY is religious truth set forth in formal order. Christian theology is the knowledge of God revealed in Jesus Christ, the orderly arrangement of Christian truth, the science of the Christian life in its natural and supernatural relations. Genetic theology is the science of the source of religion. In Christian theology it sets forth the genesis of the Christian life and its generic faith.

Science is as necessary in theology as elsewhere. And theology is as praiseworthy as any other science. Natural science often gains glory for that which does not belong to it. It is often lauded for its inventions. As a matter of fact most inventors are not scientists at all. However, the information gained by inventions and discoveries may be scientifically classified and given its place in the growing accumulation of scientific knowledge; but the task of the scientist is not that of inventing, but of verifying and arranging in exact order knowledge from any source. Theology, "the Queen of the sciences," least of all has need of inventing material. Its place is to clarify and systematize the great body of truth that is known about God, man, and the religious life.

I. The Effort to Belittle Theology

Very unwisely some imagine that to belittle and deride theology is for the help of religion. The theologians who do this cannot be of the best type, for no man can be a good workman who does not respect his work. Referring to this H. R. Mackintosh says:

"Dynamic Monachianism, we can see, has certain points of resemblance to modern liberal theories, and is on the whole a tolerably clear example of how often they are not the best theologians who profess to dispense with theology."[1]

Recently a well-known writer and editor has been arguing for what he calls untheological Christianity. The editor of another religious paper remarks that one might as well plead for a boneless body. This is simply the plea for unregulated, disorderly thinking; for untheological Christianity would be Christianity without its thought set in order; and there is no particular vice or danger in order.

The theologian presents an amusing spectacle when sawing off the limb he is sitting on, by telling the world how unnecessary he is. It has become the penchant of a certain type of preachers and writers to taboo theology on every occasion. All their skill is utilized to depreciate theology. A recent article says:

"Clearly a line must be drawn between religion and theology. One is the truth of life in its warmth and radiance, its joy and pathos; the other is a system of reasonings and conjectures, symbols and traditions by which a man seeks to justify, clarify, and interpret the faith by which he lives. Religion is poetry, theology is prose. It is the difference between a flower garden and a book of botany, a manual of astronomy and a sky full of stars. As one does not have to know the facts of botany to enjoy a bed of violets, so one does not need to be an adept in the mysteries of dogma in order to live the religious life."

Practically every statement in this is misstatement. The fair inference from it would be, since to little intelligence some satisfaction is possible, let us get along with as little intelligence as possible. Is not "the sky full of stars" vastly more enjoyment to the man versed in astronomy? Does not botanizing add to the enjoyment of the flower-bed? This man was himself botanizing when he identified the violets. Yet he pleads for ignorance as bliss.

To "draw a line" does not call for maligning. Religion is not "the truth of life": it is life itself. Theology is the truth of life verified and classified. Asserting that the theologian is "an adept in the mys-

---

1. The Doctrine of the Person of Christ, p. 149.

teries of dogma," is itself dogma without much mystery to it, and not of a very high order.

It is untrue to say that theology is "conjecture." No science can be that. Moreover theology may be as poetic as is "Paradise Lost"; but true religion is not all poetry by any means. Madame de Staël says: "A religious life is a struggle and not a hymn."

II. Christian Theology Not to Be Despised

Those making a business of decrying all theology have reason for adopting as their slogan: "We don't need theology; we need religion." Doubtless their theology has added to their need of religion. Be that as it may, their plea is proof positive of the need of the Christian religion that does not discount intelligence in orderly arrangement.

Of course, knowledge alone is not Christianity; but it is essential to it. Only ignorance or perversion can claim that knowledge is necessarily a hindrance to the Christian religion. It is nothing but sheer quackery to array religion and theology as naturally opposed to each other. It is the quack who derides medical science as naturally opposed to medical practice. Christianity cannot possibly be the worse for an orderly setting forth of its cardinal and fontal truths.

At bottom the trouble is not with theology at all, but with those who have ceased to hold the fundamental truths of Christian theology, without being candid enough to say so. To cover up their retreat they use this smoke-screen—"the hindrance of theology to religion." Their real objection is not to theology as theology, but to the theology which is founded on the Bible. This they would fain replace with the theology founded on the Babel of modern thought. They loudly decry all creeds; but they have a creed of their own; and to propagate it "they compass heaven and earth."

One of their choicest methods is to laugh down theology. They know there are not a few people with whom a loud laugh weighs more than a train-load of logic. This sort of laughter is an old story. When Jesus was here upon earth "going about doing good," He came one day into the home where the little daughter lay dead. The tumult of professional wailing was hushed long enough to hear Him say, "The child is not dead but is sleeping."[2] Utterly misunderstanding Him when thus interrupted in their business of weeping, the professional mourners "laughed him to scorn." Literally, they laughed him down. (Katagelao.) But He would not be laughed down. "And he put them all out." Then He raised the child from the dead; and forthwith great astonishment replaced the derisive laughter. Would to God that today might see a similar replacement!

Because utterly misunderstanding the theology of Christ's redemption from death in sin, the unbelieving world would laugh it down. Often quoted is the saying, "Laugh and the world laughs with you." In return we need not laugh with the world when it laughs at the highest order of truth that has been revealed to the mind of man. Better that we should "weep alone" because the world and so many of its teachers know so little of Jesus Christ and the theology of His Redemption.

III. That in Theology Never to Be Forgotten

"In the beginning God,"—and creation came forth. "In the beginning was the Word,"—and revelation came forth, the revelation of Redemption. There was no fiat creation in the sense that all God did, was to speak the magic word, and magically the worlds sprang into existence. The Eastern or Semitic mind naturally thought of the word as the symbol of power, just as they took a name to mean what an individual shows or will manifest himself to be.

In a similar way "the Word made flesh," does not mean a magic redemption. The cost of suffering was

---

[2]. It is worthy of note that later on, after the death of Lazarus, Jesus spoke in precisely the same way of death as a sleep In the presence of His power of resurrection any of the dead are but asleep As easy for Him to awaken them from death as for us to awaken a child from sleep

to be paid to the uttermost. It cost God a tremendous amount of power to make the universe. Matter, we are told, is but His Almightiness stored up. And what shall we say of the ether filling all space, and though structureless and atomless yet able to vibrate with waves of light! If the First Genesis was in every way more costly to God than we are able to estimate, so was the Second Genesis. The New Creation in Christ Jesus has its mysteries and vastnesses reaching further than those of the universe, visible and invisible. Its story of divine cost we call the Gospel.

The heart of the Old Testament lies in the meaning of the name "Jehovah." It means, not "I am," but "I will be." It was not ontology, not existence, but promise of revelation. Jehovah, Davidson says,

"is not an ontological name, but a redemptive one . . . What He will show Himself to be to those in covenant with Him . . . I do not think there is in the Hebrew Bible a case of the imperfect of this verb having the sense of the English present. The imperfect must be rendered, 'I will be.' " [3]

The challenge of Davidson to find a case where the Hebrew imperfect of this verb "to be" means the present, remains unanswered. In His name as "Jehovah," God was announcing the coming manifestations of Himself. It meant, not "I am an existence," but "I will be revealed." It is in the emphatic form of repetition. "I will be, (most emphatically) I will be manifest."

The fulfilment of this name of promise began when Jehovah manifested Himself in the deliverance of the chosen people from Egypt. This was but preparatory to other and successive manifestations leading up to the consummation of revelation in Jehovah-Jesus, "God manifest in the flesh." The name "Jehovah" was really the promise of the Incarnation and the Redemption that was to follow it. The prophetic vow in the name "Jehovah" was fulfilled in Christ crucified

---

3. The Theology of the Old Testament, pp. 47, 55.

and risen from the dead as the Saviour of the whole world.

The heart of the New Testament lies in the meaning of the name "Jesus." This He was called in view of the promise, "He shall save his people from their sins." In Christianity the great outstanding thing is *salvation from sin*.

Unquestionably man is a sinner. The "one thing needful" is his salvation. That can never be put in a second place without denaturing Christianity, not to say, de-Christianizing it. Theology can rightfully lay claim to being Christian only as it features as its fundamental truth man's deliverance from iniquity by Jesus Christ.

In the theological world a serious and recurrent trouble is the type of theologian who has forgotten "the rock from which he has been hewn, and the hole of the pit from which he has been digged." Much of salvation itself is lost when the consciousness of it is lost, when the remembrance of it is gone.

The less a man counts himself a sinner saved by grace, the poorer theologian he becomes, the more he is something else than a theologian. For us all a thundering theological "Recessional" is ever needed, "Lest we forget, lest we forget." To forget this one thing paramount, is to forget the soul, substance, foundation, and genesis of all Christian theology.

IV. THE THEOLOGY OF SUPERNATURAL SALVATION

Christ as the Supernatural Word reveals His supernatural power to save. Men vainly talk of excluding the miracles from the Gospel, not realizing that the words of Christ are even more miraculous than any of His deeds. His revelation is as deeply supernatural as his Person.

A supernatural salvation is the only kind fully competent to meet man's need. He is a creature of two worlds, the natural and the supernatural. He has capacity for God; and God is nothing if not supernatural.

Religion would not be possible but for man's capacity for the supernatural. Those objecting to the supernatural are really objecting to the possibility and the genius of all true religion.

Sin puts us out of adjustment with the supernatural; yet our need of it is insistent. Salvation from sin must arise there or nowhere. One task of the theologian is to state helpfully the relation between the natural and the supernatural; for divine deliverance of necessity taking its rise in the supernatural needs to flow down into the natural.

Salvation like any other miracle must take place in the natural realm. Elsewhere it would not be a miracle. Heaven has never seen a miracle. What is supernatural here, is natural there.

The false antithesis between the natural and the supernatural is bound to be asserted as long as the realm of nature is conceived of as wholly apart from God as a Person. Anent this Bowne says:

"In the new conception the supernatural is nothing foreign to nature and making occasional raids into nature in order to reveal itself, but, so far as nature as a whole is concerned, the supernatural is the ever-present ground and administrator of nature and nature is simply the form under which the Supreme Reason and Will manifest themselves."[4]

Redemption is therefore no unwelcome and unwarranted intrusion of the supernatural into the natural. It is rather God doing for us by the supernatural what by the natural He could not do. What the natural could not do in that it was weak, God by the supernatural has done.

If the natural could have saved us, no supernatural salvation would have intervened. Blessed be such intervention! It is the intervention of necessity, not of intrusion. The supernatural set forth in the Christian revelation never duplicates, displaces, or needlessly interferes with the natural.

Salvation is made possible by the Supernatural Per-

---

4. The Immanence of God, p. 17

son savingly relating Himself to human persons. Here we come upon the genetic truth of the supernatural realm, namely, that God is a personal existence. Reduce Deity to impersonality, and the whole supernatural world vanishes.

If the nature of God be not personal, His order of existence is lower than ours,—which is but saying that He is not God. Personality is surely the highest conceivable form of existence. Since the personal is the highest conceivable category of human thought, the super-personal is as impossible to it as super-Deity. Says Snowden:

"Personality is the only true and worthy view of God . . . Personality in man is a reflection of the same power in the First Cause of man, and nature itself reflects the same image. Religion and revelation focus their light upon the same truth. This view is the only adequate explanation of the universe. Take a supreme Personality out of the world, and it has no inner light and meaning and no originating and sustaining cause. Put this Personality at the center of the universe and immanent in it, and it is at once lighted up as a glorious temple of science and art and religion. Deprive God of personality, and he instantly sinks below his conscious creatures or evanescent manifestations of mind and becomes a fearful specter of unconscious fate." [5]

An impersonal God is utterly incapable of filling the place of the God that Jesus revealed. A lower level of existence than our own could not be looked to for salvation. Grant that God is personal and that He made us, and the cause is adequate to the effect and can be the cause of our salvation also.

The powers and privileges of personality in the Deity provide for the whole supernatural realm and for the salvation that reveals its highest and best. The question of a supernatural salvation is therefore the question whether God is God, a Being in the highest order of existence, namely, absolute personality.

As the worst thing that can be done to man is to deify him, the worst thing that can be done to God is to de-

---
5. The Personality of God, p. 134.

personalize Him. Take away the personality of God, and the meaning of the Incarnation is gone. Take away the Incarnation, and the possibility of Redemption is gone. Take away Redemption and the heart of the Gospel is gone; and all that is left to poor sinners is but the misery of utter hopelessness, an overwhelming deluge of despair engulfing this weary world.

V. THE GENETIC FACT OF CHRISTIAN THEOLOGY

The Bible is naturally the textbook on the genesis of Christianity. It makes clear that all Christian beginnings reach back into the supernatural realm of the Personal God of Redemption. Holy Writ has its hallowed hold on the human heart because the things man most needs, are therein revealed. Its Great Gospel of God in Christ and the Love that died on the Cross for our sins, is too true to our need to be flouted as "cunningly devised fables."

The Scriptures are focussed on the genetic fact that the death of Christ is the birth of Redemption. But for the sacrifice of Calvary Christianity could not have originated as a world-religion. The Cross of Christ belongs not only to the whole world but to the whole of man's eternity. Its wrappings of time and place have within them the everlasting substance of eternal importance, because it is the saving sacrifice of God in the death of His Son for the sin of the world.

Divine revelation pictures the dimensions of human salvation as of such extent that makes it appear the greatest problem that God ever faced. It took His greatest sacrifice possible to achieve perfect Redemption. Then sin was put away in such a way that it could no longer prevent man's self-fulfilment in God. That which solved this foremost problem of the universe, is the foremost fact of a redemptive theology. Of necessity Christianity takes its rise there; and the theology setting it forth must begin there. So Christian theology takes its rise where the Christian life takes its rise. Both have the same gracious genesis.

While the grace of God in the Incarnation was infinitely wondrous, the grace that fully solved sin's problem was that which was prepared for by the Incarnation—the grace of the sacrifice of the death on the Cross. The direct and immediate means of our salvation came into being there; and the grace of the Incarnation led the way to the grace of God that provided the means of our Redemption.

VI. THE GENETIC FACT OF SIN

Looking at the genesis of Christian theology from another point of view, it has its beginning in the Redemption that adequately recognizes the fact and seriousness of sin. Medical science begins by recognizing the fact of sickness. Only a scienceless science could offer its healing by denying the need of healing and the fact that there is anything to heal. Only a Christless Christianity could offer salvation by denying the need of salvation and the fact of anything to be saved from. Such scienceless science of Christless Christianity is farthest of all removed from the true, because it denies most that Christianity asserts and asserts most that Christianity denies.

If for all physical ills there were one great cure absolutely sure, it would be the greatest fact of medical science and the genesis of medical practice. Even so, the starting point of Christian theology is Redemption's sure cure of sin. In Jesus Christ is the one great sovereign remedy for iniquity. This is an established fact of Christianity. The Great Physician cures by the transfusion of His blood into human veins. "The Redemption that is in Christ Jesus," is the beginning and perpetuation of the life and health He gives. Of necessity genetic theology begins with Christ's redemptive work—with that which made it redemptive, the divine death-cure of sin.

It is an old adage that a stream cannot rise higher than its source. Because Christian theology begins with the supernatural remedy for sin, it does not need to rise higher than its source. A better source it could not have and from a higher level it could not come. Any theology which has its source below the divine deliverance from sin, would need to rise higher than its source to be any good at all. Every system of theological thought flowing forth from a lower level than the sacrificial death of God's Son is bound sooner or later to prove a mirage of disappointment.

VII. THE DEVOTIONAL GENESIS OF CHRISTIAN THEOLOGY

Salvation by culture instead of by Christ is a delusion. Culture has its place; but its place is not that of curing the leprosy of sin. The art of a purely cultural religion may be as beautiful as a mausoleum in a cemetery; but it is never other than a total stranger to the art of raising the dead. This Christ's salvation does—it enables the dead in sin to live again, "to walk in newness of life."

The genesis of Christian theology takes place at the same time or immediately following the genesis of the Christian life. Both come into being whenever a soul comes to know God in Christ. The originating facts of the Christian life necessarily become known in its very beginning. The response to these facts by Christian devotion is the first evidence of life in Christ.

Each Christian life has its own experience and its own theology. At first it is simply the devotional story of the initial acquaintance with Jesus Christ as Saviour. From then on it normally develops into the passion and practice of bearing witness to Christ. This is one of the most important aspects of the Christian life.

Devotion discovers the deepest theological significance in the death of Christ being appointed of heaven. This explains why it has the pull and power of heaven in it, why first and last it draws devotion to it. Fully realizing this, it might be true of the devotion of us all, as was said of woman's devotion to the Saviour:

> "Not she with trait'rous kiss her Saviour stung,
> Not she denied Him with unholy tongue;
> She while apostles shrank, could danger brave,
> Last at His Cross and earliest at His grave."

The devotion born of heaven inspires such heavenly devotion. That born of earth, be it a theology or a religion, cannot lift higher than itself. When the Son of Man was "lifted up," it was the supreme lifting power of divine sacrifice then lifting the whole weight of human sin. Then and there it instituted divine Redemption. The mightiest might of the Almighty went into and remains within that "power of God unto salvation to every one that believeth." It was strong enough to burst the bands of death and bring forth a deathless Redeemer who gives His eternal life to them who trust Him. No other devotion is appropriate to respond and witness to Him who is able to keep us from falling, lift our souls to heaven, present us faultless before the Great White Throne, and bring together in His own world of divine felicity and fellowship the broken fragments of the circle of our loves on earth and build them into His own Being!

"What a world were this,
How unendurable its weight, if they
Whom death hath sundered, did not meet again!"

CHAPTER II

PHILOSOPHY AND THEOLOGY

PHILOSOPHY is of the mind: theology is of the soul. The former does its work with the rational faculty; but the latter expresses the thought of the entire life of personality in God. Much that today passes as theology is really philosophy. It takes more than mere reasoning about religious matters to produce theology. Whenever philosophy displaces theology, the foundational facts of the religious life are sure to be ignored, forgotten, or forsaken.

One of the dangers during many centuries which has menaced Christianity, has been the substitution of philosophic theories for the facts of the Christian life. When personal relation to Jesus Christ is replaced with the speculations of philosophy, barrenness and atrophy take the place of life and growth.

The Christian life never begins or exists in the mind alone. For this reason no philosophy is competent to cover all its territory. Even the best philosophic system is not sufficient to carry the full weight of Christianity. The rationality of philosophy is not enough to measure it. Reason alone is not adequate to interpret such matters as faith, love, will, hope, purpose, and personality.

I. No Genesis of Religion in Philosophy

The genetic facts of the Christian life are those sufficient for its beginning. They are the initial truths it starts with and may abide in. They are the substance of all successful evangelistic messages. As a rule strongly intellectual preachers have little success in winning converts. They are more than likely to depend upon their strength of thinking rather than upon the simple facts or truths which originate the Christian life. The open secret of great strength in reaching the unsaved lies in the simplicity which depends on the genetic truths of Christianity to do their work.

From a mental Samson the Delilah of pride finds no trouble in shearing off the talisman of evangelistic strength. Loss of vision follows, and then the preacher turns his pulpit into a pagan mill grinding out its blind philosophy. Any pulpit philosophy is essentially pagan that is without the vision of the Christian message to the lost.

Not our theorizing upon the genetic truth of Christianity, but the truth itself is the chosen instrument of the Holy Spirit in reaching and regenerating souls. As Alexander Maclaren said: "Hearts are more surely to be won by showing them Jesus crucified, than by our comments on the sight." Passion, passion for souls, consuming passion for their salvation saves us to simple faith in Christ as Saviour.

Times without number it has been proved that the converting power of Christianity lies in telling "the old, old story" of the life-originating facts "of Jesus and His love." For some reason the Holy Spirit has never cared as much for our speculation about these facts as for the facts themselves. Perhaps the speculative mind takes itself too seriously. In any case the spirit of speculative philosophy is but a dead substitute for the life-giving Spirit of God. Any philosophy which denies the need of evangelism, conversion and regeneration by the Holy Spirit bears exactly the same relation to vital Christianity that any other such hostile weapon does.

If philosophy insists on having its word on this matter, let it be the pragmatic philosophy which inquires as to what works. Jesus Himself has settled this matter. "This is the work of God, that ye believe on him whom he (the Father) hath sent." The first work is faith in Him as Saviour. Then all works to follow grow out of the same faith. The pragmatic question is not how this appears to human reason, but what faith the Holy Spirit uses and blesses to originate and relate the Christian life.

As at Pentecost the human tongue is useless without the tongue of flame, even so the tongue of flame needs the human tongue. But the tongue of flame never accompanies the human tongue unless the latter is prayerfully subservient to the former in passion and message. The mind and soul all aflame with the thought and zeal of the Holy Spirit are fitted to speak for Christ as well as by Him.

There is a deep constitutional reason why the Holy Spirit uses genetic faith instead of mere reason. No personal relation can be formed by coming to Christ reason-first, instead of faith-first; and it is through personal relation with Him that the saving power is imparted to him who needs it.

Like everything else, philosophy is all right in its place. Its place, however, is never that of originating the religious life. No one ever found salvation by swallowing the rationalizations of philosophy. Not a soul has ever been regenerated by the speculative spirit. The wings of philosophy waft no sinners to heaven.

What then, we may inquire, is instrumentally efficient in saving men unto life in God? From the beginning there has been a trinity of means which succeed. These are, the Holy Spirit, the Genetic Truth, and a human interpreter. "How shall they hear without a preacher?" These three may still be depended on to work the genesis of the Christian life in a human soul. The ultimate means is, of course, the Christ Himself. From Him the Christian life is imparted.

II. CHRIST THE GENETIC TRUTH OF CHRISTIANITY

We have said that it is not our comments on the genetic facts but the relating of the facts themselves that proves sufficient and efficient. The question may be raised, Why then any interpretation of them at all? Because the beginning of a life is not all. These initiatory facts have within them inexhaustible meaning for the life which is to follow. Besides they have their associate facts; otherwise they would not be initial. Trustworthy interpretation links all the facts and truths together, and presents them as fast as the Christian life is able to receive them.

The facts are many: the Truth is one. What Christ has done for sinners, what He has achieved for us by His sacrificial death makes Him the First Fact of Christianity. To this all other truths of the Christian life are constitutionally related. In Him all truths hold together. What vast range of truths and deep meaning are yet to be unfolded in the sacrifice of His birth and His death! Christ is not only the power of origination: He is the consummation of the life He imparts. He is as truly the Omega as the Alpha of the Christian life. *We have never really begun with Him, if we can ever dispense with Him.* When once He finds us, we are His and He is ours—forever.

"Thou, O Christ, art all I want;
More than all in thee I find."

What we have said about the Son, can be said about the Spirit also. We must begin with Him in such a way as to have Him unto the end. The Holy Spirit is ever indispensable to the Christian life. Not only is He the Spirit of regeneration; He is also the Spirit of sanctification and interpretation unto the end of holy service and growth in grace.

Only Christ's spirit can really serve Him. Only His Spirit can really interpret him. Only His Spirit can really defend Him. And He has no Spirit but the Holy Spirit. As to the interpretations of the Holy Spirit, they may be recognized by this distinctive mark—they always go into the facts about Christ, never overlay them, and never forsake them.

When in this hostile world it comes to defending Christ, Christianity's most convincing apologetic is its energetic; and its most conclusive energetic is "the power of God unto salvation." A theology dead to the power and passion of Christ to save, is itself too dead to save, and not worth it. A preacher of passion and power must receive both from the Holy Spirit. What can generate in the soul such power as that of the Spirit of God? To save the lost there is no other source of power than the empowerment of the Holy Spirit.

III. THE GENESIS OF CHRISTIAN THEOLOGY IN CHRISTIAN EXPERIENCE

A theologian who personally knows the saving power of Christ, and lives the Christian life by means of it, is not likely to conjure up a theology of inventions and vagaries—all so needless and so useless. "Knowledge" still "puffs up." A tiny bit of pride would sacrifice the whole of Christianity to its own glory. Intellectual pride seeks to substitute its self-importance. There is the false theology which has "sought out many inventions." This is no railing accusation.

For the originating truth of Christianity the modern inventions and substitutions of "something just as good," remind one of the proverbial druggist who happens to be without the desired medicine in stock. The serious trouble with Modernism is that it has forsaken the only body of facts which has ever worked the work of God in the salvation of souls. It has substituted ideas that have never yet brought peace to the heart or salvation to the soul.

There can be no Christian theology without Christian experience; and that is not Christian experience which is based on the denial of the need of it in its fundamental aspect of redemption by the death of Christ. Genetic theology of necessity begins where God began, namely, in the redemption of sinners. Undoubtedly the foundation of salvation God laid in the death of His Son. "Other foundation can no man lay." The oft repeated storm-testings of time have abundantly shown that, "All other ground is sinking sand." All substitute foundations have but quicksand to rest upon. To build on them is the double folly—in superstructure as well as in foundation. The world needs to be saved from the colossal blunder of accepting these.

The ever-multiplying number of rival faiths and salvationless religions demand that we "cry aloud and spare not." The counterfeit christs must not pass unchallenged. They should be stripped bare of their disguises. But it is a most unwelcome task; yet faithfulness to Christ and humanity must not sidestep it, because it is unpleasant work. Christ's sacrifice was not very pleasant work; and He faced and fulfilled it.

IV. THEOLOGY AS A SCIENCE

Science proves itself genuine when loyal to fact. Fake science must "fake its facts." Genetic theology must prove its genuineness by its loyalty to the facts of the genesis of Christianity. It looks for the originating truths.

To seek the origin of Christianity in modern ideas rather than in historic facts would not be scientific procedure, for manifestly *the original facts are the originating facts*. To allege that certain ideas should have been foundational in Christianity, is to desert history and science completely.

Explaining away the origin of Christianity need never be mistaken for explaining it; yet sometimes this takes place. Such explaining away should never be attempted in the name of science, for true science has neither part nor lot in it. Modern theology wears the livery of science in which to serve philosophic theory. Nowhere is there less science than in some of the claims made for science; and nowhere is there less theology than in some of that called modern. Endless philosophic fogbanks and monkey meanderings therein are set forth as the most up-to-date order of scientific theology.

Where invention begins, science ends. No science can be a fact-factory. Where speculation begins, theology ends. No theology can long succeed in making the stones of philosophy look like the loaves of Christianity. Hungry folk prefer bread; and God is the Great Iconoclast to all deceptions. No mask can stand the touch of His hand.

Though accepting evolution, Professor Henry Churchill King protests against "Philosophic speculation masquerading as science"[1]; yet this is exactly what is done when evolution is called a scientific theory. President Mullins having shown evolution to be the old philosophic doctrine of Continuity, says:

"But when they get through with religion, and in particular the Christian religion, it is at the point of extinction. They do with it what certain wasps do with caterpillars, in providing food for their young. They skilfully sting the caterpillar, and paralyze the motor nerve centers. Thus they keep it alive as food, and destroy its ability to run away. The larvae then devour the helpless victim at their leisure. In religion the law of continuity is the sting. Applied in the personal and spiritual sphere, it paralyzes the nerve centers of religion. Those centers, freedom, personality, God, immortality, lose their meaning. Then comes the end of religion. Thus scientific or philosophic absolutism, not genuine science, is converting, or attempting to convert, Christianity into food to satisfy its voracious but abnormal appetite."[2]

Being a multi-millionaire in the possession of the riches of Christian truth, the theologian has no need to counterfeit. Well does he know that the might of the miraculous power is with the truth only. "This man does many miracles. What do we?" Certainly the Gospel of Christ's Redemption keeps on doing many miracles. What do imitations, inventions, and substitutions? The currency from the mint of the theological mind cannot long escape the assay that tests its worth. God's very existence is pledge that only the theology of His own triumphant truths can represent Him in result.

V. REGENERATE THEOLOGY

The birth of every God-born soul is also the birth of a theology. No one can be really regenerated and not think about Jesus Christ. And no regenerated person

---
1. Reconstruction in Theology, p. 62.
2. Christianity at the Cross Roads, p. 171.

can think about Him and not desire that others come to know Him. The effort in some way to make Him known must state what He has done for the saved soul. Every testimony to the saving power of Christ expresses a theology.

While no one more needs regeneration than the theologian to be such, he may at times produce unregenerate presentations of theology. As even a regenerated man may sin, so a regenerated theologian may occasionally put forth some very unregenerate theology. In this matter as in others no one can be always flawless. While a truly Christian theologian may err theologically, there is always the corrective force in the genetic bond binding him to Christ and bringing him back to the true fount of Christian theology.

As there is but one origin of the life truly Christian, so there is but one origin of the theology truly Christian. The genesis of the one leads to the genesis of the other: rather they are identical. "Being born again, not of perishable seed, but of imperishable through the Word of God which lives and abides." Since the theologian is one reborn of the Word, it lives and abides in him so reborn. And a theology in which the very Word of God lives and abides, cannot go far astray.

God made man capable of knowing Him; and he is reborn in coming to know Him. The birth of faith means the beginning of a life. Faith in God begins with hearing and believing His Word. If He had not spoken to us, He would have been the Unknown God. Because His Word can never pass away, as Christ Himself said, faith in it grows on eternally. Eternal life is possible because eternal faith is possible. *Christianity is the eternal life of an eternal faith in the Eternal Word.*

Since life is correspondence with environment, the Word makes possible correspondence with the environment of God. Eternal correspondence with God is through eternal faith in His imperishable Word. The sheep of the Great Shepherd hear His voice and know it. So God's children recognize His Word, know it and know Him by means of it.

For the infinitely important work of regeneration no truth fits the hand of the Holy Spirit, so to speak, like that of Holy Writ. Between the two works of the Spirit, the inspiration of the Scriptures and the regeneration of men, there is a strong bond of affinity and unity. The Spirit-born soul and the Word-fed life are in a divine alliance from the beginning. Receiving the Word of God is an experience of God; and any experience of God must be in keeping with the Word of God. Experience which conflicts with, or thought that contradicts the teachings of Holy Writ, has another inspirer than the Holy Spirit, for He cannot contradict or conflict with Himself.

The Paraclete Presence uses His own means to impart the knowledge of God. His infinite passion is to bring men to know God in Christ. God has given the Holy Scriptures for the purpose of our coming into touch with the reality of the Spirit and Mind of Christ. The Christian life is a reciprocity with this reality. Christian experience is the knowledge of the reality of God in Redemption. As regeneration is not idealistic or theoretic, the life resulting from it has actual knowledge of divine reality. Its experience is the knowledge of God at work in the soul. The genesis of reality in theology begins with the reality of knowing God in Christ. He is the genetic reality of Redemption.[3]

VI. THE THEOLOGICAL LIFE

The theological life knows God on its own account, and witnesses to this fact. It knows Him and is known of Him. This is its meaning, its privilege and joy. Living the God-knowing life one not only sees what God has done for him, he also sees God in it and through it; and thus he comes to bear witness to the God whose glory it is to bless the needy. This un-

---

[3]. Baldwin's "Genetic Theory of Reality" in what he calls "Pancalism" is a fair sample of theoretical genesis.

selfish, sacrificial glory of God realized by and in the human soul is a worthy source of Christian theology. It finds its genesis in "Beholding the glory of God in the face of Jesus Christ."

No soul born from above is ever found blind or deaf or dumb. Being begotten of the Holy Spirit it is thereby made alive to all that may be seen and heard and experienced of God in the Christian life. "One thing I know; whereas I was blind, now I see," said he whose power of vision had just been created. His blind eyes had been touched by the hand of their Maker, and they awoke to sight.

This theological fact that God had given him sight, was the beginning of a theology, a theology of experience. Unspeakably happy because he had received his sight, this man's joy was a spring of thought about it. The joy of the Lord is our strength of thought about Him. The man receiving his sight did not stop with the thought of this work of God upon him. Spirit-led he then passed on to the inevitable inference about Him who was God's agent in the miracle. Two things—a theological fact and its supernatural implication—and lo! a theological system had begun. Rudimentary as it then was, there is more real theology in it than in acres of speculation about it. Acreage counts for nothing in a Sahara.

That the genesis of this man's theology had actually taken place, was evidenced by its immediate growth and his hunger to know more about Him who had helped him so wondrously. In the lives of all Christians their theology at this stage is systematized by the providential order of Christian experience. The orderly way God always takes in the life which has become His, secures an orderly accumulation and presentation of this divine knowledge.

As every tree declares its nature in bark, leaf, or fruit, so the theological or God-knowing life bears witness in its own way to its own nature. No pear tree puts forth fig leaves. No fig tree puts forth thorn tree leaves. Nature so fully believes in itself, it is never ashamed to witness to its identity. This is its genetic theology. Even so the nature that has come into being by knowing Jesus Christ as Saviour and Lord, will normally be true to itself in the fruit of its profession. Its acquaintance with God and the life He gives, will manifest itself generically.

Any orderly statement of a man's knowledge of God, be it written or spoken, is his theology. Nature is nature because it can be depended on, not only to witness to its kind, but also to bring forth after its kind. The divine nature in man can also be depended on not only to declare itself, but also to bring forth a theology after its kind.

CHAPTER III

THOUGHT AND SPIRIT

HORACE BUSHNELL said: "Theology can never be a science because of the infirmities of language." This, however, would apply equally to all the sciences. Language is no more infirm and unstable in theology than elsewhere. The fluid nature of human terms and the looseness or lack of precision in the use of them make exact science in any subject a difficult matter.

Since theology is one of the sciences, both the privileges and the responsibilities of science should be recognized in its field. It must be granted that no one can be an authority in any science, unless in its own field he has sufficient acquaintance so to be. In this matter our newspapers are utter anarchists. Because some man has won fame as an inventor, manufacturer, or some other non-theological pursuit, they set him up as an authority on any question of theology. But the success of an Edison or a Burbank hardly constitutes them authorities in theology. This exploitation in the interest of newspaper shekels denies the rights and privileges of theology as a science.

As to responsibilities, in theology as in any other science the exactness of verification is desirable wherever possible. For example, in treating the subject of the genesis of theology, its genetic facts or truths should be verified. To be scientifically exact the theologian should begin, not according to an order of formal logic, but with the truth which has saved him, and thus made his theology possible. Every saved life can give some account of its origin. Doing this produces its genetic theology.

The genetic truth of Christianity is personal. Jesus said, "I am the truth." He is God's Great Genetic

Fact. He is the great genetic truth of Creation as well as of Salvation. The genetic experience of Christianity is, of course, personal. A Christian might be defined as one who knows by experience the reality of Christ's redemption from sin. The testimony of every man liberated by divine Redemption is, "Thank God, it works!" But each person must verify this for himself; otherwise he is a theorist instead of a theologian.

I. THE VERIFIED GENESIS OF CHRISTIAN EXPERIENCE

That Jesus Christ lived a sinless life and died a sin-bearing death, is not hypothesis but history. While the science of history is one thing, the correlate experience of it is another. The experience corroborating the power of Christ's redemptive death has long been taking place. History means vastly more to us when its statements are verified and validated by present-day experience.

It is unreasonable to expect facts of theology not experimental in nature to be verified in experience. But the genesis of the Christian life is a matter of experience. That the power of Christ is sufficient to save, is the general experience of Christians. And this gives uniformity to the theology setting it forth.

The efficiency of Christ as a Saviour and the efficacy of His death are more than correlate; they are identical. All the virtue of His death resides in Him, and is communicated by Him. Never was there such mastery over sin as in His death, because never until then was there such a sin to master. This we shall more fully present later.

There is at least one thing to which Christian experience fully attests, namely, that God blesses faith in the sacrificial death of His Son, dwells in the human soul because of this faith, and imparts His Holy Spirit in response to it *as to no other faith*. No fact of Christian experience is better verified than the response of the Spirit of God to faith in the death of the Son of God.

As the sinlessness of Jesus Christ proved invincible during His days on earth, and even in His death by sin, so has the historicity of this sinlessness proved unassailable ever since. What enemies on the ground could not do in this matter, is not likely to be done by those at a far distance. The Redeemer can still look His enemies in the face and say, "Which of you convicteth me of sin?"

To faith in His sin-suffering death the Sinless One is somehow enabled to communicate His power to master sin. Each true Christian experience does verify this fact; and this verification is vastly important. It is infinitely more than winning an argument: it is winning the blood-bought victory over the first and worst enemy; for all the problems of human life are grounded in the problem of overcoming sin. Life has but one problem—how to master iniquity.

If Jesus had not mastered sin, to whom would we look for the solution of this greatest of all problems? Must we not see that there never would have been any Christian theology at all but for the success of Jesus Christ as a Saviour? In reality Christian theology is a verification of the efficiency of the Redeemer and the efficacy of His death?

As already remarked, there are many theological statements not yet verifiable in experience which concern us profoundly. For example, there is the story of creation, the promise of Christ's Second Coming, the Resurrection, the life beyond, and the world to come. But now we are able to verify Jesus' power to save. For the rest we wait in "the hope that maketh not ashamed."

Christianity could never have made a beginning with facts not verifiable in experience. "Taste and see," has always been God's offer of verification. "Believe and ye shall have," can be put to the test any day. In days of disintegration one should emphasize his verified knowledge of Jesus' power to save. This the Apostle John did in the disturbing days of Gnosticism. "We know," is an oft repeated expression in his Epistles.

What a flame of positive assurance lit up that mighty mind of Paul as he said, "I know whom I have believed." If we have come to know Jesus as John did, we too can and do know that "we have passed out of death into life." If the saving power of God in Christ is working in us, we need not hesitate to say so. Part of our salvation is to appreciate salvation. To any one the sweetness of the Gospel always corresponds to the strength of his experience of salvation from sin.

II. THE GENETIC AND THE GENERIC

We have been thinking about the verified genetic of Christianity. It bears the closest possible relation to the generic. The generic is that which characterizes and classifies the Christian life. The generic determines the *genera* or order to which a vital thing belongs. It is the distinguishing characteristic thereof.

The genetic always contains the generic. In other words the type of life to which anything belongs, comes into being in the genesis that gives it being. This constitutional characteristic is implanted genetically. It is never super-added. It never can be. Biology has never found a solitary instance of a thing changing generically. And so the genetic is verified in the generic. What the generic is, and where it belongs, is made plain in its development.

What we have been saying, is that which is found infallibly true according to biological law. Perhaps the theological is most helpful when it is biological; but biology is not theology. However, whatever has come into existence vitally, is told in the type of life ensuing. Certainly the genetic of Christianity is identified by the kind of life the Christian lives.

The genetic and the generic are not the only pair of correspondences in Christianity. There is also the counterpart parallel of thought and spirit. There are both genetic thought and spirit, and also generic thought and spirit. The Christian life begins when genetic thought and spirit meet together in human personality. In fact this is one of the secrets of how personality becomes Christian. It takes the two in coöperation to generate the Christian life. And it takes also both the generic thought and the generic spirit to carry it on and bring it to its full development. The Christian life grows as its generic thought and spirit abide together in the soul. What they are, we shall later consider in this chapter.

III. COUNTERPART THOUGHT AND SPIRIT

One of the most needed truths to be emphasized today in Christian theology is the counterpart character of Christian thought and spirit. This is necessary, if the tremendous need of the hour is to be met. Now, complementary or correlate existences are bound to throw light on each other; and it is therefore folly to think of them as separate in life-process.

We have just been saying that it is the coöperative union of genetic thought and spirit which determines the kind of life begun; and it is the coöperative union of generic thought and spirit which determines how far the development of life will go.

First, let us examine this parallel movement in counterpart thought and spirit. To illustrate the correspondence and interdependence of the two, let us look at them as they occur in other than the religious life. For example, there is the thought of patriotism and its counterpart spirit of loyalty. The one is of no use without the other. Patriotic thought is as helpless without the patriotic spirit as loyalty of spirit is useless without loyalty of thought. Again, a man may have brave thought. Of what use is it unless he have also the courageous spirit. Or, a woman may have a loving spirit. If its counterpart in thought be wanting, her love will prove a mushy infatuation.

Numberless illustrations of this parallelism could be provided. Here we are concerned with the fact or principle that every moral or religious thought has its counterpart in spirit. There is a constitutional correspondence between the two in every case. Every distinct moral or religious spirit has an essential counterpart in its parallel thought. Neither one can be fully understood without the other. The one exists for, manifests, interprets, and completes the other.

Any truth without its spirit lies dormant; and any spirit without its thought is impotent. In its spirit is the life of a truth. In its spirit of deception lies the power of a lie. Truth is the embodiment of its own spirit, just as the lie is the embodiment of its spirit.

Spirit has an invincible affinity for its counterpart thought; and thought has an innate adaptability to its own spirit. As the body without its spirit is dead, so would any system of theological thought be without its spirit. What the system amounts to is determined by what its united thought and spirit amount to. Then the spirit's activity uses its thought in the way that its system determines.

IV. TRUTH HALF THOUGHT AND HALF SPIRIT

Every theological system has its definite trend and character. This may be determined by the co-revelation of its thought and spirit. They work in some direction toward some goal. As to theological systems, by their fruits we know them. All fruits have their own roots, unless they are grafts.

The Bible bids us, "Try the spirits." This we may most effectually do by testing out what their counterpart thought proves to be. And we can try any theological thought by identifying the spirit that naturally goes along with it.

No theological thought ever exists all by itself, or is complete in itself. A spirit to which it constitutionally belongs is always seeking to accompany, propagate, perpetuate, and perfect it. Back of or within every system of religious thought there is a definite directing and organizing spirit. Thus it is that each spirit animates its own system of thought.

We cannot preserve the truth of the Gospel without preserving its spirit. If we can keep the spirit of the Gospel as our own, there will be little difficulty about our attitude toward the Scriptures. We never go wrong in spirit without going wrong in thought also. And the presence of wrong thought indicates that the wrong spirit is not far away.

To utter a religious thought is to tell but half the truth: the other half is spirit. Christian theology is as much a matter of Christian spirit as of Christian thought. That is hardly the Gospel spirit which denies the thought of the Gospel and asserts another gospel which is not a Gospel. The spirit which is constitutionally counterpart to the Scriptures cannot inspire the assailment of them.

When describing some great movement we may speak of "the thought that gave it birth." Some great thought may have so served; but it is surely as appropriate to say its mother-spirit gave it birth. The mother-thought of Christianity is from the mind of its mother-spirit; and its mother-spirit is the Holy Spirit; and the mind of the Holy Spirit is the Word of God. The Spirit of God gave birth to the Gospel.

Christian theologians should be as much concerned about the Holy Spirit as about the Holy Truth. Jesus said: "The words that I speak unto you, they are spirit and they are life." He did not mean that His words gave life apart from His spirit. He taught that the Holy Spirit goes with His words to give life by them. He said: "The Spirit shall guide you into all the truth."

The Holy Spirit is the great counterpart to "the truth as it is in Jesus." They are the two inseparables that together impart the Christian life. Unless we have both, we have neither. We cannot separate "the Word made flesh" from His counterpart the Holy Ghost, for when becoming manifest in the flesh the Holy Ghost conceived Him and ever dwelt in Him in full measure.

V. COUNTERPART THOUGHT AND SPIRIT OPPOSING CHRISTIANITY

The divinely designed dualism of thought and spirit, when recognized, may solve some of the theological perplexities which puzzle us about the opposition to Christianity from within the Church. This is from the disruption of Modernism denying the miraculous essentials of Christianity. The naturalistic spirit cannot be divorced from its duplicate thought denying Christian thought. "What God hath joined together, let not" theologians "put asunder."

The anti-supernatural spirit is all the more against Christianity when within the Church. Surely the spirit of any theological system is just as important and revealing as its thought. As a rule men change more quickly in spirit than in thought. Sometimes they change in spirit overnight. There is a deep reason why men are less conscious of the significance of the change when it is in spirit.

Every theological system must be recognized and finally judged by what it does with Christ in His Person, Work and Word. Its thought must be to Christ's thought just what its spirit is to Christ's spirit. Since every theological system is half thought and half spirit, the teaching which fundamentally disagrees with the Word of Christ, cannot be in agreement with His spirit. Here it may be remarked that it is impossible for men to improve on the Bible, until they have a better spirit than the Holy Spirit which gave it.

Here we find centered practically the whole difficulty which has been raised within the Church about the Bible. It is not greater scholarship but another spirit that has made the trouble. The naturalistic spirit is innately opposed to the Supernatural Spirit. Contrary spirits can never agree in fundamental thought or estimate. Nothing is more deeply revealing about a theological system or a man than the attitude of spirit to that Masterpiece of the Holy Spirit, the Word of God. The spirit professing to love the Scriptures yet tearing them to shreds cannot conceal its real nature.

Any theological system which assumes a hostile position or attitude to the inspiration of the Bible, invariably does as much about Christ's work of Redemption. Christ's Work and the Work of the Holy Spirit are so inseparable that what seeks to discredit the one, seeks to discredit the other. The anti-miraculist has as little place for the redeeming death of Christ, as he has for the inspiration of the Scriptures which set it forth.

Manifestly it cannot be by the Holy Spirit that men become "wise above what is written," and proceed to deny the most important statements of Holy Writ about the foundational matters of the supernatural—the Birth, the Death, the Resurrection, and the Return of our Lord. That it is done by those professing to be of Christ, is exactly the attempted deception Jesus warned us should come to pass.

VI. THE DOUBLE DIVERGENCE

Opposing theological systems always diverge from Christianity as much in their spirit as in their thought. The spirit of Naturalism is just as different from Christ's Spirit as its thought is different from His thought. Its miracle-denying, anti-supernatural spirit and thought doubly diverge from Christianity. Conflict between the two is irrepressible.

For one thing the Spirit of God is the Spirit of discernment. When a man forsakes Christ's Spirit and Word, it becomes impossible for him to realize how serious his loss is; and he is more than likely to resent being told.

No man on earth can harmonize Naturalism and Christianity. Their double divergence means that the further each goes, the farther apart they will be. Many part-way followers are unaware that Modernism is not Christianity in a new form but the historic antithesis to it in any form. It affects every denomination in the same way. It has no more affinity with one form of Christianity than another.

It is by the spirit which is in him that a man finds his place. If his spirit be astray, it may carry him to where he cannot return, as the mighty undertow of an ocean tide sweeps away the strongest swimmer. The disciples who wanted to call down fire from heaven to consume the Samaritans, had thrown themselves into a diabolical spiritual current that would have swept them utterly away from the thought and spirit of Jesus Christ. No wonder they did not know the thoughts they were thinking, when they did not know what spirit was moving them. If a man does not know the character and trend of the spirit which opposes the supernatural in Christ and Christianity, how can he know the character and trend of the thought which is parallel and counterpart to that spirit?

To the end of time "the deceived heart" will be led astray, and will take the deceived head along with it. In fact, according to Biblical psychology the deceived heart includes the deceived head. It is true that a man may have heterodox views and an orthodox spirit, but not for very long, as the two irrespressibly endeavor to kill each other. A man may have orthodox views and a heterodox spirit; but in this case his spirit neutralizes all the good that is in his views.

Each mother-spirit broods over its own family of thoughts. Naturally, spirit is cold and impervious to any but its own order of thought. It is like the proverbial "corked bottle" to any ideas not counterpart to it. How useless it is to argue with a spirit to which all we say is nauseous! Our thoughts indicate what spirit we have invited into the habitation of the soul.

God has so ordained it that a man's thought and spirit tend to conform perfectly with each other. A theology of the Holy Spirit can no more disagree with the supernatural, than the Holy Spirit can disagree with the miracles of Christ. A truly Christian theology can no more disagree with the Word of God than Christ Himself can disagree with the Holy Spirit. Out of the abundance of the heart-spirit the theological mouth speaketh. It is not hard to identify the spirit that moved in the soul of the Apostle Paul when he said: "We have no power against the truth, but for the truth." (2 Cor. 13:8.)

VII. A Theology Of the Spirit, By the Spirit, and For the Spirit

Theology is not for its own sake when it is Christian; nor can it then be a law unto itself. It is purely for the sake of Christ and the Christian life. Its law is that of service to both. And its value depends upon its attitude toward the Holy Spirit. If it is subservient to any spirit opposing the Holy Spirit, its place is plain and its purpose manifest.

A theology with no counterpart spirit is as impossible as a man without a soul. Since God is essentially supernatural, the theology that would be of service to Him must be in keeping with the supernatural in Christ and His work. It cannot be anti-redemptionist in spirit and pro-Christ in thought. No one can be as severe with the naturalistic theology of the modern mind as it is severe with Christ. He has made His infinite sacrifice, while it has nothing to sacrifice. So far it has lived, not by sacrifice, but by subversion.

Ultimately all things shall be measured by adaptation and response to the Spirit of God. Even so in the world to come everything must take its place according to this subservience. The Christian life is itself a reciprocity with the thought and spirit of Christ. God has saved us unto His Holy Spirit. We are never so filled and thrilled as by the Holy Spirit. And we are never so easily chilled and changed as when without Him. No wonder that those who have never had this experience of the supernatural, doubt and disbelieve as to the verity of the miraculous.

The Holy Spirit imparts the divine sanity. Unless a theologian is born of and led by the Holy Spirit, he can readily imagine that any spirit which moves him, is of God, and that his own thought is as much inspired of God as the Bible itself. Anything in the way of perverse theological thought is not only possible but probable, unless we yield ourselves to the control of the spirit of Christ.

Long ago a deeply discerning prayer was uttered by

the Psalmist: "Take not thy holy spirit from me." The New Testament has thrown its flood of light on the Holy Spirit as a Person; so believing we see that this cry is as appropriate today as when first uttered. How can we interpret Pentecost unless by observing how useless and fruitless is even the thought of Christ without the illlumination of the Holy Spirit. If only by the Spirit of Truth can we enter into the Truth, only by the same Spirit can we be kept in the truth.

God has given us the truth as it is in Jesus. Let us offer Him the worship and service of a theology of the Spirit of God! A theology of the Spirit, by the Spirit, and for the Spirit cannot fail to belong to Jesus Christ. "For of him, and through him, and unto him are all things, to whom be glory for ever and ever."

The Holy Spirit abides in those who abide in the Word of Christ. God keep us for evermore thoroughly hospitable to the Spirit and to the Word of Jesus Christ! Then shall it be possible for the Holy Spirit to "take of the things of Christ and show them unto us."

The Great Truth of Jesus Christ's death for our Redemption is powerless to do us good, until His own spirit possesses us. The sacrificial spirit of Christ's Redemption is imparted by the Holy Spirit, and impregnates with its own nature. We cannot be redeemed from the selfishness of sin unless the sacrificial spirit of the Saviour gets possession of us. In this way the truth and the spirit of His Redemption become genetic and generic in personality. The generic is brought into being by the genetic. Recognizing this we may see the importance of the place which the Holy Spirit fills in regenerating the soul and conveying thereto the nature of Christ's Redemption.

When we possess the Living Truth and the Life-giving Spirit, we have the genuine genetic and generic of vital Christianity. Once the genetic impartation of Christ's Redemption has taken place by the communicating power of the Holy Spirit, there results the generic life of sacrifice. And this is surely the very best verification of the genuineness of the Christ-life within the soul.

The Holy Spirit is the genetic spirit, and Jesus Christ is the genetic truth of the Christian life. *The generic truth of Christianity is redemption from sin: and its generic spirit is that of sacrifice serving to make known the sacrifice of Christ to redeem mankind.* This is the fundamental conception herewith to be presented.

Part Two
Divine Fulfilment

CHAPTER IV

THE TERM ATONEMENT

THE sacrifice of Christ goes down deeper in the realm of man's need, and mounts up higher in the realm of God's grace than we are able of ourselves to scan. One therefore needs much divine help to rise "to the height of this great argument" of the work beyond atonement. It is a divine work and needs to be divinely interpreted. With Milton one may well pray:

........"What in me is dark
Illumine; what is low, raise and support."

God help us to say the very best about His very best.

Men have long had their theories about the nature of Christ's Work; but Christ was confronted not with a theory but with a situation. The difficulty He faced was the most serious and deep-seated that has ever been met. The lost condition of man, his situation as a sinner, the extent of his ruin, and all the rest which the eye of God saw, called for His utmost in sacrifice.

Men used to speak of the body of the Gospel, meaning its substance. There is also the body of the Gospel, meaning the body of God incarnate, crucified for our sins. It is the latter body that gives body to the former. As R. W. Dale said in unforgetable words:

"The real truth is that while He came to preach the Gospel, His chief object in coming was that there might be a Gospel to preach."[1]

I. Many Interpretations of Atonement

Clarity of statement requires exactness of definition; but what shall we do where definition is a multiplicity of variation? Now, definition should delimit. It should

---
1. The Atonement, p. 46.

outline the boundaries of that which is defined. Then after definition comes interpretation. This should tell what is within the boundaries. Unless we agree in definition, we are not likely to agree in interpretation.

In setting forth Christ's work on our behalf there are three words constantly used—salvation, redemption, and atonement. As a rule *atonement* refers to the Godward aspect of this work, and *salvation* points to the manward. Christ atones for sin: He saves sinners. The term *redemption* includes both of these aspects; and means that those enslaved by sin are set free at the cost of Christ.

About the term *atone* there has been no end of difficulty. There is the widest variance in usage and the greatest uncertainty as to its exact meaning. In this it is somewhat like the word *cause,* which is said to have over forty shades of meaning. More than fifty words follow which have been used to explain the import of the word *atonement.*

Amends—that done in reparation for injury or loss.
Appeasement—that allaying indignation caused by offense.
At-one-ment—that fully harmonizing the estranged.
Cleansing—that removing defilement and its stain.
Compensation—reimbursement for injury or loss.
Conciliation—that bringing disaffection to an end.
Counteraction—the opposite in act sufficient to nullify effect.
Counterbalance—the moral equivalent in offset.
Counter-equivalent—the opposite equal in nature and effect.
Countervail—that making sufficient requital.
Covering—that putting out of the divine sight the offense.
Efficacy—the sacrificial efficiency in expiatory or piacular power.
Equivalence—the equal measure that effects reparation.
Eradication—that uprooting the evil.
Eternal suffering—the timeless tribulation sin causes God.
Example—a sample of suffering or a model to follow.
Exhibition—divine devotion unbosoming itself to win the lost.
Expiation—that removing guilt.
Federation—satisfactory headship to the race provided.
Fulfilment—full honor or obedience to divine law.
Identification—made one with sinners to answer for them.
Indemnity—repayment making good for loss.
Judgment—bearing the legal penalty on behalf of lawbreakers.

Mediation—the work of a daysman bringing together those at variance.
Merit—the Godward worth of a vicarious sacrifice.
Moral influence—that offering appealing to the moral sentiments.
Obedience—due recognition of the law or will of God.
Offset—that commensurately counteracting result.
Penalty—vicariously bearing punishment due.
Personality—the Atoner dedicated to redeem personality by His personality.
Placation—the appeasement of God's righteous anger.
Propitiation—full satisfaction for the offense of sin.
Ransom—the price paid in restoring lost liberty.
Recognition—due honor paid to the honor of divine government.
Recompense—reimbursement for loss or injury.
Reconciliation—alienation replaced by fellowship.
Rectification—making right a moral wrong.
Redemption—paying the price to free the enslaved.
Reparation—making good for injury or injustice.
Repentance—contrition for the offense of sinners.
Requital—a return sufficient to quit or free.
Respect—the honor paid sufficient to reëstablish God's law.
Restitution—that lawfully ending unlawful deprivement.
Restoration—reëstablishing possession improperly withheld.
Righteousness—vicariously meeting the demands of justice.
Revelation—enlightenment ending separation because of ignorance.
Satisfaction—gratification adequate to an offense.
Sacrifice—making a vicarious offering appointed by God.
Substitution—vicariously taking the sinner's place.
Suffering—the agony vicariously endured.
Sympathy—oneness of feeling manifested toward the lost.
Transaction—the effect of interaction within the Trinity.
Vicariousness—acting or suffering on behalf of others.
Vitalization—bestowing the life that suffered for us.

II. Misinterpretations of Interpretations

Unavoidably there is much overlapping in the ideas expressed by this long list of terms. To discuss them all would not be sufficiently profitable to be undertaken here. Many of them present partial and incomplete interpretation. For example, that Christ's work on account of sin was primarily revelation, would be true if He came to deliver us only from sins of ignorance. In the main, sin does not come from want of knowledge; and revelation alone cannot save from it. As Alexander Maclaren said: "It is not for want of knowledge that men go to the devil, but for want of power to live their knowledge."

On the other hand many of these interpretations have been assailed unfairly. Take as an example the term which Jesus Himself used when He said He had come "to give His life a ransom for many." Objection has been made that both ransom and redemption convey a false idea, inasmuch as there is no one to whom the ransom cost or the redemption price was paid. An early interpretation naming the devil as the recipient did not long satisfy. Later, God Himself was named. This aroused the criticism that as He made the atonement, He was paying Himself; and this was like taking money out of one pocket and putting it into another. The mistake was in forgetting that each is a figure term, and that but part and not the whole of the figure of speech was intended to apply.

We are constantly using the terms *price* and *cost* where there is no thought of a payee. "The cost of an education is application." "Eternal vigilance is the price of liberty." To whom is the cost and price paid in these cases? Manifestly to no one. So is it with the terms ransom and redemption. They are intended to convey just the thought of cost, and not the thought of some one to whom this cost is paid. To give such Scripture terms "the third degree" and torture out of them meanings not in them, is surely unwarranted procedure.

Appeasement is another interpretation objected to as of "pagan color." The similar objection is made to *propitiation*. Of course, there is the heathen way of using these terms; and so to use them would attribute to God a disposition foreign to His nature. Then the appeasement or propitiation would have no elements of righteousness or love.

Let us remember that a God incapable of righteous indignation would be morally and personally defective. The divine love incapable of resentment of wrong would be spineless and spurious. As a matter of fact there is no anger like that of a perfectly holy love. The God of Christianity is not One moved in the same way by wrong and injustice as He is by righteousness and equity.

To say, as a well-known theologian did, that "the God who propitiates Himself, needs no propitiation," is like saying the man who feeds himself needs no food, or the man who clothes himself needs no clothes. To hold that the righteous indignation of God with sin never needs to be allayed, means that it is not really righteous at all, and may just as well go on forever, or until it burns itself out.

III. ATONEMENT, AN OLD TESTAMENT TERM

The more important a term, the more imperative is it that its meaning be clear. In a former work, *The Living Atonement,* I defined atonement as that which rights a moral wrong.[2] I see now that this ethical definition, like many before it, is incomplete. Christ redeems more than moral nature for more was lost than it. All of personality is redeemed, and all of Christ's Personality went into His redemption. Love, for example, cannot be fully expressed in ethical terms; and love is surely one of the most prominent things in what has been called the *atonement.* Christ's great sacrifice does right the wrong of sin. That is saying a great deal; but it leaves a great deal more to be said.

The term atonement has long been employed in theological language. Not only has it been used in Old Testament theology; it has also been taken to designate the work of Christ on account of sin. This has turned out to be a serious hindrance rather than a help, because of its very vague and uncertain meaning. The fifty-four interpretations tabulated serve to show the great lack of agreement as to what it means; and the long list is doubtless not exhaustive.

When one sets out to find the cause of this handicap

---

2. The Living Atonement. p. 168

of uncertainty of meaning, he finds that it is mainly due to the fact that *atonement is properly an Old Testament term.* It does not once appear in the New Testament. It is true that in the King James Version it appears in Romans 5:11; but this is a mistranslation for "reconciliation" (Katallage). At the time the Authorized Version appeared atonement meant at-one-ment or reconciliation. Shakespeare so used it.

Some have argued that in the New Testament Greek text equivalent Greek terms for atone are found; and support this by pointing out that in it are found the same terms which the Septuagint translators used for the word atone as it occurs in the Old Testament. The fact is, they used about a dozen different terms to translate *atone* or *atonement,* showing that they found no more uniformity of meaning than have the authors of the many theories of the Atonement which have come down to us.

Ritschl, for example, takes "ransom" (lutron) to be the equivalent to the Hebrew word for Atonement. But the linguistic grounds for this have been denied by Wendt and many others of equal authority. Professor Stevens says:

"The Seventy use *lutron* to translate several different Hebrew words. The word does not, therefore, consistently represent *kipper* (atonement), and no presumption exists that Jesus used this or a kindred word."[3]

Other authorities agree to this. Denney discussing the matter says:

"Nothing has been gained for the understanding of this passage (Came to give his life a ransom for many) by the elaborate investigation of the Hebrew or Aramaic equivalents of *lutron* If 'He gave His life a ransom for many' does not convey His idea, it will certainly not be conveyed by any of the precarious equivalents for this Greek expression which are offered for our acceptance."[4]

That there are words used in the New Testament which are more or less akin in meaning to atonement,

---
3. The Theology of the New Testament, p 127
4. The Death of Christ, p 43.

it would be foolish to deny. Perhaps the word "propitiation" (hilasmos) is nearer to it than "ransom." The fact remains, however, that a true synonym or equivalent for *atone* or *atonement* is not found in the New Testament. The reason for this will be discussed later.

We have gone in the wrong direction when we seek the Old Testament meaning of Atonement in the derivation of this English word used to translate it. As is well known, it means etymologically at-one-ment. This does not by any means settle the meaning of the Hebrew term it has been used to translate. Discussing the meaning of the word "holy" Davidson says:

"Etymology is rarely a safe guide to the real meaning of words. Language, as we have it in any literature, has already drifted away far from the primary sense of its words. Usage is the only safe guide. When usage is ascertained, then we may enquire into derivation and radical signification. Hence the Concordance is always a safer companion than the Lexicon."[5]

Very few, if any at all, are the terms which have not changed somewhat from their original meaning. Some far outgrow it; and some even reverse it, as our word "let" has done. Once it meant to hinder, as we find in, "He that letteth will let, until he be taken out of the way." Similarly the word "prevent" once meant precede. Unless this is understood, one misses the sense of the passage: "We that are alive and remain, shall not prevent them that are asleep."

It is puerile to argue about the meaning of an Old Testament Hebrew term on the basis of the etymological meaning of the English word which has been used in translating it. In his great work on Sacrifice, Alfred Cave says:

"The idea of atonement, never expressly alluded to in the pre-Mosaic ceremonial, although beyond a doubt everywhere latent, we must carefully extract from the Law—our only instrument, of course, being the etymology and scriptural usage of the Hebrew original. They who would obtain the

---

5. The Theology of the Old Testament, p. 257.

scriptural conception of the matter in hand by an analysis of *at-one-ment* or *attune-ment*, seem to forget that the Old Testament was not revealed in English."[6]

IV. THE METAPHORICAL CHARACTER OF THE TERM ATONEMENT

As every student of the matter knows, the Hebrew verb, *kaphar,* without doubt means *to cover.* So Gesenius, Davidson, and other authorities define it. Its Piel form, *kipper,* is generally used in the Old Testament. Discussing this Davidson says:

"The word 'atone,' kipper, is not used in the Kal. In Gen. 6:14, 'Thou shalt pitch it with pitch,' the word is a denominative from the noun *kopher,* 'pitch.' The word is now used only in Piel and its derivatives. Further, the word is no more used in scripture in its literal and physical sense, but always in a transferred metaphorical sense. The original meaning of the word, however, was certainly to *cover,* and so put out of sight, or do away with . . . In all these passages the use of the word is metaphorical; the sense of literal covering no more obtains . . . Considering that kipper is used in the ritual and non-ritual sense, it is probable that even in the *ritual* 'cover' has not a literal, but a metaphorical sense; and that it is not said in regard of the blood being literally laid on the object covered; for in most cases it is not; it is brought before God, and even in the ritual it might be He (or His eyes) that is covered."[7]

The verbs *kasah,* to cover, and *machah,* to blot out, are used synonomously with *kipper.* It seems clear then that while the word "atone" means to cover, this covering was in a figurative sense; and it is this metaphorical character of its use which gives rise to two things—the many shades of meaning made possible, and the impossibility of translating it into other languages. There could be no word in another tongue that would mean all that a Hebrew metaphor does in all the shades of its use. The word "atone" does not convey purely the original idea of covering. Discussing this Piepenbring says:

"All this proves that the word *atone,* by which the verb

---
6. The Scriptural Doctrine of Sacrifice. p 98
7. The Theology of the Old Testament, pp 327, 328, 329.

kaphar is usually rendered, distorts the primitive and characteristic idea that it is intended to express."[8]

Kipper is therefore translated as make atonement, purge, purge away, reconcile, make reconciliation, pacify, satisfy, pardon, be merciful, put off, and so on. These are some of the things effected by atonement. The covering from the sight of Jehovah so removes the sin for which atonement is made that all these things follow. Most of them are therefore secondary and not primary in its meaning.

Atonement does what the Psalmist prayed for when he said, "Hide thy face from my sins." It hid them, put them out of sight, or invalidated them so that they ceased to offend. There were less figurative terms used, meaning to un-sin, cleanse, and sanctify; but atonement expressed by its figure that sin was removed from the sight of God and its effects counteracted or undone. This is true also when the persons were covered or atoned for. The covering protected the sinner from the avenging hand of God. As a rule it is God Himself who does the covering by means of the atonement. That the term atone is therefore primarily and intrinsically a figurative or metaphorical one, seems to be clearly established.

V. THE WORD "ATONEMENT" INADEQUATE TO DESIGNATE THE SACRIFICE OF CHRIST

The figure of covering by atonement is not competent to portray all that Christ achieved by His sacrifice for our sin. We have already noted that its idea of covering, or the term for it, does not occur in the New Testament. If the word atonement had been accurate and suitable, the New Testament Scriptures would no doubt have used it or its metaphor of covering. Of course the New Testament was written in Greek and not in Hebrew; but in any case the conception of the character and scope of the work of Christ is too vast, con-

---

8. Theology of the Old Testament, p 313

crete, and unmetaphoric to be portrayed by the figurative term atonement.

The Holy Spirit is the highest authority in diction. His choice of words is in infallible wisdom. When under His inspiration this Old Testament term of atonement was not used to describe Christ's work, there was adequate reason therefore. And we cannot do better than to make use of His wisdom. Certainly we cannot improve upon His chosen terms. The Old Testament sacrifices and ceremonies being more or less symbolical and figurative in cast, it was perfectly in keeping that a metaphorical word was used to designate their import. The Saviour's great sacrifice in death was no symbol or metaphor. It is the great concrete reality to which all Old Testament sacrifices and atonements pointed. The discarding of the old terminology was rendered necessary by its inadequacy. The terms of shadow no longer fit when the substance has come. The symbolic expression can be laid aside when its fulfilment has come to pass.

It looks as though theology would have fared far better and been of more use, if it had used only the terms which the New Testament employed in setting forth the meaning of the work of Christ. To take "atonement" to be the generic term depicting Christ's sacrifice for sin is really to attempt to put the new wine into an old bottle. We cannot pour all the vast meaning of Christ's death into the term atonement. Doubtless some truth can be expressed by it; but then the most of the truth is left unexpressed. More is unuttered or misrepresented by the old term than is revealed.

Looking back over the long centuries of theological discussion, we see that men have been vainly stretching the old skin-bottle one way and another to force it to hold all the new wine of the vast meaning of Christ's work on account of sin. And much of the wine has been spilt on the ground, and been trampled under foot. Confusions and misunderstandings have abounded. The effort has not succeeded. Long ago the meaning of the term "atone" has been stretched to the breaking

THE TERM ATONEMENT

point. Those who wish to use the skin-bottle for a tug of war (theological) can do little more than has been done in sheer futility. Discussing the ambiguity of the term atonement as applied to Christ's work Theodore Haering says:

"We believe in Christ as the Redeemer and Author of the Atonement. But however familiar the words are to us, words which could only be avoided with some trouble even in the short survey which we have just finished, the fact is equally undoubted that the precise significance of them is by no means fixed . . . There is no less diversity in the interpretation of the word Atonement . . . In order to put an end to this confusion of language many prefer to use the word Atonement for the change effected in the relation to God by the removal of guilt, and the word Redemption for the breaking of the power of sin . . . Thus at present scarcely any other course will be left except to set aside these words which are open to misunderstanding, because differently understood by every one, and to speak in the simplest possible way of the facts, looking at them from the most important points of view."[9]

This is going too far. It may be well to set aside the term atonement which the Holy Spirit has set aside, but to set aside also redemption or any other term which the New Testament uses to explain the work of Christ, is as unwarranted as unnecessary. The meaning of His sacrifice for us and its implications are so vast, the utmost possibilities of human language do not portray it all—and cannot. W. B. Selbie says:

"In his attempts to describe the meaning of the death of Christ on the Cross, St. Paul almost exhausts the possibilities of human speech. It is a sacrifice, a propitiation, a means of reconciliation, an atonement. In every way and by every possible kind of illustration he tries to bring home to the hearts of men this thought that in Jesus Christ's death, in the love that that death involved and manifested, there is a ground and reason for man's hope and peace, for his forgiveness, his justification, his salvation, his sanctification."[10]

VI. THE VIEW BEYOND THAT OF ATONEMENT

In the Old Testament atonement served its purpose of preparation for the thought of the New Testament.

---
9. The Christian Faith, Vol II, p 592. (Eng. Tr)
10. Aspects of Christ, p 84.

But to recognize its insufficiency is not to provide the sufficiency needed. In an earlier chapter we said that Genetic Theology is as much concerned with the Holy Spirit as with the Holy Truth, for the two must go together for adequacy. Now the terms the Holy Spirit employs to express the counterpart truth of what Christ wrought out for us, can no more be set aside than the truth itself. *There is a unique unimproveableness about Holy Writ.* We must not mar its divine adaptation to the service of the Spirit.

Lest some feel that presenting the Work of Christ as greater and better than atonement is an attempt to improve on Scripture, it will be well to point out that this is just what the New Testament itself does. For example, the Epistle to the Hebrews has as its keyword "better." The sacrifice of Christ is better than all the sacrifices of atonement. It offers "a better hope," makes "a better testament." Christ is "the Mediator of a better covenant established on better promises," and with "better sacrifices than these." By "the sacrifice of himself," "He taketh away the first that he may establish the second." This surely means that His Work is more than atonement.

Again, some may fear that this is leading to a lesser estimate of Christ's Work. But a fair interpretation will find instead a higher view and larger estimate. Fidelity to the Scriptures never leads on to a lesser appreciation of the things of Christ. It is, instead, the very thing that saves us from falling into the pit of depreciation and disparagement.

Finally, it may appear to some at first sight that not having the single word atonement as a generic and characteristic term for Christ's work on our behalf, will cause disunity of interpretation. It may seem to some that taking all the terms of the New Testament—sacrifice, propitiation, redemption, ransom, reconciliation—does away with unity of treatment. This is, however, to forget that the term atonement has never led to unity in any way. Perhaps no other word of theology has been so variously interpreted and with more failure to find agreement among its interpretations and interpreters.

A careful examination of these terms of the New Testament will find a bond of unity among them. The great idea of sacrifice itself is a synthesis of all the truths presented by other terms. And as already pointed out the word "redemption" means both the Godward and the manward aspects of Christ's work. In theology just as elsewhere respect for the Holy Spirit and His Word is bound to lead to unity of thought and spirit. A theology of the Spirit finds in the counterpart revelation of the Word of God the unity of both beauty and strength.

CHAPTER V

"A MORE EXCELLENT SACRIFICE"

AS ABEL offered a more excellent sacrifice than Cain, so did our Saviour offer a more excellent sacrifice than any or all the Old Testament sacrifices. Some of these were for atonement, some for thanksgiving, or for some other form of worship.

We may notice that atonement was made in many ways. For example, Moses made it by a prayer when Israel had sinned. "Ye have sinned a great sin: and now I will go up unto Jehovah; peradventure I shall make atonement for your sin." (Ex. 32:20.) Then the prayer of atonement followed. In this prayer Moses made one of the great sacrifices of his life.

Pointing out varied uses of the word atonement, Davidson refers to the instance in which the punishment of death was inflicted on two offenders.[1] A man and a woman were found supporting the immoral worship of Baal. Phinehas took vengeance on them, putting both to death. The twenty-fifth chapter of Numbers gives the full account, and tells how this stayed the plague. "Because he was jealous for his God, and made atonement for the children of Israel." In the sixteenth chapter of the same book we find the solitary instance where incense had atoning power. "And he (Aaron) put on incense, and made atonement for the people. And he stood between the living and the dead."

Without tracing out further the many ways in which atonement was made, we may set forth in formal order the superiority of Christ's sacrifice over all those recorded in the Old Testament Scriptures. We shall confine ourselves to portraying in seven respects how

---

1. The Theology of the Old Testament, pp. 323, 336.

His Work on account of sin was greater and better than atonement.

I. ATONEMENT WHICH COVERED LESSER SINS, COULD NOT TAKE AWAY ANY SIN; BUT THE SACRIFICE OF CHRIST BLOTS OUT ALL SIN

"For it is impossible that the blood of bulls and goats should take away sins."

"Behold the Lamb of God who taketh away the sin of the world."

"And every priest indeed standeth day by day ministering and offering oftentimes the same sacrifices which can never take away sins."

"For by one offering hath he perfected for ever them that are sanctified."

"What unto me is the multitude of your sacrifices? saith Jehovah. I have had enough of the burnt offerings of rams, and the fat of fed beasts; and I delight not in the blood of bullocks, or of lambs, or of he-goats."

"And ye know that he was manifested to take away sins."

"Yea, though ye offer to me your burnt offerings and meal-offerings, I will not accept them; neither will I regard the peace-offerings of your fat beasts."

"Who his own self bare our sins in his body on the tree."

"Wherefore when he cometh into the world, he saith, sacrifice and offering thou wouldest not, but a body didst thou prepare for me; in whole burnt offerings and sacrifices for sin thou hadst no pleasure."

"But now once at the end of the ages hath he been manifested to put away sin by the sacrifice of himself."

"Saying above, Sacrifice and offerings and whole burnt offerings and sacrifices for sin thou wouldest not, neither hadst pleasure therein (the which are offered according to the law), then hath he said, Lo, I am come to do thy will. He taketh away the first that he may establish the second."

The Scriptures abundantly make known that sin provokes God's righteous indignation. So He appointed atonements which, in a figure, covered the sinner from the divine anger. For those within the Old Covenant this was mercifully provided until the Lord should come, and the New Covenant should replace the Old. In Christ's death God manifested and established His righteousness in "passing over the sins done aforetime." But He also enabled Himself to put sin away forever and to provide the means of man's fulfilment.

As to the atonements appointed for the days before the coming of Christ, the question may be raised, which was covered, the sin or the sinner? Both! Some passages emphasize the one, and some the other. As sin could not be anywhere but in the sinner, the one could not be covered without the other.

It is well to note that God took the sacrifice and by it He Himself covered either the sin or the sinner or both. When the situation was such that God could not accept the sacrifices offered, neither the sin nor the sinner was covered from His anger. So the prayer was often offered that the sacrifice might be acceptable. "Cover our sins for thy name's sake." "He being full of compassion, covered their iniquity."[2]

Turning to the great sacrifice of the New Testament, we find far more than the metaphor of the covering of sin or sinner. Sin was neutralized, undone, put away, its existence ended, God's nature was fulfilled in relation to it, the sinner freed from it, the hate of it put in his heart, and the means of mastering it provided.

"When he had made purification of sins."

"How much more shall the blood of Christ, who through eternal spirit (the or his not in the original) offered himself without blemish unto God, cleanse your conscience from dead works to serve the living God."

"The blood of Jesus, his Son, cleanseth us from all sin."

"Unto him that loveth us, and loosed (washed) us from our sins by his blood."

"He, when he had offered one sacrifice for sins for ever, sat down on the right hand of God."

He could not be seated there *unless His work was finished*. In fact it was not finished until provision was made that not a vestige of sin would ultimately remain in man. His Work was perfected because of its perfect power to secure the utter obliteration of sin. Hence His Work was far better than the atonement

---

[2]. Davidson says· "But no explanation is given of the principle how the blood with the life in it covers the persons, i. e atones . . . New Testament scholars seem as much perplexed in seeking to discover the principle of atonement in the New Testament as we are in the Old." Theology of the Old Testament, pp. 325, 355.

which covered only the minor offenses of the sins of ignorance. This phase of the superiority of Christ's sacrifice we shall next take up.

II. Atonement was for Unwitting Fault, the Errors of Ignorance, while Christ's Sacrifice was for All Sin

According to the Old Covenant unintentional transgression or the failure of inadvertence was classed as sin; *and for this only could atonement be made.* Such sins attempted no open revolt from God, and were therefore within the covenant. Outbreaking sins that annulled the covenant with God, had no atonement provided for them. In such cases the penalty of death was alone possible. Such sins as murder, idolatry, and rebellion against the moral law had no atonement provided for them. As Alfred Cave says:

"By the atoning rites of Judaism, national and personal, forgiveness was obtained for all sins which were not committed in open rebellion against the Most High."[3]

These sins of ignorance are referred to in the Epistle to the Hebrews. Of Christ as our High Priest it was said: "Who can bear gently with the ignorant and erring." Davidson says:

"Pre-Christian sin is ignorance. And another New Testament writer seems to touch on the same idea—'The times of this ignorance God winked at, but now commandeth all men everywhere to repent' And even our Lord Himself says, 'If I had not come and spoken unto them, they had not had sin.' "[4]

Sin was missing the mark aimed at. We call all sorts of failure toward God sin. The Old Testament did not. That which annulled the covenant was not properly sin but apostasy. Davidson further says:

"It is probable that sins of ignorance were properly such offenses as were inevitable, owing to the limitations and frailties of the human mind. The idea is expressed accurately in Ezekiel 45:20 where the sin-offering is made 'for every one that erreth, and for him that is simple.' "[5]

---
3. The Scriptural Doctrine of Sacrifice, p 398.
4. Theology of the Old Testament, p. 352.
5. Ibid, p 228.

In Leviticus from the fourth chapter on we have the various directions for atonements for the sins of weakness and inadvertency. So the range of sins for which atonement could be offered was restricted. How different was the scope of Christ's work who died for the sins of the whole world.

Moreover, atonement could be offered only when it was a Hebrew who thus sinned unwittingly. To quote again from Alfred Cave:

"None but Jews were permitted to offer sin-offerings, although foreigners were legally allowed to present burnt offerings (which had a minute element of atonement attached to them). None but Jews were permitted to present offerings proper for sin or for trespass, or to participate in the great festal offerings when sin-offerings were presented, or have the smallest share in the solemn ceremonial of the Day of Atonement. One of the principal features, on the other hand, of the Christian faith, is that it recognizes 'neither Jew nor Greek, circumcision nor uncircumcision, barbarian, Scythian, bond, free; but Christ is all and in all.' " [6]

Christ's sacrifice was therefore this much better than atonement—it was for all sin and for all nations and persons on earth.

III. ATONEMENT WAS BUT THE SHADOW OF THE COMING SUBSTANCE OF CHRIST'S WORK

After a masterful survey of all the Old Testament sacrifices, Alfred Cave declares that the result first of all was the diversity of sacrifices:

"and in the second place the conviction that these diverse sacrifices, all the Patriarchial and Mosaic sacrifices of whatever kind, were but shadows of completer offerings which the future would reveal." [7]

This is but saying what is said in the Epistle to the Hebrews in regard not only to these Old Testament sacrifices but also of the law that ordained them:

"For the law having the shadow of good things to come, not the very image of the things, can never with the same sacrifices year by year, which they offer continually, make

---

6. The Scriptural Doctrine of Sacrifice. p 352
7. Ibid, p 287.

perfect them that draw nigh. Else would they not have ceased to be offered." Heb. 10:1.

And so it is divinely declared that all ceremonial atonements and the ritual of sacrifices were "a shadow of the things to come: but the body (substance) is Christ's." Col. 2:17.

In the Epistle to the Galatians and that to the Colossians the merit of Christ's work is declared to be superior in every way. It is set forth that the Old Testament ordinances served as much for condemnation as for reparation. So Christ removed them, "Having blotted out the bond written in ordinances that was against us; and hath taken it out of the way, nailing it to the cross." So also the Epistle to the Romans as well as other Scriptures take the same view that, as to the Great Coming Event, atonement was the shadow cast before. Now the shadow of the past can do no more than dimly outline the substance of the present. It is not the shadow which gives form and name to the substance, but the reverse. The tree with its fruit cannot be adequately described in the language of its shadow cast upon the ground.

Because atonement foreshadowed what would be revealed and achieved in the future, it could do nothing, and was intended to do nothing, for the future. So atonement was made only for fault or sin already committed, while Christ's sacrifice was for all time. Never was any atonement offered for sins not yet committed. Atonement looked but one way, back into the past, never forward into the future. The thought of making atonement beforehand for sins not yet committed never occurred to the Old Testament saints. How could sins be "covered" in atonement which had not yet come into existence?

On the other hand, the sacrifice of Christ was as unlimited in time as it was in the sin for which it was offered. The Redeemer made "one sacrifice for sins for ever." As atonement was only for sins in the past, Christ's Work if considered strictly as atonement would be only for the sins which had been committed before the time that His sacrifice was made. Properly, as an atonement we could have no share in Christ's sacrifice. Because it was more than atonement we do have share in it, and so will the believers of all the ages share in its great benefit.

IV. Atonement was a Temporary Expedient Serving Till Christ Should Come

Atonement served to prepare for the work of Christ. It developed appreciation of sacrifice by the sacrifices it called for. This made ready for the recognition of God's Great Sacrifice because it had awakened the Hebrew people to the place of sacrifice by the sacrifices they made to God. In his great treatment of this subject Patrick Fairbairn in speaking of the sacrifices by blood, says:

"The life-blood then which God gave for this purpose upon the altar must obviously have been but a temporary expedient."[8]

He goes on to set forth the radical defects of atonement as compared with the true sacrifices for sin by God Himself. There were—

"the imperfection and inadequacy of irrational victims . . . Nor could the sacrifice itself—which was a still more palpable incongruity—be, like the sin for which it was offered in atonement, a voluntary and personal act: the priest and the sacrifice were of necessity divided: and the work of atonement was done, not *by* the victim in willing self-dedication, but *upon* it all unconsciously, by the hand of another. Such defects and imperfections inhering in the very nature of ancient sacrifice, it could not possibly have been introduced or sanctioned by God as a satisfactory and ultimate arrangement."[9]

Fairbairn wonders whether the Jewish worshippers were alive to the necessity of the coming adequate provision, whether they realized the certainty of its future manifestation. He argues that the felt imperfection and deficiency in the appointed sacrifices could not but connect itself in their minds with the Messiah. He quotes Kurtz:

---
8. The Typology of Scripture. Vol. II, p. 267.
9. Ibid. p. 267.

"A MORE EXCELLENT SACRIFICE" 69

"When the conscience of the Israelite was fairly awakened to the insufficiency of the blood of irrational creatures to effect a real atonement for sin, there was no other way for him to obtain satisfaction than in the supposition that a perfect, ever available sacrifice lay in the future . . . How natural to connect together the center of his expectations with the center of his worship—to decry a secret though still perhaps incomprehensible connection between them, and in that to seek the explication of the sacred mystery."[10]

The same thought of the incompleteness of these atonements is expressed by Alfred Cave:

"Time after time throughout the course of this inquiry, it has been seen how large a license was demanded when the blood of bulls and of goats was supposed to take away sin; time after time has it been remarked how great a claim was daily made upon the credence of the Jew: there is no inherent impossibility in what is ascribed to the blood of Christ."[11]

Perhaps these quotations sufficiently set forth the temporary and provisional nature of atonement. It is clear from what happened, that the expedient was intended to pass away after it had served its purpose. A tent may be an expedient for a mansion, but we do not describe the mansion as a superior tent. In whatever way we may view the work of Christ, it is plain that atonement was offered because the Christ had not yet come.

Now expedients are of many kinds. Of what sort was atonement? The answer is, it was the expedient of symbol or type. It prefigured the sacrifice of Christ. It had the particular resemblance that it was offered for sin. The Passover was also a type of the death of Christ; but it was not an atonement. The lamb slain was not offered for sin. No Jew ever looked upon the paschal lamb as an offering of atonement. The lamb was eaten and its blood put on the door-posts. Thus it symbolized the deliverance and preservation from death which the death of the Lamb of God secured.

---
10. Ibid, p. 269.
11. The Scriptural Doctrine of Sacrifice, p. 402.

"For our passover hath been sacrificed, even Christ."
(1 Cor. 5:7.)

In His death Christ fulfilled both types—that of passover and that of atonement. Type is more than symbol. An accidental resemblance may enable a thing to be taken as a symbol, but the type must be specially designed in its resemblance. Atonement bore no accidental resemblance to Christ's sacrifice. It was a true type of it.

The type is naturally transitional; but the sacrifice of Christ which it typified, is permanent. The type like the law itself was a pedagogue leading to Christ. When The Antitype had come and His sacrifice had been accomplished, the place and use of the type had passed. When the sun rises the tapers are put away.

The place of the type has been well described by Adolph Saphir:

"All types are by the very nature of types mere shadows, and therefore not able to give the real substance except by anticipation." [12]

"All the types taken together are not intelligible to us, and will not bring us to a right conclusion and a right understanding of Christ, unless we always bear in mind their necessary imperfection. Jesus is the sacrifice; but what sacrifice could be a type of Christ?" [13]

"He is the true Sacrifice—fulfilment of all the varied types—was offered for us on Golgotha." [14]

"The type was necessarily imperfect; the fulfilment is perfect. The former consisted in many parts. There is a multiplicity of sacrifices; and yet even when combined, there is still imperfection. The latter possesses a marvelous simplicity, for Christ is the one Sacrifice by whom all the purposes of God, as our redemption, and sanctification, a future glory, are fulfilled. In the type the purification was legal, ceremonial, provisional." [15]

"In this way the whole dispensation of the law and the Levitical priesthood were merely parenthetical. They were never intended to remain." [16]

---

12. Epistle to the Hebrews, p. 400
13. Epistle to the Hebrews, p. 406
14. Epistle to the Hebrews, p 594
15. Epistle to the Hebrews, p. 563.
16. Epistle to the Hebrews, p 399.

V. Atonement Constitutionally Belonged to the Covenant of Works, While Christ's Sacrifice as Constitutionally Belonged to that of Grace

The Covenant of Works was between God and the Jewish people. It was based on the moral law—"Do this and thou shalt live." The covenant, not the moral law was made. Moral law cannot be *made*. It was published, not enacted. God made moral beings; but the moral law is in His own Being. It is constitutional, universal, and eternal. It is the way in which moral nature must work or act to be perfect. It tells what agrees with moral nature whether in God or in man. God so made man that what agrees or disagrees with His nature, correspondingly it must also agree or disagree with man's.

While the Covenant of Works was based on universal moral law, it was specially given to the Hebrew people. This was not done in favoritism, for covenant was possible with them alone. They alone did not displace God. Their recognition of God made possible the revelation of the moral law and the covenant based upon it. When any nation lived in idolatry, there could be no covenant of God with them.

The first thing in human morality is morality toward God, the righteousness of due recognition of Him. When this fundamental ethic is present, God can be present with His people and pledge Himself to them. "I will be your God and ye shall be my people." More than one God there could not be. There is no room for more. Another god would mean that the true God was being ignored.

In consequence of this, there was no atonement for idolatry which destroyed the foundation of all right relation to God. The salvation of the people depended upon remaining within the covenant based on this necessary recognition of God; but for the unwitting sin due to weakness and which did not destroy or abrogate the covenant with God, there was atonement. Atonement, however, did not create this covenant. It held a subordinate place within it.

In the Covenant of Grace the sacrifice of Christ is the initial and foundational thing, inasmuch as *it creates this covenant.* "I will give him for a covenant to the people." This Messianic promise is:

"Behold the days come, saith Jehovah, that I will make a new covenant with Israel . . . Not according to the covenant I made with their fathers in the day when I took them by the hand to bring them out of the land of Egypt; which my covenant they brake . . . But this shall be the covenant that I will make with the house of Israel; after those days, saith Jehovah, I will put my law in their inward parts, and write it in their hearts; and I will be their God, and they shall be my people." Jer. 31: 31-33.

After quoting this passage the Epistle to the Hebrews makes this comment: "In that he saith, a new covenant, he hath made the first old. Now that which decayeth and waxeth old is ready to vanish away." Of the perfect sacrifice founding the new covenant the Epistle says:

"And for this cause he is the mediator of a new covenant, that a death having taken place for the redemption of the transgressions that were under the first covenant, they that have been called may receive the promise of the eternal inheritance." Heb. 9:15.

The New Testament word for covenant means not only *agreement* but also *bequeathment* by a will coming in force after the death of a testator. So the bequeathment of the sacrifice of Christ's death marks the measure of the richness of the New Covenant. So the Covenant of Grace is as much better than that of Works, as Christ's sacrifice is better than the sacrifices of atonement.

VI. IN ATONEMENT MEN MADE AN OFFERING UNTO GOD: BUT CHRIST'S SACRIFICE WAS GOD'S OFFERING FOR MEN

The latter is "the gift of God through Jesus Christ our Lord."

"Who being the brightness of his glory and the express image of his being, and upholding all things by the word of his power, when he had made purification of our sins, sat down on the right hand of the Majesty on high." Heb. 1:3.

This is the measure of Christ's sacrifice, it reaches unto heaven. So the Lamb is in the midst of the throne. As Saphir says:

"Jesus in heaven, at the right hand of God, the Lamb in the midst of the throne—this sums up all our faith, all our love, all our hope. It is the crowning point."[17]

Christ with His sacrifice of Himself entered the heaven of heavens, the Holy of holies in heaven. On the other hand atonement was man's sacrifice offered by a priest for himself as well as for the people. It was made upon an earthly altar. But Christ was priest, offering, and sanctuary. As prophet, priest, and king He is Revealer, Redeemer, and Ruler. Prophets brought God's messages. Christ Himself was God's message. He was the true Apostle and High Priest of our redemption.

As priest Christ was qualified, being one among men and chosen of God. He did not become priest *till His death,* when He "appeared before the Father for us," "having somewhat to offer," even the sacrifice of Himself. "We have such an high priest," such a Redeemer!

"Wherefore it behooved him in all things to be made like unto his brethren, that he might become a merciful and faithful high priest in things pertaining to God, to make propitiation for the sins of the people." Heb. 2:17.

He was not only King of kings, He was Prince of peace and Priest of priests. He was the king-priest after the order of Melchizedek, and this forever. Through His everlasting sacrifice He is the source and substance as well as "the power of an endless life." His was no involuntary and unconscious sacrifice like that of atonement. *He offered Himself.* Only the blood of animals was taken into the earthly Holy of holies. With the blood of His sacrifice of Himself He entered the heavenly Holy of holies.

As Melchizedek was greater than Aaron, so Christ was greater than all the priests of earth. The Epistle of Christ's Better Sacrifice says:

---
17. The Epistle to the Hebrews, p. 491.

"For Christ entered not into a holy place made with hands, like in pattern to the true; but into heaven itself, now to appear before the face of God for us; nor yet that he should offer himself often, as the high priest entereth into the holy place year by year with blood not his own; else must he have often suffered since the foundation of the world: but now once at the end (consummation) of the ages hath he been manifested to put away sin by the sacrifice of himself." Heb. 9:24-26.

To quote again from the excellent Christian-Hebrew interpreter, Saphir:

"The Aaronic priesthood and the Levitical dispensation were indeed of God, and possessed glory. And our Lord who on the cross was the sacrifice, and who by His own blood entered into the Holy of holies, fulfilled all that was typified by these divine ordinances . . . But Jesus, the Messiah, having come and fulfilled that which was written of Him, and being the substance of the shadow, there has begun now the exercise of a real, living, continuous, and perfect High Priesthood, of which a type is found in the pre- and super-Aaronic priesthood of Melchizedek. Jesus is in heaven, dispensing the blessings which He purchased with His blood, and in perfect mediation bringing us to God, and the favor and life of God in us." [18]

VII. ATONEMENT WAS MADE BY THE BLOOD OF BEASTS: CHRIST SHED HIS OWN BLOOD TO REDEEM US

"This is my blood of the Covenant which is poured out for many." "Nor yet through the blood of goats and calves, but through his own blood (Christ) entered in once for all into the holy place, having obtained eternal redemption."

An Old Testament passage (Lev. 17:11) prohibited the eating of blood, and incidentally explains the meaning of atonement by it:

"The life of the flesh is in the blood; and I have given it to you upon the altar to make atonement for your souls; for it is the blood that maketh atonement by virtue of the life."

That is, by virtue of its being sacrificial life. Of all forms of physical life blood is the most perfectly and purely sacrificial. In every drop of our blood some five million little lives called corpuscles make possible

---

18. The Epistle to the Hebrews, p. 364.

our physical life by the ministry of their constant sacrifice. Blood is not a mere symbol of sacrificial life: it is *sacrificial life*. It is not only sacrifice when it dies: it is sacrifice as it lives. It has no other life than that perfectly devoted to ours. It is the perfection of sacrifice whether in life or in death.

To speak of "the blood of irrational creatures" is not accurate. They may be unrational, but are not irrational. But the blood is neither unrational nor irrational. It has the wisdom of the sacrificial nature of the Maker Himself in it. Being like the Incarnate Son of God wholly a sacrificial existence, it is as sacred a thing as can be found in the whole physical realm.

While blood is essentially a sacrificial order of life, there is one blood of fishes, another of birds, another of animals, another of men. Because of who Jesus Christ was, and the sacrificial existence for man's salvation which He was, His blood was the most sacred, the holiest that ever coursed through human veins and arteries. Because He was as truly God as man, His blood was the blood of the God-man. Scripture ventures to speak of it as the blood of God. "The church of God which he hath purchased with his own blood."

There was very special significance in the shedding of the blood of the Son of God. As His body had become part of His Person, His blood was the life of His body, and was therefore the fittest physical symbol of His divine sacrifice. The pouring out of His blood best expressed His sacrifice for us in death. It would take volumes to go into this fully. Our second last chapter will discuss it further.

The blood of the divinely appointed sacrifices atoned for the sins that were unintentional by virtue of its sacrificial and life-enabling quality. God Himself appointed the blood to this holy office, because He gave it its sacrificial nature. He put it on the altar of sacrifice when He made it. It is well to notice here that *it was the blood of an unwitting animal that atoned for unwitting sin.* An innocent victim involuntarily yielded itself up to death for involuntary sin. As its unwitting sacrifice "covered" unwitting sin, the conscious sacrifice of Christ was voluntarily offered for all sin. *He who knew all about sin and yet knew no sin,* offered Himself without blemish unto God that He might be the means of taking away the sin of the world.

In the Great Sacrifice of Christ He laid on the altar not merely His blood, but all His Person, His entire Deity and humanity. The blood shed on Calvary was the visible part of an infinite sacrifice made by God Himself. The omniscient wisdom and infinite love of God cried out in every corpuscle of that Divine-Human blood shed on the cross, "I die to redeem sinful man from sin." Horace Bushnell speaks of this in an unforgetable way:

"His blood too, the blood of the incarnate Son of God, blood of the upper world as truly as of this—when it touches and stains the defiled earth of the planet, what so sacred blood on the horns of the altar and the lid of the mercy-seat, did any devoutest worshipper at the altar see sprinkled for his cleansing! There his sin he hoped could be dissolved away, and it comforted his conscience that by the offering of something as sacred as blood, he could fitly own his defilement, and by such tender argument win the needed cleansing.

"But the blood of Christ, He that was born of the Holy Ghost, He that was Immanuel—when this sprinkles Calvary, it is to Him as if some touch of cleansing were in it for the matter itself of the world! In short there is so much in this analogy, and it is so affecting, so profoundly real, that no worshipper most devout, before the altar, having once seen Christ—who He is, what He has done, by His cross, and the glorious offering He has made of Himself in His ministry of good, faithful unto death—who will not turn away instinctively to Him, saying, 'No more altars, goats or lambs; these were shadows I see; now has come the substance. This is my sacrifice and here is my peace—the blood that was shed for the remission of sins—this I take and want no other.' "[19]

> "Not all the blood of beasts,
>   On Jewish altars slain,
> Could give the guilty conscience peace,
>   Or wash away the stain.
>
> "But Christ the heav'ly Lamb
>   Takes all our sins away,
> A sacrifice of nobler name,
>   And richer blood than they."

---
19. The Vicarious Sacrifice, Vol. I, p. 474 (1891 Edition).

CHAPTER VI

THE MEANING OF FULFILMENT

HOW shall we define the Work of Christ in relation to sin. We may bound a country horizontally, but what about its other directions? When Redemption goes down as deep as sin and up as high as heaven, how shall we bound it? As to the meaning of what Christ has done for us, there is no earthly viewpoint, no matter how exalted it may be, from which can be seen all sides and directions of the Saviour's sacrifice.

Perhaps the best that can be done, is to define successive phases of it. These aspects should be supplementary to each other. Such an interpretation by phases has the advantage that what is wanting or inappropriate in one phase, may be found in another. Certain truths fit into one aspect, and can be expressed in it better than in others.

Seven is said to be the number of completeness. This is no mere fancy. If any doubt it, let him read the convincing treatise thereon, "The Heptadic Structure of Scripture," by R. McCormack (Marshall Bros.). The seven phases of Christ's work here chosen may not exhaust the subject; but they reveal a good deal of its character, proportions, qualities, blessings, beauty, and power.

These chosen aspects are—Substance, Source, Spirit, Means, Process, Extent, and Effect. A little practice beforehand in the use of this sevenfold method of defining will not be out of place. Let us apply it on two closely related subjects, namely, Sin and Christianity.

The Substance of Sin is (negatively) ungodliness and (positively) the anti-divine; its Source is self-consciousness[1] and self-will; its Spirit is selfishness;

---

1. By self-consciousness is meant, not the consciousness of self, but the self-conscious disposition where self-consciousness replaces simple consciousness. Self-consciousness like self-will centers or focusses all the activities of personality on self. It is the consciousness of selfishness.

its Means is perversion, making use of the Good to oppose the Best; its Process is self-realization by unbelief in God or by faith in that which is contrary to His will; its Extent is measured by its estrangement from and enmity to God; and its Effect is the disability and doom of everlasting death.

The Substance of Christianity is union with God in Christ; its Source is the sacrificial Person of the Crucified and Risen Redeemer; its Spirit is the love of Christ; its Means is receiving and imparting Jesus Christ; its Process is personal realization by faith in the indwelling Christ; its Extent is capacity for Christ; and its Effect is everlasting life.

We are now ready for the phasal interpretation of the subject in hand. *The substance of Jesus Christ's work on our behalf is the fulfilment of the nature of God in relation to man in his sin: the source of this fulfilment is the self-sacrifice of the Son of God: its spirit is the love of God: its means is the personal identification of Christ with man and sin: its process is the personal realization of Christ on the Cross: its extent is the counter-equivalence to sin in Christ's vicarious sacrifice in death: and its effect is divine enablement and human fulfilment.*

I. The Ascending Scale of Fulfilment

First in the order given should be our inquiry into the meaning of the fulfilment of the sacrificial nature of God in relation to man in his sin. This will be discussed here and in the following chapter.

We find that the word *fulfilment* steadily gains in meaning as that which is fulfilled rises in the scale of existence. The higher the order or rank of that said to be fulfilled, the higher and larger the meaning of its fulfilment.

Let us glance at the ascending meaning of fulfilment on the various levels where it takes place. A time is fulfilled when it arrives, a wish when it is realized, a joy when it is complete. A prophecy is fulfilled when that which it predicted comes to pass. A promise is fulfilled when it is kept. We are accustomed to say that a law is fulfilled when its demands are fully met, a contract or covenant when its provisions are carried out, a task when it is finished, a process when it is completed, a relation when it is consummated. A personal power or faculty is fulfilled in functioning to the full; a gift is fulfilled when accepted.

A spirit is fulfilled when it perfectly embodies itself or is enshrined in some act, manifestation, or achievement fully representing it. A nature is fulfilled in being true to itself, or in reaching the full expression or end of itself. Sacrificial nature is fulfilled when it fully manifests its spirit, reveals itself in some adequate sacrificial act or state. It is then true to itself in perfectly expressing itself in an embodiment of its purpose or objectification of its desire. Then the spirit and deed of sacrifice are commensurate with each other.

II. DIVINE AND HUMAN FULFILMENT COMPARED

The difference between the fulfilment of the divine and the fulfilment of the human may here be pointed out. All created things are fulfilled when the end for which they were made is realized. Thus, and only thus, can they reach the consummation of their existence. The end of any created existence is never within itself, but in God. Its fulfilment is always in the relation and purpose of the Creator.[2]

On the other hand, the divine nature is always fulfilled in itself. It reaches its consummation in the end wholly within itself. In one way, it is always consummated and already fulfilled; in another it is always being consummated and being fulfilled in all it does. God has never had a thought, desire, or will that did not fulfil His nature. Never has He performed an act except in fulfilment of what He is. But He may have

---

[2]. We may here notice how serious is any view that displaces God as Creator A God not needed in Creation is equally not needed in Redemption Without a Creator in the full sense, there can be no purpose in creation, no end, and then no fulfilment That which gives God a part-way place in Creation, part-way displaces Him as its end and fulfilment. When we need no Creator, we can have no God In the modern view God is Creator in name only. and sometimes not even that

desires and purposes not yet realized or fulfilled. When they are fulfilled, they fulfil His nature.

The divine nature may be fulfilled transcendently, that is without any relation to anything external to itself; or it may be fulfilled in itself and at the same time in relation to something it has called into existence. In this case God's nature fulfils itself in meeting its own demands in relation to created things, it meets its responsibilities to itself. God thus reaches the goal of His own purposes in these relations. In His relation to creation God ever fulfils or fills to the full His place as God, and realizes the possibilities of His relation to created things.

Necessarily, the uncreated and divine is the highest, the supreme order of existence. Because of this, the fulfilment of the divine nature is on the highest level or of the supreme order. In His fulfilment God is true to Himself, meets the necessities of the law of His Being, fulfils the requirements He Himself has appointed in relation to all that He has made.

The manifestations of the divine fulfilment vary according to the nature of that power or attribute He uses in the forefront of any activity. Naturally some power takes precedence according to the nature of the activity. For example, God fulfils Himself in creating. But His creative power while forefront in this activity, is not the only one employed. He fulfils Himself in man's redemption. His sacrificial love is then forefront in this activity; but this represents every atom of His Being.

A fulfilment of the divine nature may be preliminary, preparatory, progressive, or final, according to the character of its activity. A lesser activity and its fulfilment may lead the way to, or prepare for, a larger activity and its fulfilment. Many activities and fulfilments prepared the way for those of Redemption.

Every divine relation has its own capacity or possibility, and is filled to the full by God. In one sense, God fully expresses Himself in all that He does; not that there is no more of Him to express, but that there is no more room in the relation and the activity within it to manifest Himself.

In another way, all God's fulfilments overflow and go far beyond the capacity of His relations to created things. He reaches on to His greater and final purposes and satisfactions. In the Work of Christ His age-long purposes which had been prepared for by previous purposes and acts, were fulfilled, and the ultimate goal of His entire sacrificial nature was reached.

There is a supreme unity in all the divine fulfilments because of the unity of the divine nature and of all the divine activities. The fulfilment of this supreme unity, the unbroken continuity of its infinite fulfilment, is the largest and highest plane and scope of divine fulfilment that it is possible for us to conceive.

III. The Divine Viewpoint Necessary to Interpret Redemption

We have already said that there is no earthly point of view from which we can see all of that which reaches unto heaven itself. In naming the fulfilment of the sacrificial nature of God as the substance of Calvary's Redemption, we have in reality taken the divine viewpoint.

As the things we survey in study rise in the scale of existence, our viewpoint should rise accordingly. The low may be studied from a high point of view to good purpose; but the high can scarcely be studied from a low point of view, and the study be really profitable.

Perhaps the foremost cause of the conflict among the various theories of the atonement has been their lack of altitude in viewpoint. The lower their points of view, the more partial their interpretations, and the more they are bound to conflict with each other.

There is but one way to avoid all this conflict, namely, to rise above it. And there is but one way to rise above it, namely, to take the divine point of view—and keep to it. Hard as it may be to take it, it is far harder to keep to it, just as it is hard to get away down in humility before God, but harder by far to keep down.

As our Redemption from sin is wholly a work of God, it is no wonder that only the divine point of view is adequate to a satisfying survey of it. Every level has its own light; and every height has its own sight of that studied. Presumptuous as it may sound, we must look through the eyes of God to get an illuminative and lasting interpretation of His sacrifice in the death of His Son. That sacrifice was not made to raise theological problems, but to settle the problem of our sin. From the divine viewpoint human bewilderment and its objections tend to disappear.

> "That to the height of this great argument
> I may assert eternal providence,
> And justify the ways of God to men."

So Milton hoped by a high point of view to set forth the other side of this subject, viz., "Paradise Lost." Here we are considering "Paradise Regained." The great poet realized that whenever the divine is clarified it is justified, and that it could not be justified without being clarified. For Providence to give us the viewpoint of clarification and justification would be a providence concerning the greatest of all God's providences—that which provided our Redemption.

God has always been ready to take our point of view when needed. In the Incarnation He has done this permanently. We need a vast uplift of God to get His viewpoint. We must have regeneration, sanctification, special endowment, and new illumination of the Holy Spirit even to prefer the divine viewpoint. Alas, our sanctification is so unsteady and unripe, our endowments so tiny compared with the task, and our illumination so feeble compared with that of the mighty men of old who have presented this subject, we find it anything but easy to attempt it, let alone see eye to eye with God in it. And yet we dare not turn back from the task.

Of course, it is never possible for us to see just as God does. But we can take His viewpoint, even though we cannot see fully as He does and all He does. He has taken our place in the sacrifice of Calvary. Would it be a strange thing then, that He permits us to take His place in studying the meaning of the Death on the Cross? Unless the grace of this privilege be received, we are never in any measure in a position to speak for Him on this greatest of subjects.

IV. THE MYSTERY OF SIN'S FULFILMENT

There is one fulfilment which no height of viewpoint can ever enable us to understand or explain. This is the fulfilment of sin. To all other fulfilments everywhere it is the absolute antithesis, the infinitely opposite. Its absolute contrast strikes us blind and dumb.

It is God in all things which makes them intelligible and explainable. Because sin has nothing of God in it, it remains "the mystery of iniquity." Nothing that God has ever created can find the tiniest, the most infinitesimal particle of fulfilment in it or by it. And not this only, for sin is the absolute opposition to all fulfilment of God and in Him.

Here, then, is contrast astounding! While sin's fulfilment has nothing of God in it, *divine fulfilment has nothing but God in it.* Iniquity's fulfilment is all darkness; God's fulfilment is all light. And we are just as unable to see where it is all light, as where it is all dark. Moreover we carry unconsciously something of the darkness and blindness of our sinful nature into whatever we study. Blessed be God! we may carry something of the light of divine fulfilment into the darkness of sin's fulfilment, as we seek to understand it.

To behold the undimmed brightness of the white light of divine fulfilment in relation to sin, we need "eyes as a flame of fire." These our Lord has, but not man. No mortal eyes can look upon this celestial glory "above the brightness of the sun," shining forth in the personalization of the sacrificial fulfilment of God, and not be blinded. That white and dazzling radiance of the Person of the glorified Christ came from His having fulfilled the infinite sacrifice in God's purpose. Having become this Sacrifice, He entered upon it in everlasting state. The vision of Him who is God's sacrificial fulfilment is the greatest blinding power in the two universes, the physical and the spiritual. But a most blessed blinding this always proves to be. We can well afford to be blind to many things of little importance, if we are enabled thereby to see the King in all His glory. And to Him and the Father and Holy Spirit with Him, there is no glory so bright as that of His sacrificial fulfilment in relation to man in his sin. By His sacrifice of Himself Christ has clothed Himself with the garments of God's most dazzling glory.

V. THE TRANSFORMING VISION OF DIVINE FULFILMENT

On his way to Damascus Paul the Persecutor was blinded by the vision of the white light streaming forth from the Person of the Risen and Radiant Christ. The effect upon him was far more than physical. The resultant blinding of the eyes of his body may be taken as the outward and visible emblem of the blinding of the eyes of his soul, except for this particular—the former passed away while the latter never did. All the rest of his days Paul was blind to anything that would compete with Christ; incurably blind was he to self-will and every pursuit of self apart from Christ.

Yes, Paul was blinded, but only that he might see as never before. He exchanged the eyes of the sinner for those of the saint. He became permanently unable to see except in the light of the spirit and life of Christ. Ever after he proved to be totally blind to interests other than those of the service of Christ. Nevermore could he see gain except in the gain of Christ. Thenceforth all things became but dross and loss that he might "win Christ," who to him had become the Living Gold of God, infinite and imperishable in worth.

That wondrous light of the glory of the Lord of heaven and earth imprinted upon the retina of the eyes of the Great Apostle's soul the majestic form of the glorified Christ. All the rest of his life everywhere he looked, he saw Christ in the center of his field of vision. The indellible imprint had burned itself into his soul. Thenceforth he projected it into all that he saw.

An effect similar to this takes place when one comes to see undimmed the full glory of the divine fulfilment in man's redemption. But this depends upon beholding it in its celestial brightness as it flamed forth on the altar of God when Christ offered up the divine sacrifice of Himself for our sins, "paid the debt and set us free."

To behold Calvary's meaning and message, to see the process of Christ's sacrificial suffering on the Cross, fulfilling the divine passion, passing through the agony of death, the blinding from this vision may be so thorough and permanent that nothing but the divine fulfilment will matter ever after. Only at the Cross of Calvary can this glory of redeeming love be seen in its full splendor. The unquenchable glory of the humility of God the Son suffering sin's last and worst torment for us, is too much and too deep and too wondrous for any one to behold and forget or remain unmoved and unchanged.

It was the similar vision at "the Burning Bush" which changed Moses from a run-away failure into the great national deliverer, statesman, and law-giver. (See Stephen's interpretation, Acts 7: 25.) But "only he who sees" as Moses did, "takes off his shoes." The rest sit around and make theological sand-piles. The "blackberries" have dried up and disappeared ever since naturalism camped on the ground for "critical research."

Isaiah had a vision similar to that of Moses when he "saw the Lord sitting on a throne high and lifted up." The vision of God as enthroned blinded the young courtier-prophet to the hope he had in an earthly king in the agony of the sad hour when his smitten relative, King Uzziah, lay dead. Then Isaiah saw God fulfilling Himself by establishing the larger hope for the whole world in the coming Messianic King. Then, too, Isaiah looked upon Him and His glory who was to become in the fulness of time "an offering for sin," because there would be laid "on him the iniquity of us all."

VI. THE BLINDNESS THAT IS VISION

All prophets, preachers, and other servants of God become such by the blinding which enables them to see with God and for Him. This was true even in the most illustrious instance of all, that of our blessed Lord. These words apply to Him as to no one else: "Who is so blind as my Servant?" Because He was deaf and blind to anything but the fulfilment of His mission as the sacrificial "suffering Servant," He "was bruised for our iniquities," "wounded for our transgressions," "despised and rejected of men," became "a man of sorrows and acquainted with grief," was "oppressed and afflicted," "with whose stripes we are healed," was "taken from prison and from judgment," "brought as a lamb to the slaughter," had "travail of soul," was "stricken for the transgressions of the people," "bore their iniquities," "bare the sin of many," "poured out his soul unto death," was "numbered with the transgressors," was "cut off out of the land of the living," "yet it pleased the Lord to bruise him," "He hath put him to grief," but "he shall be satisfied," because God could say of Him, "My Righteous Servant shall justify many." Was there ever such a remarkable and perfect pre-picture? Isaiah's vision of Christ's work reads like history.

How utterly blind was our Lord to any and every inducement leading to self-reservation from self-sacrifice that fulfilled the Father's will! The eye of the soul of the Son of God had indelibly imprinted on its retina the unalterable end to His existence on earth, the consummation of the remedy for sin in His death on the Cross. Blind to all that entrances the eyes of sinful men, He saw clearly from the beginning of His ministry the goal of man's redemption by His sufferings and death on Calvary.

VII. The Light Seen in the Light of Fulfilment

The Cross was no afterthought to Him who saw the end from the beginning. He knew the meaning of the fulfilment of His self-sacrifice. As He Himself said, He came "not to destroy but to fulfil," or as He proclaimed at the very beginning of His brief ministry, "to fulfil all righteousness." So in due time "He set his face steadfastly to go to Jerusalem," and there be "perfected" as the propitiation for sin.

The light by which Jesus saw the fulfilment of His life, was the same light by which He saw the coming fulfilment of His death. And the same light gleamed in the eyes of His risen body. To the two disciples on the way to Emmaus He explained the depths of the necessity for the death of the Messiah, as foretold in the Old Testament Scriptures. Could we have the help of that exposition of the Old Testament, it would do more to enlighten us than all the books and commentaries men have produced. Unless He walks with us too on our way to the meaning of the Cross, and provides the light by which we may see the light of the sacrificial fulfilment of God's nature in His Son's death on Calvary, it is bound to be to us one of the most puzzling and misunderstood events in all human history.

"In thy light shall we see light." This is the light of God for the eyes He opens; and for it there is no substitute. The glowworm lights of science and philosophy have their place, and we need not despise them; nor on the other hand need we be so infatuated with them that practically we come to despise "the light of the glory of God in the face of Jesus Christ."

The light of man's wisdom in such a matter as the death of our Lord cannot do more than make the surrounding darkness visible. Thank God for the light of the fulfilment of His sacrificial spirit, turning the gloom of the Cross into a white radiance, and casting its far-reaching beams of glory over all history and the whole universe! It is the revelation of the meaning of all things past and present, the center of the two eternities. It is the light that never fails on sea or land, in life or death. To see it is to see by it, and as God sees. We know we have God's viewpoint when we see *His light*. If by means of it we study the meaning of Calvary, our quest of its truth will not be in vain; and to its heavenly vision we can never be disobedient.

CHAPTER VII

TRIUNE DIVINE FULFILMENT

THE threefold personality of the Godhead is a teaching due to Revelation alone. No human mind of itself could ever have found it out. Of necessity God is His own interpreter. He alone can make plain the mystery of the Trinity.

The coming of Jesus Christ and His manifestation of Deity compelled the doctrine of the triune Godhead. He was the Word, and the Word was God. He said, "I and my Father are one." In the Greek original "one" is neuter in gender. He must have meant therefore, "I and my Father are one substance." The nature of Christ's Person must correspond with the character of His work; and this has been the work of God which none but He himself could do.

Here we cannot enter upon the statement of proofs for Christ's Deity and the Trinity. It is sufficient to point out that the Trinity and Redemption are interdependent doctrines. No article of our faith more depends on the threefold personality of God than the Work of Christ in Redemption. Whenever one of these teachings has been thrown overboard, the other was immediately sent after it.

I. No Fulfilment in Redemption Without the Trinity

God is personal. The effect were infinitely greater than its cause, if impersonal Deity created persons. It is unreasonable to say that God is personal but not a Person. One might as well say that He is intellectual, but has no mind, or that He is loving but has no heart. The Pantheistic interpreter is often guilty of the folly of attributing personal qualities and powers to God, while at the same time denying His personality.

God is tri-personal. Elsewhere I have presented two

arguments for the tri-personality of God.[1] First, the psychological consideration that "other-consciousness" is necessary in perfect personality. A self-conscious God would be worse than a self-conscious man. Only selfish personality is fundamentally self-conscious. Unselfish "other-consciousness" requires persons in the Godhead. Second, the impartation of divine Redemption is a divine function, and requires that the Redeemer be divine. Christ could not impart the benefit of His redemptive work unless He is Deity. Only God can give the Spirit of God; and Christ does give the Holy Spirit.

Here we come face to face with a third consideration, namely, that it requires as much the Divine to make Redemption's sacrifice as to impart its benefit. Taking the substance of Christ's work to be divine fulfilment, this is utterly impossible without the tri-personality of the Trinity.

When God is thought of as but one Person only, fulfilling Himself in Himself is inescapably the staleness of self-repetition. And self-repetition in place of self-fulfilment means utter stagnation of Being. For example, Divine Fatherhood cannot fulfil itself in itself. An eternal Father and no eternal Son is a nonentity of nonsense.

II. GOD'S FULFILMENT THE MEANS OF OURS

The difference between divine and human fulfilment may be considered a bit further. As already said, God's self-fulfilment is of an entirely different order from that of man. *Only God can fulfil Himself in Himself.* His fulfilment is as much higher than ours, as His uncreated nature is higher than our created nature.

Only God can in righteousness be the end of His own existence. Nothing created by Him can be the end of its own existence, and God still be God. He can make nothing with an existence independent of His. His creative nature would fail to fulfil itself, if He brought

---

1. The Virgin's Son, p 129 sq

anything into existence with an end for it lower than Himself. "He cannot deny Himself."

We never so fool ourselves as when we try to fulfil ourselves in some other created thing, such as riches, power, or praise of men. We really attempt to be gods when we try to fulfil ourselves in ourselves. The devil has well been called "the Ape of God." Even so might any sinner be described, for the essence of sin is seeking fulfilment in other than God.

God, because He is God, must be the end and fulfilment of all creation. He is left with no choice in this matter. It is not selfish in God to be the end of all things. Nothing else is worthy and capable of being the consummation of created things. The welfare of all things is secured by making Him their end. Thus God is absolutely unselfish in seeking His own glory, for only out of His glory can come glory and blessedness to all. So God is absolutely true to Himself and at the same time absolutely true to all things in seeking His own glory in the fulfilment of all things in Him.

We would be perfectly selfish in seeking our own glory and satisfaction apart from that of God. The sinner acts as though he had created himself and that all things exist primarily for his sake. When we attempt to fulfil ourselves in ourselves, we must assume that all other things can find their fulfilment in us too. But the whole universe is framed for God. He is as indispensable as inescapable. We cannot ignore Him without undoing ourselves.

III. Redemption's Sacrifice Within God

When God is said to fulfil Himself in created things, it is in them and not by them. It is *where* He fulfils Himself, not by what. He fulfils Himself in Himself; when, for example, the Father fulfils Himself in the Son; and this fulfilment is carried into the divine relation to created things, and enables them to find their fulfilment in Him.

The divine is a means to an end, only when the end is

divine, that is, when it is in God Himself. Because Christ's sacrifice is God fulfilling Himself in Himself, *this sacrifice for our sin is not so much unto God as in God or by Him.*

The old objection to propitiation that it is something offered to God *ab extra,* from without, loses point in the fulfilment-interpretation. Since the sacrifice of Himself makes Christ the propitiation for our sins, it is within God, and a commercial theory of it would be *faux pas.*

Because the essence of Redemption is divine self-fulfilment, it is a process of the very Being of God. It is therefore as profound a subject as was ever thought upon by the mind of man. Its substance being wholly within the movement of the Being of God, no one can think into its heights and depths without being awed into a profound reverence for it. This subject can be saved from superficial treatment by beholding in adoration its profound meaning in the deepest and highest process going on anywhere, that of divine fulfilment. A day of irreverence is always one of shallow thinking. The swaggering self-sufficiency of intellectual conceit is never more out of place than before the Cross of Christ. Pride would be a poor interpreter of God in humility fulfilling Himself in the sufferings of His Son on Calvary.

"When I survey the wondrous Cross
 On which the Prince of Glory died,
 My richest gain I count but loss,
 And pour contempt on all my pride."

IV. ALL PERSONAL FULFILMENT NECESSARILY RECIPROCAL

We may next consider the mutual or reciprocal character of divine fulfilment. Fulfilment within the Trinity is an eternal reciprocation. Eternally there has been the fulfilment of the Father in the Son and the Holy Spirit, the fulfilment of the Son in the Father and the Holy Spirit, and the fulfilment of the Holy Spirit in the Father and the Son. This partly explains what is meant by God fulfilling Himself in Himself.

When God fulfils Himself in relation to created things, this mutuality of fulfilment necessarily continues. It is then carried into and manifested in the divine relation to these things. So every divine fulfilment in created things expresses to some extent the reciprocal life and interrelations of the Holy Trinity.

It is in these personal and reciprocal relations of the Godhead that we find the unlimited resources of God to do what He will in Creation. At first sight the *Kenosis,* the self-emptying and self-limitation of God the Son in the Incarnation, and the deeper sacrifice of His death, the deeper *Kenosis* at Calvary than at Bethlehem, may look like a vast impoverishment of the Trinity; but seen from the fulfilment point of view, they express as nothing else can do the unlimited richness of the sacrificial nature of God.

Everything of value in created things is such at the expense of the sacrificial nature of God. And the more it is worth, the more it has cost in divine sacrifice. Out of the riches of the divine interrelations they were all called into being; and out of them the whole universe is sustained. It is by sacrificial relation that God has ever fulfilled Himself in the Trinity, and by this sacrificial relation carried into the whole realm of nature fulfilled Himself there. When God fulfilled Himself in relation to man in his sin, it was out of the riches of the resources of the Trinity, that this was done. The mutual fulfilment of the Persons of the Holy Trinity is the pattern of all personal fulfilment. Since personal fulfilment is correlative and reciprocal in the Godhead, it is correlative and reciprocal in all other personal relations. As God the Father could not fulfil Himself in God the Son without the Son fulfilling Himself in the Father, even so God could not fulfil Himself in man without man fulfilling himself in God. Since sin is a personal thing, God could not fulfil Himself in relation to it without it fulfilling itself in relation to Him.

V. Sin's Fulfilment Interacting with Divine Fulfilment

As to the fulfilment of sin the difficulty is apparent that it is not something made by God and with its end in Him. As already said, its fulfilment is just the reverse of this. *Its end is to end God.* In the absolute and ultimate sin must therefore be ever unfulfilled. Because of the anti-divine nature of sin's fulfilment it is very easy to involve ourselves in a tangle of contradictions in setting it forth.

This much, however, seems indisputable: though sin is in nature absolutely opposed to the divine, its fulfilment interacts with that of the divine. For its fulfilment sin is dependent upon the divine fulfilment. We must beware of the danger of thinking of sin in the abstract. *Sin in man is man in sin.* God fulfils Himself in relation to man in sin, and thus to sin in man; and sin in man is thus enabled to fulfil itself in relation to God.

It is one thing for God to fulfil Himself in relation to man as man; and it is another for Him to fulfil Himself in relation to man in sin and sin in man. The former took place at Bethlehem; and the latter at Calvary.

As to man, God fulfils Himself in life given, while sin fulfils itself in death inflicted. Only as God fulfils Himself in giving life is it possible for sin to fulfil itself in the death inflicted on this life. More specifically, when God fulfilled Himself by giving the life of His Son to save man in his sin, this gave sin the opportunity to fulfil itself in direct relation to God Himself.

It looks as though the sacrificial nature of God could not fulfil itself, and God fill His place as God, without giving sin this opportunity to fulfil itself in relation to Him, who was the means of the divine fulfilment in relation to it. His fulfilment in sacrifice to destroy sin enabled sin so to interact with it that it could fulfil itself by meting out death to Him who embodied the divine sacrifice. So God could not fulfil Himself in giving His Son to man in his sin, without subjecting the life of the Son to death at the hands of sin.

When in the beginning of human history God gave life to man, sin made full use of its opportunity to fulfil its anti-divine nature in bringing to pass man's death to God. It then fulfilled itself in relation to the gift of God, that is to God as far as He had gone in giving life to man. When in Redemption's great sacrifice God went much further, and gave His only begotten Son to bring back life in God to man, sin could also go further; and when this opportunity was given, it did not hesitate to inflict death on the Son sacrificed for man.

This was the price which man's Redemption cost God in establishing the new means of man's fulfilment in the Son. And it cost the Son His submission to the death by sin. Only by permitting sin to slay His Son could God provide the new basis of man's fulfilment in His sacrifice. This is the dark shadow sin cast across the sacrificial work of our Lord and Redeemer.

VI. How Sin Fulfilled Itself in Christ's Death

Man's physical death which was possible to a physical body, sin made inevitable and put its sting in this death. Long had sin been fulfilling itself in man's death both physical and spiritual. The patience of God had waited long for the fulness of time when He could fulfil His sacrificial nature, and give back to man both divine life and a death-overcoming body.

Sin being not an abstraction but a living, concrete thing in man, it was man's sin. How did sin in man or man in sin fulfil sin's anti-divine nature in direct relation to God Himself? Being an uncreated existence, eternal and immortal spirit, God as such could not be made to suffer death. Moreover God the Son could not die to the Father and the Holy Spirit, any more than God the Father could die to the other two Persons of the Holy Trinity. But God the Son Incarnate, the Word made flesh, the Redeemer in a mortal human body, could die physically. We see that God found it necessary, the cup could not pass, if He brought to pass man's redemption, that sin must be given the chance to bring to pass the death of the body of His Incarnation. In other words, the life God gave in the Incarnation gave sin the chance to fulfil itself in relation to it.

At Calvary sin did its utmost possible to the divine Person of the Incarnate Son. Strange to say, only as God opened up the opportunity to sin to do its worst, could He do His best. In making man as moral and personal, He could not thus do His best without giving sin the opportunity to do its worst. In sending the New Adam, God could not do His utmost for all the descendants of the Old Adam, except by opening the door of opportunity to sin to do its utmost. And it surely did all that!

Sin in man is the supreme audacity of infinite sacrilege reaching up to the highest it could ever attempt. It made the utmost possible assault upon God Himself, laying hold upon the Person of God the Son. When sin entered His incarnate experience as a death-dealing power, it reached its most daring and utmost possible fulfilment.

In His sacrifice of the Son on the Cross God made the fullest, the greatest manifestation of His sacrificial nature possible. Then sin was able to make the fullest and greatest manifestation of its nature, its anti-sacrificial opposition. Then it showed most clearly, *it stops at nothing possible in enmity to God*. Then its deepest meaning was revealed most plainly. Then it completely unmasked itself. The naked demon resident in every sin then and there stepped out in full view of the whole world. The fiendish enmity of utmost hostility to the absolute perfection of the most loving sacrifice of God for man took hold on man, used man for whom this love was given, that sin's anti-divine attitude and magnitude might strike its most awful blow at God Himself. It was the very goodness of God in Christ, the infinite condescending humility of His grace that lent possibility to iniquity to manifest to the uttermost its innermost. So sin fulfilled itself!

Calvary's disclosure of the inwardness of sin will be more fully discussed in a later chapter on "Sin's Treatment of Christ." Here in passing it may be briefly remarked that the Cross is the last word on the Godward meaning of sin. The whole trend and inner character of its existence was there fully established for all time. Then irrefutable proof of the final and adequate exhibition of the sinfulness of sin was furnished in full view of heaven, earth, and hell. For the first and last time in all history all that was in sin fully manifested itself in man. After its long career of ungodliness it had at last brought mankind to commit the most awful deed in all the ages. And all this was possible because the richest manifestation of God's grace, of all that was in God, of God Himself, was taking place. There on the Cross sin's deepest and worst was face to face with the deepest and best in God.

VII. The Fulfilment of the Father, Son, and Holy Spirit

The perfect fulfilment of the divine nature at Calvary was manifest. It is impossible to imagine God doing more for us than the giving up of His Son to die for us. Then it was that the Father Himself made His infinite sacrifice. More and deeper He could not suffer than a Father's agony in sacrificially taking the part He must in His Son's death. There He was doing the utmost of His best in filling His place as God in sacrifice. Then He fulfilled His nature as Father in doing all His part in solving the problem of sin's destruction and man's liberation.

The Son also fulfilled His sacrificial nature by obediently suffering the pains of death, so dedicating Himself personally, and placing Himself utterly at the disposal of man's need of redemption. And not only manward, but also Godward did He fulfil His divine-human nature. All the riches of His righteousness suffering for us and because of our sin, all the power of His vicarious humanity, all the resources of His sacrificial Deity were put at the disposal of the work of restoring man's self-fulfilment by His own self-bestowment.

The Holy Spirit also fulfilled Himself as the Spirit of divine sacrifice. In all the eternity of the past He had fulfilled the Sacrificial will and purpose of the Father, and went forth from the Son in all His sacrificial activity. He is the Great Spirit of *divine fulfilment*. The Scriptures tell of His part in the Incarnation. In the next great sacrifice of God, that of the Death on the Cross, He fulfilled His own nature as the indwelling Spirit of the Son, ministering to Him and sustaining Him in the dark hours of the suffering and death on Calvary.

CHAPTER VIII

SOURCE AND SUBSTANCE

WHEN substance is important, its source must also be important. Of course, substance must be like its origin, as a stream is like its spring. The fountain-head of the River of Redemption being the sacrificial nature of God, this explains much about its volume, depth, breadth, direction, and beauty.

When the fulfilment of the nature of God is regarded as the substance of Christ's Redemption, naturally the sacrificial nature of God *must* be taken as its source. Genetic theology must make much of sacrifice, for it is the most important genetic factor in God or man. All good things in heaven or earth find in it not only their source, but also much of their explanation.

Source and substance naturally make mutual revelations about each other. The sacrificial nature of God reveals much about Christ's work of Redemption, even as His work of Redemption reveals much about the richness of the sacrificial nature that gave it origin. Shakespeare tells us:

> . . . "Great floods have flown
> From simple sources."

This means there are hidden deeps in even simple things. How immeasurable then the depths of the profound things of God. "Deep calleth unto deep." The depths of the divine sacrificial nature broke forth in the River of Redemption.

I. THE SACRIFICIAL FOUNDATIONAL

The deepest thing in the nature of God is His sacrificial character; or putting it the other way, His sacrificial nature is the deepest thing in God. He is fundamentally or foundationally a Sacrificial Being. This is deepest in His very holiness.

Holiness or wholeness in God means more than in man, even as wholeness in man means more than wholeness in an animal. The holiness of God is highest in two senses. It is highest in Him as the Most High. But it is also highest in Him as sacrificial, a holiness not for its own sake. Righteousness is ethical; holiness is personal; sacrificial is both.

The sacrificial nature is the exact opposite to the selfish. It is the unselfish nature at work in all the undertakings of God. In general it is the vicarious nature which undertakes at its own cost something on behalf of another. It lies back of all creation. It is the source of all loving interest and devotion. As the philanthropist, John Howard expressed it:

"My superfluities ought to give way to other men's conveniences; my conveniences ought to give way to others' necessities; and my necessities ought to give way to other people's extremities."

The reason for sacrifice to God is because it is the most fitting way to recognize His nature. It pays respect in kind. That is an intelligent order of worship which says by sacrifice, "I understand Thee, my God." Our original and constant debt to divine sacrifice requires appreciation in kind, just as divine forgiveness requires that we forgive each other.

Sacrifice is foundational in worship because it is foundational in the nature of God and in the Christian religion. Christ "by eternal spirit offered himself unto God." The sacrificial nature of God expresses itself by its own spirit, its own devotion.

On our part sacrifice to God is the most fitting way to express our standing before Him as sinners. It should be offered humbly with the contrite spirit, for the spirit of the deed counts much. "The sacrifices of God are a broken spirit; a broken and a contrite heart, O God, thou wilt not despise."

Sacrifice to be fitting should be of our best, because Christ gave His best for us—even Himself. His sacrifice on our behalf met every condition and requirement of acceptability to the Father and of redemption toward us. "Without blemish" He gave Himself in the way the Father had appointed, and this way fully recognized the fact and extent of our sin. For this reason it was "a sacrifice acceptable, well-pleasing unto God."

II. THE MEANING OF DIVINE SACRIFICE

The immediate source of Redemption is the Son's self-sacrifice, and the mediate the sacrifice of the Father and the Holy Spirit. While self-sacrifice is possible to God the Son, sacrifice is possible to God the Father. The surrenders of the Father's sacrificial nature reached the greatest possible to Him in giving His only begotten Son; and the surrenders of the Son's sacrificial nature reached the utmost possible in His self-sacrifice when in death "He gave himself up for us all."

The two main ideas in self-sacrifice are self-renouncement and self-dedication. Sacrifice itself means the latter. There can be no true sacrifice which is not an expression of self-dedication. God always first gives Himself in all that He does, and all that He has ever done is expressive of His having given Himself as far as it is possible according to the capacity of that to which He gives Himself.

Self-renouncement and self-dedication are more than negative and positive aspects of the same thing. Self-renouncement is more than self-denial, even as denial of self is more than self-denial. In self-denial one refuses himself something enjoyable or profitable. In denial of self he refuses to consider himself. In self-emptying he sweeps himself bare of powers and privileges. In self-renouncement he casts himself out. Self-emptying pictures Christ's incarnation, and self-renouncement His death on the Cross. In the former He dedicated Himself to man as man; and in the latter He dedicated Himself to man as a sinner.

Sacrifice and self-sacrifice are the same in nature. It may cost a mother her utmost in sacrifice to give up her son to die in some great cause. For her it would be easier by far to die herself. Because of his death she dies daily. To rate sacrifice as always far below self-sacrifice is not necessary. They may be equal to each other.

The Father could not in Person die on the Cross, any more than He could become the Babe of Bethlehem. It cost Him His utmost to give His Son in death, even as it cost the Son His utmost to die for us. The latter sacrifice so brought death into the experience of the Son that its effect lives forever in His Person. And the former sacrifice so brought death into the experience of the Father that it left an everlasting effect upon Him, the mark of which upon His heart will remain to all eternity.

W. M. Clow names three things in the Father's sacrifice: first, the impoverishment of the Godhead in the Incarnation; second, the infinite sympathy of the Father with the Son during His suffering on the Cross; and, third, the share which the Father took in the Son's agony on the Cross.[1] In this matter the same might be said of the Holy Spirit as of the Father.

All the Godhead had real share in this great sacrifice; but the Son offered up Himself. The Father and the Holy Spirit fulfilled their natures in the giving of the Son and by response to the Son's self-giving. His self-sacrifice is the heart and source of Redemption.

III. The Universality of Sacrifice

The divine sacrifice on account of sin cannot be well understood apart from the universal and eternal sacrifice of God. Sacrificial is that nature which devotes itself to the good of another. In God this nature has eternally manifested itself within the Trinity. He would be God to more than Himself. Being eternally sacrificial He was true to His nature in creating all things. How many systems in the infinite past He called into being, He alone knows. But we do know something about the creation to which we belong, for

---

1. The Cross in Christian Experience, p. 17 sq

He has told us about it. That His revelation is denied by some, is to be expected. There is nothing else about Him that has not been denied by some one. It is not that the deniers know more, but that they know less, and publish and perpetuate it by refusing this direct information from God.

The making of the universe and all that God does in it and for it, represent sacrifice on His part. He could not create anything without cost to Himself. He must enter into the limitations of His relations to all creation. And He cannot care for all He has created without the constant sacrifice of His Providential regard. In a similar way He could not redeem man from sin without entering into certain definite limitations of sacrifice.

Everywhere in the universe sacrifice is necessary. This is true not only as to its origin but also as to its perpetuation. Then, too, sacrifice lies as deeply in the relation of created things to each other as it does in the relation of God to all He has made. The universe would not be the unity which makes it a universe, but for the embedded nature of sacrifice put into it by the Creator, and which everywhere pervades it. All things "consist" (hold together) in Him who is the divine sacrifice personalized and incarnate.

The necessity for sacrifice has been thought by some as due wholly to the presence of evil in the world; and were there no sin, there would be no need of sacrifice. But the normal and necessary relation everywhere in creation is that of sacrifice. What sin has attacked is the foundational relation of God and the universe, and the constitution of the universe itself.

IV. THE NECESSITY AND PATTERN OF ALL SACRIFICE

Sin did not originate the necessity of sacrifice, but the necessity of special sacrifice. Even though there had been no sin, sacrifice would have been the substance of God's relation to us and of ours to Him. Even in a sinless world sacrifice would be as necessary as love, as necessary as in heaven itself. In fact, it is sacrifice that makes heaven heaven. Love without sacrifice would be immature and incomplete and devoid of proper source.

In Nature nothing exists without its own meaning and contribution to the rest of the world. No part of the universe exists for itself alone. As in a bee-hive, each bee has its own sacrifice to make for the good of the whole hive. No other principle of existence is permitted. When the drones have no longer any contribution to make, they are forthwith dispatched. Nature seems to have anticipated this fate for them by furnishing no weapon of defense, no sting to protect themselves. All this economy cannot be due to the struggle with environment, for those who reproduce, the queen and drones, are completely shielded from all such struggle; and the workers, the undeveloped females, have all the hardship. If by chance one does lay an egg, it is sure to turn out a drone.

That sacrifice is essential to the universe, and its necessity is embedded in all Nature, is one thing; the necessity of the special sacrifice to cope with the unnatural thing called sin, is another. The latter necessity is threefold—grounded in the nature of God, of man, and of sin. The objective necessity in sin and man for adequate treatment of the problem of sin, and the subjective necessity in the nature of God being true to His sacrificial relation are after all, but phases of the same necessity. The necessity of reintegrating man into the unity of the universe and bringing him into harmony with God by imparting sacrificial nature to him, and constituting him thereby a sacrificial order of personality, is grounded in the primal necessity of the sacrificial nature of God as the pattern of all creation.

Sacrifice is the law of the relation of the Three Persons of the Trinity. Each exists as a sacrificial personality, in the permanent and constitutional relation of One Sacrificial Being. As there is one perfect "other-consciousness" in the triune Godhead, there is also one perfect nature of sacrifice in all Three Persons of the Trinity. Sacrificially the Three "Other-Selves" exist for each other, as they have existed for all eternity. This sacrificial inter-relation carries its fulfilment into all the relations with Creation. It was this sacrificial nature of the Son who gave Himself to the Father and the Holy Spirit, that offered up the sacrifice on Calvary. Christ's sacrifice was not therefore a mere pattern of the divine sacrifice; it was the divine sacrifice itself, and involved all Three Persons of the Holy Trinity.

V. The Sacrifice of Redemption

As the universe could be constructed in but one way, on the constitutional principle of sacrifice, this was patterned after the sacrificial unity of the Trinity itself. Hence the only way that the enemy which had attacked the sacrificial nature and principle, could be successfully met, was by the same sacrificial nature and principle which had laid the foundation of the worlds.

One may speak of "throwing good money after bad," meaning that a further investment is useless. This is the case where there is no foundation left in the enterprise. It was a similar necessity which God faced, namely, that of providing a new foundation of special sacrifice for man. Because of sin, the first foundation had been swept away. The new foundation cost a greater sacrifice than that of Creation. The divine Person of the Creator had to be Himself dedicated and sacrificed to become the new foundation.

In a later chapter the extent of the redeeming sacrifice of Christ will be discussed. Here it may be said briefly that the vast proportions of this sacrifice necessary are evident even from the preparatory sacrifice of the Incarnation. Then human nature was sacrificially taken into the personal nature of the Son, and became a permanent part of His Personality. This may seem like rushing into a statement that angels fear to make, but they desired to look into this great sacrifice.

But the more amazing sacrifice was that God Incarnate should suffer the torture of a physical death by crucifixion at the hands of sinful men. There is good reason for the Scriptures saying that Christ "can save unto the uttermost," for His sacrifice for the lost went to the uttermost. In this death of His Son, God has given Himself in the largest way and fullest measure possible.

Sacrificing to the utmost possible is perfectly in keeping with the divine nature. *God is nothing if not sacrificial.* This explains why he made man, though foreseeing that man would sin and cause the necessity of the final because fullest possible sacrifice. God's sacrificial nature did not shrink from calling into existence the human race, though it would fill the history of all the centuries with its sinning.

It would seem that only the infinite, internal compulsion of the sacrificial, divine nature would undertake the tremendous problem of man and his sin. Nothing else than sacrifice can satisfy and fulfil sacrificial nature. In no other way can the beneficent bent within the blessed nature of God be met. When the need called for the last and greatest in sacrifice, nothing else than the last and greatest in sacrifice could satisfy the sacrificial nature of God.

VI. WHEN GOD'S SACRIFICIAL NATURE FULFILLED ITSELF

When, we may ask, does the sacrificial nature of God fulfil itself in relation to sin? In preliminary reply it may be said, *when all that is in God is fulfilled in relation to all that is in sin.* Some theories of the Atonement fail to recognize all that is in God, and others all that is in sin. "The Moral Influence" theory fails in both of these, but it is not alone in this respect.

All of God's nature being sacrificial, and all that is in sin being manifest at Calvary, then all that was in God was fulfilled in relation to all that is in sin.

In one way the view nearest akin to that here presented, is that Christ's work on our behalf fulfilled the broken law of God. This is true as far as it goes; but it does not recognize God's sacrificial nature as much as His judicial power; and sin does more than break law, it breaks souls.

Take another example in "the Judgment-Death" theory, which is similar to the one just mentioned. This presents the thought that Christ bore on the Cross God's judgment on sin. God does in some measure judge sin in His every act in relation thereto. As the sacrifice of Calvary was His greatest work in relation to sin, He thereby most fully expressed His judgment upon it. That this was the sole end of the divine sacrifice, the ultimate purpose of it, is not so evident. All the divine nature is not expressed and fulfilled in passing judgment; and the sacrificial nature of God is not fully expressed in either inflicting or bearing such judgment. God is vastly more than a judge in the work of Redemption. He was more than judicial toward sin; He was the bearer of *it*, not merely judgment upon it. Christ was the suffering sacrifice that bore sin "in His own body on the tree." If but the legal matter of passing judgment on sin were all that was needed to be done, the problem would be comparatively small. The sacrificial sufferings on the Cross have deeper meaning than the spectacle of the Father inflicting penalty on the Son.

The penal theories doubtless have something in them, but the infliction of penalty cannot fully represent the sacrificial nature of God. This will be dealt with later. It is often asked, on the other hand, why forgiveness of sin is not enough. Some, like Moberly, have looked upon repentance as the substance of Christ's work for us. That Christ died on the Cross in repentance or contrition for our sin looks rather artificial. There is little to support this view.

Further, it may be pointed out that all God's nature is not fulfilled in forgiveness, even as all that is in sin is not manifested by repentance for it, especially when the one who repents is not the one who sinned. Neither of these ways provide for the restoration of the means of man's fulfilment in God. An outstanding thing about the sacrificial fulfilment of the divine nature in relation to all that is in sin and in man, is that it is in no sense a fragmentary view.

VII. THE SETTING OF REDEMPTION'S SACRIFICE

The sacrificial is the largest and most complete of all the forms and instances of divine fulfilment; and the death for sin is the largest and most important instance of divine sacrifice. Its fulfilment is the total view, because all fulfilments other than the sacrificial are partial. It alone comprehends all. It may also be asked how was it that the death on Calvary fulfilled God's sacrificial nature? *Because there God's nature went to its utmost on behalf of man and on account of his sin, and when His utmost was needed.*

God's nature would not be fulfilled in sacrificing superfluously. It is fulfilled in sacrificing to the utmost only when the utmost was needed. Since nothing less than God's utmost in sacrifice could fill the need of man, nothing less would satisfy His love and fulfil His nature. We may well crown Christ Lord of all, because His death on the Cross was the crowning fulfilment of the whole nature of God. *It sums up all sacrifice.*

In view of the general unity of all the divine fulfilments, there were other fulfilments which prepared the way for that on Calvary, and others following it. To this Paul referred when he represented the fulfilment of Nature as depending upon that of Redemption and waiting for that to reach its own. "The whole creation groaneth and travaileth together in pain until now." This was because the consummation of Nature's existence had to wait "Till all be fulfilled in the Kingdom of God."

The same holds true in regard to the fulfilment of man's nature. Though we "have the firstfruits of the Spirit, even we ourselves groan within ourselves, waiting for the adoption, to wit, the redemption of our body." "That consummation devoutly to be wished for," shall then come to pass, even "the manifestation of the sons of God."

In the midst, then, of a setting of many successive relations of God and their respective fulfilments does the fulfilment of His sacrifice for sin forever stand. He fulfilled His creative nature in calling the world into being. Having created man He fulfilled His providential relation and nature in caring for him, and His kinship relation in the Incarnation. Having made His sacrifice for sin and finished this part of His redemptive work, He goes on to fulfil His leadership relation and His Kingly office in the Kingdom of the Redeemed.

As all sin is a sacrifice to the devil of selfishness, Redemption is the sacrifice of all the unselfishness of God to end sin. We must fulfil our relation to it as well as by it. Unlimited confidence in and supreme devotion to Him alone can fulfil our relation to His supreme sacrifice for us.

When Alexander the Great during a long and weary march refused the drink of water offered him, lest his men who had no opportunity then to quench their thirst, should be discouraged by his draught, they cried out as one man:

"Let us go forward! We are neither weary nor thirsty; nor shall we think ourselves even mortal while led by such a king."

Alexander conquered the world because he had soldiers who could be inspired to such devotion and confidence. In this instance he did it by sacrificial identification with them. How much more should our confidence in and devotion to the Great Captain of our salvation rise to the height that would make it possible for Him to save the world through His great sacrificial fulfilment manifest on the Cross of Calvary!

"Be this our song, our joy and pride,
'Our Champion went before and died.'"

CHAPTER IX

THE SACRIFICIAL SOURCE

THE sacrificial source of the divine fulfilment in Christ's work of Redemption will in this chapter be further considered. The subject of sacrifice is an inexhaustible one. He who understands it, understands God; and he who understands God, has the way open to all Knowledge.

The clue to the meaning of the universe lies within sacrifice. The clue to the meaning of God lies within personality; and the clue to the meaning of personality lies in sacrificial nature. Personality means more in God than anywhere else. Nowhere else is it essential in so many ways. In the personal world an impersonal divine existence could not function as God.

Sacrifice in God means more than anywhere else. All personal existence in well-being is due to it. The perfection of God's sacrificial nature is the highest and holiest order of perfection known to us, for our Redemption is wholly due to it. Perfection means more in God than anywhere else. Without it there, it could not be anywhere.

Personality perfect ontologically is the perfect existence; for the absolute in perfect existence makes all other existence possible. This we see in the perfect personality of God.

Personality psychologically perfect is other-conscious. This we see in the consciousness of the Persons of the Holy Trinity.

Personality socially perfect is sacrificially loving. This we find present in the relations of the Persons of the Trinity to each other, but also in all the divine relations.

Personality ethically perfect has the righteousness of sacrificial holiness. This too we find in God, most of all in His Work of Redemption.

I. Sacrificial Righteousness

There are as many levels of righteousness as there are levels of things that are righteous; but the righteousness of divine sacrifice is the highest of all. This is because the level of God and of His sacrificial nature is above all. The righteousness which keeps to the road of holiness is irreproachably good; but the righteousness which goes into the ditch in the spirit of holy sacrifice to extricate the sinner and reëstablish righteousness in him is of an order so good, that we cannot conceive of better.

Such sacrifice in God is, so to speak, the very quintessence of righteousness. It is the genetic source of all the righteousness of Christianity. While, natively, this righteousness has always belonged to the very highest realm of holiness, namely, within the triune relations of God, it went down to the deepest depths of unrighteousness to rescue the lost.

To fathom the depths of the nature of sacrifice is very difficult, because it is so profound. It is not only the highest in holiness; it is, so to speak, the holiest in the Highest. If there can be such a thing as the deepest in God, the sacrificial nature is deepest in Him because deepest in His holiness. His goodness is not only over all but for all. If God had foreknown only that man would sin, it would have been unexplainable for Him to create man. With the knowledge that His own sacrificial nature had far greater resources than sin had power of destruction, He could in all righteousness proceed to call man into existence.

The unlimited depth of righteousness in the sacrifice of God to save the lost stands over against the unrighteousness of iniquity as competent to overthrow, outdo, and undo it. So it came to pass that sacrifice laid the foundation of the new world of God in Christ. It refounded and reconstructed in man the righteousness native to life in God.

II. Christ's Righteousness

The self-dedication of Christ to the sacrifice which poured itself out for the redemption of the unrighteous, is the highest righteousness with which we have come in contact. Christ's sacrificial spirit, fulfilling itself in His self-sacrifice at Calvary, surpassed in righteousness all other righteousnesses in relation to us. This explains the deep meaning of the Biblical expression, "The Lord our righteousness." Jer. 23: 6, 33: 16.

> "Righteous Advocate with God,
> Grant forgiveness through thy blood . . .
> In my heart I now believe,
> Thy atonement I receive;
> Freely with my mouth confess
> Thee, my Lord, my righteousness."

While Christ was righteous for His own sake, this did not hinder Him from being righteous for the Father's sake. While He was righteous for the Father's sake, this did not hinder Him from being righteous for man's sake; rather it enabled Him so to be. All the righteousness of His Holy Person was sacrificially at the disposal of the need of man; and being wholly self-sacrificial He was wholly righteous for the sake of the lost.

The limitless power of Christ to redeem us from the unrighteousness of sin lies in the limitless Godward righteousness of His self-sacrifice for us. In part, this is because of its identity with the sacrificial spirit and nature of the whole Godhead. So to speak, all the force and merit of God's eternally sacrificial nature gathered itself in one great concentration and objectification in Christ on the Cross. All the sublime righteousness of God's eternal holiness was fully active and manifest in the sacrifice of Calvary. It was no negative redemption. Christ could not deliver us from all unrighteousness without redeeming us unto all righteousness; and all the righteousness we need is in Christ, in whom by Redemption we live and move and have our being. All righteousness rests upon giving the God of Righteousness His place. This the Work of Christ established and secured.

The Godward righteousness of Christ's sacrifice for us is manifest in the power of its manward efficacy. It does that which no other form of righteousness can do in penetrating and permeating personality and imparting its life-giving benefit. Some dislike the idea of Christ's righteousness being imputed to us. If formal, external imputation were all that took place, their dislike would be justified.

There is never any divine imputation without impartation. The sacrifice of Christ has a twofold righteousness—that which answers before God for us, and that which enters into us to enable us to become personally righteous. This is known as Christ's work for us and in us. One of our old hymns so speaks of it.

"Be of sin the double cure,
Save from wrath and make me pure."

The first is the righteousness imputed, and the second is the righteousness imparted. After all, it is but one righteousness in two inseparable tasks. Imputation means to say that the sacrifice of Christ on our behalf counts before God, that it is not in vain there, that its righteousness has brought into existence that which makes our standing before God entirely different. Impartation means that the sacrifice which gives us acceptance before God, has power to communicate itself to us. "The contagion of Christ's sacrificial spirit" but feebly expresses its ability to enter the life of sinful personality and change the spirit, trend, and the very character of its existence.

III. The Incomparable Sacrifice

There is one thing in eternity about which we shall never weary thinking and talking—the incomparable sacrifice of God in Christ for us. It will be all the sweeter as a story as the endless aeons go by. Then we shall appreciate, as we cannot now, the divine devotion that led the Son of God all the way from heaven to earth, then over the rough and pathless wastes of the chaos caused by human sin to that rocky mound of tragedy and triumph outside the gates of Jerusalem.

If the first triumph of Christ's sacrifice was its acceptance with God, its ultimate triumph is the fulfilment of human nature in it. This comes to pass by making us sacrificial to the end of enabling His sacrifice to reach the world for which it was made. During the dark days of the Great War one of the specially strong editorials in the *British Weekly* (April 13, 1916) was on "The Acceptance of Sacrifice." Sir William Robertson Nicoll said:

"When we accept as our own the sacrifice and oblation for the sin of the world, we accept it in the sacrificial temper. We identify ourselves with the divine suffering. Each heart says Amen to God in Christ. Our deliverance does not deliver us from sacrifice; rather it binds us to sacrifice."

The immeasurable sacrifice of Christ were worse than wasted, if its spirit never entered those for whom it was made. Then it would only have injured where it sought to help. Instead of lifting souls out of the mire of selfishness it would, by no fault of its own, have added guilt and weight to sink them to deeper depths of depravity.

One stands in the place of utmost peril and responsibility when in the presence of a great sacrifice on his behalf. Christ's sacrifice is bound either to end our sin, or, alas! to multiply it. Sin unrepented may trade on the very sacrifice meant to end it.

There was a joy set before Christ in His sacrifice; and there is a joy we can give Him by responding to it. The more a sacrifice costs, the greater the satisfaction when it proves not in vain. For God or man there is no joy like that in triumphant sacrifice.

> "My brothers, 'neath the eternal Eyes
>   One human joy shall touch the just—
> To know their spirits' heirs arise,
>   And lift their purpose from the dust:
> The father's passion arms the son,
> And the great deed goes on, goes on."

What unfathomable depths of sacrifice there were in the Incarnation! Think of the Omniscient Mind of the preëxistent Son which, in a way utterly beyond our comprehension, began functioning as the tiny intelligence of an embryo in the Virgin's womb! And this is His Kenotic sacrifice in but one power—that of intelligence. When one adds to this the sacrifice of His other personal and divine powers laid aside in the *Kenosis,* he begins to approach the fuller conception of it. What a sacrifice it was to lay aside the infinite reaches of His divine life and to focus it all in the tiny life begun by incarnate union with human life! Even the wider circumference and area of the larger life of manhood was a sacrifice to His infinite Godhood, limited thus to this finite scope of manifestation.

All this does not more than touch the edge of the infinite sacrifice of taking into His very person created human nature to become a permanent part of His divine nature and existence. Besides the sacrifice of His life on earth there was the sacrifice of His death on the Cross; and part of the latter was the sealing forever the sacrifice of the Incarnation.

The extent of what was laid aside was equal to the extent of what he endured for our sake. What extensively was left behind when He came to Bethlehem, went intensively into the sacrifice of His fulfilment in relation to man and sin. O the depth of the riches of the sacrifice of God in Christ! How utterly is it beyond the grasp of our human minds! Only eternity itself is long enough to unfold its vast and many-sided meaning.

IV. The Depths of God's Sacrifice

We have already noted that Redemption's sacrifice is not so much something offered unto God, as a fulfilment in God. This fulfilment of the divine nature within itself was carried into God's relation to man and sin. Their eternally sacrificial relations to each other enables the Persons of the Trinity to exist for each other absolutely. It was as an expression of this that

God was pleased to call the universe into existence. Especially, when making man, He is the sacrificial Creator.

If God's sacrificial nature was true to itself in creating, it was also true to itself, and in a deeper way, in providing for the redemption of the lost. The sufficiency of this great sacrifice is of God; and its glory is that it is inseparable from the innermost of God's nature, as it is revealed unto us.

"He hath done all things well." There are various depths immeasurable in all God's sacrifices. Never has He acted except in utter unselfishness. To whatever He calls into existence, He gives Himself as far as possible. His glory it is to give the Highest, even Himself.

The sacrificial should not be thought of as a part of God's nature. It is the spirit and disposition of all His nature. This shows us that we have not been redeemed by some attribute of God to some other attribute which He has, but to all of God by the spirit of the entire nature of God.

We have been speaking of the righteousness and holiness of the sacrificial nature of God. Now the holiness of God is that perfection to which nothing can be added and from which nothing can be taken away. This is true of the divine sacrifice in the Incarnate Son. To it nothing can be added, and, bless God! nothing from it can be ever taken away.

As sacrificial holiness is in our human way of looking at it, the best of God's holiness, so the perfect sacrificial righteousness in Christ's incarnate life made it the best ever lived and His death the greatest blessing to sinful men. In it God exercised the very heart of His holiness on behalf of the unholy. "Him who knew no sin, God made to be sin on our behalf, that we might be made the righteousness of God in Him."

From first to last, every part of Christ's nature functioned sacrificially. He personalized perfectly the spirit of divine sacrifice. Since He lived a life wholly for the sake of others, it is no wonder that He was ready to suffer a death wholly for the sake of others. If there can be a sacrificial life, surely there can be a sacrificial death. Strange to say, some can see the merit and meaning of the former, only to deny the merit and meaning of the latter.

Touching upon objections, one might here say that this divine fulfilment answers the old difficulty with the commercial theory that Redemption is like taking money out of one pocket and putting it into another. Money is external to, and no part of, personality. The sacrifice of God in our Redemption does not take something external to His Person and appear to give it away while really giving it back to Himself. In any case, the reality of sacrifice depends upon the reality of its cost.

If all the nature of God shared in this sacrifice, then all of His nature shared in the satisfaction of it; and its highest satisfaction is in giving, not in receiving. This is not saying that all of God's nature had precisely the same order of satisfaction. The mind has its own satisfaction, and the heart its own. Some of the divine nature shared in the satisfaction called in Scripture *propitiation.* God's sense of indignation with sin, His moral repugnance to it, has its own satisfaction in the solution of the problem of sin. If there are varieties of satisfactions possible to finite human personality, why is not as great variety of satisfaction possible to the infinite and divine?

V. The Excellencies of Sacrifice

No line of thinking really interests us when quite out of keeping with the kind of life we live. Truths are agreeable and, so to speak, digestible when they are counterpart to our spirit. Only sacrificial nature can assimilate sacrificial thought and transmute it into personality. Naturally a selfish nature turns away from such thought in disgust. The great truth of Christ redeeming man to the sacrificial is more than indigestible to unchanged selfish nature: it is nauseous to it.

Everything begins or ends with spirit. We never

understand or appreciate the Sacrifice, *par excellence*, as long as its spirit is foreign to us. The spirit of the sacrifice of Calvary is indispensable to its true interpretation. And the more of its spirit dwelling in us, the more Christ's great work on our behalf becomes a compelling subject of thought, and the more we revel in its excellence.

That Christ's sacrifice can redeem us unto God by imparting its sacrificial nature when all the rest of the divine sacrifices had failed in this respect, is positive proof of its supreme excellence. This greatest truth about Him who is The Truth must remain unpalatable as sawdust, until its spirit lays hold upon us. We are redeemed unto real delight in His sacrifice as soon as He imparts to us His nature. Receiving the sacrificial spirit of Christ lays the foundation of reciprocity with this joy in God.

Another excellence of sacrificial nature lies in the life it imparts. It gives man a life-giving life; and the more this life gives of itself, the more life it has. This is because its inexhaustible source is in the love and life of God. By His sacrificial death Jesus Christ became the great and only source of life in God for the whole human race. From Him by the Holy Spirit comes the quickening of His sacrificial spirit. "The last Adam was made a life-giving (quickening) spirit." So Paul also says of Him: "I live, yet not I; Christ liveth in me."

Still another excellence of sacrifice is the enduring permanence of the work done by it. Things done by any other nature have to be redone or undone, or of themselves they pass away. All wrought in real sacrifice is preserved in the very permanence of the Being of God. Because the worth of the sacrifice of Christ in death endures forever, it need not be repeated, any more than the sacrifice of the Incarnation need be repeated. Isaiah represented the Messiah as saying, "I will work a work, and who will reverse it?" This has its parallel word in Hebrews,—"One sacrifice for sins for ever."

Sacrifice as a personal nature has another excellence in the power of possession it gives. Usually we think of sacrifice as loss; but it is the only way to gain. Nothing is ever possessed in reality except by its spirit. Any other order of possession is a deep deception, a dark delusion. A selfish nature but seems to own. Nothing can be owned except in God. Even God Himself possesses all things by this spirit. By it in the first place He came to own us; and without its presence in us He lost us, and we lost Him and with Him all else worth having. Only by a still greater sacrifice could He re-possess us, and by its spirit give us possession of ourselves and all in Him for us.

Lastly, the sacrificial spirit has the excellence of being able to exalt and enthrone. Only by sacrificial nature can men reign with Christ, for only they are fit to do so. All others exploit in selfishness all unselfishness. Christ reigns in all righteousness for the good of that or those ruled over; and therefore in Him sacrificial rulership can be trusted with unlimited scope. Because the sacrificial spirit found in Him adequate room for itself, it led Him to the crowning sacrifice of all eternity, and then to His own place of honor and power at the right hand of God.

"Behold I see the heavens opened, and the Son of man standing on the right hand of God."

"He, when he had offered one sacrifice for sins for ever, sat down on the right hand of God."

"He endured the Cross, despising the shame; and hath sat down at the right hand of God."

CHAPTER X

THE SPIRIT OF LOVE

LIKE the attributes of God, the great phases of Christ's Work fit perfectly together. Omnipotence, Omniscience, and Omnipresence go naturally together. So do Substance, Source, and Spirit. Substance is essence; Source is genesis; and Spirit is motive or genius.

Sacrifice is the genetic spirit of divine Redemption, while love is its generic spirit. Sacrifice and love are complementary to each other. Only sacrificial nature is capable of real love. And love is the true motive of sacrifice. We should distinguish between sacrificial nature and the sacrifice it brings forth. Love lives and moves in the making of sacrifice or in the sacrifice made. Without both of these there is no real religion. As Froude says in "Sea Studies,"

"Sacrifice is the first element of religion, and resolves itself in theological language into the love of God."

Love is the natural activity of sacrificial nature. Love is sacrificial nature expressing itself in appropriate spirit. As the Holy Spirit is called "the Proceeding Person" of the Holy Trinity, so love is the proceeding spirit of personality. Love is always a going forth. It is never stored as personal nature, never static or inactive. It goes forth in spirit. It is like breath. Love is the breathing of God. "And he breathed on them and said, receive ye the Holy Spirit."

The spirit of love appropriately expresses itself sacrificially. Love is naturally a sacrificial spirit. The sacrificial spirit of love is the soul of the Christian religion. By it was offered the sacrifice of Christ on the Cross. There "Christ through eternal spirit offered Himself without blemish unto God." His love for us is so great, it makes us ashamed of our own poor love in return.

> "Our love to thee so cold and faint,
> And thine to us so great."

I. Love as a Spirit

All God's nature is spirit; and it is all holy spirit; but there is the distinctive Person in the Godhead, the Holy Spirit. Jesus does not speak of His love of the Holy Spirit but of His love for the Father, because the Holy Spirit is His love and the Father's love. The Holy Spirit is the love of the Father and the Son going forth to the end of indwelling.

As already noted, the fulfilment of spirit is by a perfect, permanent, and commensurate objectification or embodiment of itself. Spirit is always seeking that expression which fulfils it. When the intent of the spirit and the extent of the expression correspond, then the spirit counts itself to be fulfilled.

Christ's sacrifice of Himself on the Cross is a permanent and perfect embodiment of the Holy Spirit— the spirit of God's love for sinners. It is commensurate in extent and content with the intent of His sacrificial spirit. Only the spirit of love can redeem those lost to it and beget love in return. Only sacrificial love could reëstablish love in the life of man. And the further man is lost to the spirit of love, the greater must be the sacrifice of love to restore him. So God's sacrificial nature in the spirit of love made its own appropriate and sufficient sacrifice to save man from sin's destruction of him as a personality to live by love.

The spirit of love was the motive which moved in the heart of God to make the sacrifice of His Son. This is the genius of divine Redemption. To this the very existence and nature of Christianity testifies.

The entreaty of the love and sacrifice offered on Calvary has proved adequate to touch the sin-sodden hearts of men. The Cross is the greatest possible appeal to a world of sin, because it is the greatest possible visibility of the meaning of the spirit of divine love and sacrifice.

> "His Cross like a far seen beacon stands
> In the midst of a world of sin;
> And stretched out are His bleeding hands
> To gather the wanderers in."

II. LOVE IN THE FORM OF GRACE

God's love-letters to man, called the Scriptures, make known abundantly the love which wrought out our salvation. The passages teaching this are all familiar to us:

"God so loved the world that he gave his only begotten Son."

"Herein is love, not that we loved God, but that he loved us, and sent his Son to be the propitiation for our sins."

"But God commendeth his love toward us in that while we were yet sinners, Christ died for us."

"Christ also hath loved us and gave himself for an offering and a sacrifice for a sweet smelling savor."

"The Son of God who loved me and gave himself up for me."

"That he by the grace of God should taste death for every man."

The last quotation and a great many other passages of the New Testament use the word *grace* for the word love. Grace is love at work in Redemption, love "carrying on" in spite of sin, love reaching down to the level of the unworthy and guilty.

Grace never means that love is blind to the loathsomeness of iniquity; but, on the contrary, it sees this fully, and brings the only remedy. Grace is love paying the price of passing down to the depths of degradation in human depravity, descending to the level of the lost to bear their sin and blot it out.

Grace is the fulfilling of the divine nature in relation to those sunken below the level of life in God. It is love bringing forth the sacrifice adequate to redeem man from all corruption. George Eliot says: " 'Tis what I love determines how I love." The beloved of God being sinful, lost in the depths of iniquity, this determined how His grace loved them—even redeemingly, savingly.

The grace of God is the theme of the music of the Gospel. It is the refrain of the hymn of sacrificial love, "The Song of Moses and the Lamb." It sings of love fulfilling itself, overcoming the supreme difficulty of destroying sin and establishing a lasting, loving, living way for the fulfilment of human nature.

III. Love as Grace Abounding

Whenever love and sin meet, there is bound to be desperate difficulty for love. Sin is its inveterate enemy. Iniquity is the fiendish foe of the love of God and all the love it begets. We may find it hard to understand how God in the perfect righteousness of His absolute holiness could love the unrighteous and unholy, even to the extent of offering an infinite sacrifice for their sins. Then how difficult for Him to do this very thing, so hard for us to comprehend. It was not easy. It was the hardest of all hard roads to travel. It was the *via crucis,* the steep, rough, ruthless way to Calvary.

However, sin is not all there is in the sinner. Buried beneath its rubbish and filth is capacity for God. When He made man, God meant to glorify him in power and privilege at His right hand. Because iniquity is totally foreign to the essentials of human nature, the divine love for sinful man is righteously possible.

To err is human—but it is not always so. When it is the error of iniquity, it is inhuman. Sin is out-and-out inhumanity in humanity. Burns' lines here come to mind:

"Man's inhumanity to man
Makes countless thousands mourn."

The exceeding sinfulness of sin has made God mourn for countless days. The genuineness of His love proves itself by His unvarying hate and unwearied detestation of iniquity.

Despite the repulsive nature and disgusting appearance of all our sin, we are still precious in God's sight.

Instead of it driving Him away from us and causing Him to forsake us, He comes all the closer to us to save us from it. The divine love bends over the soul sick unto death with the loathsome disease of iniquity, even as a mother might bend over her sick and suffering child. She hates the sickness, but she loves her sick child. The more she loves her child, the more she hates the dangerous disease from which it suffers. So God loves not sin, but His sinful child. Where the sickness of sin abounds, the love of God the more abounds. The smaller the spark of likeness to God remaining in the human soul, the more does divine love expend itself to save the spark from extinction. Who has not witnessed a mother wrestle with death as long as a spark of life remained in her child? Of all loves on earth it is the most like God's. But the best earthly reflection of it can never surpass the radiance of the Father's love. We should remember that while sickness is misfortune, sin is guilt; so the interpretation of it as disease is always "short-weight." And when the interpretation of sin is deficient, so is the interpretation of the love that loves in spite of sin.

> "And as feeble babes that suffer,
>   Toss and cry and will not rest
> Are the ones the tender mother
>   Holds the closest, loves the best—
> So when we are weak and wretched,
>   By our sins weighed down, distressed,
> Then it is that God's great patience
>   Holds us closest, loves us best.
>
> "O great heart of God whose loving
>   Cannot hindered be or crossed,
> Will not weary, will not even
>   In our death itself be lost—
> Love divine! of such great loving
>   Only mothers know the cost—
> Cost of love, which all loves passing,
>   Gave a Son to save the lost."

IV. LOVE'S LEVELS AND ITS VARIOUS ORDERS

In more than one way *love* is the greatest activity in the world. It is the greatest of all such greatnesses.

Now, the measure of love's greatness in any case depends on four things—the personal measure of the lover, of the loved one, of the relation between them, and of the need within it that love sets out to fill.

Love always imparts something of its own native greatness to the beloved one. This is largely where our human greatness comes from. It is more blessed to love than to be loved; but this is true only when we are considering loves on a level—between equals. It is more blessed to be loved than to love, when we are loved of God; for His love is immeasurably greater and better than ours, and awakens it, and saves us unto loving. Our love is never worthy of being compared with His. Not our love for Him but His love for us *constrains us*. Paul seldom referred to his love for Christ, though no man has ever loved Him better. His comprehension of the love of God revealed in Christ Jesus our Lord was so great, it prevented him from thinking of his own love in return. In this he is like the Apostle John. Let us link their thought together:

"Herein is love, not that we loved God; but that he loved us . . . We love (him) because he first loved."

"While we were yet sinners, Christ died for us . . . While we were enemies, we were reconciled unto God through the death of his Son . . . The love of Christ constraineth us . . . The love of Christ which passeth knowledge."

Love does not always live on the same level. Its levels are as various as the relations it fills. Some of these are higher, and some lower. While it affects these relations very much, they too have their effect on it. As it flows along the channels of these relations, it takes on something of their qualities and characteristics. This is one of the things that causes love to be so varied and distinguishable—as the love of a man for his friend, of a teacher for his class, of a brother for his sister, of a man for his wife, of a mother for her child.

Every love finds its fulfilment on the level of the relation in which it moves. The relation that God bears to us as God, determines the level on which His love finds its fulfilment. His love adds character to this relation, and this relation adds character to His love. The divine love bearing the rich qualities and characteristics of the relation which God bears to us, fulfils itself on this level.

Love is the master-mind, the major-general who musters and directs all the forces of personality. It arranges their place and orders to suit its campaign. And love always dresses itself up in the regimentals of whatever power it puts in the forefront of its work.

When love in its activity uses most prominently the mind, we call this the *love of admiration*. Sometimes love puts desire forefront. This we call *the love of complacence or satisfaction*. There is that order of love in which the sympathies are most prominent. This is *the love of pity or compassion*. When it uses foremost in its activities the social powers, we have *the social loves* as those of patriotism, friendship, and the home. When the executive powers are in the lead, we call it *the love of devotion*. When the ethical or moral powers lead the way, we call it *the love of rectitude*. When the nature of self-giving is exercised, we call it *sacrifice*. When love leads God, we call it *self-sacrifice;* and when God leads love, we call it *self-fulfilment*. "Greater love hath no man than this, that a man lay down his life for his friend." That is its limit. Greater love God could not have than to lay down the life of His Only Son for us whom sin had made such enemies that we sent Him to His death on the Cross.

V. Love Fulfilling Itself

God fulfils Himself in His own love: we fulfil ourselves in His. God's love enables the consummation of our existence through receiving His love, and then giving back our poor love in response. No love is so fitted to awaken love as that of the sacrificial sort. If this fails, nothing can ever succeed in arousing or begetting love.

God loves us into loving, and makes love the ruling principle in personal realization. For divine love to have done its part in fulfilling itself in its sacrifice for our sin, is one thing; for us to receive this fulfilment is another.

For the refusal of love's supreme divine sacrifice, there can be no further sacrifice. And even though there could be, it would be useless to those who had trampled underfoot the sacrificial blood of divine love.

When any one refuses to drink of the water of life, the divinity of the source and the infinity of the supply cannot save him from dying of soul-thirst. "Passing out" from pulmonary tuberculosis a patient by an open window in a hospital gasped to the attendant nurse, "More air, more air!" What the poor sufferer needed was more lungs. But more lungs depended upon less tuberculosis. Lungs are fulfilled by filling themselves full of air, and extracting the oxygen which is needed. This fulfilment tuberculosis effectually stops.

God's love is more abundant than the atmosphere. The air reaches out beyond the earth some thirty miles, while the love of God reaches up to heaven itself and fills the universe. What we need is not more of God's love, but more soul to take it in, and less of the unbelief in it that has honeycombed our hearts. The curse of spiritual ill-health due to selfishness can be cured only by receiving into the heart the infinite unselfishness of divine love. God can never be sick. The sacrificial is the secret of the eternal health of the divine nature and of its life abundant.

We have said that God fulfils Himself in love. This fulfilment can become ours only as the love of God comes to its own in us. When the love of God fulfils itself in us, we receive it into the soul as the lungs receive the air. When this divine fulfilment passes into ours, then God's song of joy also becomes ours. The music of heaven can be played on the harp-strings of a sacrificial soul. Self apart from God passes out of existence when divine love tunes man's heartstrings. Then self-in-God, vibrant to the touch of the divine fingers, makes that music of love which keeps step with the march of God, and the sweet harmony of heaven's love-melody is wafted down the highways of human life.

> "Love took up the harp of life,
> Smote on all the chords with might;
> Smote the chord of self, that, trembling,
> Passed in music out of sight."

CHAPTER XI

THE SPIRIT OF FULFILMENT

IN THIS chapter the subject of love as the spirit of divine fulfilment will be continued. We may begin further discussion by referring to love's greatness. Here it may be said that love has a cumulative greatness in its three great aspects of self-expression, self-giving, and self-realization. Love is the greatest way in which personality can assert, impart, and construct itself. We have said it is the greatest way in which it can fulfil itself.

"Love is of God." When we truly love, we are partakers of the divine life and nature. From its sacrificial source the divine love has poured forth in supreme manifestation and impartation of itself. But God's love is so great, only He Himself fully knows His love for us. Of this Charles Wesley was evidently thinking when he sang:

> "God only knows the love of God:
> Oh, that it now were shed abroad
> In this poor stony heart."

I. LOVE AND THE CHARACTER OF THE LOVER INSEPARABLE

Romantic minds idealize love. They separate it from the one who loves; and think of it as a perfectly pure thing independent of the moral and spiritual character of the lover. The fact is, love can be wisely considered only as a personal process which is bound to express in the fullest way the very innermost of the soul of the lover. So every love has in it the limitations of him who loves.

Love is never different from that which loves. The love of a dog can never rise higher than dog-love. A mother's love has the mother-element in it; and God's love has the divine element in it. It is the character which loves, that gives character to love. No two loves are ever the same, for the reason that no two persons are ever the same. Since persons are bound to be different from one another, their self-expressions in love cannot be the same. In other words, the self-revelations which persons make by means of their love, vary as the persons themselves vary.

Though love is inseparable from the character of the lover, it reveals this character at its best. And its best is its truest. Love has many virtues. Not least among these is this: *all the good in personality is vitalized by it*. It is naturally kindred to everything excellent in man; and so everything noble in him finds its finest and deepest manifestation in the exercise of love.

If we are to let our light so shine that God be glorified, must be by the rays of love. Love is the soul's highest expression of itself because its truest; and the truest always reaches up the farthest. What a man is within, "the hidden man of the heart," most fully displays itself when he loves. Whatever of good or evil is in him, it is then bound to manifest itself. Persons all look alike in the dark. They are not seen at all then. But in the light of love every one has his own features, color, stature, and appearance.

Because a man's moral character and that of his love are never different, pure love is impossible in an impure person, righteous love in an unrighteous person, and unselfish love in a selfish person. How can clean love come forth from the unclean? Love is malformed, mutilated, and adulterated in proportion as low moral and religious qualities are present in the lover.

Because God is perfect in every way, his love is perfect. Because He is pure, His self-expression in love is pure. His love is as holy as His nature. All His holiness dwells in it. Because His love is the going forth of His sacrificial nature in its highest manifestation, the expression of His holiness in it is unhampered.

Longfellow says, "Love is the master of all arts." Then it is master of the art of self-expression. For this reason, love best befits all that is righteous in character, all that is holy in personal nature to assert itself. In man, ability to utter one's self in love rises as good moral qualities and self-realization in righteousness increase.

II. SELF-EXPRESSION AND SELF-INTERPRETATION

This is a world of much misunderstanding because largely a world without love. Seldom is love the asserting agent within it. Yet only perfection understands us. The world is filled with imperfection struggling to understand imperfection. Anything other than love is bound to misrepresent us in self-expression; and anything but love is bound to misinterpret to us those about us.

When we are imperfect we but add more imperfection to express it in hate. In personal relation dislike of others is no more fit to interpret others than it is fit in self-realization. What if there be no love to interpret? Then the light of life has gone out; and darkness must assert and interpret itself in the dark.

Hate is a delusion of the devil. It fills and burns the heart with the fire of hell. Love invites God's presence and habitation. It is the atmosphere of heaven, the open countenance that speaks without words. It is said that babies in all nationalities cry alike. Love also is a language the whole world understands, for by it soul speaks to soul, heart to heart, man to man, and God to man.

In such a world of sin and misunderstanding God's provision of propitiation, reconciliation, and redemption would never have been understood at all, if that providing all this had not been love. Because the meaning of the Cross has not always been sought in the fulfilment of the love of God, it has been much misunderstood. Then our lack of the spirit of love by which to interpret this great love cannot fail to becloud the whole subject and tend to fetter every statement of it. Lose sight of the love of God in the sacrifice of the Cross, and the main clue to its meaning is gone.

The love which Christ's love awakens, has its own eyes to behold the worth of His sacrifice. While God has adequately expressed the purity, proportions, and perfection of His love, yet this manifestation has to wait for its fuller understanding by love. Only love can read its deeper meaning and message. True, the sinless Son of God died for our sins because of His love for us. Nevertheless the only spirit capable of appreciating this love, is the same spirit of love itself. If love is the highest and best form of self-expression, then surely the highest and best love requires the highest and best power of interpretation to make known its message. Nothing but love has ever really preached the Gospel of Jesus Christ.

III. The Righteousness Expressed by Love

We have discussed the righteousness of sacrifice. Love is the righteousness of its spirit. Righteousness is a mere abstraction till applied to something that is righteous. Unless there is righteous love, desire, or something else in personality, there can be no righteousness. The righteousness of love is therefore no abstraction. When all God's nature is righteous, His spirit of love cannot fail to be righteous.

Righteousness is not something added to divine love. It is integral in it. When love lacks righteousness, it lacks internal structure, stability, and integrity. God's love having the same righteousness as all His nature, it never needs to be subjected to an external demand of righteousness. Nor need it be subjected to an internal demand. Nothing in God can be more righteous than His sacrificial love. God's love is the fulfilling of the whole law of His whole Being, for it is His love of righteousness in the concrete. Lovelace is often quoted as saying:

"I could not love thee, dear, so much,
Loved I not honor more."

God loves nothing more than righteousness of spirit. He loves in righteousness and for it, that all whom He loves be as righteous in spirit as He is. It could not be said that "God is love" unless love is essentially holy and righteous. God could not love us other than righteously without loving us less than He does. An unrighteous love is constitutionally crippled. Love lame ethically is abnormal, just like a crippled human body. God's love fulfils itself only in righteousness.[1]

If God had been less true to His righteous nature, He would have been less true to ours. And had He been less than true to His love for us, He would not have been true to His own holiness. *If His holiness did not manifest itself in His love, it would be manifest nowhere else.* The strength of love is in its righteousness. If God's love had not been absolutely holy, it could not have stood the strain of the sufferings for our salvation.

The righteousness and perfection of God's nature most strongly asserted itself in the love that wrought out our salvation. Then no righteousness within Him was held back from manifesting itself. His love was just as competent to reveal Him as to save us. It could not be the one without being the other.

---

1. Dale of Birmingham is often quoted as saying at the close of his life· "I have preached much about the love of God, but now I feel as though I want something stronger, and I lean on His righteousness."

No matter who said it, this is a false comparison There is no righteousness of God to lean on other than the righteousness of His love. Nowhere in Him is righteousness stronger than in His love. It is a false contrast to set the righteousness of God's love over against His righteousness in something else in Him as though the former were weaker and lesser. Such is true neither to righteousness nor to love as revealed in Christ. When or where in His love was it weak or small in righteousness?

We may contrast between righteousness and love in men, but never in God There are those who think of the righteousness of penalty as that to which love must submit The righteousness of retribution is not as great as the righteousness of redemption The sinner has not ceased to be such when he receives the just punishment for his sins If Christ suffered the punishment due my sins as though I had suffered it myself, this and nothing more does not restore me to righteousness The righteousness is applied to me as the bearer of penalty, not in redemption from that which caused it A thief or a murderer is not righteous and not any the less a thief or a murderer when penalty has been inflicted on him A punished sinner is a sinner still The worst penalty is not that which God inflicts but that which sin inflicts, the penalty in being what sin makes one to be. No penalty inflicted for being such changes in the least the being such.

God's redeeming love is righteousness at its best There it is righteousness in its fullest sweep, righteousness that does not stop with inflicting penalty, but righteousness foundational, elemental, cleansing, constitutional, and final. In the love of God in Christ Jesus our Lord righteousness has its vastest possible meaning, its utmost potency, its power of deliverance and reconstruction, its ability to purify and give life in God The revelation of this righteousness is unfathomable, for it is by "the love of Christ that passeth knowledge." If the love of Christ passeth knowledge, rest assured that its righteousness goes just as far

IV. THE SELF-GIVING SELF OF LOVE

Self-giving is the second great feature in the trinity of love's greatnesses. A wholly selfish love is a contradiction in terms. A perfectly selfish person is unable to love, since self-giving which is essential in love, is impossible to selfishness.

There is some selfishness in the best of us. Each partly selfish person but partly loves, because self-giving in part only is possible in the love of a partly selfish person. Any seeming self-giving "has a string to it," where there is any selfishness. Only the perfectly unselfish person can pay the full price in unreserved self-giving.

Because we are not yet wholly unselfish, we have never yet known what it is to love fully, perfectly. Not only do we "know in part," we love in part. Now "we see as in a darkened mirror." The best of our love is but an imperfect mirror to reflect God. Because "God is love," only by love can we mirror Him. Here our poor love must be His mirror of interpretation. So it comes to pass that men see God reflected in us but darkly, at times even in caricature, unless Christ be formed within us.

As to the self-giving of love, it does not always mean just the same, because self-giving varies with the relations in which it takes place. Some of these relations offer more scope to it than others do. "Self-love" has no scope for self-giving at all.

For example, Jesus said, "Love your enemies." So He closed the only way in which it is possible for enemies to injure us in soul, namely, in causing us to hate them. But in the relation to an enemy there is less room for self-giving than to a friend, a teacher, a brother, a sister, a child, a mother. The rule seems to be that the higher and greater the relation in which love moves, the more room is there for self-giving. So love fulfils itself by the giving of self, by filling to the full with self-giving the relation in question.

The scope or measure of God's self-giving is an enlarging one because of the enlarging relation possible. The more we grow up in Him, the more Christ can give Himself to us. Long has love been recognized as the greatest means of self-impartation. The highest, deepest, and largest way in which persons may belong to each other is by love; and they belong to each other just in proportion as they have given themselves to each other.

Unless the self-giving of love fills all the relations of life, they are empty at their best. In fact there is no "best" to them without love's self-impartation in them. God has filled His relation to us with the love that has made Him ours again, since sin had lost us to Him and Him to us.

God's self-giving has made Him ours in the fullest possible measure forever. It was the most costly self-giving which our Redemption called for. "But God being rich in mercy, on account of his great love wherewith he loved us," kept back no part of the price, "that in the ages to come he might show the surpassing wealth of his grace, in kindness toward us in Jesus Christ."

V. Love in Personal Realization

The third greatness of love is in its power of personal realization. Here we may see and understand how, because of love's surpassing service in self-realization, it is most fitting that the spirit of Redemption's fulfilment should be God's love.

Love is, without doubt, the greatest factor in personal realization. It is the largest means of fulfilment for every part and power of personality. This is how love fulfils personality as a whole. It makes every lower part subservient to the highest; and thus it prevents the higher and the highest within us from being sacrificed to the desires of the lower or the lowest.

There is the diabolical old saying that "All is fair in love and war." Why are love and war linked together? Love is the only thing that can make and preserve peace. It would be strange, then, that what suits war, would suit love. But this discreditable maxim is true for neither. Only the vilest order of love and the most barbarous kind of war could adopt such a saying.

Love never can fulfil itself in unfairness. It is because the love of God is fair that it did not stop with merely forgiving sin. In His war with iniquity He could not afford to be other than absolutely just. He is as equitable in the contest with sin as in all other activity. If in love and war *all* is fair, then unfairness is fair. This is a *reductio ad absurdum*.

Man has this remarkable likeness to God, namely, he has the same means of personal fulfilment in love that God has. There is, of course, the difference that man is realizing personality. It is on its way, in process to perfection, while God is the eternal attainment of perfect personality. Man's self-realization in love is on the way to self-fulfilment, while God's personality has always fulfilled itself in love. God fulfils Himself within the Holy Trinity, and carries this fulfilment of His love into the relation He bears to man. So God fulfils Himself in the love that originates within Him. Man cannot fulfil himself in any love originating within him. He can fulfil himself only in the love which originates in God.

Man is made in this image of God, in that he was made to love and be loved. As Disraeli says: "We are all born for love: it is the principle of existence, and its only end." Even when man had sinned and become unworthy of the love of God, God could fulfil His relation to him in no other way so well as by love.

Moreover, only a divine love could reach down far enough and with grasp strong enough to redeem man unto the fulfilment of his nature in the sonship of love. It is not just our love to Christ, but the acceptance by it of the love that has fulfilled itself in relation to us as sinners, that enables us to reach our fulfilment. But the best proof of real reception of love is love in return. As long as man remains man and God remains God, love will remain the law of fulfilment in the relation between them.

VI. The Love-Measure of Personality

There is a divine skill at work in love's power of self-realization. This is its art of moulding and adapting personality to the life of love. We see the value of this skill of love as we behold what a vast world personality is, so wonderfully intricate, involved, and correlated.

One thinks of all the subsidiary lives within his own, the many kinds of them, the complicated network of supplementary operations going on within his physical nature! But what a vast domain reaches out in personality beyond this material world! We look up into the vastness of inter-stellar space, and find this little world of ours is but a grain of sand compared to the infinitely far-flung heavens. Then we waken to the fact that there is just as vast a world below us as above us. How can we adjust ourselves to it all? Thank God for the skill of His love which is perfectly competent to solve the problem of universal adjustment.

Normally, personality is a growing capacity for love, its interests and fulfilment. This capacity grows from stage to stage, and passes from power to power, and from one adaptation to another. Coördination of the powers of soul within and adjustment of it with the world of personality without depends on the ministry of love.

There are no depths within personality or far-reaching relations without and beyond, that love cannot bless and beautify. Everywhere in God it is at work in its fine art of the adaptation of perfect adjustment.

Redeemed personality is not simply that adapted to love, but that specially adapted to the love that redeemed it. In Christ's life and death it had its place in adapting the person of our Lord for His eternal place as the soul and center of a Redeemed Humanity. So the personality redeemed by Him is redeemed unto

Him; and it has thereby special fitness as part of the living world of Christ's Great Love.

God's love for us did not begin in our Redemption, though it did begin and complete the great sacrifice necessary to it. He loved us before the foundation of the world, even as a mother loves her child before it is born.

It was love incarnate that said: "It is finished!" All completion of task, perfection of ministry, and fulfilment of mission is attained by obedience to the law of love. As it was in the beginning, in the eternity of the past, so will it be in the eternity of the future— the consummation of personal existence will be by love.

Beyond the fulfilment of personality, even God Himself cannot go. Here is a divine *ne plus ultra*. That is the highest of the high,—just as there can be no higher excellence than that of the love-passion of Jesus Christ that fulfilled itself in redeeming us. That passion of God is so powerful, it subdues and carries along with it the whole current of all human life coming in vital touch with it. In so glorious a devotion to our salvation we must glory. As Wesley sang:

"Thee we would be always blessing,
Serve Thee as thy hosts above,
Pray and praise Thee without ceasing,
Glory in thy perfect love."

No higher word about The Most High could Holy Writ say than "God is love." This exhausts the resources of our language to say the best about Him. Love is His supreme excellence. Love is the final measure of God, as it is of man. It is the art of the divine heart. God hasten the day when it will be the art of the human heart also! We measure skill by the worth of its output. The divine skill of love may be measured in this, that it found the one way to reconstruct and fulfil human nature after being so wrecked and ruined by sin. This is the highest art of the whole universe. This is the supremest skill of redeeming love. This is the love-art of the contagion of the health of the love of God.

> "Ah how skilful grows the hand,
> That obeyeth love's command;
> 'Tis the heart and not the brain,
> That to the highest doth attain;
> And he who followeth love's behest,
> Far excelleth all the rest."

VII. Love's Fulfilment in Personality

From any point of view the greatest out-going power of personality lies in love. The greatest method by which it may enrich itself is by the riches of love. And the deepest resources we have in the divine are in the love of God. So is it in human life also. Men can give us nothing so valuable as their love.

For love personality can do its greatest exploits, make its greatest sacrifices, and for it all the powers of personality can do their utmost. Without as within personality love leads and unifies; and brings to pass the highest in achievement and attainment.

When God's love for man fulfilled itself in Christ's sacrifice on the Cross, the rest of His nature was satisfied and fulfilled. All the divine desires and attributes fulfilled themselves in the fulfilment of love.

Righteousness, being constituent in love, it cannot be more important than love. Jesus said, "Love is the fulfilling of the whole law." This is true not for man only but for God also. Love is the fulfilling of the whole law of His personality. Then obedience to love is the supreme law of the universe, and its righteousness is the highest.

Whether in God's nature or man's, love is at the same time the most representative and the most comprehensive fulfilment. All its fulfilments lead up to its fulfilment in personality.

Because it had God's love as its spirit, Redemption had the highest pledge of completion. Love gave this pledge of its sufficiency in stooping to the deepest depths of sacrifice to lift the lost to its own infinite height of fulfilment.

The love of Christ had a long, long descent to make

to reach our fallen estate. And it had a far, far height to climb in carrying us up to the amazing altitudes of the human heart's fulfilment within the heart of God.

> "O love divine that stoop'd to share
> Our sharpest pang, our bitt'rest tear."

Love is the greatest of all motives, the truth of all truths. Bailey says, "The truth of truths is love." Madame de Staël remarks that "Love knows no motive." Of course not, for it is motive itself. Other motives may spring from it, but it is the mother of all motives without selfishness. It is therefore the deepest and best of all the motives in God and man.

One cannot truly interpret divine personality apart from its love; and one can never know the full meaning of love, until he sees it in love's own personality in God. Love is no weak sentimentality or temporary impulse. Divine love completely possessing God comes to us to possess us completely. What Madame de Staël goes on to say about love, can most appropriately be said about the redeeming love of Christ: "It seems to be a divine power that works and thinks within us, taking entire possession of us."

In the Epistle to the Romans, one of its great triumphant challenges is to all enemies of our security in Christ's love: "Who shall separate us from the love of Christ?" Neither tribulation, nor persecution, peril, power above or demon beneath can separate us from that which is within us and making us over again into itself. We may be separated from anything not ourselves. God cannot be separated from His love for us, for *He is that love*. And we cannot be separated from the love of Christ for us, for it is His own spirit at work embodying itself in our personality, making us unalterably His for ever.

CHAPTER XII

MEANS AND METHOD

THE means by which anything is done naturally includes the method. In fact, the method is in reality the means. We should distinguish between the ultimate and the efficient or instrumental means. In Redemption Christ Himself is the ultimate means; but there is also the efficient means, the way, the method by which He became our Redeemer. The efficient or instrumental means which He used in fulfilling the divine nature in His self-sacrifice, is that of *Identification*.

The Method of Christ's fulfilment is completely congruous with other phases of it. That method is adapted to its substance, native to its source, in keeping with its spirit, and adequate to its process. Identification is adapted to the substance of divine fulfilment, native to its source in the sacrificial nature of God, in keeping with His spirit of love, and adapted to the process we shall study in the next chapter.

I. THE DEFINITION OF IDENTIFICATION

In the activities of human life persons may be drawn near to each other, or they may be more and more separated. This means that identification and separation are opposite directions in life's movements.

Identification is necessarily within some relation of life. It is not the same as unification. The latter means harmonized in a social unity; and the former means that persons are put together in the same situation or standing. For example, a husband and a wife are identified by marriage. In this social relation they are united. It does not follow that they are necessarily unified. In a similar way Christ was identified with sin, but not unified with it.

Identification binds persons together in one common bundle, makes them belong together. Then the responsibility of the one is that of the other. When it is between a person and something impersonal that the process of identification takes place, they are made to bear praise or blame together. For example, there is the identification of the worker and his work, of a picture and its painter, of a building and its builder.

Identification is the way human life does all its work. It is the *modus operandi* of every vital relationship. It is the means by which every relation fulfils itself. Each relation has its own type of identification, and its own fulfilment by means of identification. It is the instrumental means, which must not be confused with the means in substance. In Redemption identification was the operative means Christ used to become the means in substance.

II. Levels of Identification

There are higher and lower orders of identification which are determined according to the higher or lower orders of the relations in which it occurs. Identification has deeper and fuller meaning when the relation to which it belongs, is fuller and deeper. The closer the relation, the closer the identification within it.

As life's relations are in an ascending scale, so there is also an ascending scale of identification within them. Two persons may be identified as belonging to the same race. They may also belong to the same nation. They may live in the same country, state, and city. They may attend the same school. Successively they may be identified as lovers, as affianced, as husband and wife, as father and mother.

Each identification is the means by which a possibility comes into existence which did not exist before. For example, a father is never such by himself alone. The identification of a man and a woman as husband and wife brings into existence a possibility that does not exist for either alone. When by the Incarnation the Son of God was identified with us, possibilities came into existence which did not exist before. Among them was that of His sacrificial death.

When one relation leads to another, so do the identifications within them. The identification as husband and wife may lead to the identification as father and mother. So the identification of Christ with our nature was followed by His identification with our sin through His death on the Cross.

III. The Setting of Identification

The origin of Redemption's work we found in the sacrificial nature of the love of God. The origin of the means or method of identification we may also trace back to the relations of the Triune Godhead. Eternally, perfectly, absolutely, the Father, Son, and Holy Spirit have been identified with each other. The indestructability of their identification was put to the severest test in the identification of the Son with human sin. By identification each of the persons of the Holy Trinity has eternally fulfilled Himself. By complete identification the Father, Son, and Holy Spirit have fulfilled the relations which they bear to each other.

Each identification has not only its own possibility, but also its own responsibility, standing, and state. The perfect state and glorious standing by means of these divine identifications, we need not here dwell upon. Their responsibilities are within the divine realm. God is responsible to Himself alone.

God cannot be identified with created things as their Maker without attendant responsibility to Him. This He meets out of the resources of the Godhead. It was out of the resources of the divine identifications that He met the responsibility of the sacrificial identification of the Son with sin. Out of the resources of our Saviour's identification with us and our sin we may meet responsibilities which otherwise could not be met.

During the time of the divine relations to man there has been a long succession of identifications. This began in the divine purpose and plan for man. As Creator He was identified with His work of creation.

Making man in His own image and likeness there was an identification in keeping therewith. Then the divine Providence and the Immanence of God added still others. The identification of the Incarnation has already been mentioned. In His incarnate life the Son of God was identified with the lot and life of man, with repentant sinners as their Saviour, and with sin as bearing its death.

After the sufferings of the Cross there were the further identifications in Christ's death, burial, resurrection, ascension, the giving of the Holy Spirit, acting as administrator because Head of the Kingdom of God, and as Intercessor for us before the throne of God. There is yet to take place an identification of Christ with His own at His Second Coming. From all this we may see that the identification of Redemption has its place in a long series of identifications, all of which it affects to some extent.

IV. PREVISION AND PROVISION

The Birth and Death of the Incarnate One were anything but divine afterthoughts following the creation of man. When God made man through the creative power of the Son, He did it with special foresight and provision. By creating man so nearly alike to His own personal nature He provided sufficient kinship and room for the close identification of the Incarnation.

There was also special prevision and provision in fashioning the parental relation of man also vicarious in its identification. From the beginning father and mother are vicariously identified with their child. For the child's sake they gladly toil and strive. If he is sick or in danger, they do all in their power for him. If he goes astray and commits crime and in consequence brings disgrace and suffering upon himself, they suffer with him.

The closest relation on earth and the most vicarious identification is that of motherhood. Evidently God had a deep purpose in making it thus. It was by means of the motherhood of Mary that our Lord became fully identified with human nature and life. He was "born of a woman, born under the law"—of identification.

In describing one kind of identification we have been using the term *vicarious*. Few words are more frequently used in discussing this subject of the Work of Christ—and justly so. It is well that we make as clear as possible the import it bears.

It is evident that vicarious has to do with means and method, rather than with substance. As a rule it means *for the sake of, or in behalf of*. What sacrificial love is in spirit, vicarious is in identification. Generally, they are complementary in meaning. Not all sacrifice requires the vicarious method, but all vicarious service is necessarily sacrificial. Not all identification is vicarious; but all vicarious exertion must use the means or method of identification. Vicarious emphasizes the quality of the personal relation from the point of view of the actor, while sacrifice emphasizes the objective cost of it to him. The person is vicarious and his act sacrificial. Of course, the terms may be used interchangeably.

V. SUBSTITUTION

We often hear of the substitutionary theory of the Atonement. Properly, there is no such theory. Substitution is the vicarious method of several theories. It does not say what is the substance of the satisfaction for our sins. All it makes known is the efficient means or method. That a number of interpretations agree on the substitutionary method of Christ's Work is important in showing that substitution is essential as its instrumental method, the way He wrought it out.

In the old view of substitution, Christ took our place in paying the debt we owe, suffering the penalty due us, meeting our responsibility, repenting for our sins, and so forth, according to the theory held. In any case it meant that He was so identified with us that He could act for us, in our room and stead. In the penal and judgment-death theories Christ took our place to fulfil the law. He was our substitute in this fulfilment. In this legal fulfilment we have the nearest approach to the fulfilment of the divine nature in relation to man and sin.

In our fulfilment-interpretation, Christ may still be looked upon as our substitute, but in a different way. God gave in the law a basal means of fulfilment. Sin destroyed this foundation of fulfilment. Through suffering vicariously a sacrificial death Christ became the new means of our fulfilment. He became the substitute means of fulfilment in place of that lost by sin. The process by which He fulfilled our nature in relation to God will be discussed later. This is *institution* as truly as substitution. He instituted the substitute means of our fulfilment in God. Where there is such institution, it must be by constitution, and so meeting a constitutional necessity. There can be no substitute for fulfilment itself. When He was our substitute in fulfilment it was to provide new means of fulfilment. All this is vicarious in the highest degree and largest measure. Vicariously Christ provided the new foundation, the new order of sonship in God.

As already said, Jesus' life on earth was perfectly vicarious. In His great passion-prayer He said: "For their sakes I sanctify myself." On an earlier occasion He had said: "The Son of man came not to be ministered unto, but to minister and to give his life a ransom for many." Paul repeatedly taught the vicarious character of Christ's death.

"Who gave himself for us all."
"Who gave himself up for us, an offering and a sacrifice to God."
"He was delivered up for us all."
"He suffered for our sins, the righteous for the unrighteous, to bring us to God."
"He gave himself for us."
"Who gave himself for our sins."
"He (God) made him to be sin on our behalf."
"He laid down his life for us."
"He died for us all."
"Christ died for our sins."
"That he should taste death for every man."

VI. Identification with Sin

It is easier to accept the statement that Christ was identified with us than the other statement that He was identified with our sin. The latter is not so self-evident. In the Incarnation He became "bone of our bone and flesh of our flesh." This identification with human nature was essential to the work of Redemption.

Man being made in the image and likeness of the Son, this identification with the race was possible. To be identified with sin is so contrary to Christ's nature, how was it possible? We are identified with sin through sinning and possessing sinful nature. Some would have it that He inherited sinful nature. The subterfuge of Mary's immaculate conception, when she was begotten, is of no help. It but creates far more difficulty.

Perhaps the explanation is that the conception of Christ was immaculate because it was absolutely under the agency, control and direction of the Holy Spirit. It was the act of God. Perhaps Mary was not even conscious of the moment when it took place. At least she had surrendered herself and her powers to God to do as pleased Him. "Behold the handmaid of the Lord: be it unto me according to thy word."

The conception of Christ was the only one in human history where the flesh played no part. I have discussed this at length in "The Virgin's Son."[1] To this John bore witness according to the Western Version of his Gospel. From this there are quotations two hundred years older than our earliest manuscript of the New Testament. From these earlier quotations by Tertullian and Irenaus we learn that John said:

"But as many as received him to them gave he the right to become children of God, to them that believe on his name, *even him* who was begotten not of bloods (of a father and a mother), nor of the will of the flesh, nor of the will of a man (a human father), but of God."

Christ was "without sin." "He did no sin." "He was holy, harmless, undefiled, and separate from sin-

---
1. The Virgin's Son. pp. 66-68. See also note in this book, Chapter 31

ners." How then could He be identified with sin, when in character and conduct He was absolutely free from it?

All this but avows, He was not identified with it as agent or author. But this is not the only identification possible. Identification may be through acting or through being acted upon. Passive identification is a real form of it. Christ was identified with human iniquity when it acted upon Him in such a way as to leave definite mark and effect upon his Person. It crucified Him, and so wrought its effect of physical death upon Him. This was the identification of the work with the worker, of the Suffering One with that causing the suffering, of effect with the agent or cause.

Before His Crucifixion sin had entered our Lord's experience only as that utterly opposed and frustrated. Knowing it to be His Father's will He suffered the crucifixion. He permitted sin to work an everlasting effect upon Him. He allowed iniquity to identify itself with Him as its victim, as the bearer of its bitter hate and injury. He gave His consent to sin to put Him to death. While this consent was not sin, it was necessary to sin's identification with Him. His permission was full of the holiness of submission to the will and plan of the Father. But this sin was full of all the malignity and hate of the devil. There it was all drawn to a head. It was not any the less sin because the Son of God allowed it to nail His blessed body to the tree when thereon He endured the curse of sin's effect.

VII. Identification with Sinners

Jesus was identified with sinners when He was crucified between the two bandits. He was sharing the same fate with them. It may have been sin to put them to death. It was certainly sin in all its terrible reality and highest height that He should be crucified by it. How then did this identify Him with all human sin?

As Jesus' birth by one mother identified Him with all humanity, so His death by this sin of sins identified Him with all sin. He did not have to be born of more than one human mother to be identified with all humanity. He did not have to die more than once at the hand of sin, or by more than the one sin of the crucifixion, to be identified with all sin. Every element and hateful quality of iniquity were there present in fullest measure in that terrible deed which slew the sinless Son of God. In fact, this sin reached the highest mark, the most God-assailing character. That was the utmost sinfulness of sin, the sin which identified the Sinless One with human sin.

Some have explained Christ's death as caused by God laying upon His Son in a judicial way the sin of us all.[2] There was no need of the Father laying on the Son the sin that had already laid itself upon Him. Surely it is better to say that Christ's identification with sin was due to His crucifixion and death by sin, rather than to say that His death was due to His identification with sin. Sin, not God, inflicted death upon our Lord. The wages of sin, not of God, is death.

But the Father had His part at least in plan and permission. We read that He was made sin. Peter found some of the sayings of Paul difficult to interpret. Surely this is one of them.

"Him who knew no sin, he made to be sin on our behalf, that we might be made the righteousness of God in him."

We may note that this passage supports the view that Christ's identification with sin was passive. "He made Him," not He made Himself. Yet even in the passive there was the active consent. The sacrificial Son of man voluntarily submitted. It was a matter of obedience to the will of God. He "became obedient unto death (to that measure), even the death of the Cross." Without His will to obey, it would not have been obedience. Without His consent His death could not have been at all. But His consent was not to sin as sin, but to sin as permitted by His Father. Consent is never wholly passive. While He was passive as to

---

2. Jesus Christ would cease to be a perfect revelation of the unity of God's nature in the greatest of sacrifices, if in it the Father were meting out penalty on the Son, rather than bearing it with Him.

resisting sin, He was active in permitting what God had permitted it to do.

We need to remember that He was made sin in effect, not in cause. No one can be made sin in cause or agent. Only the agent can make himself sin, can become sin by overt act. We make ourselves to become sin by sinning. Christ became sin though He did no sin, but rather refused it. We are identified with our own sin, and through it with all sin; but Christ was identified with the sin of others who put Him to death; and by it was identified with all sin.

When Christ became sin in effect, the disability of death was lodged in His body. But His body belonged to His soul; and His soul suffered the disability of this physical death. Yet it did not suffer spiritual death. "He bore our sins in his own body on the tree." Sin could thrust its effect into His soul no further than that of bodily death. He did not have to die in soul when His body died. It is impossible for any amount of sin's work *upon* a soul to kill it. Only sin at work *within* the soul can cause it to experience spiritual death.

Summing up we may say that identification was the efficient means, the instrumental way that Christ's vicarious contact with sin and sinners was brought about for the fulfilment of the divine sacrifice in relation to both. For our sake He suffered sin to put the identifying stamp of its fulfilment upon His body. Paul said that he bore in his body the *stigmata*, the marks of the Lord Jesus. These marks were the brands of sin's fulfilment. The stamp of death thus proved His body to be the prey of sin. How strange that just when sin and death could claim fulfilment in the body of the Son of God, the sacrificial love of God could claim its own fulfilment in relation to sin, through the sacrificial identification of Christ with the race that put Him to death.

> "Oh, love of God! Oh, sin of man!
> In this dread act your strength is tried;
> And victory remains with love,
> For He our Lord is crucified."

CHAPTER XIII

THE PROCESS OF FULFILMENT

THERE are vast depths to the wisdom of the Word of God. For example, it nowhere declares that Christ's death propitiated God. Instead it says through the mouth of John that "He is the propitiation for our sins"; and also by the pen of Paul it says, "Whom God set forth *to be* a propitiation (propitiatory)."

For the process by which He became this, we must go to His sacrificial experience on the Cross. He became this satisfaction which marked the fulfilment of the divine nature, by the personal process of satisfying the sacrificial nature of God. The propitiation was that of fulfilment. He became this propitiation in person by what He underwent in sacrifice. God's nature craved the propitiation or satisfaction of His sacrificial spirit in that fulfilment in His Son, which purchased our Redemption.

This personal process is founded in the possibilities brought into being by the Incarnation and by Christ's identification we have been considering. "The Word became flesh." "He was made sin." The process by which He became the satisfaction or propitiation of divine fulfilment, we may call, for want of a better name, *Self-Realization*. This is the process of personal becoming, the development of His sacrificial Self, of the Self-not-for-self. It is that self-realization which reached in Him self-fulfilment, and at the same time was the satisfaction of divine fulfilment.

I. The Mystery of the Process

Through Christ's becoming identified with sin and His experience connected therewith, our Lord became somewhat in personality which before this had not developed. He attained an adaptation of His incarnate

Person, a consummation of sacrificial nature which before did not exist. By the Incarnation He became somewhat in personality without precedent. This process Phillips Brooks poetically and dramatically sets forth:

"He remembered the unspeakable solemnity of the day when, over the rim of the fallen world, He, the pitying Saviour, when no redeemer could be found, stood and said, 'Lo, I come to do thy will, O God!' He entered back into His union with the Father. He identified their lives again. His soul mounted up and stood by God's soul, and looked over the eternal purposes with Him. And only then in this identification, seeing that the Father's glory must be His advantage too, must fulfil His most treasured plan—only then did His new submission utter itself: 'Father, glorify thy name.'"[1]

The self-existent Being of God cannot be other than an immeasurable mystery to us. All the processes of the divine nature transcend our comprehension. For this reason the process of the experience of God in Christ is largely veiled in deep impenetrability. "Great is the mystery of . . . God manifest in the flesh," and all that followed the Incarnation in the experiences and processes of the Son's person."

A judge, meeting a pastor in a local store, said before those present, "Tell me, Mr. Preacher, how could a man be born without a father!" The reply was, "Explain to me, Your Honor, how a man is born with a father." No answer was attempted. All our biological discoveries have but pushed life's ultimate mystery a little further back.

Surely there is enough of the unexplainable in natural origin to halt any one objecting to the supernatural on the ground of its mystery. It is no wonder, then, that no one on earth is able to explain how the Lord from heaven entered the Virgin's womb and became man. With but the barest rudimentary outline of the process, the mind of man staggers under its weight. When "no one knoweth who the Son is but the Father," we are in an ignorance so vast, it accounts for the

---

1. Sermons for the Church Year, p 227.

plentitude of objections and the volubility of unbelief. Sometimes men argue as though their limited knowledge were the finality of omniscience.

That was surely a wondrous process by which the Creator of this infinite universe became a Creature within it, was found in a manger for beasts and in fashion as a helpless babe. Let it ever remain a welcome wonder, for it was a poor welcome the Lord of Life and Glory received when He came, and ever after, even to this day. Blind unbelief may rebel against this mighty mystery and measureless marvel; but a religion without either mystery or marvel is without God and worship; and without these it is not a religion. Let us frankly admit our lack of knowledge, and also that mystery in all the things of God is unescapable because essential. It is essential because the processes of the divine Being must ever remain infinitely greater in scope than the mind of man can encompass.

What man is sufficient in intelligence to plumb the depths of the process within the soul of the Son of God when He hung dying on the Cross? Only God can fully explain it, and then only to one with a mind as great as His own. About this He has many things to say unto us, but we are not able to bear them now, nor are we able as yet to receive them—and in their deepest may never be able. Great is the mystery of how our Maker stooped to the level of our nature to lift us up, and to the depths of our sin to blot it out.

As there was no birth like Jesus' birth, there was no death like the death of the Lamb of God to take away the sin of the world. We cannot measure the downreach of the grace of God when the only begotten Son submitted to most shameful indignities from those to whom He came, suffered His body to be nailed to a cross, as though He were a criminal of deepest dye, and to hang there in mortal agony till His heart broke! Using the words of Nicodemus one may well say, "How can these things be?"

In this and the two following chapters a brief survey will be attempted concerning Christ's struggle of submission, His experience of suffering, His Godward self-realization, and His self-fulfilment.

II. THE PHYSICAL PHASE

First, there was our Lord's self-realization through struggle. Let us begin the study of it by considering its physical approach. The body is a larger factor in human experience than we are wont to realize. Of course the ultimate source of all our experiences of struggle is spiritual. Nevertheless we should recognize that "the body of our humiliation" is essential to our sojourn in this world. No human being comes into existence without it. We can all say with our Master, "A body didst thou prepare for me."

Because God the Son had become "bone of our bone and flesh of our flesh," the murderous enmity of sin could take deadly advantage of this. We read that, "He was put to death in the flesh." We are also told that "His own self bare our sins in his own body on the tree." Another New Testament writer mentions "the offering of the body of Jesus Christ once for all," that we might be "reconciled in the body of his flesh through death."

During all "the days of His flesh," His body was preserved undefiled, kept the perfect servant of His soul. Strange that, for the very same reason, it had to be surrendered at last to the destruction of its life in death. Both to God and to man He had presented His body a living sacrifice throughout His whole life. While this was wholly acceptable to God, it was not at all acceptable to sin-crazed man. When, finally, He gave up His body a sacrifice in death, it was that we might be "made dead to the (condemnation of the) law through the body of Christ."

To some it may seem that the physical nature of the Saviour was neither competent nor important enough to play so great a part in so spiritual a thing and of such vast significance and infinite consequence as the divine fulfilment in relation to man and sin. In reply to this it may be said: he who despises the body, despises the soul and the God who made both.

During all our life on earth we are compelled to regard our bodies as very important. In fact the greater portion of our time is spent in caring for them. God has given the human body its place of honor as it has pleased Him, and it is no mean respect in any regard. God has honored the body by giving to it an important place in the processes of soul, service, experience, religion, and life as a whole.

It was Jesus' body which made possible the fulfilment of the sacrificial spirit of God in relation to sin. While sin assailed Him in both body and soul, its successful assault was made upon His body. Whatever theories we may hold in this connection, the fact remains that but for His mortal body Christ's death for sin would have been impossible. But for His physical nature His divine nature could not have passed through the experience of suffering struggle in death. "Wherefore when he cometh into the world he saith . . . a body hast thou prepared me . . . We are sanctified through the offering of the body of Jesus Christ once for all."

III. The Unity of Christ's Experience

Because His incarnate person was a perfect unity, Jesus Christ's divine nature felt fully and shared completely all the experiences of His physical and human nature. When He descended from heaven He did not leave behind the sensitiveness of His divine nature.

Because of the reality of His Incarnation His divine nature became subject to all the limitations, restrictions, relations, and experiences of weakness imposed by His union with human nature. To this Paul refers when he says: "He was crucified through weakness."

The Incarnation opened the door of possibility leading to physical death. The Epistle to the Hebrews (2:14) intimates that to this end He was born, that He might die in sacrifice for man. "We behold him made for a little while lower than the angels, even Jesus,

... that by the grace of God he should taste of death for every man."

Christ's two natures fused together at the moment of His conception were thenceforth and forever inseparable; and they became all the more to each other as they shared together all His experiences and, finally, that of death itself.

While there was the peculiar suffering due to the righteous sensitiveness of the divine nature which it brought to Christ's human nature, there was also the suffering due to the limitation and weakness of His human nature which the latter brought to His divine nature. If He had not been human, His divine nature would not have known the experience of death. If He had not been divine, His physical human nature would not have had to die for the sin of man and by it.

In the experience of the Cross of Suffering Sacrifice His divine nature brought His human nature through it in a way impossible to the human alone, and a personal realization resulted that otherwise would have been utterly impossible. Later, we shall discuss how this self-realization in sacrifice brought to His physical and human nature the glory of supreme exaltation to the place of power at the right hand of God. While "He was put to death in the flesh," "His flesh saw not corruption," but was changed and fashioned into a kindred resurrection glory that fitted it for its place on the throne of God. Christ in His glorified body has entered into His place of rulership over all. "But this man, after he had offered up one sacrifice for sins forever, sat down on the right hand of God."

IV. The Struggle of Surrender

The great sacrificial self-realization through struggle was because of the converging difficulties met at this point. Christ had to make three very difficult surrenders just then: the surrender of His body to death by torture, the surrender of His person to the will of sin, and the surrender to the inevitable in self-sacrifice appointed by the will of the Father. From the first moment in Gethsemane to the last on Calvary it was a triple struggle in body, mind, and soul. He was the center of the greatest struggle that ever took place between the powers of evil, humanity, and Deity.

The first conflict of the Christ was long before His last days on earth. How early the Tempter met Him, we do not know. In the wilderness temptations just after His baptism, the struggle was first of all whether He would undo the Incarnation by using His divine powers to extricate himself from the difficulties attendant upon His mission. Not to subject Himself fully to human conditions and necessities would have made the Incarnation an empty shadow. To pander to the people's expectation of the spectacular, and to avoid the sacrifice of suffering death, the way of the Cross, was to surrender to Satan. Then, as at Calvary, He refused the temptation to use His superhuman powers for His own personal needs, to escape from hunger and danger, hate and death.

There was the morning struggle to start right; and there was the midnight struggle to end right. The struggle of existence is no empty metaphor even with Jesus. The higher the order of life and its mission, the harder its battle. The struggle of Incarnate existence to fulfil Himself both as Son of man and as Son of God was the highest conceivable fulfilment with the highest mission possible. His sacrificial days were lived in the midst of blind unbelief, cunning opposition, plotting officialism, and bitter hate that could be satisfied only with His death. There, at the close of His brief day, the enemy had surrounded Him; His back was to the wall. The only way out was death or defeat, by abandoning Himself to this sacrifice or abandoning the salvation of man.

The struggle not to defend Himself with supernatural means was real. "Thinkest thou that I cannot now pray to my Father, and He shall presently give me more than twelve legions of angels. But how then should the Scriptures be fulfilled that thus it must be." He had said of the Scriptures, "They testify of me."

Here He testifies of them. It is noteworthy that not only did He appeal to the Word of God, but felt that it was within His mission to fulfil its prophecies. All divine fulfilments are inter-related, inter-locked, and inter-dependent. When the Incarnation was fulfilled, so were the Scriptures predicting it. When the Scriptures and the Incarnation were fulfilled, the fulfilment of the sacrifice of God for sin became possible.

Jesus could not fulfil the will of God and save Himself from death. He did not resist their laying hold upon His body when the enemies came to take Him. Nor did He resist the cruelty of the crucifixion. To possess the power of deliverance from His enemies and death, and not to use it when they were about to nail His body to the tree, was a struggle. He did not even ask His Father to deliver Him, for He knew that it was the way that the Father had planned to let sin work its way and will in His death. The body He took when He came into the world, sin now took and crucified to put Him out of the world. He surrendered it to sin and death that man might be delivered from both.

V. THE STRUGGLE WITH SIN

Next we may think of His surrender to the will of sin. It had conquered all the rest of the human race. Here at last was one life it had not entered. Great was its power; but greater was His who had defeated it. It had utterly failed to master the Master at any point during His days on earth. Now it was in its last dread grapple with Him.

Sin is the insignia of the powers of evil. Let no one say that sin is an abstraction, a personification. It is the personalization of the God-opposing spirit. This we shall discuss later. Here we may say that it is no exaggeration of statement to declare that at Gethsemane and Calvary the mightiest moral and spiritual forces of both worlds were gathered in decisive conflict. The One Person on earth who had proved pure and strong enough to resist all the powers opposed to God, was meeting their last onset.

Because Jesus Christ was God incarnate, He was the incarnation of loyalty to God and of loathing for that which opposed Him. In one way, the intensity of the experience of the Incarnate One was due to the intensity of His love for those duped by sin into putting Him to death. In another way, it was due to the infinite, innate repugnance of His soul toward the hateful will of sin.

There was bitterness in this struggle. This was meant in what He said about the cup He must drink. Every drop in it to the very last one was bitter. The biting bitterness of the struggle was because of the coincidence of the Father's will with the will of sin. For the one He had infinite regard; toward the other, infinite repulsion. His experience of revulsion to sin and devotion to God met in that bitter cup He must drink to the dregs. This put His soul on the rack, and made all the severer the conflict with that which He loathed with every atom of His being. The struggle over surrendering Himself to sin was all the more intense and painfully difficult because of His perfect sinlessness.

Down through all the ages of human history the severest struggle of the saints has been at this point. One of the older books of the Bible is a record of just this struggle. It was no small victory for Job to recognize that God was God as much in taking from him as in giving to him. He did not dethrone God by blaming it all on the devil. He knew Satan could not touch him or his without divine permission. With his children dead, his property all gone and himself thereby socially degraded, looking up through the bitterest tears he had ever wept, he said with an inimitable tremor of voice and pathos of soul, "The Lord gave; and the Lord has taken away. Blessed be the name of the Lord." By name he meant what God had revealed Himself to be. What Job said was, "Blessed be God in taking all from me, in sweeping me bare." That is drinking his cup of bitterness dry.

When the will of God delivers the three from the

fiery furnace, all the faithful rejoice. When His inscrutable purpose permits thousands of equally faithful witnesses to be burned at the stake, is it easy for them to drink the cup of fire? Sin is no less sin, and fire is no less fire, and death is no less death when God permits them. To Jesus Christ sin was all the more terrible in that the Father had willed that it should be permitted to work its wicked will on Him. How bitter the struggle was, the two cries, one in Gethsemane and the other on Calvary, show. "My soul is exceeding sorrowful even unto death." "My God! My God! Why hast thou forsaken me?"

VI. THE INEVITABLE IN SELF-SACRIFICE

Christ's struggle with the inevitable in sacrifice was another important factor. The inevitable in self-sacrifice is the ultimate. And the ultimate is reaching the utmost limit of suffering. It is drinking the last drop of the cup the Father does not, and, in a way, cannot remove.

Self-sacrifice is the straight gate and the narrow way. It offers no room to turn around and look back. It refuses all escape from the full cost of self-surrender. It is never achieved except in prayer, and that prayer a battlefield. Body, soul and spirit all take part in that struggle. "He prayed yet more earnestly." "His sweat was as it were great drops of blood falling down to the ground."

Facing the full cost of self-sacrifice the soul must struggle over the possibility of some other way. So the Saviour prayed, "O my Father, if it be possible, let this cup pass from me." "All things are possible unto thee." No one ever better understood that it is all things in keeping with God's nature, that fulfil it, which are possible to Him. The possible with us which is impossible with God—is sin. God has possibilities that we have not; and we have possibilities that He has not. It is dangerous to attribute all our possibilities to God's nature. It is also dangerous to doubt the divine impossibilities.

President Augustus Strong asked a class in theology whether it is possible for God to lie. A student replied, "All things are possible with God." He could better have quoted, "It is impossible for God to lie." We need not wait to discuss the difference between a metaphysical impossibility and a moral one. An impossibility of reason or thought is different from the constitutional impossibility of a nature producing something not in it. God "cannot deny Himself." The things that are possible within a nature, have been made so by God. But God cannot be God and make anything with a nature contrary to His own. All things are possible to God that are within His nature, not outside of it. If permitting Jesus to escape sacrificial death was within the sacrificial nature of God, then it was possible. But that would be plain contradiction. Jesus did not say it was possible. He found that it was impossible. *There was no other way!* "Father, if it be possible." It was not possible!

An exact answer to just what we prayed for, is impossible when we pray for the impossible. When we learn this, we pray the more appropriate prayer, "Thy will, not mine, be done." This is not only possible but it is also the highest possibility—that of self-sacrifice.

There was as much impossibility within the soul of the Son as in the nature of the Father. So to speak, in His incarnate life He had been building up moral and spiritual impossibilities within Himself. That states it negatively. Positively, He had realized in personality all Godward possibilities. His self-realization in sacrifice made it impossible to refuse God and possible to fulfil God's sacrificial will.

Christ referred to His self-fulfilment in self-sacrifice when He said: "But first He (the Son of Man) must suffer many things and be rejected of this generation" (Luke 17: 25). The prayer of Christ on another occasion referred to this impossibility of escape from the ultimate in self-sacrifice: "Now is my soul troubled; and what shall I say? Father, save me from this hour? (No!) But for this cause came I unto this hour. (This will I pray) Father, glorify thy name." That is, "Glorify thyself in what thou art showing thyself to be." His name was *sacrifice*. That was His revelation in Christ. His name was *love*. That was His glory in the Son. And the glory of sacrificial love is its fulfilment. So Jesus prayed instead that the Father might fulfil His glory in the sacrificial death of the Son Himself.

These two things were inseparable—Christ's self-sacrifice on the Cross, and the glory of God to come by it. That glory in the end would come by His death, did not lessen the struggle to submit to this death. There is bound to be struggle when injury and agony are in the present, and the glory by them still in the future.

Only when the injury and agony lie in the path of the permissive or directive purpose of God, is there complete assurance that they will bring glory to Him. "He makes the wrath of man to praise him: the remainder thereof he doth restrain." Only that which God can use, can glorify Him.

There is the struggle to discern the Father's purpose as to the evil that surrounds and assails us. We pray for deliverance from it and for victory over it. The intense struggle comes when we find that victory over evil may be achieved only by suffering its worst. God answers our prayer as He did that of His Son—according to the purpose He has in us. When my soul is troubled, shall I pray, Father, save me from thy purpose in me? A thousand times, *No!* That would be a salvation to be saved from. This rather shall I pray, Father, fulfil thy purpose in me!

VII. GOD-GLORIFYING SACRIFICE

Jesus was the one perfectly normal soul. If He had wanted to die and had willed His own death, it would have been not only abnormal, it would have emptied His self-sacrifice. Self-sacrifice unto God begins by emptying out our own will and choosing His. The will of God has absolute right of way in every sacrificial

THE PROCESS OF FULFILMENT 163

life. To suffer any extent of injury and loss will really be gain if the Divine Will permits it in order to work out the deep purposes of God.

When Jesus made the glory of God the one petition of His prayer, "there came therefore a voice out of heaven saying, I have both glorified it and will glorify it again." The Father had glorified His sacrificial Fatherhood in giving the Son in the Incarnation; and now He was about to glorify it again in giving up His Son to die for the sin of the world. The full import of that "again" Jesus well knew. Knowing it to mean nothing other than His death, He went on to say, "If I be lifted up from the earth, I will draw all men unto me." John immediately adds, "This he said, signifying what death he should die" (John 12: 33).

For the Son of God the path of glory led but to the grave, not to end the glory but to begin it. The people hearing the voice from out the heavens, thought that an angel was speaking, while some supposed that it had merely thundered. None of them knew the language of heaven save the Son.

The native tongue of heaven is that of sacrifice. No other speech shall ever be heard there than the Language of the Lamb. To the unsacrificial in soul and spirit it may still look like a strange way for God to glorify Himself, namely, by the death of His Son. Joseph Parker, in his autobiography, tells of a contest he had with a man who was lecturing against Christianity. The lecturer said one could hardly believe in the God of Stephen who permitted this faithful servant to be stoned to death. Parker (then a young man) did not know what reply to make. He prayed God to tell him. Immediately there flashed into his mind this rejoinder: the God who enabled Stephen to forgive his murderers, and to pray for them in his death, did a greater thing for him than to deliver him from death at their hands. Even so God did a far greater thing for His Son in enabling Him to die the death of sacrifice for sinners than to save Him from this death at the hands of sinful men.

Paul must have caught great glimpses of the glory of God in the death of His Son, for he said, "God forbid that I should glory, save in the cross of our Lord Jesus Christ." All who have been redeemed unto its glory in sacrificial spirit, can sing not in word only but also with the understanding of the spirit:

> "In the Cross of Christ I glory,
> Tow'ring o'er the wrecks of time;
> All the light of sacred story
> Gathers round its head sublime."

The death of Christ on the Cross, having such significance, fastens the eyes of eternity upon it.

> "The Cross my all,
> My theme, my inspiration, and my crown!
> My strength in age, my rise in low estate!
> My soul's ambition, pleasure, wealth, my world!
> My light in darkness, and my life in death!
> My boast through time—bliss through eternity—
> Eternity too short to speak its praise."

CHAPTER XIV

SACRIFICIAL SELF-REALIZATION

IN THE Godhead the Son was the One adapted to enter incarnate existence on earth. In the Incarnation there was adaptation of Person to His work of Redemption. This adaptation was to the divine end which His sacrificial death had in view.

Personality in the Godhead needs no growth. It is eternal attainment of absolute perfection in personality. All created personality is capable of endless self-realization. Our personal fulfilment is by unending personal realization. There is no fulfilment for us which ends personal becoming or growth.

When "the Word became flesh," He adapted His person to the order of existence in which self-realization grows and personality becomes. "It became Him" to enter upon a becoming existence. And within this existence "it became Him" to be "made perfect by suffering." His sacrificial self-realization endured the Cross. He became "Christ crucified." So the Cross became the symbol of all He became by it. This we shall consider in the next chapter. Here we continue the discussion of the personal process by which Christ became "the propitiation for our sins."

Self-realization may be either good or bad. It is simply the process of change, growth, or realization. The addition to personality which it brings, depends upon the order of the self-realization and the source and nature of the elements built into personality. In the process of perfecting the person of Christ for His office of Redeemer the following five things will be considered: the purity of His person, the range of personal powers brought into exercise, the nature and power of that which He experienced in His death, the generic order of His experience, and the personal effect of the sufferings which He endured.

I. A Law of Self-Realization

The many-sided greatness of Christ is a vast subject in itself. He was so great there is no one on earth with whom we can compare Him. His flawlessness strikes us dumb. In one way, His sinlessness was His greatest greatness, for it indicates the quality and range of all His other greatnesses. A personality of such purity and power had never before nor has since passed along the pathway of human life.

One important principle in this connection is, *the purer personality is, the deeper are its experiences.* Because of His sinlessness the channels of Christ's experience ran far deeper than those of other men. The experiences that naturally make for depth of personality are clogged by sin and become superficial.

The law of personal life seems to be that the purer its experiences, the more of God is in them; and the more of God is in them, the deeper they are. Moreover the greater a personality, the greater the scope and variety of its experiences. "To him that hath shall be given." And the greater any experience, or the deeper its movement, the greater the personal realization by means of it.

Because of the greatness of Christ, the perfect purity of His soul, the unlimited fulness of God in all His life, the unique quality and immeasurable depth of His experience on the Cross, the power of self-realization must have been very great, very exceptional, very effective in adapting and perfecting His person as our Redeemer.

II. Personal Powers Participating

The personal powers of Christ brought into action during his experience on the Cross determined in no small degree the character of His self-realization at that time. The nature of His motives and their infinite outreach should be taken into account. The power of His unflinching purpose, the almighty pull of His desires, the intensity of His devotion, and all the rest of

His powers exercised in His experience on the Cross help to indicate the extent of the personal realization which then took place.

Christ's processes of soul were as balanced as His character. In them one power was not over-used and another unduly repressed. Never was His mind more active than when He hung upon the tree. He had refused to be drugged. His brain was never more clear than at that time.

His mind took a puissant part in the process of personal realization. The deeper one's motives and other coöperating powers, the deeper tends to be the thought which is constitutionally a part of them; and the deeper the thought of mind, the deeper the effect upon personality. Who can guess what depth of feeling and range of thought took place during the intense hours of the Crucifixion?

Nothing can be greater in power of pure self realization than the activity of the sacrificial spirit. We are never so much ourselves as when we utterly forget ourselves in unselfish devotion. And we never grow so fast as when we put all of ourselves into the good of others.

Suppose three nations are engaged in the same war, and that one is a ruthless aggressor, another defending its right to the freedom of national existence, and the third supporting the weaker nation in the interests of righteousness and humanity. The three different motives will lead to three different orders of national self-realization in the same struggle. As the thought and motive of sacrifice is highest, the realization by it is highest. When our Lord for the sake of all mankind went up to Jerusalem and to His death, His unselfish self-realization was in proportion to its motive.

As already said, the self-realization of Christ was of a self-not-for-self, a self for God, a self for man. Everything recorded about His life shows an undying interest in man and parallel devotion to God. During His life He had been growing a soul for others. Now he had a soul ready to die for others. But it grew then too—perhaps most of all then, for the self-not-for-self came then to its largest opportunity and exercise. The soul that never failed God or man could not fail itself in realization by its sacrificial experience. For such a time it was raised up. *It came to the Cross for such a work as this.* Because His was a fully prepared personality for this experience He realized in soul all the more out of it, as well as all the more for others by it.

With unflinching purpose and unfailing desire the Redeemer went forward into the sacrificial experience of Calvary. His love and interest nailed Him to it far more securely than the Roman spikes. It would have been easier to drive the crucifixion nails through hardened steel than through His hands and feet, had He not yielded His body to this death. His obedience to the Father, His own desires, purposes, and love nailed Him to the tree of death. Because of this His sacrificial self-realization thereon was all the greater.

III. SELF-REALIZATION IN MASTERING SIN

There was the struggle which engaged the soul of Christ to submit Himself to the will of sin which He detested with all His nature. The struggle did not end with the act of submission, for it delivered Him to constant contact with it, and to the steady struggle of revulsion to it.

The nature and strength of this opponent of the sacrificial nature of Christ determined in no small measure the character and extent of the personal realization through bearing in His body and suffering in His soul the contact-effect with it. In Part Three, self-realization in sin is dealt with at some length. Here we need to make the distinction that Christ's personal realization was by sacrificially enduring the torture of sin unto death. His soul was bared to death-dealing contact with the powers of evil arrayed against Him. His self-realization was not in sin but in bearing it for others.

Genetically, the struggle of sin is to deceive. For its inception it is necessary to delude. All its other powers depend upon the success of this. Once the process of self-delusion begins, all other self-realizations in sin are possible.

Sin must arraign God in some way and deceive thereby. It uses its own blackness of darkness to work in. In the very contrast of its infinite vileness with the immaculate purity of Him who faced its death, it accuses the God who permits this. How can He be righteous and permit such glaring unrighteousness? Has He not infinite power? Why does He ever let sin have its way? Why let it work its will on the Beautiful and Best in its bitterest and deadliest way of utter humiliation and fiendish torture? What kind of a God must He be to surrender perfect goodness to perfect evil?

To sit in a comfortable chair and ask such questions in an academic way, is one thing; to be hanging on the cruel nails driven through His outstretched hands and the spike transfixing His feet, and to be suffering the long drawn-out agony of such a death after a life of utter unselfishness and absolute purity, is another. Never before had sin such an argument of unfair, inhuman, ungodlike treatment to set against what Christ knew of the Father. But He could not be deceived. Behind the cloud and beyond it He saw the Father fully. He could not at all be induced to lose faith in Him. When sin's power of deluding rose to the highest, the faith and knowledge which successfully resisted it, rose to the highest in self-realization thereby.

The sense of mastery over sin betokens a divine order of personal realization. This consciousness of being above iniquity, even when He was submitting to its murderous assault, never left Him. He was proof against all its wiles. He did not doubt God. He could not be in the least misled about the Father. He knew how to overcome sin by undergoing its death. And thereby He would be enabled to deliver us from all its delusions and all other evils and from the Evil One. Iniquity might do its worst to Him, but it could not budge His loving loyalty to His Father, nor make Him swerve in the least from doing His best for us. So strong was the Godward trend of His nature, so perfect was His emptying of His own will and His realization of His Father's plan and purpose, He realized within Himself only that which was all for God.

The storm of hell beat hard upon Him, but it could not wreck His faith or love. His sacrificial existence pushed on in the teeth of the gale of fury which sin had aroused against Him. The last, even as the first, of the beating billows of evil failed utterly to affect the adamantine stability of the Rock of Ages. Poor dupes of iniquity's madness may jibe and jest, wag their heads and mock, but no other response could be provoked than the measureless love that prayed, "Father, forgive them: they know not what they do." Sacrificial love was the only response He offered to the murderous hate that surrounded Him.

Strong as sin was to carry humanity so far hellward that men could treat the "Altogether Lovely One" with the utmost malignant enmity, it was not so strong as His love for man. The deep, strong, steady movement of His soul Godward was far greater than all the power of iniquity hurled against it. When He was dying for us and because of our sin, He lived the fullest toward the Father in all His incarnate life.

Because of the new order of His experience with sin, there was a unique self-realization toward the Father. He realized that in His soul which could come in no other way than by the sacrificial bearing of iniquity on the Cross. There He met the full force of sin's antidivine power, and, out of its pressure upon Him, attained a sin-defeating, sin-destroying power He could thenceforth communicate to man.

IV. THE SACRIFICIAL STRUGGLE

Ability to live and suffer and achieve for others rises in proportion as personality increases in sacrificial development. Only the sacrificial person can have sacrificial experience. The wholly unselfish, fully sacrificial person of Christ could have, and did have, a wholly sacrificial experience. That was therefore the generic quality it had. The order of Christ's self-realization was so generically sacrificial, it reached heights and depths, breadths and lengths which are beyond us to survey.

Fundamentally, His experience was one of sacrificial struggle with sin. The severity of the conflict was due to its importance; and its importance was due to the tremendous issues at stake. The difficulty lay in the paradox of Christ's experience. He could not meet sin with sin, but with sinlessness. Without sin He suffered sin. He bore the anti-sacrificial sacrificially. *Righteousness was His only response to the unrighteousness that slew Him.* He had to smother the most devilish hate in the divinest love. He had to let sin break, and death still his heart that it might impart its life to man. He was so human that He could die, and so divine that He could destroy death and sin and hell. He permitted His person to be the battlefield where God overwhelmed all that was in sin with the infinite forces of the resources of all that was in God.

Christ's sufferings and death were infinitely more than those of martyrdom. The martyr is helpless in the hands of the enemy. The Son of God could at any moment have overwhelmed the enemy. Yet He withheld this power, that He might overwhelm sin in a far deeper and infinitely larger way.

Had the Saviour been helpless in the grasp of sin, there would have been no voluntary submission, and a very different order of self-realization. To withhold the power He had to deliver Himself from the Cross and its death, meant that every moment was itself a battle. His perfect self-renouncement of divine powers by which He could have freed Himself from this torture, preserved the integrity of His Incarnation, but it left him, in one way, at the mercy of the merciless powers of evil. His refusal to save Himself from the long drawn-out conflict and suffering secured a new self-realization in self-mastery.

In human experience there come dreary days which seem to stretch themselves out into weeks and months.

And there are crushing hours when time itself seems to have come to a standstill. Then there are moments in which we seem to have lived days. So with Christ in "the hour and power of darkness." The power of personality to create atmosphere is well known. The presence of evil lives which surrounded Him and their attendant spirits of evil created a foul, choking atmosphere which pained the sensitive soul of the Christ as much, if not vastly more, than His physical agony. That human life, for which He was dying, could gloat in His sufferings, made His sufferings all the more severe. Because of who He was and how they slew Him, this was the most awful murder in human history.

The very wolves of hell seemed to have gathered about the dying Lamb of God; but the Lamb overthrew them by the blood of His sacrifice, overcame them with the testimony of His unbroken faithfulness. Out of the effort of evil to crush Him, He realized a strength. Out of this death in the hands of sin He realized more life in the Father, not for Himself alone, but for all who should come after Him, and by union of faith draw life from Him.

V. THE ADAPTATION OF SACRIFICIAL SUFFERING

While all the earthly experience of our Lord entered into the sacrificial development of His Person, it was His experience with sin as He hung a-dying on the Cross which completed the process by which He became *The Solution of Sin's Problem.* To this He, Himself, referred when He said: "Behold I cast out demons and perform cures today and tomorrow, and the third day I am perfected." The completion of this process going on within His Person is referred to in the Epistle which describes it and Him as "The Son perfected for evermore." The Holy Spirit by the Author of Hebrews further says:

"For it became him . . . to make the author of their salvation perfect through suffering . . . Who in the days of his flesh, having offered up prayers and supplications with strong crying and tears (in Gethsemane) unto him that was able to save him out of (ek) death, and having been heard for his godly fear, though he was a Son, yet learned obedience by the things which he suffered; and having been made perfect (having been perfected) by the things which he suffered, he became unto all that obey him the author of eternal salvation." Heb. 2:10 and 3:7-10.

Here we find once more reference to His becoming. We have spoken of the paradox of His experience, for both sorrow and joy entered into it at the same time. There was a joy set before Him as "He endured the Cross." As Charles Cuthbert Hall has said:

"We may look, as if with His eyes, upon some part of that great landscape of Joy which He saw from the eminence of the Cross. He rejoiced in the doing of the will of the Father. He rejoiced in the reconstruction of Human society. He rejoiced in the communication of the spirit of victory to individual lives."[1]

While this joy did its work in His soul, suffering most intense was also at work. He needed the adaptation which came by them. The adapting effect by both could not come except by the experience of both. The effect of suffering comes only by suffering. The experience of sin in sinlessly suffering its death was necessary to the process of personal realization in making perfect the Author of our salvation. By that experience of utmost self-sacrifice He became the sufficient sacrifice for our sins.

After all it is not only the experience, but how it is borne, the spirit which governs the experience, which determines what is realized in and by it. And His, we learn from the same Epistle of Hebrews, was the eternal spirit of sacrifice. It was without beginning in God, and will have no end.

Whatever the eternal spirit of God as fundamentally sacrificial meant to the Son of God, it was new to the nature of man, as new to Christ's human nature as that nature itself was new to Him. By suffering His human nature was fitted by this eternal spirit for its ultimate place in the person of the Redeemer in His

---

1. The Gospel of the Divine Sacrifice, p 134.

ministry of Redemption. His humanity thus infinitely enabled shared with His Deity all the sacrificial experience and process of sin-bearing. His manhood and Godhood bore it as one.

In one way, the Incarnation wrought no greater change in Christ's Person than did His death. Our Lord could not pass through the intense, soul-searching experience such as that of the Cross, and come out of it unchanged. And this change represents the depth and scope of the process of His self-realization. This personal effect of transformation was the very substance of His adaptation to Redemption, the perfecting and fulfilling of His Person in this sacrifice.

VI. Experiencing and Becoming

The effect upon the Person of Christ was according to the law of personal realization, that is, according to the uniform way in which this law works. Another fundamental law of self-realization is—*what we experience we become.* Because personality is personality, it can never receive an effect in a wholly passive way. It must react to it to some degree.

To what extent personality becomes what it experiences, depends upon how far the experience goes, and how much similar self-realization preceded it. When we experience sin by sinning, we become sinful. And the extent of the sinfulness must be commensurate to the nature, extent, power and experience of sin and according to the momentum of previous sinning. Contrawise, when we experience the will of God accomplished in our lives, we become a divine realization to the extent to which the obedience carries us and with the momentum of similar previous self-realizations by obedience to God.

Our Redeemer had the experience of His own personal reaction to the sin that nailed Him to the tree of shame and death, and at the same time this was a divine realization of the will of God. When His soul suffered sacrificially, it became sacrificial to the extent of the measure of His sacrifice, and added to it the

SACRIFICIAL SELF-REALIZATION

accelerated movement of His previous sacrifices. When He experienced death, there was a self-realization of soul commensurate to the extent of the death, its nature and power.

Christ's sufferings on the Cross we have sought to interpret in terms of personality. The pangs of His sinless self-realization were caused by suffering in perfect righteousness the unrighteous death which sin inflicted. Such pangs necessarily attended the birth of Redemption. That sacrifice of suffering overcame sin fully—and in a most personal way. It brought forth a Person who had conquered the enemy, not for Himself only, but for all mankind. The Vicarious Victim emerged from His death the Vicarious Victor.

When Christ experienced the sacrificial death on the Cross appointed of God, there was a sacrificial development and attainment corresponding. This was a divine realization to the extent of the sacrifice and added to it were the realizations from all His previous sacrifices. Rather, all His previous self-realizations by sacrifice had added to them the greatest realization of all, that in His sacrificial death.

Everything that had happened in the incarnate experience of our Lord, had its own effect upon, and was registered in, His Person. The process of self-realization stored up in His person the accumulated result and attainment of all the experiences through which He had passed. The experience during His crucifixion and death stored up in His Person their own effect, result, and realization which is still there, and shall be for evermore.

Each period of suffering made, so to speak, its own deposit in the soul of Christ. The agony of Gethsemane, the trial, the scourging, and journey to Golgotha, the nailing to the Cross, His suffering while the Crucifixion was perfecting its work of death, and last of all the death itself, made Him "the man of sorrows and acquainted with grief." No wonder that His "countenance was marred" so much, for "He was bruised for our iniquities."

We may conclude this chapter on sacrificial self-realization by pointing out that, in the incarnate life of our Lord, every self-realization was a self-fulfilment. His generic life-principle of sacrifice had secured in His Person the invincible habit, so to speak, of fulfilling Himself in God. *In His death He as faithfully fulfilled Himself in God.* In His death for sin His unchanged order of self-realization in God became forever unchangeable. Everything which had been realized in His soul during life and death was in God, and therefore was absolutely true to God. His death itself was the supreme experience of being absolutely true to God in every particular. Because the Saviour died in self-fulfilment in God, God perfectly fulfilled Himself in relation to sin in Him and through Him.

NOTE —A differing statement in a prominent religious paper has recently put the issue this way: "*It is not what Christ is, but what Christ has done, that saves men.*" This is an attempt to separate the inseparable. To us Christ is what He is, because of what He has done. Ontologically He cannot change. Relationally He can. The Scriptures do not separate the Christ from what He has done. In fact they name Him from what He does. Paul combined both Him and what He had done when he said, "We preach Christ crucified." The view that Redemption is in an act, not in a Person, necessarily misses the truth that all the redeeming merit and saving power of Christ's death rests on *who He is* and consists in *what He became* by that death. In a similar way we might consider the Incarnation as an act alone, and thus lose all its meaning. But the Incarnation gets all its meaning in Him who "became flesh and dwelt among us." All the virtue of His birth and the efficacy of His death dwell in the Person of the Son of God. We therefore conclude that Christ apart from His death, or His death apart from Christ is not the Gospel.

The old penal view seems to be at the bottom of this misconception. The paper mentioned goes on to add: "Without (Christ) dying to pay the penalty of every man's sin, every human being since Adam's fall would have been lost forever." Here we have repeated the old false confidence in redemption by penalty. If suffering penalty were all that Christ did, the human race would still be lost. There is no converting, renewing, or redeeming power in penalty, no matter on whom it falls. Bearing the penalty for sin has the effect of sin. It is sin's power rather than God's. Inflicting on a criminal the just penalty for his crime does not make him just. It gives no new nature in place of the old criminal nature, which is the worst penalty of his crime. If it be held that punishing a sinless substitute redeems the sinner, just as if the sinner had borne it himself, we are still a long, long way from redemption. All the penalty of eternity cannot change or redeem the lost. It lacks the power of liberation from sin in nature. Sin's penalty is death. The sinner has already suffered its penalty. Things would not bring forth after their kind, if the penalty of death brought forth life. *Life comes only from life.* In Christ the gift of life comes from the life that sin could not put to death, even when bearing the suffering of physical death at its hands. In Christ's death God did vastly more than fulfil the law of sin's penalty. The Son bore this penalty that, passing through it, He might bring to us the fulfilment of the sacrificial nature of God. Had only sin been fulfilled, this would have offered no hope. In Christ's death sin finds God in another place than as judge or avenger. He is the bearer of it and its suffering, because the redemptive virtue is not in the penalty of sin, but in the sacrificial divine person who bore it. No thanks to sin and its penalty! All praise to the self-sacrificial nature of Christ and its fulfilment on Calvary! By it we are redeemed from the worst of all penalties—that of being sinful in nature. What we need is redemption from penalty, not by it, for the latter is obviously impossible.

CHAPTER XV

THE CROSS OF CHRIST

SO IMPORTANT and many-sided is the process of the self-realization of Christ on the Cross, we may well consider it somewhat further. Every Christian century has endeavored to set forth something of its meaning. No wonder that the Cross has so supremely occupied attention, for it is the very symbol of divine Redemption. On it took place the most important and significant death in the history of the world. It stands therefore as the emblem of the experience Christ passed through, the sufferings He endured, the forces He overcame, the success of His whole mission.

But the symbol is not the substance. The Cross is not Redemption. It has been taken as the emblem of Christianity, because it was the instrument by which the Redeemer was put to death. Having accomplished this, the Cross could go no further. The power of Redemption is in Him who died, not in the wooden instrument of His death. Christ offered up, not His death, but Himself by means of His death. As the wondrous accuracy of Holy Writ puts it: "He gave himself for our sins......He offered up himself......He offered himself without spot unto God."

I. THE CROSS A COMPLETION

Coming face to face with Christ's death on the Cross there arises that great question of the human heart, What was it His death accomplished? Perhaps the clue to the answer lies in what He became by it in divine fulfilment.

In fact, the effect upon us of Christ's death depends upon the effect it had upon Him. His sacred sufferings could not redeem us, had they left no impress upon Him, wrought no adaptation in His Person. Only a death that became a means of self-realization in Him, could become a means of self-realization in us.

Suppose the process of Christ's self-sacrifice had stopped short of His death, and instead of accomplishing "His exodus" on Mount Calvary, He had passed to the world beyond from the Mount of Transfiguration, what would have been the difference? More than we can measure! His sacrifice for us would have been arrested in the flower and before the fruit of Redemption had a chance to form and mature.

In a way the Cross was necessary to complete the Christ. Certainly it was necessary to complete His righteousness for us. Sinless as was His life, there was still a righteousness for Him to achieve, a sacrifice to finish. Not until He was dying could He say, "It is finished." Then He had realized a new order of righteousness by suffering the unrighteousness of the crucifixion and its death; for, as already said, righteousness was His only response to the unrighteousness that slew Him.

The Cross was the fullest possible demonstration that His righteousness was unswerving and invincible. There and then it was proved to be invulnerable, while He bore the wounds of death for us. It was a righteousness that grew to completion when everything in earthly circumstances was unfavorable and antagonistic. To grow in soul a vicarious righteousness when suffering in body and dying in torture by the greatest unrighteousness was the greatest triumph of the self-realization of the Cross.

Never was a life so searched as that of Christ. Never was a death such a quest of evil. But the "Prince of this World" found nothing in Him. During His lifetime Jesus had used the various oppositions He met. He made use of them as occasions for doing good to man for God. But for the antagonism of enemies we had never read some of the most helpful sentences which fell from the lips of the Master. Many of the greatest revelations from the Great Teacher came in this way. Somewhat in the same way He used the unrighteousness of the Crucifixion as the occasion for realizing within Himself a redeeming righteousness for us all.

II. THE HEART-BREAK OF THE CROSS

The death of a great love is naturally attended with great convulsion of feeling and revolution of thought and with corresponding effect in self-realization. But Christ's love was not dying. Rather, it was passing through and overcoming death and the sin which had inflicted it. This could not fail to have proportionate effect upon the process of His personal realization. His love had all the greater power in self-realization because it could not be put to death. His love was never further from dying than when His body died. He died because of the greatness of His undying love for mankind. Little use in sin killing Him when it could not kill His love. But God saw immeasurably deep use in permitting sin to slay Him. Never did sin more outwit itself than at the Cross.

How bitter must have been the cup of death which Christ drank to the dregs! How unspeakably hard to be slain by the very ones loved so deeply! On Calvary Divine Love was baring its bosom to the stroke of death. But in truth this was other than a death by crucifixion. On the Cross the Son of God died of a broken heart.[1] Who can tell the depths and heights

---

1. The "blood and water" which flowed forth from the pericardium (heart-sack) when pierced by the Roman spear, taken with the fact of the unusually brief time our Lord remained alive on the Cross, may be allowed as evidence that our Saviour's heart broke under the intense strain of the agony of soul He was then enduring
In literal heartbreak, we are told, there is first a weakening through dilatation, an abnormal dilation or stretching of the heart chambers. Physical overstrain or mental agony may cause this We remember that Christ had been for three years under severe physical strain The night before the Crucifixion there was no opportunity to rest How weakening the bloody sweat was in Gethsemane, we do not know This was followed by the flight of the disciples, the denial of Peter, the scourging by the Roman soldiers, and the fainting under the Cross when Simon the Cyrenian was pressed into service The mental and spiritual agony during the hours on the Cross is utterly beyond us to estimate Heartbreak is accompanied by such awful pain that a scream or shriek accompanies it. Such was the cry that startled the spectators of His suffering.
Of course there is spiritual heartbreak besides the physical The former is possible when no physical heart-rupture has taken place Many a heart-broken woman has lived years of agony. We are not compelled to ascribe physical heartbreak to our Lord, though the evidence is all that way. Something stopped his heart from beating At some point the physical mechanism broke. It could not endure the strain longer under which both body and soul were suffering What perfect sacrificial mind could realize the enormity of

and breadths and lengths of the richness of redeeming realization in the soul of Christ through suffering for us the agony of a breaking and finally broken heart? What experience possible could be so intense as this? The suffering self-realization of the breaking heart of Jesus on the Cross spells the process of the Redemption of God in Christ.

III. THE LAST STEP IN SELF-SACRIFICE

The character of the personal realization on the Cross may be suggested to us by the fact that it was the last step possible, and the greatest in accepting the will of God in His program for the Incarnate life of His Son. It was the supreme and final test of the Son's faith in, and of His absolute loyalty to, the Father.

The more difficult and costly the effort to carry out the Father's will, the greater the personal realization by it. In accepting the Cross and suffering its death Christ obeyed the will of God on a scale never before possible and in circumstances and conditions of unparalleled difficulty. This must have been perfect self-realization in perfect self-fulfilment in God.

Not only in difficult and trying obedience to the will of God, but in any obedience to it there comes an increase of one's entire capacity for good and the power to do it. One of the best things about it is that it increases capacity to know God, even as one of the worst things about disobedience to God is its decrease of ability to understand and know Him. We not only come to know Him better and understand more fully the wisdom of His will, when we act as the conscious agents of it, but our entire powers are lifted into a higher state of efficiency; and not least among them is that of personal realization.

---

sin, feel it with the infinite sensitiveness of God, and the physical structure not come to rupture and death? Whatever may have taken place in His body, it was a heartbroken soul that uttered itself in that sudden outcry, "*My God, my God! Why hast thou forsaken me?*"
There may be spiritual heartbreak without physical, and physical without spiritual; but surely there may be both at once where the physical is because of the spiritual In any case the spiritual has the vaster significance. If Jesus died only with physical heartbreak, then it explains little more to me than the physical cause of His death If He died spiritually heart-broken because of human sin, this explains to me how He bore sin, to what extent, and what effect sin had on God in His death. "It broke His heart on Calvary."

In some cases the divine will is so deep in the majesty and mystery of its purpose and meaning, it is but partly comprehended at the time it is obeyed; and the only way to the full comprehension of the depths of its wisdom is by gaining the enlightenment of passing through it. The victory of its revelation is on the other side of the battlefield of obedience. The contest must be fought all the way across. The fact is that in what we are doing there is a greater wisdom than we are capable of realizing at the time we obey the divine will. God can say to us when we obey Him, "What you do, you know not now; but you shall know hereafter."

IV. THE QUESTION OF HIS AGONY

Jesus knew that it was divinely appointed unto Him to die on the Cross uplifted between the two eternities of the Past and the Future. He knew this clearly, fully, unmistakably. He had no agony in trying to discern and decide what was the will of God in this matter. He had intimate and perfect knowledge of the Father. To Him the Father's will never seemed in the slightest to be arbitrary, unwise, or unnecessary.

On the other hand, having accepted by His *Kenosis* the finite compass of existence within the Incarnation, He was living within the limits of the human way and capacity of apprehension. For this reason He was no more omniscient about the infinite meaning, infinite purpose, infinite process going on and centering in His sacrifice on the Cross, than He was omniscient about the program of the *Parousia*.

Most certainly Jesus Christ knew the nearest to omniscience that was possible. Sometimes it is said the only thing Jesus confessed as beyond His knowledge was the date of His Second Coming. But in Gethsemane He did not know whether another way than the way of the Cross was possible, consistent with the end the Father had in view. Here too on the Cross we find another instance of the limitation of His knowledge.

Christ was achieving that with more wisdom in it

and reason for it than He knew. This is evident from the question of utmost agony uttered when dying. Yet He must have gained something in self-realization by the struggle to understand the mighty mystery which then puzzled Him.

Perhaps the most agonizing cry that ever burst from human lips was that which echoed up the tense vault of heaven from the dying lips of the Crucified One, when He moaned in the groans of the last agony, "My God! My God! Why hast thou forsaken me?" Small wonder that what puzzled Him to understand, has puzzled men ever since to explain.

V. Interpretations of the Forsaking

Some interpret this "forsaking" as proving that Christ was dying not only a physical but also a spiritual death. Such reasoning is strangely oblivious to many patent facts. For one thing, if the Saviour were dying spiritually, He would not be asking such a question, He would not be seeking to know the mind of God in this matter, and He would not be praying at all. When one is dying spiritually it is for the want of such prayer and inquiry, not in and by the actual exercise of them.

It must be most blessed to die spiritually when one can say in his last breath, "Father, into thy hands I commit my spirit." To die into the hands of the Father, is that a spiritual death? As a matter of fact, the Son was never more alive to and living in and by the Father than at the instant when He asked this question—except this: His body was ceasing to live in and by God. It was because His soul was all alive to the Father that He asked this. The very question grew out of and came forth because of His life in the Father.

Passing over whether it is ever possible for God the Son to die spiritually to God the Father, we have the teaching of Scripture as to the exact nature of His death. It says specifically, "He was put to death in the flesh." While the soul is very much affected by the death of its body, the soul itself does not die in sin because the body dies by sin putting it to death. Even

Christ's body died by sin, not in sin. It suffered the curse. It did not commit the cause of it.

Another explanation of this "question of dereliction" is that Jesus was at the moment suffering a delusion due to the mental strain caused by His suffering. This means that a temporary mental break-down had taken place. But Jesus was never deluded as to the relation of the Father to anything, least of all as to the relation of the Father to this supreme event. And the Incarnate One could not be mistaken as to the process of the presence of God without a corresponding realization in His soul. This would be the self-realization of an imperfection. And with that having come in, out goes the flawlessness of the Son of God. Self-realization in delusion could hardly perfect the sacrificial Person of Christ. Certainly it would not be a fulfilment in God. We therefore conclude that, when the soul of Christ was "made an offering for sin unto death," His soul did not die. It but experienced the death of its body.

The penal theory of the Atonement has its own interpretation of this last question of the Incarnate Christ. According to it the Father was meting out in His withdrawal the penalty due to sin, and was visiting this penalty on His suffering Son. Surely He was suffering penalty enough without imposing any more by the direct act of God! Because of who He was and the nature of this death all sin was resting upon Him by the contact of the Cross. Christ had put Himself under the whole of that load. There was no need that more be added.

Those who interpret this last experience of the Cross as due to the Father placing or attributing to Christ by direct act such a responsibility for sin as called for the penalty of forsaking the Son, are welcome to all they can get out of such an interpretation. If it helps them, who can deny it to them? When they insist that those to whom the interpretation is a hindrance, adopt it as the true and only one, that is quite another matter.

The Judgment-Death theory is another phase of the

penal interpretation. To most men any such personally inflicted penalty appears mechanical, unnecessary, and unlike the Father. That in this awful moment when the sin-bearing Son was already dying, that the Father functioned in measuring out penalty of any amount upon Him, is scarcely satisfying. If it be replied that this satisfied God and was for His purpose, we must respond that it could satisfy only the God of a mechanical theory, not the God of the New Testament which Jesus revealed.

But Jesus did suffer penalty. So too did the Father. Who meted out the penalty to the latter? The same one that meted it out to the former. The penalty the Son suffered was not suffered for the sake of penalty, any more than the Father's suffering was for the sake of penalty. A mother suffers penalty in bringing to birth her child. She does not give birth to her child for the sake of suffering this penalty. Her penalty suffered is not personally imposed as judgment upon her. "A woman when she is in travail hath sorrow, *because her hour is come.*" Christ's Hour of Death had come; and the Father was standing by Him. The unavoidable suffering which neither the Father nor the Son, nor the Holy Spirit could escape, was borne, because it was inextricably involved in the process of Redemption.

Was the forsaking a myth then? By no means! We find that the mind of the Master was ever suffused and filled with both the thought and the expressions of Scripture. Even here, in the agony of death, He used the words of the Twenty-Second Psalm. A glance at this psalm shows that these opening words were *not the forsaking of desertion*. As an answer to the necessity which the Father Himself faced, He could have said, using the words of another Scripture: "For a small moment have I forsaken thee."

VI. THE WITHDRAWAL NECESSARY TO DEATH

What then was the forsaking our Lord suffered? This interpretation is here offered: *it was the divine forsaking or withdrawal always necessary to the process of physical death.* In spiritual death there is also a withdrawal, which we need not here consider, as such was not the order of Christ's death.

In the death of even the smallest insect God cannot be a mere spectator, any more than He can be a mere spectator to its life. He gives life to all that have it. And when this life comes to an end, its cessation could not take place without the withdrawal of that which made the life possible. God's withdrawal of it is death. Jesus Himself said: "Not a sparrow falls to the ground without your Father." He did not say, without your Father knowing about it. This would be true, but it would be far less than the truth which Jesus uttered.

If even a sparrow could not die without the Father, without His withdrawal, without His taking part in the process of death, how much more could not the body of the Son of God die without the Father taking part in the process? When Christ's heart broke, God's ordained way of sustaining the life of the body was gone. Then He must withdraw. *He cannot give and sustain life through a broken heart, and be the God of Nature.*

It was when Christ's heart broke and death struck Him, that He uttered this piercing cry. It was when He felt the awful agony of the pang of heartbreak. Then He felt His body dying. *He was dying,* and He knew it, and called out to Him who as God must share in His death, must take the part of withdrawal in it. There is of course the difference that in the sparrow's death from natural causes, God's withdrawal is not untimely and forced, as it was in the violent and unnatural death of the Great, Conscious Victim of iniquity. In the latter case the mystery lies in why the Father coöperated with the evil sin was inflicting. It is easy to see why God coöperates with the processes of Nature, which are but His laws over again. But in sin's lawlessness! Why does He coöperate with it?

During His lifetime on earth Jesus frequently saw the hand of God where others saw naught of it. And some of the events they claimed to be the acts of God, Jesus denied that they were such. His perfect union with the Father and the Holy Spirit (the Mainspring of all sensitiveness in created things) enabled Him to discern clearly the divine movement in the death of a sparrow, and in "the everywhere" of God's working.

At times we become more or less conscious of God's presence, and are able to see that His hand is intervening here or there; but the Son of God was constantly conscious of the Father's presence, and to a degree impossible to us. All His days He saw the Father's hand at work. Had His sensitiveness to God been as dull as that of most men, He would have died without discerning the divine withdrawal and without understanding the part that God was taking or compelled to take in His death. There are the unexplainable compulsions of God. So we face the old thought that it was the very sinlessness of Christ which added to the sensitiveness of His soul, to the keenness of His sufferings, the agony and certainty of His Death. Christ's sensitiveness to the presence and meaning of sin had worn Him out, physically exhausted Him.

God is the sustaining force underneath and within all life. He upholds and makes possible the continuance of all created life. Not a life, however microscopic or however great, continues to exist except by the sustaining hand of God. The Incarnation would not have been real, if the physical life of the Son was not made possible by the upholdings of the divine presence. The natural is a world far more dependent upon God than we are wont to realize. To the Old Testament saints there were no secondary causes in Nature. God did everything immediately. Scientifically we have made a little gain at this point, and lost religiously, lost most seriously.

God is much more intertwined with and immanent in Nature than we yet realize. He dwells in all, save sin. There is so very much of God in even the most ordinary of human relations, we smite Him terribly when by sin we cause His withdrawal from them. Little did Christ's enemies know how they crucified the Father in crucifying the Son. Not a speck of knowledge did they seem to have of the pain they brought to the Father by causing His withdrawal in the physical death that followed the Crucifixion.

Without the divine withdrawal Jesus could have lived on indefinitely, and suffered even unto this day on the Cross. There was a manifest mercy in the withdrawal which ended His sufferings. But the passing was pain, excruciating pain, because the Son felt the awful wrench when the sustaining presence of God withdrew. Immanuel's own Deity supported that. We say "excruciating." *The Cross of Christ gave us that word.* (Ex—out of, and cruce—the cross.)

VII. THE DEATH OF DEATHS

Jesus did not ask God whether He had forsaken Him. What He did not know was why God seemed to fail Him, why God helped in the very process by which sin was putting Him to death. Knowing God to be unalterably opposed to evil, He could not but wonder why God let sin use Him to accomplish its work of death.

Sin has never forged a tool of its own. For its accursed work it always snatches one out of the hand of God. But why does God let it? When David like ten thousand other sinners commits adultery, why must God coöperate with the sin to bring forth a child of shame? Who is able to explain why God is compelled to be helper in the detestable work of iniquity. Why must He as God take part in the very unrighteousness He hates? Sin would unseat Him from His throne, yet He makes possible the completion of the crime and murder sinners initiate, even the murder of His own Son.

God is so interwoven in the fabric of this world, the wonder is that sin is permitted at all, and especially when it can never work without a certain kind of coöperation on His part. Why is it that sin can safely make use of His faithfulness, trade on His very righteousness to complete its work of faithlessness and unrighteousness? Why must sin in putting the divine Son to death use His own Father-God? Why in that death of His Son must God seem to be true to sin rather than to Him? Why did God let it even appear that He sided with such evil against the Incarnate Good? Why support and complete devil-inspired unrighteousness against the Righteous One? To answer all this one needs to have the mind of the Father Himself. He alone understands the infinite mystery of iniquity. Only Omniscience understands how the Being of God is involved in relation to the existence of sin, and how because God is God sin can take such terrible advantage of His very Deity. Any attempt at final answer to all this is the futility of delving into the essence of the unexplainable.

It is worthy of note that for the first time, as far as we know, Jesus calls the Father, God. He did not say, My Father! My Father! His death had evidently brought Him to the place where the Father was acting as God to Him as never before. After the resurrection He couples the two expressions: "I ascend unto my Father and your Father; and to my God and to your God." Perhaps His death put Him, as incarnate, constitutionally in a relation to God He had not borne before; and His place in the Godhead felt the disability and last agony His sacrifice for sin had imposed. From the beginning the Father had been imparting to and sustaining the Son's life. Now, for the first time, the Father withdraws His support to the physical life of the Incarnate Son. This brings death into the Son's experience.

While Jesus suffered the agony of seeing sin seemingly tie the very hands of the Father from delivering Him from death, He bore it to free our souls. He hung in mortal pain by His loving arms held fast to the tree, that we might be sure in the hour of death of dropping into "the everlasting arms." He died with this agonizing "why" upon His lips, that we might die with no question upon ours.

That startling cry, misunderstood then as now, made

the spectators shudder. One last upward look, one last word of prayer, and the death of deaths has come! Forward falls the noble brow, thorn-scarred and bloody! The noblest, purest soul that ever dwelt in human body is gone! The lifeless form hangs limp on the Tree of the World's Shame! The Author of Life is dead!

Never again could crucifixion have such a victim! Never had death such prey! Loving hands that had wrought in every possible good, their work is done! Poor blood-stained limbs that in love trod so many a weary mile while serving man, their last step has been taken! Great busy brain through which had pulsed the thoughts of the Infinite, its thinking is over! World-embracing heart beating in rhythm with the measureless love of God, the Roman spear will soon lunge needlessly into thy divine tenderness! Farewell, Sovereign Soul through which Deity surged and suffered in quest of a lost humanity! O world of my sin, the sin of the world has slain the Son of God! What a Cross! What a death! What a love! "My God! My God! Why didst Thou die for me?

"Cross of Jesus, Cross of sorrow,
  Where the blood of Christ was shed,
Perfect man on thee did suffer,
  Perfect God on thee has bled!

"Here the King of all the ages,
  Throned in light ere worlds could be,
Robed in mortal flesh is dying,
  Crucified by sin for me.

"O mysterious condescending!
  O abandonment sublime!
Very God Himself is bearing
  All the sufferings of time."

CHAPTER XVI

THE EXTENT OF FULFILMENT

THERE are three outstanding directions in which the extent of divine fulfilment in Redemption may be portrayed. These are—toward sin, toward sinners, and toward God. In the first of these we find the commensurative characteristic. In the second the qualitative feature of its extent. In the third its effective extent. These are in order—counter-extent, vicarious extent, and enabling extent. The first two will concern us in this chapter. The third will be considered under the effect of fulfilment.

The severest test of all interpretations of Christ's work of Redemption has always come at this point—its quantitative aspect. The more insufficient any theory of it, the more unsatisfactory will be the way of stating its extent. Of course, when men differ widely in setting forth the substance of Christ's work, they are sure to differ just as widely in explaining its compass, reach or measure.

I. COUNTER-EQUIVALENT EXTENT

When the substance of Christ's work is thought to be divine suffering, moral influence, penitence, penalty, satisfaction, and so on, those so interpreting it are under the necessity of depicting in some definite way the amount of suffering, moral influence, penitence, penalty, or satisfaction necessary to measure up to adequate extent.

When its essence is taken to be eternal divine suffering, we have over-extent. The question naturally arises, why should God in all the eternity of the past be suffering in anticipation of sin, even as He must be eternally suffering in the future in remembrance of it?

In the moral influence theory we have as certainly

under-extent. No amount of moral exhibition on the part of the one wronged, can be redemption of the wronger. Exhibition is not impartation, nor is it fulfilment of the nature of God in any satisfactory way.

In the penitential interpretation it is as difficult to state how much penitence Christ had on the Cross, as to explain in the penal theory how much punishment He suffered. One might go on to point out how the many theories get in trouble with the extent of that they take to be the substance of Redemption. And yet we cannot dispense with the idea of extent, for the sufficiency of Christ's work depends upon the adequacy of its extent; and it is therefore a fundamental feature of it.

Having named sacrificial divine fulfilment as the substance of Christ's work, we need a consistent interpretation of its extent? We may first say that the divine fulfilment in relation to sin is necessarily its counter-reach as a counter-equivalent. It must have equal counter-content. It must counterbalance sin in every way.

The fulfilment of the divine relation to sin provides that which is commensurate in counter-compass. It cannot be less in extent counter to that of iniquity. Stating this in another way, as far as sin has gone in preventing divine fulfilment, destroying the foundation thereof, so far must the divine sacrifice go in counter-action. Since sin has destroyed the foundation of man's fulfilment in God, the divine sacrifice must lay a new foundation for this fulfilment.

Christ's sacrifice of Himself is the counter-equivalent to sin in every way that sin has interfered with fulfilment in God. We may be specially interested in some particular way, and fashion our interpretation accordingly; but full divine fulfilment means that whatever sin has done, Christ can undo; and whatever sin has undone, He can recreate. Being the Creator-Redeemer, man can be created anew in Him. It may be asked, how can Christ do all this in the face of the irrevocable past? Alas! Even God cannot change the past; and "lost time is never found again."

While nothing is more certain than the unchangeableness of the past, this has nothing to do with the scope of divine redemption. God is not seeking to save history. He is seeking to save sinners. And while He cannot change or undo their past, He can make their future more than counterbalance it. He can bring a greater gain than all the loss by sin. Redemption puts man on a far higher plane than though he had never sinned.

II. The Law of Balance

The sufficient extent of divine fulfilment in relation to sin is according to the law of balance. In the spiritual as well as in the physical world the law of balance is at work. A ready illustration of this in the heavens is the perfect counterpoise of centripetal and centrifugal forces which determines the path of the planets. The perfect equation of these forces acting in opposite directions holds the planets steadily in their orbits.

Somewhat in the same way the unselfish sacrifice of Christ and the selfishness of sin it counteracts, determine the orbit or place of the saved soul, and prevents man from becoming "a wandering star reserved unto the blackness of darkness for ever."

All systems of equity and jurisprudence are built upon the law of balance. The *quid pro quo,* or equivalent is not in legal usage only: it is a principle which is used also in commercial and social systems everywhere.

When two things of a kind are equal in extent, they are said to balance each other. When they are of mutually opposing natures and equal in extent, they are said to counter-balance each other. They are then counter-equivalents. The amount or extent of the sacrifice for sin is determined according to this law of balance.

In Part Three of this book there will be discussed how the divine nature is opposed by sin. Here we may briefly say, the selfishness of the one and the unselfishness of the other, the unrighteousness of the one and the righteousness of the other, the lawlessness of the one and the law of the other, the destruction of the one and the fulfilment of the other, stand over against each other as perfect opposites. Here, then, are opposite natures, counter-existences. Christ's sacrifice is the countervail to sin, counter-commensurate in counter-extent.

The extent of a nature is measured in its fulfilment. There is no more comprehensive way of interpreting the extent of sin's nature than in its fulfilment. There is fulfilment of sin in the sinner, but no fulfilment of the sinner in sin. Human self-realization in sin can never reach self-fulfilment, for the sufficient reason that it travels in the opposite direction.

There is no fulfilment for man but in God. We see the extent to which sin has gone in destroying the basis of this fulfilment in God. To equal counter-extent has the Great Sacrifice gone in re-founding a new basis of man's fulfilment in the Redeemer. Here we see the depths of the depravity of iniquity and the heights of the riches of Redemption. "God hath set the one over against the other." "Neither height nor depth, nor any created thing shall be able to separate us from the love of God which is in Christ Jesus our Lord."

III. Extent Toward Sinners

Turning to the extent of Christ's work in relation to sinners, we may consider *the extent of the constitutional quality of this relation.* In this direction of His work, such quality reveals it depth; for mere extent without quality would be like length without depth.

Redemption's essential quality in relation to man is *vicariousness.* Its richness lies in this sacrifice being foundationally on behalf of men as sinners. It is fully for them. This is the fundamental altruism of its fulfilment. It tells how far God goes in our behalf, to what extent He is for us, and what fulfils His relation to us. In the vicariousnesss of Christ's sacrifice there is a double fulfilment. While He fulfilled the divine nature, at the same time Christ vicariously fulfilled human nature.

Pope's expression could be well applied to the Work of Christ: it "extends through all extent." Especially is this true as to the distance it goes on man's behalf. God has undertaken for man to the full measure of his need; and He has borne the full cost in meeting it.

The Son of God has gone to the extent of putting Himself where He could effectually destroy iniquity and restore man. As much as sin was against man, Christ's sacrifice was for him. It was and is the full counter-equivalent to sin's robbery, injury, and enmity. The redeeming love of God has reached full counter-extent to the hostility of iniquity. The Son took man's nature, and in it He fulfilled Himself in relation to sin as the enemy of both God and man.

The manward extent of Christ's work is indicated by this—God came all the way to man as a sinner, and in the Person of His Son gave Himself fully to man, underwrote the whole of his liabilities, underwent all the sacrifice and suffering necessary in undertaking all his responsibilities. Christ sacrificially fulfilled Himself in relation to man by fulfilling man's nature in relation to God and sin.

IV. SUBSTITUTION AND INSTITUTION

We never go very far or very deep in the study of Christ's Work without coming upon some form of its substitutionary aspect. This is because it is fundamentally vicarious in its constitutional quality. We have already noted the substitutionary method in discussing the instrumental means. There it was pointed out that substitution is *"the how"* not *"the what,"* the efficient method not the ultimate means. For this reason substitution may be taken as the method in any theory of Christ's work which makes room for His vicariousness. Few of them give room for more than a fraction of the extent of the vicariousness there is in His fulfilment.

THE EXTENT OF FULFILMENT 195

As the doctrine of the Second Coming of our Lord has been beclouded by various millenial thories, so the teaching of substitution has been handicapped by its association with penal and like theories. That the wrath of God inflicted penalty upon Christ as our Substitute, is a limitation of substitution to a doubtful interpretation, to one with far less room in it for substitution than there is in the sacrificial fulfilment of the divine nature.

The fulfilment interpretation of Redemption has so much in it, we do not need to make up for any lack in it by belaboring defective interpretations. It is always a waste of time to point out defect, unless in the spirit of appreciation for that manifestly deserving appreciation.

The largest room for substitution is in institution. The fulfilment interpretation might be called the institutional theory of Christ's Work. Not only as our substitute did He fulfil all that should be fulfilled, He also became the substitute means of our fulfilment in God in place of that lost by sin.

By the Cross was the institution of such substitution. Christ was not only our substitute in death: He is still our substitute. By His death grace was established in place of law as the basis of God's dealing with the sinner. The spirit of sacrifice and its foundational righteousness were re-integrated in human nature. In this the righteousness of His sacrifice was established. It was not only set up: it was set in operation—the institution of the redeemed life in God.

The extent of Christ's work in its manward direction is also helpfully expressed by the term *vicarious*. The two terms—substitutionary and vicarious—have practically the same meaning, but the former has come to have a penal ring to it. We need not deny there is the phase of penalty endured in Christ's work of Redemption, though it is not by any means the most important one. Vicarious, as a term, covers all the extent of His manward sacrifice. It sums up how far His sacrifice went in its relation to us. Toward sin it reached equal counter-extent. Toward us it reached full identification with us in perfect vicariousness. So the Vicar of our souls blots out our sins, is the ground of our standing before God, and the means of our fulfilment in God.

V. Fulfilment Toward Man

In estimating the manward extent of Christ's redemptive Work we may begin from either the divine or the human standpoint. From the latter we might consider how He brought to pass the divine fulfilment in human nature, that is the fulfilment of Christ's human nature in relation to sin and to God. Through sin we had lost the power to fulfil our nature in God, and at the same time he had lost the power or ability to fulfil it in relation to our sin. Yet this alone could meet the whole situation. A constitutional necessity was met at this point. This will be discussed at the close of this chapter.

To fulfil our nature in relation to our sin is possible only by fulfilling the will of God and, in fact, the whole plan of God concerning it. So, One sharing our nature, One just as truly human as we are, One even better—normally human, and who therefore had not lost this ability of fulfilling human nature in God in relation to sin, was needed whose vicarious Work and Person was great enough to meet the situation and solve the whole problem.

We have earlier noted the interacting or reciprocal nature of fulfilment. God could not fulfil Himself in relation to man without man fulfilling himself in relation to God. And God could not fulfil Himself in giving the life of His Son without allowing sin to fulfil itself in inflicting death. If the Son's life is to be given in death, sin get's the chance to inflict this death.

There is a third side to this interacting fulfilment—the fulfilment of human nature in God in relation to sin. Because man was in sin and sin in man, sin was using man to fulfil itself in relation to God. Because all human nature was under the curse of sin, God had to provide a human nature free from sin and the curse, that it might sacrificially and vicariously fulfil itself in God in relation to sin by bearing the curse of its inflicted death at the same time that God was fulfilling Himself in relation to both sin and man.

Sin is fulfilled in death, God in life, and man in sonship. God made man to fulfil himself in the sonship of obedience to the divine law. He made him in the image of the Son. This sonship man lost by his disobedience.

The Eternal Son was not only the Son of Obedience: He was also the Son of Sacrifice. In obedience to the Father's will, He fulfilled both. Then His humanity was as vicarious as His Deity, He became flesh for our sake. Vicariously He fulfilled His dual nature a Son of Man and Son of God. For the first time human nature was perfectly fulfilled in God, fully attained its consummation in God.

Here we find man's nature fulfiling itself in the sonship of perfect obedience. But this involved that His humanity in obedience to the will and plan of God be a sonship of sacrifice also. The insignia of the Sonship of Sacrificial Obedience was stamped on the Son's death. "Though He was a Son, yet learned he obedience by the things which he suffered." "He also himself in like manner partook of the same (human nature in flesh and blood); that through death he might destroy him that hath the power of death, that is the devil." Heb. 5:8 and 2:14.

Christ's perfect obedience and sacrifice as Son of God and Son of Man fulfilled the will and sacrificial nature of God in relation to sin. Existing in the form of flesh and in the nature of man He fulfilled in His vicarious sonship the will of God for human nature in relation to sin. So the manward extent of Redemption is seen in Christ's vicarious human sonship, vicarious obedience, and vicarious sacrificial fulfilment in relation to human sin.

VI. THE VICARIOUS EXTENT

The extent of Christ's vicarious work must be measured by the depth of its righteousness. What He said at the beginning of His ministry was characteristic of both its conclusion and the inauguration of His heavenly ministry. He "fulfilled all righteousness."

The righteousness of the sacrifice of the Son of Man when He suffered obediently and vicariously for man, as already said, is the highest and most potent righteousness human nature can fulfil, and the highest in man it is possible for us to conceive. It established a righteousness on a plane higher and more secure than that which sin had destroyed. A sonship more stable, with deeper security became possible to man by the redemptive Sonship of Christ. The Son of God, thinking it not degradation to exist for sacrificial ends, in the form of man, by His vicarious death put sin and death potentially to death for all who would believe in Him; and thus He secured the new order of sonship in Himself that is nothing short of eternal life in God.

The perfection of Christ's Sonship, the rich resources of His vicarious sacrifice, and the righteousness of His fulfilment in each of the three ways,—of God toward man, of man toward God, of God and man toward sin—mark the measure of His glorious work of Redemption. The vicarious quality of His Sonship and sacrifice relate them to the whole human race. "He died for all." No sinner need remain dead to divine sonship, for the right to this sonship has been purchased for him at a great price. Christ's redemption is sufficient in vicarious extent to answer for sin, to destroy it, and to put the sinner in possession of the blood-bought sonship in God. "Sinship" is now replaced by Sonship.

As Westcott says:

"The will of God answers to the fulfilment of man's true destiny; and this, as things actually are, in spite of the Fall. Christ as Son of Man made this will His own, and accomplished it."[1]

---

1. The Epistle to the Hebrews, p 311

All the necessities arising out of our guilt and responsibility in general are provided for in the divine and human fulfilment of Christ who vicariously undertook for us all that we could not do for ourselves and for God. In a real way He assumed in His sacrifice of Himself the obligations and possibilities as Son of man, the federal Head of the new race of humanity in Him. Because He went to the utmost extent in meeting these obligations and inaugurating these possibilities and privileges, He was able "to save unto the uttermost all that come unto God by him." This obligation Horace Bushnell expressed thus:

"Do we then assume that Christ in His vicarious sacrifice was under obligation to do and to suffer just what He did? Exactly this! Not that He was under obligation to another, but to Himself. He was God fulfilling the obligations of God; just those obligations in the eternal fulfilment of which God's perfections and beatitudes are eternally fashioned."[2]

VII. THE CONSTITUTIONAL NECESSITY MET

Constitutional necessity is the necessity for that which constitutes, or for that which is called into being. There is also operative necessity, for the enabling that which has been called into being to work, or to achieve the end for which it was made.

There was the constitutional necessity that a new relation of God to sinners be called into being, that He be not only the God sinned against, but also the God who has borne our sins in His incarnate Person. There is also the operative necessity that the new relation being established, the Holy Spirit could operate through it in reconstructing man to conform to this new relation and to give him life in the Son of God.

God is a constitutional necessity as well as an operative one. He is a necessity to man, to the very humanity of man. He is a necessity to man from his lowest to his highest possibility. He is a necessity to man's place in the universe, and to man's relation to his fellow-man.

---

2. The Vicarious Sacrifice, Vol I, p 58.

God is a necessity to man's life, to his spiritual health and growth. He is the bread of man's soul. He is necessary to man's self-realization in righteousness, and to the spirit of man necessary to the wellbeing of his entire nature. He is a necessity to man's unity within himself, to what man should arrive at in personality. God is always the absolute necessity to man's personal fulfilment.

The infinite insanity and ruin of sin lies in its inspiring man to act as though God were not a necessity at all. Sin attacks the constitutional and operative necessity of God. It brings man to act toward God as an intrusion, a superfluity, a hindrance. By iniquity man becomes constitutionally disqualified as a son of God, for only they who "are led by the Spirit of God, are the sons of God."

The extent of the necessity met by the Work of Christ may be realized in this—He met both the constitutional and the operative necessity created by sin. In Christ the new relation to God was established for sinners, the constitutional enemy of God and man destroyed, and man restored to the state and place where God may meet all his necessities. The Work of Christ constitutionally provided for God's fulfilment in relation to man as a sinner, and to become the means of man's fulfilment in the situation where sin had placed him.

Why was the death of Christ necessary? For many reasons both constitutional and operative. First, it personally related God to man's sin in the constitutional way of bearing the utmost possible personal effect of it in the physical death of His Son. Second, it constitutionally related the holiness of God's sacrificial nature to the unholiness of man's selfish personality. Third, it put the Son of God at the very center of sin's effect in man, and at the heart of the problem of reaching the place where once underneath sin He could lift and carry the whole load of it, "bear away the sin of the world." Fourth, His death constitutionally enabled Him by the sacrifice of Himself to become the complete cure for the constitutional disability of sin. Fifth, His death was the constitutional fulfilment of both human and divine natures, bringing both together in the solution of the problem of sin, where otherwise they must have been apart forever. Sixth, His death not only demonstrated that the unity of the Godhead and the unity of Christ's human and divine natures were strong enough to stand the strain, the utmost strain that human sin could put upon them, but it also organized the nature and power of this unity into direct personal contact with sin's disunity in man. Seventh, the death of Christ met the constitutional and operative necessity of permanently relating and instituting the sacrificial life of God outpouring itself upon the sinful souls and lives of men. It established the *modus operandi* of the Holy Spirit in redemptive relation to and in man for ever.

Summing up we may say, the extent of the necessity met by the death of Christ is evident in that it provided a way of escape, a ground of acceptance with God, and a means of fulfilment for sinners. The Son, "the same yesterday, today, and forever" in holy divine nature, "became flesh" and lived our life, "was made sin" and died our death "that we might become the righteousness of God in him." All that He attained or became by His sacrificial suffering and death expressed the change of relation to the unchangeable holiness of God. By permitting sin to put to death the Body of His Incarnation the foundation of the changed relation to God was laid, and a constitutional necessity was perfectly fulfilled, for it was filled to the full with the sacrifice of God in Christ. The meeting of this necessity is the heart of the Gospel. Some say the center of Christianity is the penal transaction of God's wrath visiting upon His Son the penalty of death for us. The necessity of fulfilling all that is in God in relation to all that is in sin, and the provision of new divine means of human fulfilment, could hardly be met by penalty of any sort. Rather, sacrificial love is that fulfilment. Its suffering of death was necessary, but not the penal interpretation of an angry God inflicting it.

CHAPTER XVII

THE GODWARD EFFECT

THE close relation between the effect and the extent of the Work of Christ has already been mentioned. Obviously, there are two directions of its effect which remain to be discussed more fully. These are the Godward and the manward. The latter will be the subject of Part Four. Here the Godward effect will be considered.

It has already been noted that by preventing man's fulfilment in God sin is an immeasurable injury. Since Christ's sacrifice counter-balances sin in every way, it must therefore be of equal extent to sin's Godward effect. In attempting to portray the Godward effect and extent of Christ's sacrificial fulfilment in relation to sin, we are compelled to deal with incommensurables.

I. THE TRINITY IN REDEMPTION

Necessity here compels us to point out that the two doctrines of the Work of Christ and of the Trinity are inseparably intertwined. Neither can be profitably discussed or presented anywhere without the other. Even though genetic theology is not called upon to set forth the doctrine of the Holy Trinity, yet some mention of its nature and necessity must be made. This, as already said, is due to the fact that the genetic doctrine of Christ's redemptive Work is inextricably intertwisted with the doctrine of the threefold personality of God.

It has long been noticed that as belief in the Supernatural rises or wanes, so does belief in these two doctrines. This is because both are supernatural in nature and revelation. Never in the history of Christianity have such combined forces of Naturalism been arrayed against them as today. When the Word of God teaching them is not believed, how shall we expect genetic theology to fare better? Our task is not to offer a system of apologetics defending the fundamental doctrines of Christianity, but to state the genetic relation of them.

The Scriptures themselves present no arguments for the existence of God. They begin by assuming or revealing it. All lines of thought begin with an assumption. Besides a dependent existence is not called upon to prove the existence of that upon which it depends. A baby could not be called on to prove its mother's existence. This proof is not necessary to the beginning of its existence. And no babe is half as much dependent upon its mother, as we are dependent upon the Father in heaven.

Moreover, the Bible presents no arguments in support of belief in the tri-personality of the Godhead. It simply reveals it in the course of the story of Redemption. The latter would not be interpretable without this revelation. Redemption by the fulfilment of the divine nature makes the doctrine of the Holy Trinity more than ever indispensable. God as one person cannot fulfil Himself in Himself, for this would be only the staleness and stagnation of self-repetition instead of self-fulfilment. And the Godhead unable to fulfil itself in itself is neither absolute nor transcendent.

The question may be asked, if God is three persons, why do we so frequently speak of Him as one? Because He is one, though not one person. The usage of Holy Writ warrants this mode of expression. While God is tri-personal, the absolute unity of the Godhead not only permits but requires us to speak of God as *He*. He is one God, not three. The unity of the Trinity is such that the Three act as one, for they are one in three inseparable otherselves with one other-consciousness, the mark of perfect personality.

There are no individuals in the Godhead, for individuality is the boundary line of the finite. It is the distinctive or delimiting characteristic of finite personality, while personality is at the same time inclusive. The individual is one of the race: the person is the race in one. But the Deity is not a race; nor is it the solitariness of one personal existence, making personality impossible. If there were individuals in the Godhead, there could be more than three—any number in fact, as in humanity. Constitutional tri-personality is not the same as common personality in indefinite numbers.

No interpretation of the Trinity makes divine self-fulfilment more impossible than the Modalistic, so much revived today. Modes cannot fulfil themselves in one another. It is impossible for one mode of personal manifestation to exercise the full functions of personality. And three modes of manifestation of one person are infinitely removed from three fulfilments of three persons.

A term when turned inside out and emptied of its contents, ceases to be of any use whatever. When the Father-Mode is said to love the Son-Mode, father and son cease to have meaning. In this view, God being but one Person, the Father is His own Son; and the Son is His own Father. Such interpretation not only empties the terms of their essential meaning, it makes them supremely ridiculous. If God were but one Person, the divine self-fulfilment in Redemption would be forever impossible. What God could not do for Himself, He could not be to others.

II. The Effect on the Holy Spirit

As the Godward effect of sin and Redemption counter-balance each other, what is the effect and extent of the Work of Christ in its Godward direction? Any presentation which leaves this out, misses the very virtue and power that it has to redeem us, for its merit to God gives its meaning to man.

We have been considering in preceding chapters the effect upon the Son in His Godward self-realization. The Father and the Holy Spirit, because in perfect unity with Him, must have shared in this effect as far as their nature and office made possible. Their eternal nature of sacrifice had reaction to the sacrificial crucifixion of the Son.

The Word of God does not undertake to reveal the effect the Cross had upon the transcendent Persons of the Father and the Holy Spirit. There are many reasons why the nature and extent of this effect upon them is not portrayed, while the effect upon the Son is set forth. He is in Person adapted to be Sacrifice, Revelation, and Redemption. In the Incarnation His self-sacrifice is inaugurated. In His life and Person He is the Revealer. And in His sacrificial death He is the Redeemer. It was He who was born, lived a human life, and died a sin-bearing death. But He could not pass through all this without effect upon the Father and the Holy Spirit. Otherwise the unity of the triune Godhead would be without meaning.

We are bound to infer this from what the Scriptures reveal of that which is known as "the passability of God." This means that He is capable of feeling, suffering, sacrifice; for such exercises without effect upon the divine Persons rather depersonalizes them, and these passabilities would be without half their meaning, if they have objective but no subjective effect.

The passability of the Holy Spirit means the possibility of effect upon Him. This would be in keeping with the nature of His Person and the closeness of His union with the Son—and with the Father too in His sympathetic union with the Son. The Spirit of God is infinite personalization of sensitiveness. He could not but share in the experience of the suffering Son. That this suffering and death had great effect upon the latter is clear. It follows that the Holy Spirit must have felt some parallel effect to the sacrificial suffering of the Son.

The work of the Spirit of God is not to bear witness to His own suffering, but to Christ's. We learn from Holy Writ that this Great Mysterious Person of the Trinity can be affected or grieved in a way peculiar to Him. Because of His nature, His place or office is to enlighten the soul from within, and a sin against the Holy Spirit has a constitutional effect upon Him which it has not upon the Father and the Son.

May it not be that similarly the death of Christ wrought an effect peculiar to the Holy Spirit? Was not the reaction upon the nature of the Holy Spirit as different as His Person, place and office are different from that of the Father and the Son.

We know very little about the inner processes of the Trinity. Their always mutual undertakings have always mutual effect. He who eternally proceeds forth from the Father and the Son, and is therefore known as the Proceeding Person of the Trinity, could not fail to have His goings forth in sacrificial experience during the Great Sacrifice of Calvary. What beyond this His share was and what its effect and extent, we are left to speculate; and from this we may well shrink. We are safe in saying, however, that the effect upon the Holy Spirit through His coöperation in the sacrifice of Christ's death was that of His own sacrificial self-fulfilment.

III. The Effect on the Father

To the Father, the death of the Son could not be other than an agony unspeakable and immeasurable. That He sent the Son to die for sin, did not make this death any the less painful to Him, rather more. To Him death was death when the Son was "obedient unto death." His sympathy with the Son was as perfect as the Son's obedience; and the heights and depths of sympathy are plumbed as we suffer with the suffering ones.

"Oh, the deep, deep depths we fathom!
Oh, the lofty heights we scale!
When we share our loved ones' anguish
When their drafts our own lips pale."[1]

While appointing the Son to the humiliation and suffering of the Cross would bring pain to the Father, the greatest suffering would probably be from the inevitable part He must take in the death-process itself.

---
1. Ethel F. Parsons.

No doubt the use which sin made of the Father in putting to death "the Son of His Righteousness," brought the keenest agony to Him. Then He appeared to be but God rather than Father to "The Son of His Love."

The nails of the Cross could not pierce the Son without piercing the Father too. Even the spear-thrust into the broken heart of the Son's dead body wounded the Father's heart. Perhaps the agonizing hours during which the suffering Son was hanging on the tree must have seemed to the Father to stretch themselves out to all eternity. All the pain the Father had ever known must have seemed to gather itself together into one at that awful moment when He withdrew His sustaining presence from the physical life of the Crucified and Heart-broken One. Then He appeared God rather than Father to His well beloved Son, that He might be both God and Father to the sinning sons of men.

IV. THE ETERNAL ATONEMENT THEORY

It is a pity that the poignancy of the pain of the Father should be obscured by the doctrine of eternal divine suffering, based on the mistranslation, "The Lamb slain from the foundation of the world." In The Revelation the expression, "from the foundation of the world," appears twice. Each time (13:8 and 17:8) it refers to the Lamb's Book written from the foundation of the world. The Epistle to the Hebrews denies this eternal suffering, using the very same expression: "Else must he often have suffered since the foundation of the world." In fact the whole epistle seems to have anticipated this error: . . . "But now once at the end of the ages hath he been manifested to put away sin by the sacrifice of himself . . . But he, when he had offered one sacrifice for sins for ever, sat down on the right hand of God." Heb. 9:26, 10:12.

That the Cross has been eternally in God's heart if taken to mean that God is eternally sacrificial, is true; but taken to mean that God eternally suffers in anticipation and remembrance of sin, diffuses and evaporates the meaning and significance of Calvary.

Anticipation is not realization. The anticipation of death is not death. This teaching reducing the sacrifice and sufferings of the Cross to a mere sample of "eternal atonement," takes the heart out of the Gospel. Normal Christianity can never regard the tragedy of Calvary as but a show-window sample of eternal divine suffering. Some may reply that Scripture teaches that it was the Son who suffered but once while the Father suffered eternally. This would mean that at the deepest point the Son did not manifest the Father. And as to the Scripture teaching that the Father suffered eternally, it will be time enough to discuss it when such a Scripture is found.

V. THE FATHER'S FULFILMENT

What must Father Abraham have felt on Mount Moriah at that moment when he raised the sacrificial knife to end the life of his son, his long promised son. Imagine his feelings when the confiding eyes of his well beloved child, looking up into his inquiringly, changed at that moment of discernment to the stare of dread terror! But no human analogy can take more than a tiny step up the steep heights of the suffering of the divine heart when Calvary's death took place.

The Father in heaven went all the way through the sacrifice of His only begotten Son. No angel could stay His hand. An awful necessity, deep as the abyss of eternal death, gripped Him. A necessity as unbending as the Holiness of His immeasurable righteousness was before Him. Never was His heart more yearning in love and pity. But even the infinitely plenteous pity of the Father's loving heart could not arrest the painful process of This Incomparable Sacrifice.

To the suffering Saviour how terribly tense the last moments which broke His heart! To the Father witnessing it all how slow must have seemed those awful moments! The Eternal Father was suffering an eternity of painful sympathy with the Eternal Son. If in the personal powers of God there is that which corresponds to human weeping, it must have been with more than moist eyes that the answering love of the Father looked down into the dying eyes of His Son, gazing upward in the enveloping darkness of death, and searching for the meaning of the divine withdrawal.

Upon those who had sought Christ's death, there had fallen the curse of obdurateness. Their callous hearts were insensible to the enormity of the crime of the crucifixion. Truly, they knew not what they did. But the Father knew what He did. No insensibility was in Him. He, too, was sensitiveness infinite. How deep were the processes of the all-enveloping mind of God! And mind runs deepest when it is actuated and accompanied by the deepest feelings.

Had the whole universe dissolved suddenly with one awful, ear-splitting explosion, it could not have sounded worse than the infinitely piteous cry, "My God! My God! Why hast thou forsaken me?" And this from the loving lips that had ever before called Him Father! How terrible the wrench to the heart of the Father when the Great Heart of Immanuel, that had never failed to love Him to the uttermost, broke on Calvary. If no one but the Father knows in the ultimate who the Son is, surely only the Father knows the ultimate extent of the effect that the death on Calvary had on Himself. And yet, from its very nature He would be the very last to set about calculating it.

The sacrificial nature of God the Father fulfilled itself in all its relations—to sin, to man, to the Son and the Holy Spirit. There were both the sacrifice of His suffering and the suffering of His sacrifice. He gave the greatest gift ever given, the one that cost most to the Giver, as well as the one greatest in itself. There was His sublime suffering,—that is, it was without measure. There was His supreme sacrifice—that is, it was without end, without limit.

VI. THE EFFECT ON THE SON

Turning to the effect on God the Son, we touch the whole movement of the divine sacrifice. The Godward effect here was self-sacrifice. There was self-sacrifice in the Incarnation. The measure of the sacrifice at this point is beyond our capacity to imagine. We are able to imagine a situation only by recombining what we have already seen or known. For this reason we are utterly unable to imagine how the eternal pre-existent Son could limit Himself in the microcosmic existence of an embryo in the womb of a virgin. What a sacrifice to function in its infinitesimal intelligence, for intelligence is constituent in all life, and the higher the order of life, the higher the order and range of its intelligence. What a sacrifice to wait upon the slowly widening area of embryonic and prenatal life! And yet in relation to infinity, it is but one degree of limitation compared with another even in incarnate manhood. No wonder the angels desired to look into this infinite wonder. They see the world from which our Lord came, and have greater capacity to wonder because of greater knowledge and deeper reverence.

Christ's death was still another kind of self-sacrifice. It was more than the sacrifice of His power to resist the assault of sin upon His Person. It was a sacrificial birth into another world—the world of ministry, not now of a beating, but of a broken heart. He, too, fulfilled every relation, the relation to man and to God and to sin.

If Christ had laid on Him in a mechanical or idealistic way the load of our sins, the effect would have been in kind. Literally He took our sin upon Him when He laid aside the power to resist its crucifixion and death. Then He received from it both upon and into His person an everlasting effect. For the first time sin had intruded its effect upon the person of a divine Being and entered into the very relations of the Trinity. It put the Son under disability to understand the Father for the first time in His eternal existence. How much further His place as Deity was laid aside and sacrificed in this second Kenosis, we do not know.

How did the Son fulfil His new place as sin-bearer? What was the extent of this fulfilment? He bore sin in actual effect. He felt its power, suffered not only physical disability, but mental and spiritual. The interference with the Godward processes of soul during such suffering must have been real. And yet this was not in any sense failure. Rather it was the reverse. There on the Cross as He bore sin, He realized its meaning as only the Son of God could. *He fulfilled Himself as Son of Man, Son of Sacrifice, and this fulfilment was in heartbreak.*

What a chain of effects wound around the Cross. The effect of sin is hate; and of hate, murder. The heartlessness of sin broke His heart. The effect of this on God was marked by His withdrawal. God was not wanted in His own world. Sin had long been trying to drive out God from this world. It had been seeking to have men live without heart. But as infallibly as God must leave a loveless soul, so must He leave a heart-broken body. So effect follows effect clear up to the throne of God, and rebounds to bury itself in the depths of the heartbreak of God in Christ.

Not long ago I listened to a Canadian friend relate his sorrowful search for the grave of his nineteen-year-old son "somewhere in France." The brave lad had won his commission as lieutenant in the English army. He had been for quite a time at the front. He had been granted furlough to go to his home then in England. But he voluntarily went with his comrades for one night more in the struggle. Before daybreak he was shot through the forehead. Though I had known this brave soldier when but a babe in a neighboring parsonage in Canada, though I had two boys in the same struggle, I found myself unable to enter into the experience of my brother minister of the Gospel. I had never been through the agony of searching from place to place and grave to grave for the resting-place of my boy "gone West." My boys returned alive. My heart had followed them for nearly two years as far as they had gone in a division that had thirty-five thousand casualties. This friend's son had gone to the Great Beyond. Only a broken heart could follow him there.

So the faithful father-heart fulfilled itself in the only way possible—in heartbreak.

If we could feel the meaning of sin as Jesus did on the Cross, our hearts would break too. Heart-break comes in one way only—by a grave dug in the heart. Only those who suffer it, know the pang of its effect. At Calvary sin dug a grave in the very heart of God. Bless God! it is deep enough to bury the accursed grave-digger in it.

Christ's heartbreak did more than interpret the heart of God. He was God incarnate bearing our sin. He was the heart of God fulfilling its own sacrificial nature in bearing sin to the point of heartbreak. The heartlessness of sin was more than the heart of God incarnate could stand. "Christ crucified" carries the Cross today in His broken heart.

VII. THE OPEN WOUNDS OF CHRIST

The effect upon the Eternal Son went far enough to dedicate, designate, and constitute Him as the "One Mediator" and "Only Judge." It put Him forever between God and human sin. Never more can sin be dealt with as though the Redeemer had not died for it. All the divine relations to man and sin now center in Him.

This effect cannot be obliterated. The effect of death was undone in the case of Lazarus and the two others whom Jesus raised. Not so was it with Christ Himself. He came back in a changed body, but with all the marks of the crucifixion upon it. His physical nature entered into a new realm, living by the spirit and in spite of the broken heart. "I am he that liveth and was dead; and behold I am alive for evermore." "And I beheld, and, lo, in the midst of the throne stood a lamb as it had been slain."

The change in His body is indicative of the change in the rest of His Person. Rising from the grave with new powers, His very wounds became avenues of His new power of self-impartation. It is no wild mysticism to say that out of the wounds of His risen Person His sacrificial life-blood still flows. Once the blood of His body flowed in crucifixion: ever since the blood of His sacrificial soul has flowed in Redemption.

The wounds of Christ's Risen Person may be likened to five outlets which pour out from the infinite reservoir filled from the springs of divine life in Him—the life fulfilled in relation to man and sin. If the fulfilment of the divine nature changed His body to a state of such power, service, and glory, what was not done for the rest of His Person? What, think you, was the Father's fulfilment in relation to the heart-broken Deity of the Son? But there was one thing He could not do for Him, because it was part of the very enablement of the fulfilment of Redemption. *His wounds were left unclosed and unhealed, for they are incurable till the world's Redemption is accomplished by means of the sacrificial life of God pouring out through them.*

"The timeless suffering of God" is a faulty expression The eternal is not timeless, any more than the omnipotent is powerless The infinity of anything is not its negation Timeless suffering means that it never occurs Any experience must have order and succession to be such This is but time over again Timeless experience or suffering is a contradiction in terms

The Bible could not be at the same time a book of Revelation and a book of argument and proof That which comes by reason needs no other revelation That which is by Revelation comes from a world where in the nature of the case all the facts are not available, and without all these facts reason can offer no safe conclusions All the facts are not available about the Trinity "No one knoweth who the Son is but the Father, etc " Hence the Trinity must be a doctrine of Revelation

Personality is never dual or triple In itself a personality cannot possibly be more than one In a person there may be dual natures, as material and spiritual, or there may be dual consciousness, as when in reading one's mind may be quite elsewhere Some might prefer to call this the mechanical and the conscious minds Personality is not in itself more than one, even when possessed by a spirit, whether good or bad (To deny the possibility of the one is to deny the possibility of the other) Such inhabiting or controlling spirit belongs to another or is another personality No man ever had more than one soul or can be more than one personal entity Personality is the sole or soul-entity Ontologically, multiple personality is impossible

The unity of the passability of God makes it impossible for the Father to have opposite passion to that of the Son The Penalist has never been able to explain how the Father could be angry with the perfectly obedient Son, perfect in every other way too, when bearing the suffering of sin on the Cross There is Scripture for "The wrath of the Lamb," but none for the wrath of God with or upon the Lamb

The Ritschlian conception of Christ having for us the value of God is more or less a philosophic vacuity "Value judgment" is of no use to interpret the incommensurable in other things as well as in value What is the value of a child? a mother? No value can be set upon them because utterly beyond measure So the Scriptures present it "What shall a man give in exchange for his soul?" his life? himself? There can be no exchange value for the incommensurable in value One might as well set out to measure the heavens with a yardstick Even though he could so measure it, there would be considerable in the heavens not so expressed

CHAPTER XVIII

THE ENABLEMENT OF FULFILMENT

ONE important effect of the divine fulfilment we are studying, is its enablement. This is more than empowerment. The railway engine in the ditch may have as much power as when it was on the track, but its ability is gone. It needs enablement.

Nothing can be added to the divine power. Nothing need be added to it. But the divine ability is another matter. Is God in the ditch then? Is it not the sinner who is in the ditch? Yes, sin put the sinner in the ditch, and he lost thereby both power and enablement. To save the sinner God needs the enablement which will relate not only His power but all else in Him that man needs. The only way He can enable Himself to enable the sinner, is by going into the ditch where the sinner is. So what had disabled the sinner, enabled God. Going into the ditch of man's sin enabled God to get under man's disability. This put God in a position to remove the disability.

Sin in man is a disability to God. Any power in man moving in the opposite direction to divine fulfilment is a disability to God. This relative disability is what the Work of Christ removes. It removes the disability of man in being unable to fulfil himself in God, and the correlate inability of God to fulfil Himself in man. The sacrificial nature of God at Calvary blotted out God's and man's disability because of sin. Because of this God has become to us preëminently the God of Redemption.

I. THE ENABLEMENT OF LOVE AND SACRIFICE

God's sacrificial nature enabled Him to do exceeding abundantly, above all we could have asked or thought. His sacrificial spirit turned all His power into redemptive ability. It took man out of the ditch of sin, and put him back on the track of fulfilment.

Had not God been preëminently sacrificial in nature, He could have fulfilled Himself in some other way— in judgment and penalty, for example. But Christ came not to judge the world but to redeem it. When at last He must judge those refusing His sacrifice, it will be the judgment of sacrifice. The throne of the Lamb will then be compelled to condemn those who have trampled underfoot the sacrificial blood of the Lamb.

Christ's sacrifice constituted Him Judge over all for whom He had made His sacrifice. Because His sacrifice is final, His judgment is final. Redemption is the enablement of God to save from judgment all who accept it; and it enables the judgment of God to remove every appearance of being unnecessary, harsh, or vengeful toward those who refuse it.

Redemption also enables God to put judgment on its basis—that of men's attitude to the sacrifice He made for them. In consequence men are now lost, not so much because of sin, as for refusal to respond to the Redemption from it. Scripture tells us that sin is charged up to men only where the law of God is known; but sin is so serious, men perish by it without knowing God's law against it. (Rom. 2: 12, 4: 15, 5: 13.)

To refuse Redemption is not possible to those who have never heard of it. What will be the verdict of sacrifice upon those who never heard of it? Must they perish forever without opportunity to know of it? This was due them—to hear of it. In one way they are in a more defensible position than the Christians who could have told them, and did not.

Sacrifice is the enablement of love to meet a need. God's nature being essentially sacrificial in all its relations, how about His relation to sin? His opposition to it is the opposition of sacrificial nature. Since sin is in genius opposed to sacrifice, what does divine sacrifice do about it? Nothing in God is more affected by sin than His loving spirit and sacrificial nature.

Since nothing in Him is more opposed by sin, nothing in Him more opposes it, and can so effectively express His attitude to it and will concerning it. So love's sacrifice does this about it: it does everything that God can do.

II. Love's Sacrificial Fulfilment

From nothing else in God can spring forth a fulfilment of such nature and extent as that which came forth from His sacrificial nature. The enablement of this fulfilment arises from the utterly unwithholding nature of sacrificial love. Either this means nothing at all; or it means that nothing needed from God and His resources is held back. Because God is love and His nature sacrificial, no part of the price of Redemption was kept back. This Redemption by the fulfilment of divine love and sacrifice is thereby the pledge of its absolute sufficiency.

Sacrificial love by its fulfilment is the enablement of the whole divine nature to dedicate the infinity of its sufficiency to meet man's need. It enabled God in Christ to put all of Himself into it. No wonder then that it was sufficient to bridge the chasm caused by sin.

In an earlier chapter it has been noted that love has the ability to interpret itself in a way which can be understood. In such a world as this, divine Redemption would never have been understood at all, if sacrifice had not been its source. The larger the sacrifice, the plainer its meaning. The greater its sacrifice, the more love's genuineness is established. Utterly blind selfishness may not comprehend it; but its integrity is exhibited in such a way as to make successful denial of it impossible.

The enablement of possession by sacrifice has also been noted. This enablement meets the requirement which lies in the reciprocal nature of all real possession. A man cannot have wealth without his wealth having him. Literally, he must give himself to it to have it.

The sacrifice of His Son is the price which God paid

to repossess us, to redeem us from being sacrificed to sin. From its slavery the love of Christ redeemed us, that we might become the slaves of the love of God. The greatest slave of love this world ever saw was Jesus Christ.

"Know ye not that to whom ye give yourselves as slaves unto obedience, his slaves ye are whom ye obey." Love to Him makes it a delight to belong to God. Sacrificial love enables obedience to Him to be a joy. It set before the Saviour the joy that enabled Him to endure the Cross, despise the shame, and when His sacrifice was complete to sit down with God in the sacrificial equality of heaven. Sacrificial capacity measures the extent of heaven possible. It enables God to enter into fellowship with those for whom His sacrifice was made. Sacrifice lays not only the foundation of heaven: it builds the whole superstructure thereof. Love and sacrifice is the enablement of heaven to be heaven, of God to be God and of man to be man.

III. The Enablement of Attitude

Nothing can ever change God's attitude to sin. Any change would mean that God is less God or sin less sin. The change of attitude possible is to the sinner; and this can ultimately come to pass only as the sinner is separated from his sin, or provision is made to secure such.

The attitude of the sacrificial love of God toward the sinner is most manifest in its fulfilment. Its character is best expressed in the New Testament word *grace*. Many things affect men's attitude to one another; but one thing affects man's attitude to God. Grace means that God refuses to let anything but His sacrificial love express His attitude to the sinful sons of men. His love controls in determining the divine attitude toward sinners.

Attitude is more than the angle of approach: it is the array of powers, the cast of countenance, the position assumed, the posture of intention or relation. It tells how God meets the sinner, how He looks upon him in his lost condition, how His heart reacts to man's fallen state.

Grace indicates God's supreme feeling. It is deeper than the expression on His features: it shows the sweet lines in His face which come there only by suffering for us. Grace is the smile on the face of the Father meeting His prodigal son "while yet a great way off." Its attitude is the welcome home to him who exchanged His presence for that of swine. No recrimination, no reproof, no accusation, no complaint. Grace is the kiss of welcome, the ring of restoration, the shoes of salvation, the robe of rectification, the feast of fellowship, and the music of rejoicing when God's good heart is made glad by the poor sinner's return home.

The attitude of grace is more than in look or feeling, even as sacrifice is more than sympathy. Grace is that which was back of the melting look which our Lord gave to perjured Peter after his denial with an oath. Grace is that spirit of sacrificial love which forsook not the disciples when they all forsook Him and fled. It is the godliest quality in God, that in Him which yearned to save the enemies of His Son even when they reviled, scourged, mocked, crucified Him and broke His heart. It is that wealth of richness of compassion God has toward the whole human race. It was in sacrificial attitude that Christ ate with sinners that He might bring to them the Bread of Life. He "received sinners."

"Sinners Jesus will receive;
Sound this word of grace to all."

His sacrificial soul suffered to see them lost; and then it suffered on the Cross for the lost that the way might be opened up in Him to redeem the whole world. Grace is the great word to explain Calvary.

"That was compassion like a God,
That when the Saviour knew
The price of pardon was His blood,
His pity ne'er withdrew."

Grace marks the extent of God's solicitude on beholding the peril of those who persecute themselves in persecuting Him. It enables Him to approach them with the gift of life to save them from the penalty of death. The attitude of Grace is made efficient and permanent by its fulfilment in the death of the Cross. Then, too, its source is a permanent one. Moreover it leads to something permanent—even to everlasting life.

Grace is the greatest attitude possible. It costs the very most in every way. All the highest and best of God has gone into His love's sacrifice. Grace is that in God He has most to give, though it is His very best. It enables God to turn loss into gain, to give life by a death, and to stand before the whole world with outstretched hands pierced for us and representing the permanent attitude of the Cross of Christ.

> "Measure thy life by loss instead of gain,
> Not by the wine drunk, but by the wine poured forth;
> For love's strength standeth in love's sacrifice;
> And whoso suffereth most, hath most to give."

IV. THE ENABLEMENT OF RIGHTEOUSNESS

There is a suffering sin brings both to God and to man which has no saving power in it. It is a wrong not a righteousness. No amount of such suffering could ever redeem us. But the voluntary suffering of Christ's sacrifice is in righteousness and in the interests of righteousness. The voluntary element in Christ's Work on our behalf has an intrinsic righteousness in it.

This voluntary, vicarious sacrifice enables the infinite holiness in God's nature to flow out in it and by it. That sacrificial righteousness is the supreme order of holiness, has already been set forth. As John Bunyan remarks, righteousness is not an attribute of God, because it is an abstraction. As we cannot have whiteness without something that is white, so we find righteousness in God only by naming something in Him that is righteous. *Righteousness is therefore more properly named as an attribute of all God's attributes.*

From this we may infer that the only way that God

could enable His righteousness, was to enable something in Him which is righteous. He cannot enable an abstraction. Because sacrifice is that supreme order of righteousness on behalf of others, God can most of all enable His righteousness by enabling that in Himself which is most righteous.

Because sacrifice is the spirit of His whole nature, its righteousness is the righteousness of His whole nature. It is a righteousness which takes no short cuts. It pays the full price. It meets the constitutional requirement of a generic righteousness that is genetic in redemption from sin and generic in that to which man is redeemed.

What in God is so exalted in His nature as sacrifice? Where is His righteousness so vast in extent, so effective? It is as constructive as sin is destructive, as justifying as sin is damning, as purifying as sin is contaminating, as satisfying as sin is unsatisfying, as life-giving as sin is death-imparting, as successful in fulfilment as sin is in defeating it. But it is more than a match for sin. Where sin and its unrighteousness abounded, sacrifice and its righteousness did much more abound.

Sacrifice in grace is a higher righteousness than the legalistic. Why is it that when it is recognized that Christ redeems men *to* a higher righteousness than that of the law, it is not also recognized that this is done *by* a higher righteousness than that of the law? The law which Christ fulfilled in His great Work was a higher one than the law of the Old Testament, the law of works, of moral or ceremonial requirement, of the natural standard of the sonship of obedience. The law He fulfilled had to go far beyond this. The law of commandments had no provision for reconstruction and the laying of a new foundation of righteousness. The law of the divine sacrifice in Christ had this possibility. It had this righteousness: it had the power to lay the foundation of a deeper righteousness.

As love is the fulfilling of the whole law, so sacrifice as it is in the death of Christ is the fulfilling of the

Higher Law. This is the law of reconstruction, of re-establishment, of redemption. As love cannot be fully portrayed in terms of right and wrong, so much the more cannot love's greatest sacrifice. It contains a righteousness which passes beyond legalistic standards of righteousness. The standard of righteousness inherent in the nature of divine sacrifice is the highest we can conceive of. It lies back of and is really the genetic foundation of all other righteousness. In the divine sacrifice of Christ God enabled this genetic righteousness to do its perfect work.

This righteousness of divine sacrifice is so great that faith in it is itself a righteousness. We are made righteousness in a super-legalistic way by the super-faith in His super-righteousness.

"Being justified freely by his grace through the redemption that is in Christ Jesus; whom God set forth as a propitiation through faith in his blood, to declare his righteousness for the remission of sins......to declare at this time his righteousness: that he might be just, and the justifier of him that believeth in Jesus...... It is God that justifieth. Who is he that condemneth: it is Christ that died, yea rather that is risen again."

During the late war the question was often asked whether the righteousness of a soldier's self-sacrifice is sufficient to save him. It may be questioned whether it is perfect self-sacrifice when a man is doing his best to kill others, and gets what he is giving. To say the least, it is very different from the self-sacrifice of Christ.

Waiving the matter of the self-sacrifice in a soldier's death in battle, there is no need that one should compare it to, or think of it as replacing, the divine self-sacrifice. Real sacrifice is always acceptable with God; but it is not possible for sinful man to offer any sacrifice to God with the power in it that God's sacrifice has for us. It would be safer to take the ground that the soldier's sacrifice in death for the sake of others is an unconscious acceptance of the divine. "When saw we thee hungry and feed thee, etc.?" If such service was unconsciously unto Him, why cannot a supreme sacrifice be unconsciously unto Him? Whether it is enough unto Him to be a saving acceptance of His Great sacrifice as the foundation of our righteousness and acceptance with God, is for Him to decide. War and its slaughter is the nightmare of Hell. God save us from any more of Hell's delirium! May no man risk his acceptance of Christ's righteousness to the sacrifice war calls for.

"Oh, poor, brave, smiling face made naught,
  Turned back to dust from whence you came;
You have forgot the men you fought,
  The wounds that burnt you like a flame;
With stiff hand crumbling a clod
  And blind eyes staring at the sky,
The awful evidence of God
  Against the men who made you die."

CHAPTER XIX

SACRIFICIAL ENABLEMENT

AS TO sin, nothing can ever change the judgment of divine discernment from unqualified condemnation. Otherwise God's discernment would be defective. Nothing can change God's feeling toward sin from perfect hate. Otherwise His moral indignation would cease to work in unison with His moral intelligence. Nothing can ever change the attitude of God's holiness from infinite revulsion against sin. Otherwise His holiness would cease to be of His entire nature, or no longer absolute.

On the other hand God can provide that equal in extent to His revulsion toward sin, and His hatred and condemnation of sin. This provision can have as much righteousness in it as there is unrighteousness in iniquity, as much love in it as there is hate of iniquity, as much satisfaction in it as there is revulsion toward iniquity. The divine satisfaction in the sacrifice for sin equals the extent of the divine dissatisfaction caused by sin.

Scripture terms this satisfaction "propitiation." It means that God is as pleased with Christ's sacrifice of Himself as He is indignant with sin. Propitiation is the great term of Scripture for the satisfaction of God in what Christ has become by His death. It expresses the extent to which the divine desires in this respect have been met. In view of the righteous anger of God with sin and His dissatisfaction aroused by it, propitiation is the enablement of counter-equivalent satisfaction. This satisfaction is not only in sin's extermination but also in man's restoration.

I. The Enablement of Satisfaction

When there is an infinite and unchangeable dissatisfaction, the only solution is an infinite and unchangeable satisfaction to counter-balance it. While the whole nature of God is a unity, each of its powers has its own desire and satisfaction. The satisfaction of His mental nature is not the same as that of His moral nature. The desire of His love is not the same as the desire of His mind, but there is never any conflict between these desires and their satisfactions. All His powers and attributes are unified in being alike sacrificial. All His desires of mind, heart, will, and moral nature are made one in this—they are equally the desires of sacrificial personality.

In addition to this there is the reciprocal satisfaction which every part of the divine nature gives to every other part. This is the mutual satisfaction of the parts, powers, and attributes of God in each other. But it is His person which has satisfaction in the desires named. He has satisfaction in the thought of His mind about all the rest of His powers. And He has satisfaction in all the rest of His powers from His mind. In perfect personality there is constant mutuality of satisfactions from every part. God's sacrificial spirit and its nature pervading all His nature and powers secures unity and continuity in the satisfactions of God. It brings complete satisfaction from every part, because sacrifice is the highest conceivable activity of personality. Perfect sacrifice like perfect love is its own satisfaction. It is the highest possible satisfaction of personality as a whole.

The mutual satisfaction which the persons of the Trinity render to each other, has been previously mentioned. Being counterpart and inseparable "otherselves," each of the Persons of the Godhead ministers constant and complete satisfaction in every relation and work. Father, Son, and Holy Spirit live and fulfil themselves in this mutual satisfaction. In absolute sacrifice they exist for each other. Unreservedly and infinitely they belong to each other. Each Person has his own adaptation to this mutual contribution.

We have already remarked that the Son is God in relation, God in Creation, Revelation, and Redemption. There is therefore in Him the special adaptation to self-sacrifice in these works and purposes. It is possible therefore for Him to give sacrificial satisfaction in keeping with His personal adaptation. This satisfaction is in counter-content and counter-extent to the loss of satisfaction caused by sin and the dissatisfaction to the divine nature due to sin's existence. Such satisfaction in Him as the self-sacrifice on account of sin is called *propitiation*. More and deeper cannot be said than, "God hath set forth Him to be a propitiatory (sacrifice)," for "He is the propitiation for our sins." His self-sacrifice is the enablement of the divine satisfaction in Him as the satisfaction of propitiation. This is fulfilment of God's holiness by its satisfaction in the self-sacrifice of God the Son for human sin.

II. THE ENABLEMENT OF SELF-GIVING

The life of the Godhead is a transcendent process carried on by means of the reciprocal self-giving of the Persons of the Godhead. This process internal to the Deity is carried into the divine relations to Creation. While God made man to give Himself to him, and made man for man in return to give himself to God, this is possible only by the reciprocal self giving of the Persons of the Trinity being carried into the process of man's relation to God and God's to man. Without this divine reciprocity within the reciprocity in relation to man, the self-giving of God's life to man and of man's life to God would be impossible. In Creation there was a self-giving of the Son to the Father, of the Father to the Son, and of the Holy Spirit and to Him. In Redemption there was the self-giving of the Son to the Father in relation to man and sin, and the responsive self-giving of the Father in the same relation and also that of the Holy Spirit made possible the sacrifice of Redemption.

Sin had made it impossible for God to give Himself to man in fatherhood, because it had disqualified man as a son of God and replaced the spirit of sonship with its evil spirit. God's tender mercies, continued as far as possible, but He could not give Himself in the process of man's personal realization going on. His self-realization in sin made it impossible for God to give Himself to man in the fellowship which is necessary to sonship-life in God.

What sin had made impossible to God, it could not but make impossible to man. Perhaps among all sin's effects of disability in man the one which best sums them up was his inability to give himself to God. The very genius of sin lies in this withholding from God the self belonging to Him. The resultant in paralysis of the power of self-giving to God was inevitable.

The only possibility left to God in self-giving was that of providing a new order of sonship and a new order of the divine self-giving in it. The Father could give Himself in the Son, and by His self-sacrifice establish the new order of sonship in which God could give Himself in a new and living way. This redemptive sacrifice enabled the self-giving of God to sinners. It enabled God so to give Himself that sinful man could be awakened to giving himself to God. It enabled God to give Himself so sacrificially to man that this sacrifice became effectual in imparting His spirit of sacrifice to man, and thus enabled him to become a son of sacrifice, a son of God on a higher plane. Then the paralysis of sin preventing man's self-giving to God was cured by sin being destroyed; and the very genius of the sacrificial sonship established is that of self-giving to God, for as many as are led by the spirit of sacrifice, they are the sons of sacrifice, and are most like the Son of God.

The sacrifice of Redemption enabled God to become a life-giving source to man. The life-giving spirit of Christ's sacrifice enabled God to give Himself to those who had lost the desire to receive Him. It enabled the divine life to be transferred or imparted to those who had lost it. Christ in fulfilling God's desire to give Himself to the lost, enabled Him to become "the desire of many nations." His risen life became the light of men by having passed through the darkness of the valley of death for sin.

On the Cross Christ's power of self-giving was perfected and, so to speak, universalized. The Second Adam became a quickening, which means a life-giving spirit. His quickening by the Resurrection enabled Him to become the quickening spirit to those dead in trespasses and sins. His death enabled the Son to impart to man His own spirit of Sonship which has been eternally alive to the Father, and to give eternal life by it. As He has ever given Himself to the Father, so do all in Him ever give themselves to God.

At the Cross of Christ there met that which was worse than the impoverishment of sin in human life, and that which was better than the riches of man's sacrifice for man. The richest of all God's self-giving was then both enacted and inaugurated. At Calvary there met every opposite in God and sin to their fullest extent. At the Cross there came into direct contact immeasurable self-giving and selfishness, wondrous love and bitterest hate, infinite worthiness and utter unworthiness, glory unutterable and shame unabashed.

> "Upon that Cross of Jesus
>   Mine eye at times can see
> The very dying form of One
>   Who suffered there for me;
> And from my smitten heart with tears
>   Two wonders I confess—
> The wonders of His glorious love
>   And my unworthiness.
>
> "I take, O Cross, thy shadow
>   For my abiding place;
> I ask no other sunshine than
>   The sunshine of His face—
> Content to let the world go by,
>   To know no gain nor loss,
> My sinful self my only shame,
>   My glory all the Cross."

III. THE ENABLEMENT OF ATTRACTION

Jesus Himself said: "I, if I be lifted up from the earth, will draw all men unto me." This is not merely a manward enablement. There can be no manward enablement which is not grounded in a Godward. If sacrifice had no attraction to God, it never would have any to man.

We know something of the place of attraction in the physical world. Gravitation expresses the law of attraction. If the electro-dynamic theory of matter be the true one, the nature of the attraction in gravitation must correspond. Be that as it may, the attraction of chemical and electro-affinity reigns in the physical universe. Even this is patterned after the affinity and attraction within the nature of God.

Sacrifice within the Godhead is similar to the law of attraction in the physical world. Nothing has weight with God that is not sacrificial. The sacrificial principle of the universe making it a universe is the spiritual counterpart to the physical law of attraction. Sacrifice is the great attractive thing in God, man and the universe. Because Redemption is the greatest of all possible sacrifices, it will be to all eternity the greatest of all attractions. The throne of the Lamb by the law of spiritual attraction will hold together the whole spiritual universe of God in the world to come. "In him all things hold together."

It is an unfailing law of personality that the more anything has cost, the more interest it has. The more of ourselves we have put into a thing, the more hold it has upon us. Because of what Calvary cost God, it has more hold upon Him, more interest and attraction to Him than anything else.

When we behold the cost of the Cross, we are attracted by the beauty of its love, the grace of its unselfishness, the grip of its vicarious sacrifice. We are drawn by the attraction of its worth, for its worth is just what it cost, what God put into it—of Himself. But no man can come unto God except by the attraction of divine sacrifice. So Christ *draws* all men unto Him. If crucified, "I will draw all men unto me." Jesus did not mean that all would come to Him and be saved. That would be universalism. What

He meant was that all who come to Him as Saviour would be attracted to Him by His self-sacrifice. Because Jesus Christ Is Sacrifice Incarnate, Divine Sacrifice Dying For Us On The Cross, Rising From The Dead, And Enthroned In Heaven, He Is Forever Lifted Up As The Center Of Universal Attraction. *He draws all men unto Him and into the divine movement of sacrificial existence.*

NOTE: In 1846, Gardiner Spring, D.D., of New York City, published a volume on *The Attraction of the Cross.* The author says the Cross most fully reveals the true character of God and of human sinfulness; and it alone shows how a man can be just with God, for it is the last revelation of God's will to man. The Atonement is defined as, "that satisfaction to divine justice made by the sufferings and death of Christ, in the room and stead of sinners, in virtue of which pardoning mercy is secured to all who believe the Gospel."

IV. THE ENABLEMENT OF HUMILITY

Of our Lord it was said: "He humbled himself, and became obedient unto death, even the death of the cross." Surely this means that His humility made Redemption possible: it enabled God to redeem us.

In Creation all the divine enablings come through humility. Even in making the world He submitted to lowly limitation. In Redemption the divine enablement is through weakness. God Himself can say as well as man—and better, "When I am weak, then am I strong," and "My strength is made perfect in weakness."

Of the Incarnate Son of God it was written, "Because of weakness he was crucified."[1] What is this weakness but the strength of the enablement through humility? What a measureless humility the Incarnation was! What a glory the Son of God enjoyed in the pristine power of His Deity! What impotence He submits to as the babe within the Virgin's womb!

As the humility of the Incarnation enabled God to reveal and manifest Himself as never before, so the humility of the death on the Cross enabled Him to make

---
1. II Cor. 13:4.

still greater revelation and manifestation because of still greater sacrifice there. He took a mortal body to dwell in. He submitted to its last weakness in death. He was in humility ushered out of this world by a criminal's death. But this enabled Him to destroy the power of death and to deliver sinners from the bondage of everlasting death unto everlasting life. Coming forth from the grave He said: "All power is given unto me." Surely that was enablement. "Able to save unto the uttermost," He proved to be by His Humility fulfilled in empowerment.

The pride of sin and the humility of sacrifice stand over against each other as absolute opposites. Pride weakens: humility strengthens. The presumption of iniquity puts on airs of superiority; but humility is meek and lowly in heart; and so is able to give rest unto our souls.

A railway engine must become weak to be strong. It must begin in weakness that enablement may come. If it is started at full speed, inefficiency and damage result. When the throttle is pulled wide open, the wheels but spin around instead of going forward. In humility the engine must begin slowly with but a little of its power in use. So does its humility turn its power into ability.

When Omnipotence would relate itself to weakness and inability, it must humbly reduce itself to helpful contact. The full energy of Omnipotence unreduced coming into contact with weakness would prove to be but obliterating. On the throne of the universe the full measure of infinite power is quite in place; but in the ditch of sin Omnipotence would be worse than useless. Only the adaptation of humility would fit there.

God empowers by means of partial power. When "out of weakness men are made strong," it is at the price of Omnipotence itself being made weak. So was it with the humility of God in Christ's birth and death.

"Who being in the form of God thought it not a thing to be clung to (grasped at) to be equal with God: but made himself of no reputation, and took upon himself the form of a servant, and was made in the likeness of sinful men: and being found in fashion as a man, he humbled himself, and became obedient unto death, even the death of the cross.''

God in Christ is God in humility. Sin in man is man in humiliation. The Son of God humbled Himself in becoming the Son of Man. Then He further humbled Himself by suffering the humiliations that sin inflicted. But the shame of the Cross was changed to the glory of full divine ability in Redemption. Suffering sin's fulfilment He became the glory of the divine fulfilment enabling life and glory to be purchased for man. This fulfilment was divine enablement to the nth degree.

CHAPTER XX

THE FULFILMENT OF ENABLEMENT

SOME years ago there appeared in *The British Weekly* an especially remarkable editorial on "The One Fact More." Suppose that about any matter a survey of the available facts leads to a certain conclusion. Unexpectedly, it may be, there emerges "the one fact more." It changes the whole face of the matter, and the former conclusion is reversed. Such a situation is as possible in theology as elsewhere. This may happen in interpreting the Work of Christ. The fulfilment of the divine nature, we have been trying to explain, may be *the one fact more*.

Redemption itself is "the one fact more" about the problem of sin. It is sufficient to reverse the conclusion of hopelessness, as we survey the facts of sin's power, prolific productiveness, pestilential persistence, deep-rootedness, and unrelaxing hold on humanity. For all who believe in the Redeemer the one fact more of Redemption changes the whole situation. It enables great enheartenment. But it has also other enablements which we may continue to study.

I. The Enablement of Mastery Over the Evil One

In a time of the prevalence of anti-supernaturalism the existence of evil spirits is sure to be denied along with all other supernatural matters. Here it must suffice to say that Jesus Christ's revelation on this matter as on all others is taken to be entirely trustworthy. One cannot read the impartial treatment of "Demon Possession And Allied Themes" by Dr. John L. Nevius, who was for forty years a missionary in China, and not see that scientific scholarship has its verification of the teaching of Christ on this matter that is truly startling.

Jesus was no fraud or self-deceived enthusiast professing to exorcise non-existent spirits of evil. He clearly manifested perfect and easy mastery over all the spirit world. He never struggled to perform any of the miracles of casting out demons. The demons themselves never questioned His authority. Intuitively they knew Him and whence He had come; but He refused their testimony. They still know and fear Him, as Dr. Nevius shows. The power of the world of evil spirits is evidently far more than "the malign influence of a dark superstition to be cast aside in more enlightened days." Days of unbelief in the revelation of Christ never prove thereby to have much enlightenment. As Jesus said there is a light which is darkness in disguise.

As I have elsewhere said about sin as "the mystery of iniquity,"[1] demon existence is as unexplainable as is sin, for the fallen angels are the perfect personalization of sin. God is not in it or them; and anything without God in it is without the one thing that makes it interpretable. It is God in all things which makes them understandable. Great, therefore, is the mystery of sin and Satan.

We may not be able to explain the essence of darkness. When out of it comes the rattle of machine-gun fire and the fumes of poison-gas, and we see comrades swept down by the hail of hell or gasping in their last agony, we know enough about the situation to be aware that it is not created by mere imagination.

While we cannot explain how there has come to be the unslumbering opposition of the demons to God, this makes the trustworthy teaching of the Master all the more indispensable. Moreover there is a profound reason why in such matters we should not "lean unto our own understanding," especially when it contradicts the revelation of Christ.

That the human demon exists, there is surely evidence enough. While he differs in some respects from the fallen angel, sin is the maker of both. Manifestly, fallen humanity is bedeviled by sin. Iniquity in us is

---

1. The Virgin's Son, p. 35.

the devil's own territory he never fails to occupy. To dislodge the demons from their entrenchments in humanity is one of the hardest difficulties of God. Only by destroying this territory can they be dislodged.

We should have too much regard for humanity to charge it with producing unaided all the fiendish atrocities, hellish inhumanities, multiplied perversities, and gigantic ungodliness in human history. There is no adequate explanation for the slow and inadequate acceptance of the grace of God in Christ other than the mysterious, stubborn hold which the powers of evil have in human life.

II. "WHEN SATAN'S EMPIRE FELL"

The strategy of the enemy is no accident. The cunning and repeated assaults by evil not only Job but every child of God has met. The coöperative ability and strong power of the evil spirits are doubtless due to their exalted rank and high endowments before they fell. In His vision of Redemption our Lord saw Satan fall as lightning from heaven. It will be a good day when he is bound and thrown out of the earth. Through Christ and Him alone the Great Outcast from heaven will one day be the Great Outcast from earth as well.

The enablement of Christ's fulfilment meets the problem of the serious complicity and terrible alliance with evil spirits. Christ has faced the fact that the identical process of self-realization in sin that made the devil what he is, is going on in man. There can be no overthrow of sin that is not therefore an overthrow of the whole presence of evil spirit and its power of opposing God through man. The Word of God tells us that, "To this end was the Son of God manifested, that he might destroy the works of the devil," (1 John 3: 8. See also the stronger statement, Heb. 2: 14).

The demons were not only aware of the entrance of the Son of God into human life: they knew also what it meant to them. They quailed before Him, except when the Great Adversary personally encountered Him. The struggle in the wilderness temptations put

Satan behind Him as vanquished. When at Cæsarea Philippi the devil in Peter sought to block Christ's way to the Cross, he was dismissed as vanquished: "Get thee behind me, Satan!" But it was only for a season that Satan left Him. He inspired all opposition to Him as he does to-day. The demons wanted anything but the sacrifice of Christ's death, but sought to make it as crushing as possible. At Calvary the Titanic Contest took place. The Cross was the great vortex of the struggle to overcome the Christ. Satan found no foothold in Him. He found nothing in Him to which he could appeal successfully. He could not bring Him to use His divine powers to deliver Himself from death and suffering, nor could he break the Son's faith in the Father's will that He should be an offering, a sacrifice for sin unto death. The Godward growth of Christ's soul, went on all the stronger and deeper because of the encompassing power of darkness about Him. His infinite sacrifice went all the way through; and "Satan's empire fell."

When the Son of God entered the battlefield of human life, He met there single-handed, so to speak, the whole force of evil making havoc in this domain of God. His sacrifice was a victory Satan could not withstand, for it provided a means of self-fulfilment the devil cannot assail. It overthrew Satan's use of sin to make demons out of men. It was a great victory Christ gained for God and man.

In Christ no one can be overthrown by evil. The fulfilment of Christ's sacrifice has put the weapon of victory into our hands. We have no business to wrestle with the enemy in our own strength. When the devil catches us on the battlefield armed with only the painted lath of self-confidence, instead of the Sword of the Word, how he loves to smash it to splinters, take us by the neck and rub our face in the mire.

"He that committeth sin is of the devil." In the Greek original, this means, *keeps on* committing sin. Sin is the closest possible affinity with the Evil One. To some our Lord said, "Ye are of your father, the devil; and his works ye will do." We never pray the Lord's prayer as He gave it, unless we say, "Deliver us from the Evil One." In the field of the world Satan is busy. "The enemy that sowed them (tares) is the devil." Those unrepentant who share the devil's work, must share his fate: "Depart into everlasting fire prepared for the devil and his angels." To save man from so terrible a destiny, the Saviour died," that through death He might bring to naught him that hath the power of death, that is, the devil." This was Redemption's enablement of power over the Evil One and all his hosts.

III. THE ENABLEMENT OF RELEASEMENT AND EMPOWERMENT

Jesus' life was a constant battle. It was a war unto death with all evil. He made peace for others "By the blood of his cross," and for Himself also but in a different way. As He trod this vale of tears He became the Son of Sorrows, the Man of Miseries, acquainted with all our grief. After such a life as He lived, His death was release, rest and rapture.

Christ's death set Him free from the limitations of this life, when He passed out to the infinite freedom of the greater world from whence He came. He was like a prisoner who in his escape carries away his prison bars with him. "He led captivity captive." His death enabled Him to "give gifts unto men," most of all the gift of Himself as the means of fulfilment.

As they come to the hour of death, some are happily surprised to find they do not have to go to heaven: heaven comes to them. But heaven had always been about Him who is the Maker of heaven and earth.

That was relief—to cease from suffering as He hung on the crucifixion nails. After the pang of heartbreak how pleasant to pass into the joy unspeakable and full of glory surging all about Him like an infinite ocean of divine delight! There the Son of God was at home in that immediate world of God filled to the

THE FULFILMENT OF ENABLEMENT 237

full with measureless manifestations of His presence. How holy the world overflowing everywhere with the gladness of obedience to the will of God! How empowering to enter that world of God so full of God that nothing can go wrong in it, nothing but the joy of God possible to it!

Freed from the exhausting conflict of the Cross, He bathed His weary spirit in the restfulness of the perfect peace of Paradise. Its refreshing atmosphere fanned His face as He was caught up into the rapturous rejoicing over His heaven-thrilling triumph. The satisfaction of having completed His sacrifice for the sinful world filled His soul. He had the divine thrill of having fulfilled Himself in the will of God unto the uttermost in that which is uppermost with Heaven.

Blessed was that release from the devouring agony of death, the cruel mockings, the desertion by even the devoted, the poignant pain of spirit, the suffering of soul in such grief as man had never known! The presence of the hosts of evil and the multitude of enemies that had gathered about the death-rood of the Son of God, He exchanged for the transcendent presence of the Father, the greetings of the holy angels, and the shouts of the hosts of heroes now at home after their struggle and victory even then through Him.

Like a lamp flames up when no longer turned low, now the living flame of His Deity shines forth in full splendor like it did on the Mount of Transfiguration. The Son was re-empowered with all the possible prerogatives of Deity. His suffering self-realization of Godward fulfilment on the Cross had added its own glory and power to Him on its completion. If a *kenosis* was possible before His birth, surely a *plerosis* was possible after His death. As Redemption's song in The Revelation puts it:

"Worthy is the Lamb that was slain to receive power, and riches, and wisdom, and strength, and honor, and glory, and blessing...... Blessing, and honor, and glory, and power be unto him that sitteth upon the throne, and unto the Lamb for ever and ever."

IV. The Enablement of Personality

This points to the provision for perpetuity. Redemption for persons by God in Person is of course a personal matter. The finished sacrifice on the Cross was the inauguration of a sacrificial existence and a sacrificial impartation. Redemption by the death of Christ lives in the Person of the Redeemer.

In a former treatise on this subject of the Work of Christ (The Living Atonement) the thought was presented that Christ by His death became our living Redemption. "He ever liveth to make intercession for us." "He is the propitiation for our sins." In His person is stored up all the potency of divine Redemption.

This interpretation delivers us from the old problem as to whether Christ died for the elect only. When we behold Christ Crucified as the fulfilment of God in relation to human sin, we see that if but one had believed on Him, He could not have done less; and if all the world should have believed on Him, *He could not have done more.*

God's provision for our Redemption is perpetuated in the Person of Christ, and its manward effect in those who receive Him. In His Person the eternal weight and might of divine personality came into direct contact with sin in such a way as to overcome it, destroy it, and turn its loss into a gain.

So to speak, the atomic energy of a divine personality was released in the death of Christ, and being let loose it became the dynamic of divine Redemption. Its enablement became permanent in the Person sacrificed to it. The infinite strength of God in Sacrifice went into our Redemption and became available to all. This dynamic of Deity, this transcendent energy existing eternally in God wrought itself into the Person of the Christ as Redeemer. Hence this enabling of His Person was in the main a matter of adaptation. To that phase we shall next turn.

CHAPTER XXI

ABLE UNTO THE UTTERMOST

EVERY fulfilment is by an enablement, an enablement to reach the end designed; but there is also an enablement because of having reached fulfilment. There are two fulfilments in Redemption, the fulfilment in providing it, and the fulfilment in its reception.

Necessity in substance precedes necessity in operation. Internal necessity comes before the external. The internal necessity that God should be true to His sacrificial nature, is one thing; the necessity of adaptation that His sacrifice might become effective in the hearts and lives of those for whom the sacrifice is made, is another.

There is the necessity arising out of the three natures, of God, of man, and of sin. There was the necessity that the divine sacrifice be brought into contact with sin and fitted for the destruction of it within the springs of human self-realization. There was the necessity of adaptation, so that Redemption might be capable of entering into the process of personal realization.

So to speak, there was the necessity that Redemption turn the flank of sin's forces. Sin drove men away from God; but God planted Himself in the path of sin. Then their sin brings men face to face with the Cross of Christ standing there between them and the void. They must go by the Cross, if they pass to perdition.

I. The Enablement of Adaptation

This enablement was provided by bringing within the realm of human nature the resources hid in the sacrificial Person of God the Son. The power of personal adaptation is one of His distinctive marks. His birth was His adaptation to Revelation; and His death was His adaptation to Redemption.

Christ's death had the effect of separation; and His resurrection had the effect of union. But both had the effect of an adaptation. The change which took place in His body by this death and resurrection may be taken as indicative of the change in the rest of His Person. Empowerment by adaptation to Redemption is the measure of the transformation of "Christ crucified and risen from the dead."

His resurrection completely conformed and equipped His body for His new state of existence and place as Redeemer. Death had sent Him out of this world leaving His body in its hands. His body was dead because of sin; but His spirit was alive because of righteousness, to which He had added the righteousness of His sacrifice in death.

On the one hand, there was the adaptation in His Person to meet all that God required in fulfilling Himself in relation to sin. On the other, there was the adaptation of His Person to the end of sin's destruction. This was the change which took place in Him by His death and resurrection. We may liken this adaptation to becoming an anti-toxin for sin. It has been found that the dead of their own kind is most deadly poison to all bacteria. The serum of blood having the dead germs of a disease has been found a sure means to destroy the living germs of the same disease when injected into the body of the patient.

When Christ was smitten by sin and identified with it in His crucifixion, something similiar to the innoculation with the germs of this "disease of the devil" took place. So to speak the sin of the crucifixion innoculated the body of His Incarnation with the germs of sin. That all His blood might be turned into an anti-sin serum, He suffered the sin-death. But in His death all the germs of sin died; and His resurrection made His blood available as the serum of salvation. All this is but the physical figure of the spiritual adaptation of Christ's person. Because of its sacrificial nature, Christ's blood was well chosen as the symbol of His sacrificial spirit and life. The shedding of His blood expresses His poured-out life; and the application of it means the contact of the sacrificial spirit of Christ, which is death to sin. "The blood of Jesus Christ, his Son, cleanseth us from all sin." "They washed their robes and made them white in the blood of the Lamb."

The Saviour said that the Holy Spirit could not come unless He went; but it was the way He went that determined what the Spirit brought. The Holy Spirit could not be poured out from His wounded Person till after it had been so wounded and His blood shed; for without the sacrifice of the shed blood, there is no adaptation to destroy sin. Nothing but the pouring out of His sacrifice can cure sin's curse.

What Christ became by His death, the Holy Spirit has the power of conveying to us. One drop of that sacrificial life-blood which has borne sin for us, has more potency than all nostrums of men and religions of man. One touch of His life sacrificed for us, and this touch by His Holy Spirit made effective within us, and sin is ended and the soul cleansed.

No Redemption can be complete apart from the cleansing of the sinner. In Christ Crucified the very life that died on the Cross ends sin in the soul, and cleanses it from all unrighteousness. The transfusion of His blood into our souls kills the love of sin and implants the instinctive hatred and dread which His sacrificial nature has toward iniquity. "How much more shall the blood of Christ who through (His) eternal spirit offered himself without blemish unto God, cleanse your conscience from dead works to serve the living God."

It takes spirit to destroy spirit. It takes a nature to destroy a nature. The adaptation of spirit and nature to destroy spirit and nature depends upon the destroying one being stronger and naturally destructive to the other. The self-sacrificial spirit and nature of Christ were adapted by His death for sin to destroy it; and

His spirit and nature has ever had the innate power to blot out iniquity. The adaptation of vicarious sacrificial contact was needed.

Christ's sacrificial and sacrificed Person, because of being absolutely opposed to sin in every way, and having passed through the adapting process of the death on the Cross, can be depended upon to destroy both the nature and the spirit of iniquity, whenever He comes into saving contact with the sinful soul. Of the eight songs in The Revelation perhaps the one which most praises the Work of Christ is in the fifth Chapter; but the opening song of ascription found in the first chapter has the very same note: "Unto him that loved us, and loosed us from our sins by his blood."

The giving of Christ's life for us in the sacrifice of death is often mentioned in the New Testament in the language of the blood. "In whom we have redemption through his blood." "Thou hast redeemed us unto God by thy blood." "Ye were not redeemed with corruptible things......but with the precious blood of Christ, as of a lamb without blemish and without spot."

Reconciliation is one of the great words of the New Testament to describe the enabling power of Christ's death. Its sacrifice is adapted to bring reconciliation. God is reconciled to all sinners who accept His sacrifice for sin. Sinners being the offenders need a different kind of reconciliation, the reconciliation of repentance by faith. The goodness of God in His Great Sacrifice leads to this repentance.

II. THE PERFECTION OF ADAPTATION

Christ's sacrificial death on behalf of sinners thereby adapted Him to be an object of their faith and love. After what has been said as to the adaptation within God by sacrifice, it hardly need be said that the manward adapation was not the only one. The fact is the adaptation of the one is the adaptation of the other. Christ's adaptation to be the object of faith and love was because He had done something for sinners that was needed, and had thereby become something to them that could be appropriately met only by faith and love.

Even the sinful can believe in sacrifice for them; and, moved by the Holy Spirit, may be led to love Him who thus loves them. Faith in His giving Himself to us calls for the giving of ourselves to Him. God in Christ being love's utmost sacrifice, it is the largest adaptation to eyes blinded by sin, but opened by this grace. God being so manifested in the death of His Son is adapted and enabled "to reconcile the world unto Himself," or Himself unto the world.

No change could take place in the Being and Nature of God, but a change in His Relation could and did take place. And this was brought about through God Himself bearing sacrificially the sin of man.

In this enablement by adaptation, the divine adaptation of the sacrificial, we see something of the wonderful wisdom of God. We cannot help believing in the man who pours out his blood unto death for us. *Not to believe in that is to turn enemy to ourselves.* How much more then must we be enemies to ourselves not to believe in the Son of God who poured out His divine blood unto death for us! The church itself comes into existence through His blood shed for us: "The church of God which he hath purchased with his own blood."

There is not space here to dwell long upon how Christ's shed blood adapted Him to be Mediator between God and man. Because He gave Himself a ransom for all, and is the perfect God-man, He is the "one Mediator between God and man." So reasons the mind of Paul illumined by the Holy Spirit. And so writes the inspired author of the Epistle to the Hebrews.

"By his own blood he entered in once into the holy place, having obtained eternal redemption for us...... And for this cause he is the mediator of the new covenant...... This is the blood of the covenant which God commanded to you-ward You are come......to Jesus, the mediator of the new covenant, and to the blood of sprinkling...... Wherefore

Jesus also, that he might sanctify the people through his own blood, suffered without the gate...... Now the God of peace, who brought again from the dead the great shepherd of the sheep with the blood of the eternal covenant, even our Lord Jesus, make you perfect in every good thing to do his will, working in you that which is well pleasing in his sight, through Jesus Christ, to whom be glory unto the ages of the ages. Amen!''

In all three directions of adaptation, then, toward sin, sinners, and God, Christ's shed blood is the Spirit-chosen symbol. The hope of the world is in the blood of the Cross. Christ without His crucifixion is Christ without His adaptation, and without His adaptation He is without His power. With divine wisdom the great apostle said, "We preach Christ crucified." Then he could add: "Christ the power and the wisdom of God." There are the two wonders; one, why all men do not see this, and instead add their own crucifixion of Him by refusing faith in His crucifixion. The other wonder is, how man could have crucified Him in the first place.

"Jesus, the Master came down from above,
Born in a manger, the Saviour of love,
Sent by the Father and pure as the snow;
Why did they treat my Lord so?

"They crucified Him: they crucified Him;
But Jesus died for me;
The off'ring made, the ransom paid,
He saves and I am free.

"Out in the highway or down in the street
Healing the sick ones who fall at His feet,
Blessing the needy who pass to and fro;
Why did they treat my Lord so?

"Nailed to the Cross, I can see Him just now;
Scorned and forsaken, the thorns on His brow;
Wounded and bleeding to die from the blow;
Why did they treat my Lord so?

" 'Father, forgive them!' I hear my Lord cry,
'I must redeem them, for them I must die;
Down in the valley of death I must go';
Why did they treat my Lord so?"

III. THE ENABLEMENT OF RE-CREATION

There are three Biblical accounts of Creation: in the opening words of The Epistle to the Hebrews, the Gospel of John, and the Book of Genesis. There is a divine dignity in the language of all three. The Word of God offers as its initial message, "In the beginning God created the heavens and the earth." If one throws into the discard the truth that God is Creator, other important truths must follow it. Surely it is more in keeping with Christian faith to look up to God as our Creator than look down along the hypothesis of evolution. To adapt Spurgeon's witicism, we pray better when we can say, "Our Father who art in heaven," than when we fold our hand and repeat, "Our father who art up a tree."

Holy Writ not only reveals God as Creator, but also gives the Eternal Son the place of Agent of Creation.

"All things were made by him; and without him was not anything made that was made." "By whom also he made the worlds." "For in him were all things created in the heavens and upon the earth . . . All things were created through him and unto him." "Thou didst create all things; and because of thy will they were, and were created."

All this adds immeasurable importance to Redemption. The Person who purchased it was no less than our Creator.

"When Christ, the mighty Maker, died
For man, the creature's sin."

We have already noted that Creation was a divine sacrifice—the sacrifice of limitation by His necessary relation to it, not only in calling it into being but also in upholding and preserving it.

Having been for ages creating worlds upon worlds, the stupendous sacrifice comes, in which the Creator turns aside to become a creature within this little world of man and sin. "He was in the world, and the world was made by him; and the world knew him not." Alas! even yet it does not know Him. "He came unto His own," not only nationally but creationally, "and his own received him not." Though He was Creator sacrificed for creatures, His sacrifice they would not. Blindly they killed Him who had given them life—and all else of good they had.

In the profound thought of the Epistle to the Romans Paul tells us that sin has affected all creation. In consequence "the whole creation groans and travails together in pain until now, waiting for its redemption," that must wait on that of man. Then the curse of being the habitation of sinful men can be removed.

When Christ sacrificed Himself in death for us, He thereby dedicated all His powers to the work of Redemption. This included His creative skill and energy. Being the Author of life, He could not be held by death. "Whom God raised up, having loosed the pangs of death; because it was not possible that he should be holden of it." "Destroy this sanctuary and in three days I will raise it up." His resurrection by new creation is the pledge of ours. "And God both raised up the Lord, and will raise up us through his power."

As Creator-Redeemer Christ is the Contractor and Completer of Christian personality. He is "the beginning of the creation of God." His redemption by re-creation is thus stated: "If any man is in Christ, there is a new creation." In other words, Christ's sacrifice has harnessed His creative powers into the reconstructive work of Redemption. "The new man that is after God created in righteousness and holiness of truth," is the result of having a Redeemer-Creator, for we are his workmanship, created in Christ Jesus for good works.

When the Son of God said, "I go to prepare a place for you," this no doubt meant that there also His creative skill and resources would be employed. But it is greater to prepare us for our future, than to prepare a future place for us. The extent of creative reconstruction in the future is inseparably connected with Christ's Coming Again.

"Looking for and earnestly desiring (hastening) the coming of the day of the Lord, because of which the heavens being on fire will be dissolved, and the elements will melt with fervent heat. But according to his promise, we look for new heavens and a new earth; for the first heaven and the first earth passed away." "And he who sat upon the throne said, Behold I make all things new."

IV. THE ENABLEMENT OF UNITY

The Trinity is not all transcendent. It has a unity that is both transcendent and descendent. This is a unity which to us comes down out of heaven. The Son is the One dedicated to the great task of unifying all things in Creation. He is not only Creator and Redeemer but also Unifier. He is enabled to do His work of unification by communicating and imparting from within the eternal harmony of God's nature. In His Person this harmony was brought into corrective contact with the chaos and disharmony of sin, and the transcendent unity of the Triune Godhead was in Him applied to the disruption of iniquity.

We have already pointed out that the secret of the infinite unity within the divine nature is because of its transcendent and immanent spirit of sacrifice. And this unity is reflected in all that God has done. If two cannot walk together unless they are agreed, the infinite works of Christ in the universe could not hold together, unless they all belonged to each other and to Him in sacrificial relation to the whole and to Him. "In him all things hold together."

The unity of the Persons of the Holy Trinity is marked by their perfect identification with each other. There is but one Being in the eternal repose of absolute unity. The constant fulfilment of this unity made its sacrifice to meet the problem of sin's disunity. Its stronger unity in fulfilment overcame the fulfilment of sin's disunity.

When the Son of God was identified with human life and nature, the transcendent unity of the Godhead came into redeeming contact with all the disruption and disharmony of human life, and overcame them. The starry heavens *portray* on the largest scale the wondrous unity of the universe. That is extensive. In intensive unity the fellowship of the Son of God with the Father manifested the irrefrangible harmony of the Being of God. Against this intensive unity the disruptive, chaos-creating power of sin hurled itself in vain during the dying experience of the Son of God. The organization of the same unity in humanity is manifest in the organism of the Kingdom of God. The life-giving rule of the Redeemer is His Redemption manifest in a divine organism.

From the divine unity there came to disintegrated and disunited humanity the restoration to a new unity. The divinely cohesive nature of divine sacrifice became the basis and substance of this new unity. Thus the transcendent unity of God's eternally sacrificial nature reached out and took within itself the shattered and severed fragments of humanity, and re-related and re-integrated them by the sacrifice of the Son to this end. His sacrifice has within it potential unity sufficient to harmonize every person within himself and to God, and the whole race with itself in the Kingdom of God.

That this unity was the goal of Christ's sacrificial work, He made known in unmistakeable terms in His great prayer recorded in the seventeenth of John. This was His valedictory as He faced the fulfilment of His sacrifice in death. He not only prayed for this unity, He died for it. He died to fulfil His own prayer: "That they may be one, even as we are one; I in them and thou in me, that they may be perfected in one." As long as men remain small in soul, with small interests and pursuits, they are bound to be fragmentary in feeling, disunited in interest, and missing the greatness God intended, record their loss in multiplied disharmonies. Christ redeemed man to the greatest enterprise ever undertaken by God or man, and unified man with God and man with himself in the great things of God and man.

Peace with God and that alone must propagate all successful peace movements for the world. No more can the world be pacified apart from Christ than it can be redeemed from other sins apart from Him. We have a more complicated and powerful world enmeshed in things that lead to war, than the world that John Milton saw. And though blind *he saw these things in the large,* and accordingly said:

"O shame to men! devil with devil damned
Firm concord holds; men only disagree
Of creatures rational, though under hope
Of heavenly grace; and, God proclaiming peace,
Yet live in hatred, enmity, and strife
Among themselves, and levy cruel wars,
Wasting the earth, each other to destroy:
As if (which might induce us to accord)
Man had not hellish foes enough besides,
That day and night for his destruction wait."

Part Three
The Need of Redemption

CHAPTER XXII

THE FACT OF SIN

LOGICALLY, the need of Christ and His Work should come first in the order of our discussion. To follow the exact order of formal logic is not always most helpful. Having studied the nature of Christ's Work, we can the more advantageously consider the need of it.

The seriousness of sin makes it a very important subject. Any presentation of Redemption resulting from a superficial survey of sin is worse than useless. Any system of religious thought which minimizes the sinfulness of sin, at the same time minimizes the meaning of salvation from it.

One superficiality naturally leads to another. A superficial survey of the nature and consequences of iniquity must result in a superficial survey of the nature and consequences of Christ's Work on account of it. A discriminating, well-balanced view of the need which has been caused by sin naturally goes along with an equally discriminating and well-balanced view of the sacrifice of God in Christ to meet this need.

I. Moral Discernment

Sin exists because God and man exist. God and man cannot exist except in some kind of relation to each other. And man would be other than man without the possibility of His choosing to be untrue to the true relation which he bears to God. In other words, self-realization without self-determination would not be personal in fact.

Man being made for God, it disagrees with him to disagree with God. Now, there is no nature with which everything alike agrees. If every nature agreed with all other natures, there would be no such thing as nature or agreement. Differentiation in nature would be gone.

Intelligence is necessarily a part of life. Man is alive and a creature of intelligence. He knows when things disagree with his physical nature. He knows also there are things which disagree with his spiritual nature. To deny this is to deny his intelligence. And to deny this intelligence is to deny the intelligence of this denial.

Every part of human nature has its own appropriate intelligence. Moral nature has as a necessary phase its moral intelligence. Man knows right from wrong. He knows the evil and the good he does. If he had not the power to distinguish between good and bad, right and wrong, he would be an unmoral person —and then he would not be a person. The very thing which makes moral nature moral, is the ability to discriminate between the moral and the immoral. Moral nature is as essential to personality as intelligence is to life.

He is no farmer who cannot distinguish between weeds and grain. He is no artist who cannot tell black from white, beauty from ugliness. He is no musician to whom harmony and disharmony sound alike. In the same way religious life is possible because we can tell good from bad, right from wrong, sin from righteousness, religion from irreligion.

Perversion of mind does not prove that mind does not exist. Perversion does prove itself to be such by its deranged thinking. The self-induced moral insanity denying that sin exists, shows that a forged folly is preferred to frank intelligence in religious discrimination.

He who refuses to let his moral faculty function, enters upon a voluntary moral insanity. A man walking midst the smouldering ruins of a great city burned to the ground, may conjure up arguments to prove that fire does not exist. He is either wilfully perverse or woefully insane. The man who, walking in a world where the ruination of human lives is everywhere going on, and beholding the disorders of war, murder, robbery, immorality, and all manner of inhumanities, conjures up his proof that sin does not exist, is as obviously deranged or as wilfully perverse as is the other.

In a world of sin, one would think the existence of sin is about the last thing that needs to be proved. A man lost in the forest is not much in need of proof that trees exist. He is in a poor place to deny this. Not long ago we saw the trench-torn earth reeking with human blood, nations cloven to the heart, the fairest flower of manhood ruthlessly mowed down by war's barbarous scythe. Since then a crime wave has been sweeping over our land. A multitude of post-war evils infests the world. He who calmly sees all this, and then positively declares that there is no sin on earth, is either a callous rascal or a self-made fool in moral judgment. Patience with such has long since ceased to be a virtue.

II. The Fool Trusts a Fool

Wisely was it said that he who stops to argue with a fool, proves there are two of them. The perversity that denies that wrong is wrong, is never cured by argument. He who persists in taking the light of moral discernment to be darkness, must be left in his darkness. Any man having put out his eyes need not be permitted to take up our time telling us of the impossibility of seeing unpleasant sights. But we have a duty to perform in seeking to save those in danger of committing similar self-injury, because misled by this dangerous propaganda.

Wit and wisdom said, "When a man says, everybody is honest, pity him! When another says, few men are honest, watch him! When a third says, no one is honest, search him!" A blind optimist says, there is nothing but good in this world. To him you would commit nothing of value for safe keeping. When one comes to you arguing that no one can do wrong, take him at his word. Accordingly, it will not be wrong to lock him out. Spurgeon tells us he was on the point of lending money to a man, when he was providentially prevented by the man's remark, "You know, Mr. Spurgeon, I can do no wrong."

No religion is fit to be trusted to set the signals along life's railway line, which has as its creed, "There can be no danger." Folly it is to follow a guide who cannot see for himself. "I see the wrong that round me lies," said the poet. Let us follow the poet that sees, rather than the pest with his denial of sight. Those who see cannot follow the blind without turning blind. When the blind follow the blind, the ditch will get its own. When those who see follow the blind, the devil will get his own.

III. Sin Denying Sin's Existence

A religion denying the existence of sin, is really denying the need of its own existence. If we cannot go wrong, why should we permit any one to make a religion out of telling us how to go right.

All these efforts to blot out the distinction between righteousness and iniquity can come only from a wilful blindness arguing against light in the terms and logic of midnight darkness. That setting out to discredit the trustworthiness of the moral and spiritual faculties, would wound humanity in a most vital spot, damage it in a most fatal way.

True religion cannot be based on the denial of truth; and nothing is more valuable and vital than this: our moral nature does truly discriminate between right and wrong. Nothing is more dangerously untrue than that denying the reliability of our power to perceive truth. And basic in the truth of Christianty is the recognition of the fact of sin's existence. That is a figment in religion which calls sin "a figment of the religious imagination." That is itself mortal mind dying in deadly error which classes iniquity as "an error of the mortal mind." Its result is necessarily death to the power of spiritual discernment. And with that dead within us, what else would really be alive?

THE FACT OF SIN

The ability to recognize sin as sin lies at the very foundation of the truly religious life. If the reliability of this ability we doubt, there is no reason why we should not doubt the reliability of every power we possess—and the reliability of this doubt too.

Any religion which accuses our discrimination of sin of being unreliable, in so doing accuses itself of unreliability. It cannot sweep away the reliability of this power, without sweeping away the reliability of all our powers, for all reliability of powers rests upon precisely the same basis—*faith in them*. Poison and so put to death faith in the fact of sin, and only a dead faith remains for all else. What use is it to say that the cook poisoned only one of the dishes we have eaten? What good then is the rest to us?

The man who says agnostically, "We know nothing and can know nothing," has really said we do not know and cannot know that we know nothing. To doubt that we doubt is more than doubtful procedure. As some one has said, we cannot carve a goose and carve the carver at the same time. We cannot distrust our moral intelligence without first trusting it to enable us to distrust it. We are compelled to use our moral intelligence in order to decide that our moral intelligence is not trustworthy. So we thus both credit and discredit the same power at the same time. This is about as wise as trying to run in opposite directions at the same time.

A man can say there is no wrong or sin only as he claims to be moral personality. If he denies he is such, then he invalidates his statement. And if he denies there can be wrong or sin, he invalidates his moral intelligence. What is the use of eyes if there is nothing to see? What is the use of power of moral discrimination, if there is no righteousness and sin to discriminate between?

A non-moral judgment cannot make denial in moral matters, any more than an ignoramus in law can make a safe legal decision. If all men were without eyes none of them would ever be found denying the existence of light and darkness. If all were without the consciousness of sin, no one would or could deny the fact of sin.

There is no more striking proof that sin exists than the denial of it. This denial is itself a sin—sin against the light of spiritual intelligence. It shows that the moral consciousness exists, and is at work in the bad work of abusing itself. A man coming home rather late one night, descried his henhouse door open. Going to it he put his head inside and shouted, "Who's here?" "Nobody!" came the answer in a voice that sounded almost white. So sin in denying that it exists, proves that it does.

IV. Moral Discernment to be Trusted

If the power of spiritual discernment cannot be trusted to say there is sin, it cannot be trusted to say there is no sin. If its affirmations are not to be believed, how comes it that its denials are to be trusted? It has been long and well established that affirmations are far more likely to be correct than denials.

Every normal person does accept his sense of right and wrong as trustworthy. Persistence in sin may blunt its edge and interfere with fineness of discernment. It is wholly another thing when this spiritual sense "is lost on purpose to meet the demand of a sophistry denying sin's existence."

Denying the existence of sin is the denial of the existence of righteousness. Denial of the possibility of the immoral is at the same time denial of the possibility of the moral. If there can be no wrong, there can be no right. If iniquity be impossible, conscience is a superfluous power. Why should God give us an unneeded ability, without a realm for it to work in, and its exercise untrustworthy?

The denial of the fact of sin never goes alone. It is bound to lead to other denials—the denial of God, or, maybe, the personality of God. There are certain existences which do not need to be proved—our own, for example. As a rule the existences which do not need to be proved, cannot be, as far as formal logic is

THE FACT OF SIN

concerned. One must trust his powers when proving God's existence, but to trust them is to account as trustworthy the one who gave them; and to account the Giver of what powers we have to be trustworthy, is to assume His existence. Thus we must assume His existence to attempt to prove it.

God's existence is like that of a mother's—to be depended upon rather than to be proved. He is primarily not an object of reason and logic, but of faith. So is it with the powers He has given us. Their existence and work are to be depended upon. The spiritual sense of sin and righteousness is not primarily an object of proof, but of faith. We are dependent upon our powers. If they were not trustworthy, then we could never reach any trustworthiness. Faith in God and our God-given powers lies at the basis of all. Doubt Him and His reliability in the powers He has endowed us with, and there is left nothing but an infinite void of independability and doubt. In the ultimate *it is faith in God which compels assent to the fact of sin.* Those who depersonalize God and hold that we construct all our world, are able to destroy for themselves all dependence and dependability but their own. They are then in Hamlet's contradictory subjectivity: "There is nothing either good or bad, but thinking makes it so." This gives away their whole case, for it assents that thinking can be bad. Suppose, then, that thinking makes this subjectivity itself bad, thinks it bad! Then it is so! It must be bad, for according to this it may be bad to think that thinking a thing is good, makes it good; or if our thinking this subjectivity good makes it good, then it can be good to make things bad by thinking them so.

V. The Reality of Experience at Stake

The fact of sin is no different from all the other facts of observation and experience. Its effects are real, and real effects can come only from real causes. Moreover sin answers every test of reality that we ask of anything else in experience or observation. As some one has said: "It infects and infests those things in ourselves which we count most real—love, desire, will, purpose, mind, and all the rest of our powers."

The world is not far astray in its rough and ready way of estimating men according to their estimate of right and wrong. In Boswell's life of Johnson, in discussing a certain person Samuel Johnson says:

"If he does really think that there is no distinction between virtue and vice, why, Sir, when he leaves our houses, let us count our spoons."

Sin would scarce be sin, if it did not inspire in some the denial of its existence. The actuality of its presence is shown by its definite characteristics and effects. By such spiritual intelligence recognizes it. Its prolific productiveness and deep rootedness can hardly be credited to a nonentity. The vacuum interpretation of this difficulty tacitly acknowledges that something is wrong, while it has no vacuum-cleaner treatment for it. But the vacuum is in this interpretation of non-existence, not in the fact of sin. Here then are two religions diametrically opposed: one says, "Deny your sin!"; the other commands, "Confess your faults."

"Come, now again, thy woes impart,
Tell all thy sorrows, all thy sin;
We cannot heal the throbbing heart,
Till we discern the wounds within."

CHAPTER XXIII

VARYING VIEWS OF SIN

THE origin of sin, though an interesting subject, is a matter of speculation. Divine revelation gives us no information as to where it came from. On such subjects how helpless we are where the Word of God is silent! An ounce of revelation is worth a ton of speculation.

Genetic theology is concerned with the beginning of the Christian life, not with the beginning of speculation about it. Genetic philosophy is welcome to deal with the subject of sin's origin. The inquiry of Greek philosophy dating a long way back was, "Whence evil?" (Pothen to kakon;). Modern philosophy has broadened the inquiry to "Whence everything?"

The genesis of evil is utterly beyond us to explain. Even if we could disclose the mystery, the explanation might offer no practical help in overcoming iniquity. Not where sin came from, but where the sinner is going to, is of more importance. The seriousness of sin is revealed not so much in its origin as in the destiny to which it dooms the sinner.

A never failing effect of sin is its blinding influence. And no victim of it is for this reason able to realize how blind it has made him. One of the first things which Christ's Redemption enables in man is the recovery of ability to apprehend with all the saints the atrocious character of iniquity. The measure of power to realize how injurious and guilty sin is, indicates the measure of our power of fellowship with Christ and of our power to make progress in the Christian life.

I. THE DAMAGE OF THE DEFICIENT VIEW

In the Christian life our personal relationship with Jesus Christ is vital. This relation is deeply affected by our view of sin. In other words what we think of sin affects our Christian life at its very center and source. The importance therefore of our view of sin can scarcely be exaggerated.

The more we feel the greatness of sin's transgression and guilt, the more do we feel we owe to Him who redeems us from it. In the Christian life there is no substitute for this gratitude, any more than there is a substitute for love to Christ. We love much when we realize we are forgiven much. Christ's Redemption from sin goes much further than our understanding of sin's seriousness, but our appreciation of His work on our behalf cannot go one whit further.

No one can prevent defective views of sin from leading to defective views of the divine sacrifice for sin. When the demerit of iniquity seems unimportant or small, the merit of Christ's sacrifice cannot seem great. They are bound to balance each other in our thought about them. The heights of grace we behold in the Cross of Christ always correspond to the depths of depravity we decry in iniquity. Most of the impoverished and feeble interpretations of Redemption are directly due to weak and inept views of the seriousness of sin.

The view of iniquity we take affects not only our personal relation to the Saviour and our appreciation of His sacrifice for us, it affects also our love of God the Father. We see how far His grace has reached down in proportion as we see the depths of sin's degradation. For this reason underrating the seriousness of sin devitalizes the grace of God. Sin must appear sin that grace may appear grace.

Moreover, our view of sin determines our attitude to it. A shallow estimate of what it means, leads to shallow repentance for it. And the worth of repentance, like that of all other religious acts, depends upon its depth. It is wholly impossible for a superficial estimate of iniquity to lead to a deep sense of guilt. "No serious view of sin," "Not seriously convicted," and "Not soundly converted," follow each other in natural sequence.

VARYING VIEWS OF SIN 263

When David saw how his sin seemed to God, he could never forget it. "My sin is ever before me." He was a man after God's own heart, not in committing sin, but in his adopting the estimate of it which God's own heart takes. This made him humble and patient with other sinners like himself. Even so our attitude to our fellow men is affected by our sense of the seriousness of our own sin before God.

II. THE NATURALISTIC VIEW

In this very important matter of coming to the divine estimate of sin, it is a bad day for us when instead of this we turn away from the teaching of God's Word to the teaching of Naturalism, which invariably cocaines the conscience by belittling the seriousness of sin. But the effect of cocaine soon passes off. Would to God this were so with the effect of Naturalism!

Nothing has done so much to revive Naturalism as has the hypothesis of evolution. Whatever we may think of evolution in other respects, we cannot give it credit for bringing any conviction of the guilt and the seriousness of sin. According to evolution man has kept God's law. He has evolved. He has come a long way up, not out of evil, but out of primeval state. Evolution being the standard, he is not only guiltless but praiseworthy for standing at the top of the process.

Why should the evolutionist like another Naaman go down to the little Jordan of Redemption for any cleansing? Should there chance to be some microscopic particles of the dust from which he has evolved, still clinging to him from former stages of his development, these can with far more dignity be washed away in the nobler streams of the Abana of Philosophy and the Pharpar of science. 'Twere a pity to spoil this evolutionary pipe-dream. But what about pity to man who is infinitely more important than all the dreams of Naturalistic philosophers? For it so turns out that sin, instead of being a little innocent soiling of evolutionary dust, is a deadly disease, a spiritual leprosy, and like Naaman unless the sinner is supernaturally cleansed and healed, he will die in his sins.

Any system of thought that obscures the curse of sin and the cure of Christ is itself a curse. When God and the world are completely separated in thought, a sin-ignoring Deism is then the danger. When God and the world are considered identical, a sin-denying Pantheism is then the danger. When God and Determinism are identified, a sin-excusing Fatalism is then the danger. When God and Nature are identified, a sin-minimizing Naturalism is then the danger.

A man's vocabulary tells a good deal about him. So does the vocabulary of the evolutionist tell much about him. Many are the evolutionary expressions which belittle the seriousness of sin. It has been described as "the unavoidable jostling in the march of human progress," "mere inconvenience like cold or dirt," "the opposition necessary to moral development," "slips in the climb of attainment," "incomplete development," "natural imperfection," "the effect of finiteness," "mere infirmity," "a momentary cloud before the sun," "dirt on the image of a coin," "absence of good," "negativeness," "good in the making," "a blessing in disguise," "a fall upward," and even "a search after God." How the man-destroying, God-defying nature of sin is obscured in all this! Great God of Heaven! Why are men blind to the trend of all this? It is neither the hand nor the voice of Christianity. As President Patton of Princeton says, "Our difficulty is with those who are trying to unite Christian faith and anti-Christian philosophy."[1] That can be done only as Christianity ceases to be Christian.

III. THE INVARIABLE DISABILITY OF SIN

How different is the God-given estimate of sin found in the Scriptures! "The wages of sin is death." Then a cause of death cannot be an addition to life, all naturalistic philosophy to the contrary notwithstand-

---
1. Fundamental Christianity, p. 179.

ing. Let God be true, even if we have to conclude all contrary philosophy closely related to Ananias.

In what way must, lying, theft, hate, treachery, lechery, blasphemy, brutality, bloodshed, lawlessness, viciousness, vice, selfishness, and other forms of ungodliness are in anywise helps to human progress, it is impossible to show. Down through the centuries all the slow advance man has made, has been in spite of sin's hindrance. From first to last it has ever been the relentless enemy drawn up across the path of human progress; and from its deep-dug entrenchments there it is still stubbornly resisting every attempt at human improvement.

The Scriptures tell us that the demons were once good and pure in the service of God; but by sin they fell. With neither angel nor man has sin ever been known to lift upward. It can but reduce beauty to ashes and moral grandeur to ruins.

True, iniquity has been compelled to serve in some way good purposes entirely foreign to its nature. So has the devil himself been used. An enemy is none the less such when his hostility has been overruled to good ends.

No thanks to sin that it has called out the reserves and resources of God, and developed man's religious nature in conflict with it. Praise is not offered to wolves for making farmers good rifle shots. War may make military heroes; but it is none the less hell. Sin may make good spiritual warriors, many religious heroes; but sin is none the less of the devil.

At the beginning of this chapter the effect of defective views of sin upon the Christian life was mentioned. In concludng we may point out the help that comes from adopting the same estimate which we find in God's Word. This view given by the Holy Spirit who convicts of sin as sin, helps us in that it drives us to draw more deeply and fully from the wells of salvation. We do tend to drink more deeply at the fount of the water of life when the Word and Spirit of Christ stirs our souls as to the diabolical character of iniquity. This is true to Christian experience.

When the Word of the Lord grips our minds, it is always with a beneficent effect. Instead, when we excuse our sin, and depend on our self-righteousness, pride, learning, or anything that leaves us "corrupt and contented," we are certainly not moving in the direction of "the life abundant."

God has no varying views on the subject of iniquity. Nor can we have, the more we receive the enlightenment of His Spirit and Word on this matter. The more of death we behold in sin, the more of life may we find in the Redeemer who died to bring us His life.

We must beware of reading God's thought through the colored glasses of proud philosophy or scientific knowledge. Knowledge still puffs up. Sinful human nature is, as it has always been, blind in its resistance of the light of God that shows the serpent gliding away for safety. Any attitude that makes sin safe puts us in danger. A quaint conversation between John Newton and Doctor Taylor, one of the great Hebraists of his day, may close this chapter.

"Mr. Newton, I want to tell you something. I have collated the Hebrew Scriptures fifteen times, and I have never found the doctrine of the Atonement in the Hebrew Scriptures."
"Dr. Taylor, Once upon a time I tried to light my candle with the extinguisher on; and so I am not at all surprised that you have not found the doctrine of the Atonement in the Hebrew Scriptures. And not until you find yourself to be a filthy, lost sinner, although you are a Hebraist, will you find the doctrine of the Atonement in the Hebrew Scriptures."

CHAPTER XXIV

THE MEANING OF SIN

THE meaning of sin is known to us in part only. "Now I know in part," is most appropriate to say at this point. Probably the full meaning of iniquity will never be known by us. The deeper meaning of all things lie in their relation to God; and sin is no exception to this. The fullest revelation of its meaning therefore comes out in the sacrifice of divine Redemption, for this is the fullest expression of sin's meaning to God.

In his monumental work on *"The Christian Doctrine of Sin"* Julius Müller says:

"Evil is not an unintelligible thing, seeing that we allow the *possibility* of it to be a necessity...... Yet, notwithstanding all this, the real point in question, the *realization* of evil, cannot be fully understood. We must acknowledge that evil is in its nature inconceivable, *i. e.*, incomprehensible, seeing that it is realized by arbitrariness, and arbitrariness is a violation being only by usurpation, and in the face of the exclusive claims of moral good. We can understand the connection of its particular manifestations with its principle, but this principle is itself a perversion, it is that which ought not to be. We know that as an action of behaviour it is brought about by means of motives of various kinds, but these motives, when viewed in the light of the divine necessity of moral good, are proved to be shadowy and false, a sphere of unreality which nevertheless exists, and wherein even that perverted principle obtains realization in a world created by God. Evil is the inscrutable mystery of the world; it ever remains in its inmost depth, impenetrable darkness...... Sin in itself still remains incomprehensible, and this incomprehensibleness will of course present itself most clearly when the sin is, in the strict sense of the word a *first sin*, or a *commencement* of sin, wherein the pure will becomes impure by self-determination The truth of the old saying, that 'Satan is the ape or counterfeit of God,' *causa sui*, to make its commencement from itself alone, and to have only itself as its presupposition...... We can conceive of the most perfect perception of evil, that of God, to be only the most thorough recognition of its utter arbitrariness and its violation of all rational connection."[1]

I. POSITIVE AS WELL AS NEGATIVE

Though sin is the Great Negative to God, it has its positive side. The negative can be looked at in two ways at least. There is not only the injury which it has wrought; there is the good it has prevented. Think what a Garden of Eden this earth would be to-day, if all its wealth, resources, and human lives which have been worse than wasted in sin, had been conserved! Had all that man has squandered in bitterness, been used in brotherhood, all hate been love, all ungodliness been devotion to God, at what magnificent altitudes might art, invention, science, education, and human achievement be found to-day!

Both positive and negative aspects are set forth by Principal Fairbairn in the following way:

"Sin is in its positive character the substitution of self for God as the law and end of our being; in its negative character it is transgression or violation of law. We refuse to obey God's will, and instead we obey our own—*i. e.*, we make ourselves into our god, and attempt to force Him and all He has created into servants to our wills, means to our ends. There is therefore, to speak with the older theologians, something infinite in sin."[2]

Dr. Fairbairn goes on to say:

"It is, as it were, the creature attempting to deny to the Creator the beatitude he was created expressly to give. If man misses his mark, so in a sense does God...... Sin is the reign of unfilial feeling in the heart that was made for filial love and where this reigns the created sonship can never fulfil its end, or the creative Fatherhood be satisfied with its unrealized ideal."[3]

Principal Fairbairn had earlier classified the term used to designate iniquity, saying that sin is a religious term, evil a philosophic term, vice an ethical term, and crime a legal term. These terms other than sin may be employed "in a system which knows no God, but with-

---
1. Vol I, p 173, sq
2. The Place of Christ in Modern Theology, p 453
3. Ibid, p 455

out God there can be no sin." In another work he describes sin as follows:

"It is bad as seen in the individual; it mars the Godlike beauty which is native to the soul; it steals away the charm which made it seem to the eye of its Maker very good; it isolates it from the source of life; it removes it from the breast of the Almighty who breathed it into being It grows by what it feeds on, for in sinning there is no cure of sin, there is only increase of the evil."[4]

II. Sin's Immeasurable Meaning

How poorly portrayed by human words is this uncompromising enemy of God, this incomparable foe of man, this unalterable obstacle to human progress! Telling fitly the clog and curse of sin one needs terms that would glow like molten lava, for this Protean thing called iniquity is infinitely more than defect. It is human deformity set on fire of hell; it is the spiritual brimstone burning in the crater which cannot burn out, the volcanic fire of a lost soul. If one could fully feel the ruin and despair to which it finally leads, the burning torture of endless remorse on account of it, his lips might blister and his tongue burn to the roots as he tried to express the words of flame and the thoughts of fire fitly depicting it.

In the most prosaic portrayal of sin one meets this difficulty at the start—it is a maze of bewildering contradictions. It is a builder and a destroyer; it is perfect imperfection; a reality and an unreality; a presence and an absence; a development and a withering; a growth and an atrophy; the impersonal and the personal; the inhuman and the human; a trend away from God yet assailing Him; the denial of God yet the mimicry of Him; and the depreciation of the values of God yet the counterfeiting of them in every way possible.

Some of the meaning of sin may be seen in the attitude which it begets in man toward the God of love and sacrifice. It is moral atheism, the refusal of all

---

[4]. The Philosophy of the Christian Religion, p. 151.

the rights of God, man's alienation and defection from Him, opposition to Him in purpose, antagonism to Him in motive, enmity to Him in feeling, contradiction to His thought, frustration of His affection, perfidy in place of faith in Him, and the dislocation which prevents man from fitting into God's will and desires for human welfare.

Iniquity as a term means that which is wrong, wrung, or twisted out of shape. The term sin, as already said, means missing the true aim, not hitting the mark or gaining the prize God set before us. It prevents man from reaching the goal of his self-fulfilment in God. It is the bane which stops man from coming to his own in God and God from coming to His own in man. It is the worship of self, the vain attempt to elevate something else than God to the throne of God.

The deception of iniquity makes deceit seem a virtue, all good appear evil, all evil appear good, when sin has made personality fully its own. It is spiritual defection, deflection, subversion, moral mal-adjustment, twist of being, the selfial turned into the selfish, the false axis of life, its wrong orbit, lawlessness, unholiness, unrighteousness, culpability, malignity, viciousness, vitiation, violation, outrage, debasement, destruction, knavery, slavery, the abomination of desolation, the pestilence that walketh both in noonday and in darkness.

Sin is poisonous in principle, venomous in spirit, virulent in contagion, and pernicious in penetration. It is vitriol in the eyes of the soul, "ought-not" to the conscience, corruption to the heart, unbelief to the mind, disruption to the affections, blight to moral sense, dissatisfaction to desire, enervation to the will, disintegration to spiritual power, and death to the soul.

III. THE EMPIRE OF EVIL

Sin may be considered from the point of view of the method, aim, and measure of its confederacy. This may be estimated by the nature and extent of its opposition to God. The measure of iniquity is the distance between its deed and what God would have us do, between what it makes us and what God would have us be.

The method of sin, once its deception works, is to use the good in such a way as to make it the enemy of the best, to make use of the good to such an end that it ceases to be good. Its great aim is to displace God. Its spirit is that of rebellion against righteousness, the spirit that makes us "children of disobedience." It is essentially corrupt and corrupting, the soul of untruth dwelling in the true self, and exterminating all that is good and true within it.

Sin is the soul of the great under-world. It opposes confidence in "the Great Oversoul." While it must borrow life from human life, it seems to have a diabolical vitality all its own. It is totally foreign to the essentials of human nature, and totally contrary to divine nature.

Iniquity has organized a confederate world of ungodly spirits. Schleiermacher calls this "the Kingdom of Sin." Haering also says:

"Individual wills are merged into a kingdom of sin."[5] "Not as a sum of self-centered unity, but in conformity with the general laws of our spiritual being, as a communion of wills reacting upon each other."[6]

This innate affinity of spirit in sinful souls is the secret of the homogeneity of the world of all sinful nature. Because of the universality of its spirit, the uniformity of its aim, the identity of its attitude to God, the Word of God calls it, "the kingdom of Satan," and "the world."

IV. COMPLICITY AND MULTIPLICATION

That there is an organized world of evil, finds ample corroberation in human experience. Sinning we find ourselves in the grasp of not only the evil done, but at the same time of an evil beyond it, its kindred evil in the allied world of iniquity. Those who smile at this

---
5. The Christian Faith (Eng Tr), Vol I, p. 541
6. Ibid, p 441.

should undertake some serious work of moral reform or attempt deliverance from invested evil. Every real reform quickly finds that Pilate and Herod become friends, and the confederacy of opposition will have widespread ramifications. It was this coördination of evils which united against our Lord during his life and death, and is the same united power which has always made the battle for righteousness so difficult.

There is an inexplicability in the ubiquity of evil, that world of ungodly spirit present in spite of the surrounding presence of God. Because of it no one sins by his own unaided power. There is an inspiration to evil, a pervading power with a gravitation downward. The pull of this evil attraction is like the undertow that has so often swept the strongest swimmers to a watery grave. Standing on the edge of a tall building with flat roof one feels the suction into space. In somewhat the same way the void of the bottomless world draws and pulls our souls to death.

Sometimes the pressure of this presence of evil is intense. One of our missionaries facing an idol in a heathen temple in China, shook his fist in self-confident threat of its extinction. Immediately all his joints seemed to be unloosed, and a strange weakness overpowered him in so uncanny but complete way that he was glad to drag himself from the place.

At the moment of consent to sin, this evil presence becomes an inflow, and is no longer merely external. Each sin committed seems not only to be a point of contact, but also a link of complicity with the whole collective world of iniquity. The soul by sin is annexed to its territory.

One of the most terrible things about sin is its irresistible power of multiplication. *No one sins once and stops there.* Any impregnation by evil never results in a solitary offspring. Invariably it brings forth a brood. As a Welsh proverb says: "One sin draws a hundred after it." Coleridge presents the same thought:

> "This is the curse of every evil deed
> That, propagating still, it brings forth evil."

The prolific productiveness of sin is one of its worst penalties. That is one awful retribution, the certainty of yet more sinning. Jesus said, "He that committeth sin is the bond-slave of sin." The servile degradation of existing to multiply the accursed progeny of iniquity, is the fate of every sinner. Archbishop Trench has said:

> "Evil, like a rolling stone upon a mountain top
> A child may first impel, a giant cannot stop."

CHAPTER XXV

THE GODWARD EFFECT OF SIN

THE strength of an opposition depends upon that which opposes. In this chapter we shall consider the opposition of sin to God and how far this opposition goes. This is a prime consideration in any serious treatment of the subject.

Primarily, what we think of sin arises from what we think of God. When Deity is taken to be impersonal existence, the resultant estimate of sin is bound to be depreciated to the vanishing point. This is similiar to what happens about prayer. To an impersonal God it is useless to come with requests. The most that can be done is to think high thought, in fact pray to ourselves, and then call that prayer which has ceased to be prayer. In a similar way when God is taken to be but impersonal principle, sin against mere principle ceases to be sin in any real way. Its existence is the futile fancy of foolish fiction—of mortal mind. Supplication and intercession are replaced by mental concentration, in the case of prayer; and transgression and guilt are replaced by assertion of unreality, in the case of sin.

I. THE SOCIAL INTERPRETATION

Not only does abandonment of faith in the personal nature of God destroy the meaning of sin; any viewpoint with diminished range of vision as to its Godward effect proportionately diminishes its meaning.

Just before the World War began, one of our foremost writers and teachers of the social side of Christianity published in the daily press his prophecy that a great revival of the Christian church was about to be ushered in by a re-definition of sin in terms of social obligation. Without doubt this sincere man believed what he said.

Of course we know now that Professor Rauschenbusch was mistaken. What he saw ushered in was the war that broke his heart. His great strength and zeal in this special line of thinking had led him to a false position and a mistaken confidence.

Never has a revival of the Christian Church come by any other than the power of the Holy Spirit; and He invariably uses His own body of truth, the Word which He has inspired. And Scripture does first and last insist on the Godward meaning of sin. The Holy Spirit is not likely to revive the Church with a definition of sin that leaves God out of account. The agelong struggle of the Holy Spirit has been to get men to see from the divine point of view, because it is the true, the essential viewpoint. That sin may appear sin, it must be brought up into the light of the divine presence. Sin has never been known to be sin, except as God has been known to be God.

Our responsibility to God is foundational to all other responsibilities. Because we have obligations to Him, we have obligations to each other. Very little meaning is left in the social obligations when the divine are let out. Our failure to man has far more meaning when we understand it to be because of failure toward God. The deeper meaning of sin is not expressed by social terms, but by the terms of relation to God.

There is no necessity that either the social or the Godward effects of sin be presented in such a way as to obscure one another. In the social we find its horizontal direction, and in the divine its vertical. Multiplying the one by the other we have the solid consideration of its proportions.

II. The Change in Emphasis

Iniquity is a wrong from every point of view, but the greatest of these is the Godward. As already suggested, the most important viewpoint is sin's effect on divine fulfilment. Even in a sinless world man could not fulfill himself in his fellow-man. If we were to confine our view of sin to its social wrong, the Cross of

Calvary would then seem to cast but a dim shadow athwart the earth in place of the full light of Redemption by and unto God.

For many years the absolute sovereignty of God was emphasized and the free-will of man obscured. With less profit this emphasis was reversed. While there is some religious benefit in emphasizing our own will, there is not nearly so much as in emphasizing God's will. It makes a great deal of difference whether in such matters our attention is directed to and centered upon God, rather than upon ourselves; for attention is directive in growth, and is therefore bound to be a controlling factor in the Christian life.

For years the Godward effect of sin was emphasized and its social effect obscured. To less profit and with greater mistake the reversal of this has taken place. We possess far more power to master sin when our attention is fastened upon Him who alone has solved its problem.

It is said that every painting of Nature with no clear outlook to the sky leaves on the mind an impression of repression and confinement. Without what is called "atmosphere," the effect is stifling. Similarly when the heavenward view of sin is left out in our portrayal of it, the sense of its seriousness is more or less stifled, it guilt belittled, and power to combat it is proportionally lessened. The experience of the Church shows plainly that all conceptions of iniquity that ignore its Godward meaning tend to slow down and repress rather than strengthen the Christian life.

III. THE MANWARD EFFECT

Having said all this, let us think of Sin's Godward effect as revealed by its effect on man. Here its injury to God may be calculated by what man is to God. While sin's injury to man is determined by its injury to God, we should realize that sin is far more against man in being against God, than it would be if it were against man alone—if this were possible.

Because of what man is to God through being created to be His child in His own image and likeness, what must the effect upon God be when sin produces in man moral insanity, deranged intelligence about God? To God sin cannot be other than unreason. Even we can see that in proportion as sin enters into man's mind, he cannot reason and think as God does. He cannot regard iniquity in his heart and think divinely.

To know God is the beginning of wisdom and the end of insanity. To begin sin is to end wisdom and to head in the direction of moral imbecility. The fool not only says there is no God; he acts as if there were none. Positively painful to God it must be to see men afflict themselves with this moral and spiritual madness which may become chronic and eternal. Hell is the madhouse of the universe into which God must gather and confine all the incurable from sin's imbecility.

Human nature being spiritually patterned after and grounded in the nature of God, sin has all the more painful effect upon Him because of its disastrous result in man. It could not affect God in one way and man in another. Sound the great depths of man's likeness and relation to God, the vast Godward possibility of his nature, and there we have revealed the depths of the measure of how sin affects God.

Sin directly injures God because it breaks man away from normal relation to Him. Instead of living by faith and love toward Him, receiving love and life from Him, and enjoying filial relations with Him, man becomes His antagonist and realizes an abnormal growth of personality, a self-realization of nature absolutely at variance with Him.

Besides this there is the damage within the social relations. There is so much of God, far more than we think or feel, within the most ordinary of human relations, when sin disrupts any of them, it affects God to a further extent than we are aware. God is so necessary everywhere and so infinitely great, He presents infinitely vast area for injury through His relations to man and among men.

IV. THE PSYCHOLOGICAL VIEW

If the sociological estimate of sin is more or less insufficient, the same is true of the psychological. For example, a psychologist has declared that, "All evil is but misplaced good, all sin but perverted righteousness, and it is as natural as lapse of memory." Here the insufficiency comes from this conclusion utterly outreaching the scope of psychological study. Here the psychological microscope is being used as a telescope. Necessarily it is all out of focus, and is nowise adapted to the use to which it is thus put. When the psychologist paints beforehand his theological picture on the lens of his microscope, men can but laugh when he tells them in all seriousness what he sees as he looks through it. Laplace said he had swept the heavens with his telescope and had not found God. My revered teacher, President Sawyer of Acadia University, remarked that Laplace might as well have swept the kitchen with a broom. What if Laplace had said he swept the heavens with a microscope? That would have been like the psychologist's estimate of sin.

The great psychologist, Professor James Ward, has warned us that "Psychology is not biology." Nor is it theology. In Behavorism it has reached its lowest yet. Psychology has "gone to the dogs" to find out what man is, and how he should live.

True, sin is perversion. We knew that much before the psychologist arrived on the scene. That it is only perversion, and how far its perversion reaches and its effects go, psychology has no means of determining. Sin is sin because of our relation to God, and our relation to Him unavoidably involves the Absolute. Perversion of relation to the Absolute is not a subject for psychology. The psychologist as a psychologist has no business to venture into the realm of the Absolute. The divine is absolute or nothing. Since the shoemaker is wise enough to stick to his last, the psychologist would do well to keep out of theology.

It has become the fashion to-day that, if a man invents some superior order of toothpick, straightway the newspapers send a reporter to interview him as to the wisdom of colonial representation, as a statesman task in framing the policy of the British Empire. Psychology instead of studying perversion within its own defined realm, has itself become perverted.

V. THE ABSOLUTE IN SIN

The Godward effect of sin involves the Absolute, we have just said. Let us think of this a little further, for sin is God's absolute opposite, and its Godward demerit is nothing less than infinite.

In the physical world we find many relative opposites, such as short and long, cold and hot, light and heavy, far and near, weak and strong, small and large, rest and motion. All these being but different degrees of the same thing, are but relative opposites.

Rest and motion may seem to be absolute opposites, but there is no point of absolute rest to be found in the physical universe. Some one may reply that something and nothing are absolute opposites. True, but nothing is an idea, not a physical existence. It is clear then that no absolute opposites can be found in the physical realm. For this reason the more materialistic and naturalistic science, philosophy, or theology becomes, the more out of touch with the Absolute must it be.

The spiritual world is the home of the absolute, while the relative opposite may be found in it too. Here we find the absolute opposites such as, willing and unwilling, true and false, good and bad, honor and disgrace, hate and love, right and wrong, sin and sinlessness. These are not degrees of the same thing. They are all absolutely, not relatively, opposed to each other.

Spinoza said that God has infinite attributes 'in number, though he could name only two, thought and extension. God is the Great Absolute, and sin is the Great Opposite to the Absolute. In no way that we can conceive, are they not absolutely opposed to each other. As in the moral world goodness is infinitely removed from badness, right from wrong, love from hate; so sin is infinitely removed from conformity in any way to the nature of Deity.

VI. Sin's Godward Meaning

Sin is sin because God is God; and God is God only where sin has not had its way. If God could be left out of account, sin would no longer be sin, and God would no longer be God.

We wrong our fellow man. Strictly speaking we sin against God and Him alone. Joseph said, "How can I do this great wickedness and sin against God?" The Prodigal Son pleaded, "Father, I have sinned against heaven and in thy sight." Jeremiah wrote, "We have sinned against Jehovah our God." The Psalmist sang, "Against thee, thee only, have I sinned."[1] He is the unescapable God—unescapable because indispensable. The Godward demerit of sin is therefore indispensable in a true consideration of it, because foundational and fundamental in it.

God is holy: He is all God: He is God in the absolute. Holiness is vastly more than righteousness: it is the Godliness of God, the abolute integrity of Deity. Now every thing that God is in His holiness, sin is not. It is unholiness, the perfect antithesis to Godliness. As to His dependability as God, sin can be depended upon only to oppose it. Sin is faith in having no faith in Him, who is worthy of unlimited faith. The love of God is not so much an attribute of God as of the personal relations of God. There sin would put its attribute of hate in love's stead. Human loves it would empty by making them Godless; and thus answering God's love with hate, and making human love a dying slave to selfishness, it hinders the indwelling of God's love in the human love in which His love would live and move and give it Godlike being.

Withering the natural unselfishness of love in human

---

1. Davidson suggests, "The words, *against Thee only* mean *against Thee, even Thee*; as: 'I will make mention of Thy righteousness, of thine only,' that is, even of Thine (Ps lxxi 16). The words express the judgment of the conscience regarding sin; it is against God." The Theology of the Old Testament, p 233.

life, sin lessens the possibility of the greatest manifestation of God in it, for it is in the unselfish loves in which God lives that He finds the largest and best adapted room for His unselfishness to manifest itself. Iniquity in opposing and frustrating the divine unselfishness in all its sacrificial richness, manifests thereby the absolutely opposite character of its selfish and hateful nature.

If but the feeble and fractional righteouness of man were opposed by sin, it would not be so serious a matter. When it is the absolute antagonism to the infinite perfection of God Himself, the unsullied, unlimited righteousness of God and His acts, then the measure of its unrighteousness can be nothing short of infinite.

Sin's Godward meaning measures the manward need of Redemption. It indicates the source and absolute sacrifice of Redemption, if we are to be saved from the fate and fold of everlasting death. To close with this word from Tennyson:

"The sin that practise burns into the blood,
And not the one dark hour which brings remorse,
Will brand us after of whose fold we be."

CHAPTER XXVI

SIN FROM MODERN VIEWPOINTS

EACH age has its own favorite and familiar point of view. At different times different theological viewpoints have been responsible for the various theological systems which have come down to us. Approach to a man is made easier as soon as his point of view is known.

Perhaps the three most familiar viewpoints in the theology of to-day are Immanence, Experience, and Personality. Sin may be studied from them and the need of Christ and His work seen in a way that appeals to the man of to-day. G. H. Morrison says:

"To-day it is the immanence of God that is claiming the chief thought of Western Christendom. It is on the immanence of God that men insist who profess to be leading the march of human thought. It is not God above us, it is God within us, that is the watchword of the latest systems. And it is deeply interesting to discover what is the meaning of this revolution, and what are the causes that have led to it.

"Well, then, if I mistake not, the chief causes of this change are two. The one is the devotion of our age to science, and the other is the modern delight in nature. Our fathers thought far more of heaven than we do. It is not heaven men study now—it is the earth. With splendid devotion men have been studying nature, learning her laws, discovering her methods; and then when we were in danger of forgetting the wonder and gladness of it all, there have come the poets with their annointed eyes, and shown us what was behind the veil.

"It is not theologians who have been most powerful in altering the emphasis in our thought of God. It has been men like Wordsworth in the sphere of poetry, and men like Darwin in the sphere of science. For the one has taught us to feel the mystic presence that broods in the lonely places of the world; and the other has shown us in orchid and in earthworm an exquisite and unfathomable wisdom. This is why there is such intense interest now in any theology that proclaims God's immanence. It precisely meets the spirit of an age that has been trained and taught as ours has been." [1]

---
1. The Wings Of The Morning, 185

I. The Immanental View

Let us first think of sin's effect on God's immanence and the need it has created of Redemptive immanence. Even this doctrine of divine immanence sin straightway turns into dangerous, anti-christian panthesism. Dr. Morrison admits this has come to pass when it is said, "There is no God, save the God who breathes in our humanity." He goes on to enumerate that then "We cease to have a God who is a person." "Bringing God so near, the pantheist really puts Him far away." "Again, the popular pantheism of today is also fatal to human personality." "Slip the anchor of the living God, and you slip the anchor of accountability." "The popular pantheism of today is certain to put our moral life in jeopardy and must inevitably destroy the sharp distinction between good and evil." From this Dr. Morrison turns to Christ:

"The moral power of the cross of Christ has operated in a two-fold way. It has not only made goodness very beautiful. It has also made sin exceedingly sinful. A man may be a Christian though he parts with much that was regarded as vital by the fathers; but no man can ever be a Christian who treats sin in a light and easy way. 'God commended His own love to us in that while we were yet *sinners,* Christ died for us.' The meaning of that love will grow or lessen, according to our measurement of sin. And hence it is that when men have most deeply felt the wonder of the love of God in Christ, they have felt at the same time the guilt of sin, and known that it was exceeding sinful. Now it is just that moral heritage that is like to be lost in the teaching of to-day. It is a bad thing to vilify humanity; I believe it is even worse to deify it."

Looking at God's immanence in a way that does not deny or obscure His transcendence, we may say the indwelling of God is essential to all that He has created, not for its preservation only, but for its part in the great scheme of universal order and progress.

In His physical realm the Creator dwells and manifests Himself according to the measure of its capacity. Because of this immanence the starry heavens are able to exhibit their sublime, resplendent harmony. No wonder that the soul of man yearns as he beholds the solemn majesty of their perfect order. There we find Nature's greatest object-lesson on the beauty and benefit of the divine presence and control.

While the harmony of the heavens in their vast array is glorious in grandeur beyond words to describe, the very stars are far outnumbered by hosts of human sins in a world of moral disorder. One world is full of galaxies of glories; the other has chaos piled on chaos.

The disorder everywhere today apparent on earth announces that the one great source of order, the regulating presence of God, has been seriously interfered with, just where it is worth most. In a way the soul of the smallest child offers greater room for divine indwelling than does the whole material universe.

Nothing purely physical can contain the intensity and richness of the divine immanence that human personality can. By means of this dwelling of God within the soul He confers the greatest blessing and honor it is possible for Him to bestow. It grants not only privilege but also possibility — that of development, achievement, and satisfaction to man.

II. THE DISPLACEMENT OF GOD BY SIN

The presence of sin in human life means that God is proportionately absent. Iniquity is essentially God-absence, godlessness; and in this godlessness God cannot dwell. He cannot abide in that which is utterly opposite to His character, aim, and desire.

That it is possible for sin to enter human life is but the other side of the possibility of God's expulsion. The compulsion of His own nature expels God from a work of iniquity. Sin's presence is then but the other side of God's absence. We hold to the divine omnipresence in Nature; but in the moral and spiritual world where sin has found existence, we cannot hold to it. This displacement we may now consider.

It has been found that a stone weighs as much less in water as its own bulk of water weighs, for it has displaced that much water. The spiritual weight of sin may be estimated by the amount of divine displacement it has caused. In proportion to sin's extent the divine immanence is withdrawn. The greater the sin, the greater damage both to divine immanence and that from which it withdraws.

In a world of sin God cannot be omnipresent. Here are idolatry, blasphemy, theft, hate, lying, covetousness, uncleanness, torture, suicide, murder, and inhumanity and ungodliness always. Such iniquities and God do not occupy the same space or place in human lives.

To this it may be objected that since God does not occupy space as physical things do, He also does not occupy spiritual place as created spiritual existences do; and that divine withdrawal still leaves Him omnipresent in surrounding presence. There is truth in this: God cannot be put out of His world even by sin. But He cannot dwell in sin, nor can He dwell in the same place that sin dwells? He may dwell all about it; but where sin is, He is not.

God's immanence needs something in which to dwell; but sin is the condition or situation that makes His immanence impossible. Take for example the marriage relation. Iniquity can by one evil act dissolve it. God cannot dwell in this relation when it has been destroyed by sin. Sin "when it is perfected brings forth death." This death is the divine withdrawal. Out of the destroyed relations of life there is the full divine withdrawal. They are dead because dead to divine immanence.

God is the soul of all true progress. Because God and sin are mutually exclusive, sin has the power in this way to disconnect the wheels of progress from their mainspring in the divine indwelling. Where sin dwells, the power that makes for advancement is absent. In iniquity the power that makes for deterioration and destruction is present. When God dwells in the human mind by the Holy Spirit it is led on to new and greater realms of truth. When sin dwells in the mind, instead of having the light of life, its very light is darkness. "He abode not in the truth because the truth was not in him."

III. TRANSCENDENT AND IMMANENT

God may be present when not immanent. He is present in the soul He is seeking to win to Himself, but He has not become immanent in it by union with Christ. Immanence is the integration of His presence, the organization within and identification of it with the soul. This leads us to remark that perhaps it is better to say, God is not omni-immanent though omnipresent. Because God is personal and Nature impersonal, God is more present in it than immanent. Because man is personal He is never fully present in him till immanent.

Here we come to the relation of God's immanence and transcendence. Usually there is this distinction made between the two: God in relation to Creation and God beyond or above what Nature is capable of holding relation to. But there is His transcendent immanence, the immanence within the Trinity. The Father dwells in the Son and the Son in the Father, and the Holy Spirit reciprocally dwells in both.

There is that in God's Being or nature too great and high to be contained in or related to any creation, whether physical or spiritual. In this transcendence His greater greatness lies. There lie the resources of His Tri-Personal Nature. We must beware of thinking of this transcendence as quantitatively outside and beyond the universe. It is rather qualitative, the divine above and unlimited by any relation to creation.

Through God's immanence the resources of His transcendence mediately come into relation to human life. "There is but one Mediator between God and man, the man Christ Jesus." Even so there is but one mediation of God's transcendence, through His immanence.

Here we meet another view of the seriousness of sin. As it interferes with the indwelling of God, it interferes with the mediating channel through which flow down the transcendent resources of God. President Mullins expresses this truth as follows:

"God's transcendence is a truth to be kept always in mind. Its correlative truth is God's immanence in the world. God is everywhere immanent (that is, he indwells) in nature. He also indwells in man so far as his body and his moral constitution are concerned. But God is not immanent in man's sin—and guilt-consciousness as he is elsewhere. Sin has separated man from God. Yet God must dwell in man if man is to become God's holy son." [2]

Without over-refinement of reasoning, we may say, there is the immanence of God necessary to created existence, and there is also the immanence in man necessary to self-realization in God. When the channel of this divine immanence is choked by sin, the stream of God's transcendent blessings is held back and self-fulfilment in God is thus made impossible. Here the resources of the transcendent immanence to establish a new order of divine immanence came to the rescue of man. The Father and the Holy Spirit sacrificially immanent in the Son, so to speak, transferred its resources into man's devasted soul. How this was achieved we may further draw on Dr. Mullins to explain:

"The Incarnation, therefore, is the descent of the transcendent moral ideal in God into the human race. It is God becoming immanent in the race. It is the transcendent God becoming immanent in the world among free beings who are held by the power of sin, in order to its salvation. The death of Christ on the cross was thus the God of holy love projecting himself into the life of the race by overcoming the sin-death principle in the race. In other words, God's immanence thus becomes a new law of life, operating in an ethical and spiritual manner for the salvation of men. It is a new life force acting graciously for human redemption. If Christ's approach to man had stopped short of dying, if he had been translated without tasting death, he would have remained apart from man at the point of his deepest need. He would have then disclosed a shining moral goal indeed, but it would have been left suspended in midair with no point of contact for sinners. It would have remained transcendent. Men would have remained powerless to attain it." [3]

The need of Christ because of sin is thus seen to

---
2. The Christian Religion In Its Doctrinal Expression, p 320
3. Ibid, p 320.

reach from the depths of man's loss of God both immanent and transcendent to the heights of the divine transcendence which by sacrificial resources brought to him the help of a redeeming immanence. The immanence of the sacrificed Son of God in the soul of man was the extent of the need which sin had caused. So sin's obstruction was over-ridden, and God came back into human life by "a new and living way," in a new life-giving immanence of the Great Friend who died for us. Of this Theodore Parker sang:

> "O thou great friend to all the sons of men,
> Who once appear'dst in humblest guise below,
> Sin to rebuke, to break the captive's chain,
> To call thy brethren forth from want and woe!—
> Thee would I sing. Thy truth is still the light
> Which guides the nations groping on their way,
> Stumbling and falling in disastrous night,
> Yet hoping ever for the perfect day.
> Yes, thou art still the life; thou art the way
> The holiest know,—light, life, and way of heaven."

CHAPTER XXVII

SIN AND EXPERIENCE

THE knowledge we have by reason or from some purely intellectual source has its value, but some larger knowledge or a stronger mind may come and upset it and our conclusions drawn from it. The knowledge of experience is not like that. No larger experience can upset the knowledge that water quenches thirst or that bread satisfies hunger. In other words, the knowledge of experience is unassailable except by other experiential knowledge; and as a rule experience agrees with Experiential Knowledge.

Men are most impressed with the knowledge of experience. Byron refers to this when he says: "Oh, who can tell, save he whose heart hath tried." And Emerson declares, "Only so much do I know as I have lived." That only experiential knowledge is possible and real, is not so.

It is to the credit of any theology when its point of view is largely experiential. To refuse other knowledge would be foolish. If a man is going to a new country, it is well to avail himself of the knowledge of others' experience, but the possibilities, resources, and a thousand other things are not experiential knowledge of the country.

In theology the experiential method is overdone when things not experiential in nature are measured by things of experience. Iniquity is experience, however; and we may think of it from this viewpoint. The discussion of the previous chapter may suggest to us that sin's resistence of God's immanence must be a painful experience to Him. He cannot but suffer when caused to withdraw from the lives, needing Him indispensably, because made for Him exclusively.

I. God's Experience with Sin

In one important particular the divine nature is unlike ours. It is an absolute symmetry. This means that divine experience also is a symmetry in every respect. We are often made happy or unhappy over very little, often satisfied or disturbed by mere trifles. That this is largely due to unbalanced nature, seems clear. On the other hand God's feelings equal His knowledge; His knowledge equals His desire; His desire equals His wisdom, His wisdom equals His love, His love equals His power. In a word He has as much capacity for suffering as for satisfaction, for sacrifice as for holiness.

Looking at the symmetry of God's experience, we see that it balances with things affecting it. God's satisfactions or dissatisfactions always equal their sources. His feelings are always in proportion to that which occasions them. He is never over-joyous nor over-sorrowful, never under-pained nor under-pleased.

Because God's experience is perfectly balanced, His sorrow and dissatisfaction because of sin measure up exactly with the character and extent of it. His is the only experience which fully represents in exact equivalence the real character of sin and the damage caused by it. He alone perfectly comprehends the ruin it has brought to man and the injury to Himself. And He alone has the sensibilities of feeling, moral nature, and sympathy commensurate with unlimited knowledge.

The deeper wounds which sin has made are not on the sinner but on his God. In Him there is infinitely finer sensitiveness; and besides there is so much more of Him to suffer. A child may suffer the few moments of actual death—and far less than appearances would indicate. Not so with the mother! Because it is her child, she feels a thousand deaths in seeing one. It is harder to have a deeply loved one die than to die. So must it be with the God who is *love*.

What countless deaths has God felt in beholding the numberless soul-deaths of His children. We do not know how a thousand years can possibly be to God as "a watch in the night" or as brief as the bygone days, if during this time He is bearing the agonizing reaction to human sin. His love suffers far beyond that of the best mother earth ever saw or of all mothers together that ever lived. Surely this must make the days and years seem long until the fulness of time be come, when sin shall be forever cast out. And in this age-long suffering of the wrong of sin there is not the satisfaction of the suffering of the sacrifice of Redemption. There is no joy set before that suffering to help in enduring it.

Sin in God's experience inflicts the penalty of His nobility, even as the purity of Christ's self-sacrifice sent Him to the cross. He could be the hope of the world only by enduring bitter pangs of experience as He passed through the process of being perfected in death.

"Our dearest hopes in pangs are born,
The kingliest kings are crown'd with thorns."

What numberless volumes there are in the library of divine experience! What chapters of suffering in the history of God! No thought of man can travel the lengths and breadths and depths and heights of the divine experience because of sin. God alone could tell His own story of His own suffering; and then it would take the language of infinity to express it with "the groanings which cannot be uttered." Never are we more painfully conscious of the utter inadequacy of human speech than when endeavoring to portray the experience of God in penalty, suffering, and sacrifice for sin.

II. Human Experience in Sin

There are experiences of God due to our sin which are peculiar to Him, and also those He shares with us, for He suffers both with man and also on His own account. Then, too, all divine suffering and experience in general are necessarily on vaster scale and in greater intensity than ours.

Of course, to a limited degree we may judge of the divine experience by what our own has been. Sin cannot be one thing in the experience of man and another in that of God. Moreover man cannot sin and God not be affected experientially by it. There cannot be Absalom's treason and filial callousness without David's wail, "O Absalom, my son, my son! Would to God I had died for thee!" His child cannot poison himself and the fond father not be affected.

That is one side of the matter. On the other, man is dazed and stupified by his sin and proportionately unconscious of its hurt. Yet to some extent he realizes the failure and trouble it has brought into his life. Only by the awakening of Redemption are his powers quickened and enlarged to realize in the fuller way the folly of sin.

> "I know
> The past and thence will I essay to glean
> A warning for the future, so that man
> May profit by his errors, and derive
> Experience from his folly."

So said Shelley. We may say in prosaic way that the experience of man because of sin is missing the deepest satisfaction he might have known, that of the fellowship of achievement with God. Instead, one by one the normal joys of life depart. He feels a fearful famine in his soul. The vitals of his being gnaw, starving for the bread of everlasting life. His pangs of spiritual thirst are but increased as he drinks the salt waters of selfishness. He eats the cinders of burnt-out pleasures. "He feedeth on ashes."

Defiled and defiling by his sin, man wallows in the sty of his lust. He turns the palace of love into a hovel of hate. His possible heaven becomes a potential hell. To quote Shelley again:

> "For when the power of imparting joy
> Is equal to the will, the human soul
> Requires no other heaven."

The autobiography of the sinner records that at first he finds his desires a blind brood yelping for their sustenance; but later they have developed into a pack of devouring wolves, ready to destroy each other in the mutiny of conflicting hungers and impulses. Creeping paralysis of the moral nature comes on, growing callousness of soul, dissolution of faith, decay of love, the true self gradually being undone by the strengthening of the sin-self. Life is then filled with the heat and burnings of incipent hell, hating itself, wishing it had never been, it dies the living death while waiting for the lesser death, and then the death that never dies.

Such in imperfect summary are some of the features of human experience when sin has lost its power of enchantment, and its drugged conscience awakens to the filth and wreckage of sin's debauch, the hated hell within, the hopeless conflict without.

Through the little channel of man's mind it would take all eternity to pass all there is in the full swelling ocean of misery through iniquity. The horror of it all no man could feel in one moment and live. No wonder the Christ-heart broke on the Cross as He wearily, lonely looked forth upon its black and unending billows. The little about it our poor intelligence can now understand and utter, is as a broken whisper in the antechamber of the eternity where the full truth shall dawn upon us of the appaling need Our Lord died to meet.

III. SIN AS DISEASE

Another viewpoint of experience with relation to sin takes on a clinical character. James in his well-known book, *The Varieties of Religious Experience,* discusses at length "The Sin-Sick Soul." The outstanding work of this character by W. Mackintosh Mackay devotes a volume of three hundred pages to its consideration. He begins with the evisceration of experience by philosophies of religion which leave it little better than a beautiful corpse. He quotes Max Müller as saying: "A religion without experience is no religion."

Turning to the Scriptures he finds the remedial view of salvation emphasized. Paul's interpretation of it agrees with this:

"No doubt to Paul salvation appears rather as a resurrection from the dead than as a recovery from disease. In this, however, he is only speaking proleptically. The basal idea of his thought about sin is that it is a malady so mortal that its victims are already as good as dead . . . Philosophically, indeed, disease is just *death working in life*. Death and life are present side by side in every diseased organism. And the same is true of the soul. So long as it is in the power of sin it is under the power of death."[1]

The author goes on to discuss freedom from this viewpoint of sin as a disease. The sinner, he says, is limited in his freedom; but has enough of it to make him responsible. He has the same freedom a sick man has. He feels like a man in the grip of paralysis.

Mackay uses Henry Drummond's phrase, "spiritual diagnosis," in pleading for sympathetic rather than "cast-iron" treatment of the sinner. For remedy of this malady he would restate the Gospel method as based on "the experience of salvation from the disease of sin through communion with God in His Son Jesus Christ."[2] In other words the divine remedy for sin is union with God through faith in the remedial value of Christ's sufferings on our behalf.

The chapter on "The Symptoms of Sin" comes closer to our subject of sin and experience. In Tennant's treatment explaining the origin of sin as due to the conflict of "the Ape" with a higher reason which has slowly evolved, Mackay finds little promise. The symptoms he names are: depression of spirits, the sense of guilt or spiritual pain, moral paralysis, and the loneliness of hate of God and man.

Before discussing the diseases of "the flesh," soul, and spirit, the author deals with predisposition to the disease of sin from heredity's bias to evil, unhealthy environment, and propagation by personal contact. Sin may be epidemic, recurrent as in backsliding, and it is the cause of, as well as caused by, spiritual anæmia.

This incomplete though extended abstract of a very

---
1. The Disease and Remedy of Sin, p 2
2. Ibid, p 13.

interesting treatment of the experience of sin as a disease may be concluded by the quotation:

> "Thy wounds are five: two in thy feet,
> Two in thy hands and one within
> Thy side, that pierced thy heart divine.
> Yet what are thy five wounds to mine?
> The innumerable wounds of sin,
> Wherewith my death is nigh complete!
>
> "Behold my wounds transcending even
> Thine own! And heavenly Surgeon haste.
> Heal what is not past healing: yea,
> And with thy kind knife cut away
> Mortified parts that burn and waste.
> Thy probe, thy lancet, are of Heaven."

CHAPTER XXVIII
SIN'S TREATMENT OF CHRIST

SIN is essentially personal. If man were not a person, he could not sin; and if God were not a person, He could not be sinned against. The theology which dispenses with God's personality is perfectly consistent in dispensing with the existence of iniquity. And yet this is not so much consistence as persistence of incapacity. It is scarcely consistence, that the man who is blind to the heavens overhead, is blind also to the earth underneath.

The Son of God came to reveal God to man. He also came to reveal man to himself. It requires personality to make a full revelation of personality. If Christ were not God in person, the most He could do would be to make a revelation about God. And to man the divine Son could not make the Father known except by becoming a human person. His humanity He took on by the Incarnation, became the vehicle of His revelation. To reveal the pure personality of God the human vehicle of expression had to be pure. Christ's sinlessness made His full manifestation of the Father possible.

A Brahmin tells of one day watching an ant-hill. He moved so that his shadow fell upon the ants. They seemed frightened by the sudden shadow. He thought to himself, if I could become an ant without ceasing to be a man, I could tell them not to fear man. Immediately the thought seized him that this is perfectly parallel to the Christian doctrine of the Incarnation. And so he came to Christ.

I. THE LIGHT OF JESUS' LIFE ON SIN

God's perfection brought by the Incarnation into the midst of human life, was also brought thereby into the midst of the realm of sin. The Son of God could not live a perfect human life without at the same time revealing the imperfection of the lives to which He came. The perfect purity of His personality could not but stand out in contrast to the impurity about Him in human life.

Then also there is the very marked contrast between Christ's treatment of sinners and sinners' treatment of Christ. The white light of His sinless character and perfect life of sacrifice revealed the attitude of God to sinful man. The attitude which these sinful sons of men took to this revealed attitude of God, showed the Godward attitude of sin. To behold best the exceeding sinfulness of sin, it is still necessary to see it in the white light of this life of God receiving the assaults of sin from every direction. What sin did to the Sinless One tells unmistakeably its generic quality and accursed character.

Sinlessness, to be such, must be perfectly positive toward God. Everything in Christ's life and growth came there through perfect response on His part to the Father and the Holy Spirit. So He grew up sinless because of His perfectly Godward self-realization. Herein lies the great difference between His mode of living and ours: every possibility of response to God and service to man He turned into act and personality. He did not go part way, He went all the way in every sacrificial possibility God opened up before Him. In every act He reached the utmost of self-forgetful service, the righteousness of perfect unselfishness, or perfect interest in others.

In our lives at their best we realize but in part this self-forgetful, God-remembering, man-helping righteousness. Our faith in it is limited; our love to God and man goes only so far; our obedience to God in any matter is never absolutely flawless. He ever went to the utmost in faith in God, in love to God and man, and in obedience to the Father. His constant and perfect unselfishness excluded the possibility of unbelief in the sacrificial. His unlimited love excluded all chance of hate. At every step His life realized to the full the will and desires of God the Father; and thus

He emptied all possibility of failing the Father in any way.

In the "emptying and becoming" of self-realization He emptied every possibility of self-ward, self-centered realization by full and unlimited Godward realization. He did not partly prefer God's way and will. He kept back no part of Himself in the sacrifice for God to redeem man.

Compare this with the trend of the growth in Judas Iscariot's personality. He began with preferring the good to the best and ended with preferring the evil to the good. Jesus' choice was always the best rather than the good; and never the good in place of the best. The Christ-life was centered in the gain of absolute good, while His unfortunate betrayer centered his life in the relative good of personal gain, which became personal gain at the price of evil to the *best*. When a man seeks but relative good, absolute evil is present with him.

When we seek some relative good at the expense of the highest and best, we turn good into evil. This is the way the good is made an enemy to the best. To Christ the best was never centered in personal gain, but in personal sacrifice.

Judas passed from one downward stage to another, till he reached the state where he was captivated by the deception that he could gain in a material way at the expense of the highest spiritual gain. So for a shadow he traded the substance of highest value, the highest loyalty of soul to the highest and best he knew. So Jesus and Judas realized absolutely opposite possibilities of personal growth. One lived sinless self-realization, the other self-realization in sin.

II. SIN'S ATTITUDE TO CHRIST

Because Jesus Christ was a true and perfect revelation of the character of God, sin's treatment of Him was a true and perfect revelation of its character. For the first time the Godward attitude of iniquity was visibly manifested in full measure. Because of who

SIN'S TREATMENT OF CHRIST 299

Jesus Christ was, sin had opportunity and scope to reveal itself in finality.

If those who opposed Jesus Christ, denied His teaching, fought His love, and at last put Him to the most cruel death they knew, had not been badly deranged by sin, it would have been as natural for them to trust and love Him, as it is for a child to love and trust its mother. He was the most trustworthy and lovable personality that earth ever saw. Then the treatment that sinners accorded Him, limns the blackness of sin's hate against the immaculate whiteness of God's love.

There is the situation where sin cunningly hides its real character. It must always begin with deception. There it dare not show itself as it is. Then it disguises itself with the appearance of good. But in these poor dupes of sin the initial stage had been far, far passed. Sin was ending its process, finishing its work in them. Yet a worse thing they could do than put the Christ to death. They could under the inward impact of the Spirit of God refuse to accept from God this death of His Son as His sacrifice for sin. Denney says in this connection:

"All the people who had responsibility with the death of Jesus knew something of what they were doing, or they would have had no guilt and no need of forgiveness. But they did not know everything, or their guilt would have been final, and forgiveness impossible. It is remarkable that unpardonable sin in the New Testament is always represented as sin against Christ, and against God's salvation as present in Him . . . It does not need to be proved that the deliberate rejection of Christ is unpardonable; it is in point of fact the deliberate rejection of pardon."[1]

When the divine light of the white life of the incarnate Son of God shone forth fully on earth, sin in opposing and killing Him could not mask itself. It could only reveal itself. Dan Crawford related that one time he inquired of his native preachers just what they thought of Christ's death. One of them said: "In the death of Christ God was drawing sin on, until it

---

1. The Christian Doctrine of Reconciliation, p 221

completely unmasked itself." Surely this African preacher had been taught of the Holy Spirit!

When one begins to take in the proportions of that sacrificial life of the Son of God, who he was, how he lived, what He said, the way He loved, he feels that of all blindnesses this was most terrible when there was so much to see and the best ever possible to be seen.

"He might have reared a palace at a word,
  Who sometimes had not where to lay his head.
  Time was when he who nourished crowds with bread
Would not one meal unto himself afford.

"He healed another's scratch; his own side bled,
  Side, feet, and hands with cruel piercings gored.
  Twelve legions girded with angelic sword
Stood at his beck, the scorned and buffeted.

"Oh, wonderful the wonders left undone,
  And scarce less wonderful than those he wrought!
  Oh, self-restraint, surpassing human thought,
To have all power yet be as having none!
Oh, self-denying love that thought alone
For needs of others, never for its own."

The thing that perhaps most of all condemns sin is that the more self-denying the love, the more this love provokes sin's worst. God's goodness always incites sinful nature to further badness; and the greater the goodness, the greater the incitement to badness. The stronger the sacrificial effort, the greater the evil with which sin meets it. Never has there been any goodness of God on earth, but sin takes occasion by it to perpetrate some evil. For every benevolence of the Father there arises the malevolence of iniquity. The greater the grace of God, the more ungraciousness is aroused in sin to show itself.

So it came to pass that when God manifested His greatest goodness and largest love in the gift and sacrifice of His Son, sin had unprecedented opportunity to manifest its atrociousness and utter inexcusableness. "He had yet one, a beloved son; he sent him last unto them." And the ultimate in love and sacrifice proved to be the most powerful arousement of all for sin to do its very utmost. So sin crowned Him with thorns, scourged His back, spat upon His face, nailed Him to the tree of shame, mocked His dying agonies, and taunted Him till His heart broke.

III. THE CRUCIFIXION'S REVELATION

Natively, viciously, and virulently anti-divine is sin. Its demonic hate of God is such that it could not tolerate on earth the presence of God Incarnate. From first to last iniquity strained every power it inhabited to thwart His mission and destroy His life. It would have murdered Him when a babe, if divine intervention had not prevented it. From crowding Him out of the inn at His birth to crowding Him out of Human life at Calvary, sin bore one unvarying attitude toward God manifest in the flesh.

As soon as "the Word became flesh and dwelt among us," sin found as never before a faithfulness to God it could fight, a perfect righteousness it could crown with thorns. It smote the head that never went astray in thought. It spat its venom in the face of matchless love, marred by its vile vengeance. A divine form it nailed to the cruel cross, and made its spear-thrust into the very heart of divine devotion.

This treatment of Christ in crucifying Him showed the very soul of sin to be nothing less than relentless assault upon God Himself. As Joseph Parker once said in his dramatic way: "Sin is the clenched fist; the blow struck; its object — the face of God Almighty!"

It may somewhat excuse the blinded tools of sin to say, they knew not what they did, but it does not excuse sin itself. That which inspired them to do this, yet left them insensible in a measure to what they did, is all the more terrible therefor. Because it robbed them of the power of moral feeling and spiritual vision, rendered them fatally insensible to divine beauty, goodness, righteousness, and holiness as it is in God, the fatal features of iniquity in all its hideous ugliness photographed themselves on the pages of human history.

The drunkenness so brutalizing a man that he slays his loving wife and little children, is all the more terrible therefor. So sin filled men's hearts and spirits with demonic hate toward Love Incarnate. It incited them to the murderous hostility that unfeelingly tortured to death the Prince of Life. They were intoxicated with sin's devil-driven fury. The treatment of Jesus Christ meted out to Him by sin shows it to be indefensible, reprehensible, absolutely culpable. Its treatment of God in Christ reveals it as unutterably damnable.

> "Ye hearts that love the Lord,
> If at this sight ye burn,
> See that in thought, in deed, in word,
> Ye hate what made Him mourn."

CHAPTER XXIX

SELF-REALIZATION IN SIN

SELF-REALIZATION may or may not be self-fulfilment. It is simply the process of personal realization or becoming, whether it be good or whether it be evil. There is self-realization in sin, but never self-fulfilment in it. To grow in sinful personality is to be moving in the opposite direction to self-fulfilment in God.

Self may be a self for God, a self not for self; or it may be a self for self. In the latter case it acts on the thoughts, desires, ambitions, and purposes of self-will. Back of that is faith in self apart from God. This is followed by the longing after the realization according to this faith. "The thing we long for, that we are." The accumulation and organization of personal growth take form according to the character of our faith and its desire and purpose and will. This is called self-determination.

George Eliot speaks of "the miserable aims that end in self." This is an inversion of the process of life. It means the impoverishment of personality. Self-realization in sin grows incapacity for God and all good. It enlarges incompatibility with God and all that is like Him. The soul is more and more out of adjustment with God and the universe. There is increasing inability to understand God and the meaning of all things. When a man "concenters all in self," he attempts to be god and end of his own existence. He then worships the creator of his sinful self.

I. Self-Conscious Self-Realization

Every iniquity which man commits is a self-realization that falsely accuses God of not being good enough to command devotion to Him. It blames Him for not being competent as God, not dependable enough to warrant the faith in Him that gives Him His place. Sin accuses God of lack of interest in us, and differs with Him as to what is our good and for our good. The self-realization of selfishness breeds utter unreasonableness and perfect self-deception.

Being out of tune with God and disconnected from the help of His surrounding mind, the selfish mind increases the shallowness and distortion of its thinking. No man thinks deeply or sanely who keeps himself in the forefront of his thinking. Egotistic thinking is like a spavined limb. It limps in pain.

The theological thinking of today is not yet emancipated from the folly of setting forth self-consciousness as a normal process of thought. It is a strange persistence of false psychology that puts self-consciousness in place of simple consciousness. Consciousness of self differs in process not at all from consciousness in general. In consciousness of self, self must be made the object in precisely the same way that anything else would be made the object in the subject-object process of consciousness. But self-consciousness thrusts the self in between the subject and object of consciousness. It projects self into every thought and consideration. Self-consciousness is the abnormal consciousness of selfishness. It is the psychological center of a sinner's consciousness. Self-consciousness is as different from normal consciousness, as self-love is different from normal love. Other-consciousness is that which is normal to normal personality. A mother is not self-conscious but child-conscious. The selfish ego is never fully conscious of anything but itself. And the very fires of hell are lit in the unescapable self-consciousness of the sinner.

The love of self not rooted in the love of God builds a void into the soul that belongs to the bottomless pit. Self as belonging to God is slain by the love that excludes God. "For love of self his very self he slew." Swedenborg says: "Self-love and love of the world constitute hell."

Self-realization in blindness dooms a man to incapacity to see as God does, really not to see at all. The blindness of those that will not see, becomes the blindness that cannot. This is why the poverty of iniquity is preferred to the riches of Redemption.

II. Self-Realization in Delusion

As holiness is the Godliness of God, so selfishness is the sinfulness of sin. Self-realization in selfishness affects our entire nature at the most strategic point, the principle of organization, the integration and personalization of spirit.

Selfishness never wills wisely, never loves freely, never lives deeply or fully. Self-interest is the smallest and meanest possible. When self is the first and central consideration, all the powers of personality are restricted, enslaved, imprisoned within its narrow limits; and painful congestion of diseased interest then brings its own acute suffering. Life then swings out no farther than the little radius selfishness allows. It is like a horse in a field tied to a stake with a short tether, and the ground eaten bare and trodden hard within the little circle. The tether tends to get wound up around the stake. So selfishness brings life at last to a complete standstill and to starvation in the midst of plenty.

Self-realization in sin might be defined as that process by which God is lost, and the powers by which we possess Him and all else save sin are withered to complete atrophy. When a man loses God, he loses himself. By sin the soul is lost; and when a man loses his soul, he can lose nothing more.

All power of possession dies with the death of life in God. Like the dog in the fable dropping the bone for the shadow, iniquity drops the gain of reality and grasps at its shadow. So sin snatches at the shadow of selfish greatness, and drops the reality of true greatness found only in love and loyalty to God.

How fatal is the delusion which comes by iniquity! The life-quest of satisfaction apart from God is absolutely impossible of realization. This deception due to sinful self-realization reminds us of another fable. According to it, man pursues a beautiful but elusive maiden all day long. At its close the disguise disappears, and in the gathering twilight he finds her changed into a hideous old hag.

The power of sin's false attraction determines the false orbit by which the soul becomes a "wandering star to which is reserved the blackness of darkness for ever." In the second volume of Müller's great work, *The Christian Doctrine of Sin,* he quotes these lines:

> "In vain, in vain do self-willed spirits strive
> To climb the lofty heights of purity;
> Self-limitation gives the power to rise,
> And law alone can give us liberty."

III. THE PERSONALIZATION OF SIN

In early stages of its growth personality builds into itself both good and evil, but not at the same time and in the same act. We cannot move in opposite directions of self-realization at the same time. We may retrace our steps back and forth between good and evil. Soon the movement shows inclination to be less in one direction and more in the other; and one line of personal development begins to predominate over the other. Finally, it supersedes it.

Emptying the possibility of going in one direction by going in the other, personality becomes a realization of that which tends to recur in the same direction. More and more the emptying becomes completer, and the recession in the opposite direction goes further and further. The becoming is also completer in keeping with the emptying.

There is a point sooner or later reached in personal becoming where the desires of God are either reciprocated, or refused. There is acceleration of self-realization that reaches its cumulation; and then God becomes either wholly foreign to personality or permanently immanent in it. In all self-realization the gravitation of moral nature sets in either wholly to-

SELF-REALIZATION IN SIN

ward God or wholly away from Him. The Closing chapter of the Word of God so expresses it:

"He that is unrighteous, let him do unrighteousness yet more;
And he that is filthy, let him be made filthy yet more;
And he that is righteous, let him do righteousness yet more;
And he that is holy, let him be made holy yet more."

Some one is sure to object that in our survey of sin we have personified it. It is not necessary to do this. Sin personalizes itself, which is a more serious process. No objection, theory, or argument can change the fact that sin is at work in human lives transforming human personality into that which it is.

During its process sin is desire, thought, deed; but in finished product it is personality. Its process leads no other way. Self-realization, whether good or bad, must move on to some goal in its embodiment not only within but also of personality.

If there could not be completion of the process of self-realization in sin, there could be no completion of the process of self-realization in the righteousness of God. When sin has run its full course, it has captured personality; even as Christianity having run its full course has personalized Redemption, fulfilled personality in the Redeemer. Finally sin and holiness are fully personalized; and man has become the fulfilment of the one or of the other. Then the sin-self or the self for God is perfected.

"In the lowest deep, a lower deep
Still threatening to devour me, opens wide,
To which the Hell I suffer, seems a Heaven."
—MILTON, *Paradise Lost*, Bk. IV, Line 76.

CHAPTER XXX

SIN AND PENALTY

JOSEPH PARKER once said: "Sin explains the Cross; sin explains the Atonement; sin explains Christ." It does explain the need of Christ and the penalty from which He would save every man.

Two human states stand out in contrast. There is the blessed state when God has fully come to His own in man, and man has come to possess fully what Christ purchased for him by His sacrifice. Then human personality has perfected its realization of God in Christ, and man has reached his self-fulfilment in God.

In the opposite direction and character there is the unhappy state when sin has perfected its realization in man. Godward affinity and capacity is gone. Then man's true self has disappeared and the sin-self is perfected. This having taken place the sin-made soul can say: Sin and I are one, myself am sin. Thus the sin of man has become "the man of sin."

"So farewell hope, and with hope farewell fear,
Farewell remorse; all good to me is lost;
Evil be thou my good!"

If the fallen angel, into whose mouth Milton puts these words, can say "All good to me is lost," it is not quite all lost. The good of being able to discern good as such still remains. But this good is used to end all good. As Othello said when about to kill his wife: light was used to put out light. Twice he committed suicide: first in putting out the light of the life that was more than life to him, and then in putting out the light of his own life. So sin twice kills man: it murders life itself; and then in putting out the eyes of the soul it snuffs out the light of spiritual life in the power to recognize life. When one light has used the other to put it out, the second light soon goes out, and in that darkness there is no way back to light or life.

"Put out the light, and then put out the light:
If I quench thee, thou flaming minister,
I can again thy former light restore,
Should I repent me: but once put out thy light,
Thou cunning'st pattern of excelling nature,
I know not where is that Promethean heat
That can thy light relume."

I. The Sin That is Eternal

When self-realization in sin is complete, the moral code is for ever reversed. Good is then bad and bad is good. Godliness has become foolishness, and faith in God has become unbelief. In the mind of sin there is no room for the thought of God.

According to the Master the hopeless stage in sin may be reached in this life. Concerning the man to whom the light of the Holy Spirit upon the sacrificial work of Christ is darkness, and who deliberately terms it the work of the devil, Jesus said: "He is guilty of an eternal sin." (Mk. 3: 29.) It has become unchangeable personality, and must by its very existence as such keep on repeating itself for ever.

There is the death that never dies. There is the second death when the last vestige in personality, to which God might appeal, has died. Dr. Denney speaks of the second death on this wise:

"If the wrath of God is finally revealed only in the day of wrath—if it is then only that we see all that sin is to God—apparently we ought to say, not the wages of sin is death, but the wages of sin is the second death, the death involved in the wrath of God, the death which has no life on its horizon."[1]

It is a terrible thing that man imparts his immorality to sin. His immortal soul may exist forever only to perpetuate iniquity in everlasting repetition. We hold that animals die finally when they die physically. They have no powers to relate them to the eternal. Their full life is registered in the temporal, and ends there. They have no capacity to know God and the

---

1. The Christian Doctrine of Reconciliation, p 229

eternal world of God. Man, on the other hand, all the days of his life is growing a soul for eternity, developing power of contact with the eternal. In the temporal his life but feebly and partially registers itself. The very capacity of his powers spells endless existence. It may be an endless existence in God; or it may be an endless existence in that which opposes God.

Life is a choice for eternity, a lived-out choice, a development of capacity and affinity in personality immortal. Because self-realization in sin or self-realization in God predestinates the soul to its after-world, *we largely make our heaven or our hell.* This does not deny the matter of place: it asserts that existence and capacity are more important than place, and determine it. "Which way I fly is hell: myself am hell." said the fallen archangel.

> "The mind is its own place; and in itself
> Can make a heaven of hell, a hell of heaven."

Omar Khayyam says he sent his soul out into the invisible, some letter of that after-world to spell, and his soul returned to him saying: "I myself am heaven and hell."

It is the mercy of God that sends a lost soul to hell. Heaven would be a thousandfold more hell to it than hell itself. Nothing more tortures the unsaved soul than the full glory of God's manifested presence. So in mercy God sends the lost to where there is least of it, and gives them their own choice and desire; for they call upon the rocks and mountains to fall on them and hide them from the face of God and the Lamb upon the throne.

II. ETERNAL PUNISHMENT FOR ETERNAL SINNING

Let us not laugh at the representation of "the bottomless pit." In any direction, in infinite directions, space is a bottomless pit, and a body risen from the dead could fall at the rate of millions of miles a second, and never come to the end of its fall. So Milton represents it when describing Satan's setting out for earth, the Arch Enemy suddenly dropped, and "to this day would have been falling," but that a cloud interrupted the fall and bore him as many miles aloft till he found the path from heaven to earth.

There are many troubled over the justice of everlasting punishment. It looks too severe to be meted out for the sins of a brief life on earth. We must not doubt that God is fair and His sentence of the lost equitable. We are not more righteous than He.

When life's choice is irrevocable and adaptation fulfilled unchangeable, what is God to do with the lost? with those who have utterly lost capacity for Him? He can but send them to their own place, to that in place which corresponds with what they are. Could he but "give His enemies their wish, and end them in His anger, whom His anger saves to punish endless! How He can is doubtful. That He never will is sure."

There is no hint in Scripture that God can literately exterminate the lost "root and branch," unless the second death means this. If this means the annihilation of personality, does sin do it or is it the act of God? That personality is entirely dissolved by sin, is not the evidence of Revelation or experience, as witness the fallen angels. When conditional immortality is based on Christ's, "who alone hath immortality," we should remember that immortality in the New Testament applies to the body as well as the soul, and not the one without the other. Christ alone is all immortal, because He alone has the immortal body risen from the dead.

To hold that the immortal side of man's nature is withdrawn in the second death, is to say that it is not immortal. It dies to man. God is blamed often for what belongs elsewhere. The everlasting penalty of sin is inflicted by sin rather than by God. It is that which sin earns and the sinner brings upon himself.

The great mistake usually made in this connection, is in not recognizing that *eternal punishment is for eternal sinning.* For eternal sinning there can be no other result than everlasting death. The very hell of hell is in eternal inability to cease from sinning. So sin eternally carries its own penalty with it. Having made itself indestructible in immortal personality, its penalty is made eternal thereby. The worst possibility in sin is that it may lead to sinning forever and to its attendant consequence and eternal penalty of everlasting death.

About such lost souls Peter uses the expression, "that cannot cease from sin." Having no other capacity and possibility than everlasting sinning, they who have developed it, must in the everlasting fitness of things go to their own place, the bottomless abyss of the moral and personal universe. As sin did not wipe out the existence of the demons, there is little ground for hope that it may annihilate the existence of unrepentant human souls. The "larger hope" is an inverted pyramid, standing on its apex, and must be held up by other than its own support. Bishop Brooks says:

"You wonder sometimes how men can believe in heaven and hell. My friends, the wonder is, with this sight before them which I have described, men can help it. The belief in heaven and hell is but the carrying into the long vista of eternity of what men see about them every day—the law of spiritual accumulation and acceleration, the law by which sin and goodness increase each after its own kind. The more clearly a man believes in the life to come and thinks of it as under the same great moral forces that pervade this life, the more impressive grow to him its spiritual necessities. He believes in a mercy that runs beyond the grave; but unless it be a mercy which does what mercy never does now, and *compels* to goodness the soul refusing to be good, there still stretches out the possibility of a wickedness for ever obstinate, and so for ever wretched."[2]

III. THE REALITY OF SIN'S PENALTY BEYOND PICTURE

It is not like Jesus Christ to raise a false alarm, when He warns of "the worm that dieth not, and the fire that is not quenched." There is that in the spiritual world beyond the strongest figures of this world to describe. Turner's best picture of a sunset is far less beautiful than the reality it paints. So the utmost

---

2. The Law of Growth and Other Sermons, p 9

physical terms used to describe spiritual consequences, depict far less than the reality itself.

Sir William Robertson Nicoll quotes *John of the Sterngassen:*

"Everything rests in the condition in which it was born. If a bird gets into the water it dies. Throw a stone up to the heavens and it returns to earth; for the earth is its fatherland. God is our fatherland; and if we live outside God, we too must die."

Eternal death is the eternal state of being incapable of drawing life from God. It is the utter impossibility of being other than a sinner for ever. It is that state of being dead for all time to fulfilment in God. The lived-out choice of life's personal realization is as irrevocable as life itself. A lost life is never found again.

When souls have added to them the weight of sin from which they can never be detached, they must ever sink downward in the infinite void of godlessness to which they doomed themselves, because it is that only for which they have fitted themselves.

"Here, judge if hell, with all its powers to damn,
Can add one curse to the foul thing I am."

So "beholding heaven" is out of the question when "feeling hell." Instead of wishing for heaven, the lost will be wishing to remove the furthest possible from it. None of the self-doomed to perdition will ever think it possible or desirable that they be not cast out for ever.

Written clear across the expanse of eternity is this: the penalty of sin fulfilled in personality is infinite. Then we cannot think too seriously of sin. It is worse than human demon or fiend of the pit, for by it they became such. It is worse than Judas, for it made him; worse than the devil, for it made him; worse than hell, for it made it.

"Sin! What a monster she is!
Her home is in the deep, damp dark
Where things begot of hell rave and rot.
Look upon her foul progeny!"

IV. THE SOLUTION OF THE RIDDLE OF THE UNIVERSE

In concluding the discussion of Part Three in this book, we have reached the place where the seriousness of sin can be expressed only in terms of eternity and infinity, because of what it becomes in *immortal personality*. That we have the explicit teaching of our Lord on this subject, is most providential; for the sin-dulled mind of man could never of itself measure the full extent of sin's farthest and deepest desolation.

Sin is the mother of many misconstructions. Wherever it works, contradictions are sure to abound. And no wonder, for that which contradicts God, cannot but cause contradictions in our thinking about it. On the one hand, we know less about sin because we have sinned; yet on the other, if we had not tasted sin's bitter degradation, felt its awful enervation, we had not known its meaning as we do.

Perhaps the paradox of iniquity's effect upon personality must perplex us as long as it assails us, haunts our minds and hinders our thought concerning it. Taking what the Word of God says, and remembering our own experience in sin, we wait the revelation of the world to come about "the mystery of iniquity." Only the mind of God runs the full gamut of so puzzling a subject.

Some one has said that the key to the riddle of the universe is God, and the key to the riddle of God is Christ. The real riddle of the universe is neither God nor Christ: it is sin. The solution of this enigma of enormity is the Redemption of Christ from it.

Sin makes man a riddle to himself. In Pope's *Essay On Man* he expresses this enigma of contradiction in humanity:

> "Chaos of thought and passion, all confused;
> Still by himself abused and disabused;
> Created half to rise and half to fall;
> Great lord of all things, yet a prey to all;
> Sole judge of truth, in endless error hurled;
> The glory, jest, and riddle of the world."

There is no optimism like that of Redemption. While with its baneful effect sin still abounds beyond bounds, yet the grace of God much more abounds. This is the solution, not for thinking only, but for living and building up personality all the stronger and better for sharing in the war of all time with iniquity.

God is equal to the occasion and problem of sin. His Redemption from it is founded on the sure, broad base of the Rock of Ages. His solution shall stand to the end, when the earth tottering with age, and reeling from its rolling orbit will plunge into the vortex of cosmic dissolution.

We cannot but appreciate anew our need of Christ. One shudders in view of sin's horrors to think where and what we would be without Him. The storms of iniquity still rage; and the ravages of this disease of the soul call more loudly than ever for the Great Physician. Mackay in describing the issue of sin says:

"A disease does not weaken as its victim weakens. Rather it increases till near the end...... After all spiritual death does not depend on any so-called 'waste of soul.' It is due to the withdrawal of the Divine Spirit from the soul of man. No matter how much or how little 'soul-stuff' remains to be wasted, when that separation takes place the soul must die. What exactly that death of the soul is, we may never be able exactly here to say. We only know it must be something inconceivably awful: perhaps to some more awful than to others."[3]

As Mackay says, this consideration is sufficient of itself to give urgency to the Gospel message. He quotes Lewis Morris:

"They seemed alone
Those prisoners through all time. Each soul shut fast
In its own goal of woe. Apart, alone,
Forevermore alone. No thought of kin
Or kindly human glance or fellowship
Of suffering or of sin, made light the load
Of solitary pain......

".......Hopeless sin
Rots slow in solitude, nor sees the face

---

[3] The Disease And Remedy Of Sin, 112 sq.

Of men, nor hears the sound of speech, nor feels
The touch of human hand, but broods a ghost
Hating the bare blank cell, that other self
Which brought it hither hating man and God
And all that is or has been."[4]

---

[4]. Epic of Hades, 22d ed , p 6

Part Four
Redemption of Self-Realization

CHAPTER XXXI

CHRISTIAN PERSONALITY

IN PART ONE the effort was made to set forth the genetic ground of Christian theology, in Part Two the genetic doctrine of Christianity, and in Part Three the genetic need to be met. Here the genetic process of personality redeemed by Christ will be considered. *This is the subject-object process of self-realization.*

Personality can be redeemed only by redeeming the process of personal realization—that which invariably makes it what it becomes. Redemption to be Redemption must enter personality, control and possess the process that makes it. In the mediatorial work of Christ He enters into and fulfils personality by means of this process. Having fulfilled in Himself the sacrificial nature of God by His self-sacrifice on the Cross, He communicates this fulfilment to human personality. So the redemption of self-realization is the second fulfilment of Christ's work, even as His own sacrificial self-realization was the first.

In the confusion of these days we do need among other things a clearer conception of personality. For one thing, we must be sure that it is the salvation *of* self-realization, not *by* it apart from Christ, that is set forth. The naturalism of salvation by ordinary self-realization has nothing to offer Christianity.

The view taken concerning self-realization controls not only the view of personality but all other views in the whole field of Christian theology. What we think of the nature of God depends upon what we think of personality. And what we think of the Work of Christ on our behalf depends upon our interpretation of that for which He sacrificed Himself, namely, human personality.

I. THE CENTER OF PERSONALITY

Growth is surely central in all created life. For this reason self-realization should be accounted central in the life of personality. In "The Secret of Personality" George Trumbull Ladd follows a long, long line of interpreters in placing the will as the central thing in personality. The author of this work pleads guilty of having once so stated it. This he would now repudiate along with self-consciousness as normal in personality.

The old abstract method of treating the will as a separate power that of itself wills, instead of looking upon it as inseparable from mind, desire, purpose and other personal powers, is in part responsible for this mistake. When self-consciousness replaces consciousness, self-will replaces will in abnormal life of personality. Thus the will obtains in self-will an exaggerated importance that does not belong to it.

We may say that for several reasons the will cannot be wisely considered as central in personal existence. We do not exist by willing to exist. The will does not will that it should exist; for, in that case, it would have to exist before it exists in order to will to exist. Personality does not will itself into existence.

No power of personality can be named as its center of existence, because existence is not a matter of arrangement of powers. It is not arrangement of being but being itself. Existence as such is without center, circumference, or parts. It cannot be analyzed in this or any other way. The moment we start to take it to pieces, we find ourselves dealing with mode of existence and not with existence itself. The way an existence acts, is one thing; how it comes to be an existence, is quite another. Hence the modalistic interpretation of the Trinity cannot in any measure interpret it ontologically.

God is the only explanation of existence. There is the mediate cause of personal existence. Its biogenesis comes into being by the epigenesis of conception. Thus two tiny impersonal lives unite in creating or procreating personality. The mystery lies in what takes place in that epigenetic union. How two impersonal forms of life (but from persons) can unite and so uniting originate personality in embryo, it is impossible to say. Here we have one life on the mother's side from the long, long line of her heredity reaching right back to the beginning, and one out of more than a million lives with no two precisely alike from the equally long line of heredity on the father's side. These two streams of heredity coalesce in this mystery of conception, and lo! a personality has embryonically begun its existence. Microscopic though it be, all the generic of personality is genetically present there; for the generic cannot be super-added afterwards; nor can it ever be changed. Nothing has ever begun as generically one thing and afterwards became generically another. Otherwise the word *Nature* would be obsolete or meaningless.

II. Faith Central in Self-Realization

If it be said that it is in development rather than in existence that the will is central, one must ask whether the embryo develops because it first of all wills to develop? Has the embryo a will? Some would say, As well ask if it has hands, conscience, and intelligence. Well, there is no life without inherent mind on a level with its order. Mind is integral in life, whether will is or not.

If it be held that only in conscious self-realization the will is central, we must insist that this is a mechanistic and artificial interpretation. As already remarked, the will cannot be where the mind and other powers are not. The faulty consideration of abstract will lies at the heart of this conception of the centrality of the will in personality.

Kant wrote about "pure reason," while no such thing has ever existed. Even so men discuss pure will and place it as central in personality, as though there could be pure will. To-day we recognize that it was the fiction of abstract will which founded the systems known as Calvinism and Arminianism. Each is based on the fallacy of abstract pure will, which of itself wills and is central in personality. But it is personality that wills, just as it is the person and not really the eye which sees, the person and not really the ear which hears.

In self-realization faith is as central as will. In the order of time it must precede it. We believe in that which we will, before we will it; else why do we will it? Further, we believe in the act of willing, before we act in willing. Normally we first believe to will, rather than will to believe.

III. THE PRIORITY OF FAITH

In all self-determination faith is prior to will. The fount of all willing, doing, growing lies in faith that believes in so willing, growing, and doing. Faith controls the order of self-realization, the determination of the line which self-determination takes. Even self-will depends upon faith in it. Whatever faith is in, that is the direction which self-realization takes. It is impossible to act wholly contrary to faith; for even the act contrary to a faith is made possible by faith in the powers used in this act, and also in acting in the opposite way to this faith.

In personal realization will does not act apart from faith and mind. Will apart by itself can no more will, than a single feather of a wing can fly. Nor does faith ever act alone, even when it is logically and chronologically first in all the activity of personality. If mind is integral in all life, so must faith be; for without faith no mind can work. Even the life of an embryo has its tiny mind and its integral and intuitive faith that works with its mind. Any life that did not believe in itself would not continue to exist, and so could never grow.

In the self-realization of Christian personality, faith is therefore the first power to be redeemed. In its subject-object process abstractions cannot work. In this vital process concrete personality first finds faith in the concrete means of redemption. This faith exercised in the living Redeemer determines the order of personal realization that results, and effectively carries on with the other powers of self-realization its personal development and achievement.

In Redemption the concrete Christ is vitally related to the soul as *The Great Objective of Its Faith*. At the same time in His own activity in this relation to the soul He bears as Mediator, *He is the Great Subjective*. In redeeming the subject-object process of self-realization His personality and vicarious achievement awakens in man the appropriate faith and will. Then a new order of personal realization takes place. There begins the transference by which Christ communicates Himself, and re-produces Himself in the person linked with or united to Him by faith.

It is thus that faith in Him begins the process of personal realization that redeems personality. So self-realization in and through Jesus Christ takes its place as the constructive center of Christian personality. In the subject-object relation of faith he who is united with the Crucified and Risen Christ and willeth to do His will, shall know in his own soul the realization of Christian personality.

IV. THE LIFE-INCLUDING LIFE OF PERSONALITY

The inner nature of human personality is perhaps plainest in its process of self-realization. Its power of becoming is there seen in active operation. We have already noted the germinal union which embryonically calls it into being. This genetic process indicates its generic principle or genius—*the life-including life*. That which personality may become is thus indicated, though all it may thereby attain stretches away upon the horizon and far beyond it.

As personal existence begins embryonically by means of this co-inclusion of life, so does it grow up in its development. Other than human life begins in this way of correlate inclusion; but human life carries on this principle and process in a higher way, to higher extent, to higher relations, for higher being, life, and activity. So for personality isolation spells death.

All life grows by the inclusion of suitable elements; but this life-including life of personality is more than the addition of mere elements: it is the addition of life itself. It is the extension of life into life, interpenetrating, sharing, acquiring, participating, receiving, giving, co-living, and correlating. This marks the higher order which is personal life. Not only does it organize into personality each addition or realization, it also organizes its life into the lives about it and them into its life. Christian personality is thus redeemed by including and being included. *God in Christ is thus brought into it.* Thus there comes into it not only the corrective but also the constructive elements it needs. Thus it oganizes into itself the life of Christ, and is itself organized into His life.

We may say that personality is generically a life-including life, including and being included.[1] It begins in this way; and in this way it continues as long as it is personality and life. Physically and spirtually the child-life begins by being included in the mother's life. Spiritually, it includes both the father's and the mother's life and is included beyond what we see. Physically, there is conscious and sub-conscious inclusion far beyond where any psychologist has yet gone. There is a

---

1. The life-including nature of personal life throws its light on the mystery of how Christ's nature was sinless though descended from the sinful nature of Mary In the Incarnation the divine life included the human and the human included the divine embryonically This brought to pass a reaction upon both natures included The divine life epigenetically uniting with the human did so with the effect of *exclusion* as well as that of *inclusion*. Sinfulness is not essential to human nature Anything not genetically inherent in human nature was excluded The law of the inclusion seems to be that the stronger and greater nature excludes all that in the lesser nature uniting with it which is extraneous and not in keeping or harmony with the stronger and greater nature The holiness of the divine life and nature united only with that which is pure human nature. What was born was "not of bloods—of a father and mother, nor of the will of the flesh, nor of the will of a man, but of God " This is the only birth in human history where the begetting preceding it had no "lust of the flesh " It was purely a sacrificial begetting, and a sacrificial person was begotten So, not only were the natures uniting pure, but the process itself was as holy. It was not sinful life and nature including the same It was not as in all other conceptions in human history Instead the absolutely holy life of God genetically including the purity that was sacrificially submitted and dedicated to this union "Behold the handmaid of the Lord, be it unto me according to thy word " And that word was, "Behold thou wilt conceive in thy womb and bring forth a son . and he will be called the Son of the Most High .   The Holy Spirit shall come upon thee and the power of the Most High shall overshadow thee, wherefore also the holy thing which is begotten shall be called the Son of God "

great region here where God can be included and can work to the greatest advantage in all the later stages of human development. The mother-life which includes God to the full, is the greatest agent of the Kingdom of God and is thereby a most determinative factor in the measure of personality, or of personal possibility. A sacrificial humanity can never be produced except by a sacrificial begetting, either by generation or regeneration or both.

The more formative and plastic the stage of personality, the greater the influence and effect of the life-including-life process. When The Highest is included and includes, the result in personality is proportionately great. Personal life being included in the highest realm and order of existence, in the highest of ways— consciously, morally, socially, sacrificially, and permanently, it is then capable of being included and including for ever. When it includes the divine and eternal and is included by it, then personal "becoming" is lifted to the highest plane, and its realization is divine, infinite and eternal.

V. THE PERSONAL CONTENT OF LIFE

Without waiting to discuss how much of the infinite and eternal human personality can include, we may be sure it is *incurably inclusive*. In Redemption it includes that which not only excludes sin; its unalterably reciprocal life is saved to reciprocity with the world for which God intended it. Sin is the selfish order of inclusion that destroys the soul as part of the Kingdom of God. Redemption is the inauguration and establishment of the inclusion of God in Christ. This captures the process of self-realization, and dedicates it to the construction of sacrificial personality. The spirit of love implanted in the soul not only delivers it from the loss of itself but from all else resulting. Faith relates the soul to the whole world of Christ by vital union with Him who is its life and fulfilment.

Personal life must be equally content and container. It must contain as much of other lives as they contain it. Take out of life the lives of all who live in it, and mere emptiness remains. "I live, yet not I; Christ liveth in me," said Paul. What contraction and damage in other ways would have been in his life, if Christ had not come into it. Moberly's great work discusses this matter:

"I am borrowing a phrase which has become happily familiar to very many, if I say whereas 'mutual exclusiveness' may seem indispensable for the understanding of the distinction of divine persons, it is no less indispensable that we should grasp—or at least that we should see that it would be necessary to grasp—the opposite conception of 'mutual inclusiveness.'"[2]

From a different point of view Illingworth mentions this also:

"At the same time, with all my inclusiveness, I have also an exclusive aspect...... Thus a person has at once an individual and a universal side. He is a unit that excludes all else, and yet a totality or whole with infinite powers of inclusion."[3]

It is a mistake to call the differentiation of the distinct an exclusion. That is but a conclusion—and a wrong one. Personality does not vary by shutting out life, but by producing unique variety. The finite does not exclude the infinite. It does not exclude that which it cannot contain. There is no need to shut out that which cannot get in. The distinctiveness of the finite is not the exclusion of the infinite. Otherwise the distinct would mean the extinct. Where persons mutually exclude each other, they stop all self-realization in each other. It is scarcely legitimate to name as an essential in personality the very thing which would stop its growing, becoming, and acting as personality.

As to inclusion, everything depends on its spirit and how far the inclusion goes. It cannot be truly reciprocal unless sacrificial. No reciprocity is possible in selfishness. The unselfish spirit excludes only evil, and includes according to the capacity of its personal-

---
2. Atonement and Personality, p 157
3. Personality Human and Divine, p 30

ity. There is nothing else in unselfish nature to stop the range of its action. In Christian personality it can go on including more and more of Him and of His, whose we are by Redemption. There is thus intensive as well as extensive growth in the life-including life.

The more complementary lives are, the more intensive and extensive may be their inclusion of each other. There is a constitutional way in which the spirit of love builds into an organism complementary personalities according to its nature, plan, and relation of the whole. In this the inclusion goes as far as room and need determine. The love of Christ not only intensively builds Him into life which lives by this inclusion, it also builds us into His life. We are built up in Him and unto Him. With Christ there is this complementary inclusive power that fits Him to become the content of lives and to impart His Redemption according to the measure of His Person, on the one hand, and according to our need of Him and our capacity, on the other.

In the intensive aspect the vital element of the inclusion is important. How much life is in the lives we include? And how much life do other lives include in including ours? When we include "the life that is life indeed," then we have the more to impart and the more by which to receive.

Summing up this matter we may say that the redemption of personality is before all else the inclusion of the Redeemer with full reciprocal power in our lives. This inclusion rules in all other life-inclusions, and it empowers them. The personality-making power of self-realization in Christ excludes sin. It includes the remedy for its damage and disorder. Thus it brings into the soul the wealth, health, and growth of life eternal.

VI. Personality Unrepeatable

Snowden says: "Personality in man is only a gleam of personality in God......The human is only a tiny copy and pale reflection of the divine...... Personality in man is only a pale copy of a perfect pattern."[4] This is similar to the thought of Lotze: "Perfect personality is in God only; to all finite minds there is alloted but a pale copy thereof." And Dr. W. N. Clarke says: "Probably the truth is that complete personality exists in God alone."

On the other hand Illingworth says: "Man's equipment is out of all proportion to his achievement, and suggests, at least in its superficial aspect, a design that failed."[5] Bowne declares that, "We cannot believe in man without believing in God; and we cannot believe in God without believing in man...... (Otherwise) the universe is a failure, and God is a failure too."[6]

These quotations remind us that the fulfilment of the perfect pattern is through the Redemption that is in Christ Jesus. Unfortunately a great many writers confuse the distinctness of each personal pattern with the abnormal separateness of sinful personality. The uniqueness of each personality is not a seperation. The contrary is nearer the truth; for distinctness is the equipment for the unique contribution which each may make to the completeness and unity of the whole. We could not be complementary parts of this great unity in God, if we were facsimile repetitions of each other; for then we would lose our place as distinct though inseparable parts in the unity of the whole.

That which should have been named is *The Unrepeatability* of personality, instead of separateness and self-included nature. The distinctness and uniqueness of each personality is such that it can never be repeated. As Seth says: "Each self is a unique existence, which is perfectly impervious to other selves—impervious in a fashion of which the impenetrability of matter is a faint analogue."[7] While "impervious" may not fully or clearly express uniqueness or that which cannot be repeated or replaced, it is clear that Seth has something of this in mind.

One cannot but wonder at the infinite originality of

---
4. The Personality of God, pp. 41, 87.
5. The Doctrine of the Trinity, p 138
6. Personalism, p 299.
7. Hegelianism and Personality, p. 216

God in that he never repeats Himself. He takes pains to make each blade of grass, each leaf, each snowflake different in some respect from any and all of its kind. This is perhaps the reason why personality, which is of more value than all else, is made with the same love of variety and evidence of originality. For this reason no one can take our place. To fill the unique place for which we are each designed, *we need personal redemption.* We cannot be redeemed *en masse.* The fulfilment of each personality depends upon, not only the part and place that God has assigned to it, but also on its uniqueness and unrepeatability. The full development of this distinctness and the filling of the place no one else can occupy, sin can defeat. It destroys the soul's contributive originality. Unless Redemption's fulfillment does its great work in each personality, its place must ever remain empty and unfulfilled.

VII. The Fulfilment of Personality

However faint it may be, each human personality is a unique copy of the divine personality of the Son. In the triune Godhead the Father cannot take the place of the Son; nor can the Son take the Father's place. The distinctiveness of each of the Persons of the Trinity cannot be, and need not be, duplicated. The Son filled His place as both Creator and the pattern of our creation. Because of this absolute uniqueness each divine person has His own unique part to play, His own work to do, His own contribution to make, His place that only He can fill. Somewhat in the same way, no one can ever fill our place in the life of God or in any other life.

Looking at the fingers of one's hand from the viewpoint of their tips, they appear separate. From the hand's viewpoint they appear united. The hand would not have increased unity, if the fingers had been undivided or grown together to their tips; in that case their usefulness would be very much diminished. As it is, each finger has its own place that cannot be taken by another. Each finger does its utmost in filling its own place. If one finger should be lost, the hand would be marred. And yet the same life-blood is in each finger as in the hand as a whole. Even so one purpose gives to each part its place in the unity of the whole according to its capacity.

Somewhat in the same way the redemptive life of God is in all redeemed persons. One great purpose directs them all to one great end; and yet each has his own particular fulfilment. The unity not only within persons who are Christian, but also among them, is because the life of the Redeemer includes them all and is in them all. They are His fingers at work for Him, laboring together in One Great Task. Thus the hand of God works in human history.

A remarkable thing is that the more completely we include the life of Christ and are included by it, the more our personal distinctness stands out as part of the unity of the Kingdom of God. As Paul's wonderful absorption of Christ and in Him did not in the least detract from the distinctness of his personality, but all the more defined the sharpness of its outline; so we are never so much ourselves as when most in Christ. Blessed be God! Christ is "the Way" in ways not yet dreamed of by us. But we do see that He never overruns personality or submerges it, as it follows Him. He so fills it with His life that it is enabled to fill its place as a unique and unrepeatable part in the whole life of God.

The secret of each personal existence has back of it the secret of its appointed existence in God. The fulfilment of this existence is secured in the Redemption of Christian personality. Christ began by including our lives in creation. And He made each personality so like His own that it can include Him. The Father has for each His own purpose and plan as part of the whole. To redeem us to His holy purpose He provided the way by which He included us sacrificially in His life that we might sacrificially include Him in ours. The place which Christ has prepared for each of us within His own life, is then filled to the full—in fulfilment.

CHAPTER XXXII

CHRISTIAN CONSCIOUSNESS

TRUE Christian consciousness is the consciousness of personality it its self-realization of the self-for-Christ. Genetically, it is Christ-consciousness, that is, consciousness in Christ and of Christ. The consciousness in the process by which the self-not-for-self realizes and fulfils itself, is now before us.

This consciousness is more than psychological. That is to say, it is the consciousness of more than a psychological process. It is the consciousness of Redemption at work in the whole soul. More goes on in the process of creating, developing, and perfecting Christian personality than registers itself in consciousness.

We must carefully discriminate between the true and false in this matter. The so-called Christian consciousness that flouts the Word of God, denies its miracles and other revelations, and sets itself up as the only authority that is truly Christian, is anything but Christian. It is the old subjectivity of self-sufficiency. It is the self-consciousness of proud selfishness puffed up by the conceit of a little knowledge torn away from the truth as it is in Jesus. Psychologically it is the subjective, not only torn from the objective, but denying the objective. It is stagnation of the subject-object process of self-realization in Christ's Redemption. The Christian consciousness when reduced to a subjectivity becomes a futility. It never can be the consciousness of the sacrificial self—the self-not-for-self. Its genius is the exact opposite.

I. Normal Consciousness

Years ago the subject-object nature of normal consciousness was discovered by James Ward of Cambridge. The Copernican system did not more revolutionize astronomy than this subject-object discovery revolutionized psychology. But its work is far from being perfected. Theological and other writers still go on presenting self-consciousness as essential in normal personality. This may be some excuse for the repetition in our discussion of it.

Let us once more re-state this matter. According to the old view self-consciousness enables the self to distinguish itself from the external world of non-self, and therefore all self-realization is fundamentally self-conscious. Ward shows that it is consciousness and not self-consciousness which is normal in personality; and all consciousness is necessarily a subject-object process in which the subject and object are inseparable. In consciousness of self the self is made an object in the subject-object process of consciousness just as any other object might be. Self and non-self are thus distinguished from each other just as the various objects in the non-self world are distinguished from each other. We can compare or distinguish only by making that compared or distinguished an object of the subject-object process of consciousness. In consciousness the self must always act as subject. In self-consciousness the self is super-imposed where it does not belong.

If self-consciousness were the normal consciousness of self, the case would be different. Instead of being a psychological process, self-consciousness is a spiritual disposition. Abnormal, selfish, self-centered personality has self-consciousness as its psychological center. The true self, the other-self, the self-not-for-self is other-conscious. Self-consciousness is like self-will. In fact it is the consciousness that belongs to self-will and selfishness. Self-will in preference to God's will, like self-love in preference to the love of God and of others, is naturally self-conscious.

Consciousness is the ability to relate self consciously to any object. Self-consciousness is the inability to get completely away from self as an object. The exclusive self-interest of selfishness interposes its objective self in all consciousness, and everywhere overlays the subject-object process of consciousness with its self-consciousness. It is no more normal to personality than cross-eyed vision is normal to eyesight. It is the diseased consciousness of abnormal personality. There is no more need of considering all consciousness as fundamentally self-consciousness, than of considering all will as fundamentally self-will, or all interest as essentially self-interest. Consciousness of self need not be self-consciousness as a disposition. Christ came to deliver us from the curse of self-consciousness. Let us not represent the accursed as the normal.

II. Consciousness in the Trinity

Twenty-five years ago in classroom I heard Dr. W. N. Clarke confess in a manly way that his statement, "God is self-conscious,"[1] had been made in ignorance of this subject-object advance in psychology. His absorption in theology, he said, had prevented his noting this advance in psychology. So he had said, "A personal spirit is self-conscious," "Modern thought insists on the separateness and self-included nature of personality." As a matter of fact it is out of date modern thought which does this. It is modern thought with unmodern, discarded psychology.

Self-consciousness considered as normal in personality leads logically to Unitarianism. So Dr. Clarke says, "God is one person." Modalism follows the same line of reasoning. Mackintosh speaks of Christ's self-realization as completed in "finite self-consciousness." Earlier he had spoken of the New Testament as affirming, "Not the eternal being of this or that chance individual, but of the Lord Jesus Christ, with His arresting and unparalleled self-consciousness." Logically this leads him to consider Christ "as an eternal personal mode or distinction within the one self-conscious life in God."[2] In reply it may be said:

[1]. An Outline of Christian Theology, pp. 67, 170, 171.
[2]. The Doctrine of the Person of Jesus Christ, pp 497, 459, 454 Self-consciousness in place of consciousness results in putting individuality in place of personality, indwelling in place of incarnation, mode in place of the God-man, and leaves Jesus Christ not divine at His highest Personality

consciousness emphasizes personality, and self-consciousness individuality. When individuality, (the dividing in), replaces personality in the Godhead, it is impossible to have self-consciousness in its three dividings and separations without tritheism. Mackintosh would avoid this in the old way of making God one individual, though there is no one left to be divided from. We cannot take personality away from each in the Trinity and then give it back to that back of these modalistic manifestations. Nor can we make up in overplus immanence of the divine in Christ for that which is held to be lacking to Him in the generic of divine personality. No immanence in personality can equal personality itself; nor can the excellence of this immanence be for a moment mistaken for that which makes it possible, the excellence of personality itself.

III. Subjectivism in Personality

When self-consciousness is considered as characteristic and essential in personality, we are left to choose between three separate self-consciousnesses or one, three individual gods or none. As already remarked there can be no individuals in the Godhead. The Father is not God apart from the Son and the Holy Spirit. The Son and the Holy Spirit do not have and cannot have separate existences as individuals may have.

Even one personality in the Godhead who is fundamentally self-conscious would be but the misery of a self-centered existence, the utter opposite of the sacrificial.

No matter how good otherwise a divine person may be, he cannot be happy in the stagnation and stultification of unescapable self-consciousness. As already remarked, the true mother is happy because she is child-conscious instead of self-conscious. The Three

---

is the highest thing in God or man As God is one person and Christ cannot be that person, He is not divine in personality, however filled with God He may be At His highest, in the generic of His personality He is man and not God And all love and fellowship between the persons of the Trinity is so much fiction, for there can be no fellowship and fulfilling in each other between these modes of one personal manifestation.

Other-Selves of the Trinity, instead of having three self-consciousnesses have *the one other-consciousness of sacrificial Deity.* That is the consciousness of The Sacrificial Trinity. The self-not-for-self in the Trinity as elsewhere is essentially non-self-conscious.

Every gain in human thought seems immediately menaced by some perversion. The subject-object process of consciousness has been threatened by subjective idealism. This would make the process empty and futile. According to it the subjective creates its objective. The objective is not the noumena of reality, of things in themselves, but the phenomena of subjective creation.

Subjectivism tells us, we do not see sights. We project them. We do not hear Niagara's roar. We create it. Our senses are but broadcasting instruments, not receiving or recording ones. This idealism interprets self as shut up within itself and unable to be sacrificial, for it is imprisoned in the revolving squirrel-cage of its own subjectivity.

But for this application of Kant and Berkley we might have still gone on supposing we really saw the flowers in their beauty and really smelt their perfume, when according to subjectivism we were seeing our own created beauty and smelling our own smell. So this idealistic psychology sets forth the noumena of its own nonentities.

IV. ALL SELF-REALIZATION A SUBJECT-OBJECT PROCESS

What Ward discovered about the subject-object nature of consciousness is true of all self-realization. Faith, for example, is subject-object in its process, so is love, desire, will, and purpose. All personal relation and realization proceeds on this subject-object method.

Subjective idealism may offer its subjectivity of self-consciousness; but when it is attempted to carry subjectivity into all the rest of the process of self-realization, its folly becomes the more apparent. Personality does not realize itself in relation to, or out of, appearances. Phenomena will not do to trust in. Faith does not create the object it trusts in. Love does not make the person who is loved. Desire does not call into being the thing desired; and when we will to do God's will, we do not create His will.

The reality of personality makes it necessary that all additions to it come from that which is as real as it is. The subject-object relation would lead to but self-repetition and hallucination if the objective proved to be but the projection of subjectivity. As the mind could learn nothing by apprehending its own objective projection, so personality could know no self-realization by subjectivity.

We have said that the redemption of personality must be by means of the redemption of that which makes it what it becomes, that is, the redemption of self-realization. This redemption would be impossible, if this process did not relate personality to personality, the reality of the subjective to the reality of the objective. The redemption of mere phenomena of subjectivity is impossible. When the subjective soul is related to the objective reality of the Saviour by faith, love, desire, will, purpose, and all the rest of the powers of self-realization, each power receives from Him, transfers to personality in the subjective what there is in Him as the corresponding objective to it, and builds up personality thereby.

We may see this in the faith which so relates human personality to Him, that its subject-object process can do its work of trust, confidence, reliance, and bring over into personality that which builds it up through and in Him. This will be discussed at length later. Here we may say in summary fashion that self-realization in subject-object relation with the reality of the living Christ makes over the soul into what He is, brings into it the spirit and character that is in Him. His sacrificial self-not-for-self is thus enabled to impart and reproduce itself by this subject-object relation. Then the realization in us of this self-for-others passes on from stage to stage until it reaches its fulfilment in Christian personality.

It was said that in consciousness the subject cannot be separated from the object. So in all the rest of the process of self-realization the subject is never apart from its object *in the process*. Ontologically they may exist apart, but in the actual process of self-realization they are inseparable. Because this is a vital process, and by it there is living impartation, reception, and construction, both the subject and the objective are organized together in this relation and activity. The objective becomes available to the subjective in this vital way. In discussing this matter Canon Moberly says:

> "An objective fact that is not apprehended in any sense subjectively, is to those who have no subjective relation to it, as if it were non-existent. A fact objectively existing, in itself, without relation to any apprehending mind, is an impossibility in thought...... Subjective truth rather is that which is true in and to the apprehending capacity of the individual...... It is subjectively that the objective is realized...... Objective that is wholly without subjective realization, is the same as non-existent. Subjective that is not objective also, is hallucination...... How can the sacrifice of Jesus Christ, consecrated on Calvary for eternal presentation, become in me—not a personal reality only, but the main constitutive reality of my own individual personal being?[3]

V. Subject-Object Correlativity

Einstein has announced his theory of relativity. A matter more important to us at this point is the doctrine of correlativity. It is not enough that a subject and object be related, they must be related correlatively. They must be correlates. There must be kindredship between them, a congruity that fits and adapts them to each other in subject-object relation. In other words they must be "two of a kind" in self-realization.

There is the indispensable need that subject and object be correlatives to work in personal realization. Only the correlative can be contributive. Correlative is more than relative. The mother and her child are more than relative; they are correlative. The need of

---
3. Atonement and Personality, p. 141, sq

the correlative is true even with the senses. Because we have physical eyes, they cannot behold spiritual things. The physical and the spiritual are relative but not correlative.

Since we have been discussing reality, it may be fitting here to say that in the subject-object process of Redemption there must be correlative reality. We have been saying that an object of faith must be a correlative reality to its subject. For example, coming to the top of a stairway in the dark, and believing there is yet another step, faith puts its foot on the imaginary step, and a jolt results. The correlative reality was not there.

After its jolt faith refuses to go on. In fact it refuses to be faith any farther without its correlative objective. The subjective faith was so dependent on its objective, when it discovered itself without it, it broke down. If the subjective had been creating its objective, it could just as well have gone on. Objective noumenal reality not being there would have made no difference. But faith that can go on without correlative reality, is not faith. It is credulity, which is an order of hallucination.

In the subject-object process of Redemption Christ's provision of perfect correlative reality to the sinner's guilt and need is that which makes it competent to redeem us. Christ made Himself not only relative to our need; He made Himself correlative to it. The soul and its Saviour are congruous in the perfect kinship of vicarious sacrifice.

But real Redemption cannot be merely objective. That would not provide full correlativity. If there were no sacrificial spirit of Christ to enter and possess the subjective soul, its full correlativity to the objective Redeemer would be wanting.

VI. THREEFOLD CORRELATIVITY

In Part Two we were considering the personal process by which the Christ became personally correlative to our need as sinners, our need of being redeemed to sonship in God. The correlativity complementary to this is in the personal relation by which Christ comes into life and soul with His mastery over sin and His solution of its guilt and problem. The objective had first to be provided. Christ's personal adaptation enabled Him to become the objective reality of Redemption.

This adaption came through the series of sacrifices when He became man, took a human body, lived a human life, bore our sins in His body on the tree, rose from the dead, and ascended to the throne of Redemption and Mediation. This adapted Him correlatively and enabled the Holy Spirit to flow through and out of His sacrificial and sacrificed personality upon those who receive the Saviour. This provided for the impartation of the correlative to Christ within the soul. The spirit of the Crucified in those for whom Christ died is the correlative subjective for the subject-object process of redeemed self-realization.

There is the correlative of the Incarnation when Christ became "bone of our bone and flesh of our flesh"; and this is the outstanding miracle of identification. There is the correlative of the Cross when the Sinless One became the propitiation for our sins; and this is the outstanding miracle of adaptation. There is also the correlative of the Spirit of Him Crucified and Risen from the dead poured out and into sinful human hearts; and this is the outstanding miracle of Redemption. This trinity of correlation has made full provision for the redemption of personal realization.

VII. THE MYSTERY OF CORRELATIVITY IN PERSONALITY AND PRAYER

There are many phases of the correlative correspondence between the subjective and the objective in the process of the redemption of personal realization. They are not easy to understand because back of them is the essential mystery of personality itself. We are told that the Hebrew expression "the image and likeness" of God in which man was made, means that it is intensively the closest possible, the very image, the very likeness. What is this but the mystery of man made with God as his correlative. And then the deeper mystery comes when God in Redemption becomes the correlative to man in sin to deliver him and make him God's own in personality. Necessarily man thus gathers into his personality all the wonder and mystery of divine love and sacrifice. Of the mystery of personality Illingworth says:

"Though personality......is the one thing which we know best in the world, it is also the most mysterious thing we know. 'Grande profundum est homo.' There are 'abysmal deeps of personality' which startle us at times by the vastness of the vistas which they half disclose."

"Now human personality is the inevitable and necessary starting-point of all human thought. For we cannot by any conceivable means get out of it, or behind it, or beyond it, or account for it, or imagine the method of its derivation from anything else from which it can have been derived...... Personality is also our canon of reality, the most real thing we know, and by comparison with which we estimate the amount of reality in other things."[4]

There are deep unplumbed caverns, unscaled towering heights, and vast unexplored continents in human personality. Yet we are able to look further into it in self-realization than from any other point of view. We are able to watch and understand something of the mysterious process by which its subject-object process makes and perfects personality.

In the preceding chapter we considered it as the life-including life. In keeping with that constitutional reciprocity we are here thinking of the correlativity which makes it redemptive. Redemption provides its correlative in every phase of self-realization. It is to the correlativity of prayer that the sinner is first saved. This is not only "Behold he prayeth"; but how! "What wilt thou have me to do?"

All too much prayer is thought of as a begging business, endeavoring to get something out of God, trying

---

[4]. Personality Human and Divine, pp 52, 41, sq

to overcome His reluctance instead of taking hold on His willingness, as Bishop Brooks has said. By the redemption of prayer itself we are redeemed from endeavoring to convert God to our desires. Instead of insistently imposing our blind desires on God, we had better pray to be uplifted to our having His desires for us. When the self-giving God finds in the suppliant the correlative of desire for Himself with which comes all good, then real prayer begins. Otherwise we but try to make use of God.

Because prayer at its best is communion with God, it has not only initial but also constant place and service in self-realization. And there can be but little communion with Him as long as like Jacob at Jabbok we wrestle to have our way with God, as though we knew better than He what is good for us, or that we are more interested in ourselves than He is in us.

When our struggle becomes with ourselves, to put ourselves entirely in God's hands, as Jacob finally did at Jabbok, or as Jesus did so much better at Gethsemane, the correlative in the suppliant and the sufficiency in God meet together, and deep satisfactory realization in the soul takes place as a result.

The dedication of sufficient time is an important matter in the self-realization by prayer. But time is largely wasted till correlative communion begins. We not only make too little place in our lives for prayer, we make too small a place in it for God to come into our souls. And we can never suitably invite Him in except as needing His Redemption from sin. It is a poor translation which says of the publican that he smote his breast and said "God be merciful to me a sinner." What he did was that which we should all do. He kept on smiting His breast and kept on saying, "God be merciful to me a sinner." That is a necessary correlative to maintain.

The growing soul needs a good deal of time spent in real prayer-communion with God, looking into His face, listening to Him as well as speaking unto Him. It is in this way that more things are wrought in soul-building than we are ever aware.

CHAPTER XXXIII

FROM GUILT TO JUSTIFICATION

GUILT is properly a legal term. Where there is no law, there can be no guilt. It is the law which declares men guilty or not guilty. There may be sin without the law forbidding it. Then those who sin without the law, perish even though guiltless. The knowledge of the law aggravates the evil of sin. There is no personal existence without law of some kind. Man may be without statutory or legislative law, but he cannot be without the law of personal well-being written in "his members," in the constitution of his nature.

The decree or enactment of a legal authority is one thing; that which is essential to personal well-being, is another. No statutory law can bring into being the law of well-being, or change it in the least. For example, no edict of man can change the law: "Man shall not live by bread alone." That man is more than physical nature, stands forever unalterable.

Law is, in general, the *modus operandi*, the way a nature or power works. But it is not necessarily the power itself. The law of gravitation is not the power of gravitation, but the way this power works. The law of well-being is the normal way that personal nature works. Such law is integral. The ten commandments are innate in the constitution of human nature. They are not mere decrees. God made man with this law constituent in his personal nature.

I. Guilty Before God

Guilty before God is not the same thing as guilty before statutory law. One might be guilty before a law of man and guiltless before God; or he might be guiltless before human law and guilty before the law of God. All God's laws are laws of well-being. This cannot be truly said of all human laws. He who knows man, having made him, not only knows what is good for man, but expresses it in all His laws announced. His laws declare both His omniscience and infinite interest in man. In other words, all God's laws are infallible in righteousness.

We have said that God's holiness is that absolute perfection to which nothing can be added and in which nothing can be wanting. We have also said that His holiness is best manifested in His sacrificial nature, for the perfection of unselfishness dedicated to the good of others, is the highest form of holiness of which we can conceive in God. *Were God not by His very existence that which constitutes holiness, righteousness and unselfishness, there would have been none possible anywhere.* Were He not wholly sacrificial in nature, we could conceive of a better God. And had not His Great Sacrifice the end in view of founding and fulfilling in man the righteousness and holiness of a sacrificial nature like His own, we could conceive of a better sacrifice. In other words, the holiness of God and its sacrifice in Christ on Calvary are both absolute.

To be guilty before the absolute, unselfish holiness of sacrificial Deity to which we are indebted for all good and most of all for His infinite sacrifice of His Son on the Cross, is the deepest guilt possible. It is a terrible thing to be guilty before the infinite purity of the divine perfection dedicated to our good in every way. It is like the guilt of crucifying Christ, where perfect love and unbounded sacrifice met the bitterest hate, where having given all, it was rewarded with death by torture. That was not weakness but viciousness. There was blindness in it; but blindness to such heart-appealing sacrifice is itself a great guilt. But it was not all blindness. It was inexcusable to think that such a Life and Person was worthy of death. God made no man to think that way.

As all sin is fundamentally the same, so all guilt is foundationally the same. It may vary in amount; but in any case it is guilt before immeasurable goodness. We have all treated God in just the same spirit as that which hailed His Son to the Cross. Our very blindness has been cultivated and self-induced. Our selfish ingratitude and wilful refusal to have this God of love and sacrifice rule over us for our good is the guilt of perversity, complicity with enmity, failure toward that which has never failed us. Being wholly without excuse for our iniquity, our guilt is unquestionable.

Our guilt is as deep as the sacrificial holiness of God is high. Our failure to respond in kind to all God's wondrous goodness toward us is absolutely contrary to the law of both His nature and ours. We have rewarded the Father with disloyalty, mutiny, indignity, treachery, treason, and all the infinite evil in iniquity. And this crowns our guilt and seals our condemnation, that, when after all our sin, He sends His Son to redeem us, we spurn His infinite sacrifice.

As God is better than all the good works He has done, so guilt before Him is deeper than guilt before all the goodness He has done us. Because personally He is such a God, infinite in majesty yet so lowly in sacrifice, righteous in flawless love yet unswerving in holiness, guilt before Him must be measured by *what He is,* against whom we have sinned so grievously.

The deepest guilt is possible to those who have the greatest revelation of God. In another way, our deepest guilt is not in what we have done but in what we are. We are the personalization of guilt. Self-realization in sin has developed a personality with less and less capacity for God, accompanied by more and more attitude of opposition to what He is. We are guilty of the making of personality contrary in character, spirit, and aim to that of God. The law of God's nature is compelled to judge us guilty of an order of personal existence that is at war with Him as God. This is not only guilt of conduct but of state.

II. THE CONSCIOUSNESS OF GUILT

Insensibility to God is necessarily followed by insensibility to our wrong against Him. In act, the greatest guilt lies in rejecting the gift of God in His Son. This is the guilt of sin against sacrifice on the greatest possible scale. Part of this guilt lies in its being a sin against light unprecedented. The sacrifice of God in Christ has manifested God in the fullest and most unmistakable revelation. At the place of greatest light, the possibility of most pronounced attitude is possible. But the spirit of God is also light within, light on what we are, as well as light on what we have done. The consciousness of the sinfulness of what we are and our guilt because of it, is made possible by the light of the Holy Spirit within.

Self-conviction of sin is not naturally possible. The sin-self seeks to justify itself in its sin. Sin is the loss of power or ability to know self as it really is. Unless the *Undisabled Mind* is given us of the Holy Spirit, the knowledge of our state and standing before God is utterly impossible to us. Only as He imparts to us the divine feeling and intelligence can we be convinced of the fact and the righteousness of God's estimate of us. The Holy Spirit is the only One able to lay upon us the blessed burden of conviction, the consciousness of our guilt as sinners.

Sin grows all the more dangerous and ruinous the less our sense of its shame, injury, and guilt becomes; yet this is exactly the inevitable effect it produces, namely, to make the sinner insensible to the crime of his sin. Absence of sense of guilt means nothing less than unarrested decay of soul. Conscience then continues seared; and the soul becomes more and more calloused to its responsibilities.

Conviction of sin is the Great Amen to God's condemnation of sin.[1] It awakens the soul to God's estimate of sin, and lays the foundation thereby for all that is to follow in Redemption. Every sinner becomes

---

1. This reminds us of the expression of McLeod Campbell in his work, "The Nature of the Atonement," p 117, where he speaks of the oneness of Christ's mind with the Father enabling Him to make a perfect confession of our sins "This confession, as to its own nature, must have been a perfect *Amen in humanity to the judgment of God on the sin of man*" Robert S Franks marks the significance of this in his "History of the Doctrine of the Work of Christ," Vol II, p 396

a man after God's own heart, as he comes into agreement with Him about the serious sinfulness of his sin. Unless God lays in the soul of man by His Holy Spirit the permanent basis of the divine evaluation of sin, no agreement with Him on other matters can ever amount to much. *Man's self-deception there prevents his real knowledge of God anywhere.* "If we say we have no sin, we deceive ourselves and the truth is not in us." I John 1:8.

The beginning of God's work of righteousness in the soul is to bring us to face the responsibility for our iniquity, to recognize with shame our ill desert, and to accept the justice of the condemnation of God upon us as sinners. If we cannot be brought to behold the unrighteousness of our sin and to feel our personal guilt, how are we to apprehend with all the saved the righteousness of Christ's Redemption and the equity of justification by faith in the same?

The closer we come to God, the more His Spirit imbues the conscious powers of personality, and the more He enables and inspires that central consciousness of the religious nature with a sense of our unworthiness. *True conviction is not a transition.* We see this in the mature expressions of Paul. Real conviction of sin can never be forgotten. It is a foundation upon which we consciously rest as long as life lasts. The truly Christian soul never outgrows the conviction—"By the grace of God I am what I am." The only mistake in the Scripture that Paul ever made, was in counting himself "the chief of sinners." Every true disciple of Christ would contest with Paul for that place.

III. The Justification of the Ungodly

The justification of the sinner may seem to be, at first sight, a theological fiction. Unfortunately some never get beyond that superficial first view. They ask, "How can God declare a man to be what he is not?" *He does not!* In salvation there is no fiction. In God's justification there is no supposition. In this matter there are at least three things to be taken into account —the tribunal, the law, and the standing accorded in justification.

First, *the Tribunal.* Before the tribunal of God when as yet the Son of God had not borne the sin of man, no justification was possible to the sinner. Before the tribunal which required obedience to God, man could have naught but condemnation. Were no other divine judgment-seat possible, the sinner's sentence of condemnation would have to stand forever.

The judgment-seat of Christ is, however, the mercy-seat. He came not to condemn, but to deliver men from condemnation. He therefore undertook for them all responsibility before God that could be vicariously assumed. The Throne of the Lamb is now the judgment-seat of God justifying the pardon of sinners, saving them from all unrighteousness, and righting the wrong of their sins.

Second, *the Law.* This is the law of vicarious sacrifice. Sacrifice itself may stand in need of justification. Not all sacrifice is worthy, i. e., made by worthy motive and to worthy end. When sacrifice is made for the help or purpose of that which is not righteous or only partly righteous, it cannot be fully justified. Only that offering which is by righteous motive and for righteousness in full and perfect measure is justified. The perfect unselfishness of Christ which sacrificed for the holy purpose of God to establish righteousness in man is justified. The means—the self-sacrifice of Calvary, and the end—the fulfilment of personality, correspond in righteousness. In this case the means and the end mutually justify each other.

Often sacrifice has been made for a selfish object. Here the end condemns the means, no matter how good the latter may be. The selfish is always a soul-withering objective. It is the smallest and meanest interest possible. On the other hand, sacrifice may be for the highest and holiest purpose. For example, there may be sacrifice to make known the greatest sacrifice of all, that of God in Christ. This is the vastest objective possible to the Christian. It fulfils at the same time the will of God and Christian personality.

While sacrifice itself may be unselfish, it may be for an object unworthy of it. "We who are about to die, salute thee," said the brave soldiers to one who had not the holiest purpose in their death. In fact, some of the greatest sacrifices have been made to objects least worthy of them.

The Roman Catholic Church demands sacrifice of all its members. This is not wrong if the Church exists wholly for the purpose of God. If lives are sacrificed to the Church, it must be that this is justified by the Church existing wholly for the sacrificial love of Christ. The Church will not do anything then but what He does. If the Church loves as sacrificially as He did, is the embodiment of His Holy Spirit and aim, then all sacrifice for the Church is justified.

Perhaps the greatest failure of Protestantism is its failure to train in sacrifice the members of its churches. The average life is not developed in this way. The attendance at church, for example, is unsacrificial, and largely depends on the selfishness of the entertainment secured. The general conception seems to be that we are saved by the sacrifice of Christ in such a way that we can act as selfishly as we please. Yet our Lord called the Church into existence to be a sacrificial body; and it is a true Church only so far as it is sacrificial to the one great end of making effective in all the earth the Sacrifice of His Redemption.

It is one thing to justify a sacrifice, and another to justify by it the one for whom it is made. But, as is easily seen, the two are closely related. "It is God that justifieth." God does not justify without means, any more than He works elsewhere without means. The means of justifying the believer works. It is the means God has provided to end man's condemnation. He is freed from this condemnation by means of the law of sacrifice. He can be justified by this law. It is God's sacrifice, God's law, and God's justification of the sinner.

"It is Christ that died, yea, rather that is risen again." His rising from the dead was God's visible justification of Christ's sacrifice. Since the justification of the sinner depends on the justification of the sacrifice on his behalf, his possession of its benefit makes its justification his own. His spiritual resurrection is the parallel to the physical resurrection of Christ. It proves that he possesses the divine means of justification. It shows that the law of God's sacrifice is at work in him. Even the infinite sacrifice of God could not justify an unchanged, selfish sinner. The justification of Christ's Great Sacrifice before God is its power to make the unjust just, the unrighteous righteous, the sinner a saint. "Not having mine own righteousness." Not that I have possession of a sacrificial righteousness of my own, but that the sacrificial righteousness of Christ possesses me. I am justified by the law of that sacrifice. It includes me "in Christ Jesus," where there can be no condemnation.

Third, *the Standing.* Whatever standing Christ and His sacrifice has before God, he who is "in Christ," has. He is "at the right hand of God." Then so is my justification. "Who is he that condemneth?" The only One who could condemn, has made my condemnation impossible by His acceptance of Christ's sacrifice for me. The tribunal and the law have declared my standing. They have more than declared it; they have put it on the throne of the universe. The standing which was given Christ's sacrifice of Himself for me by His enthronement, is the highest possible exhibition and assurance of my acceptance with God by faith in Him. My justification is an *experience,* because it is infinitely more, even as Christ is an experience because He is infinitely more. "Peace with God" is the blessed experience resulting from my standing before God in Jesus Christ, my sacrifice and Saviour.

"On Christ the solid rock I stand;
All other ground is sinking sand."

IV. Justification by Faith

Faith in the righteousness of Christ's redeeming sacrifice is the means of sacrificial transmission to those for whom it was made. It is the process by which divine righteousness includes within itself the lives for which its sacrifice was made. Faith is personality absorbing by self-realization the spirit and substance of Redemption.

Since it is the hand that made the world and bears creation up, which was pierced for us, faith takes its favors from that pierced hand. Like John, the believer lays his head on the bosom of the Redeemer. There he learns by fellowship the humility of true greatness. Faith in the greatness of God's goodness humbles us, as we feel our own littleness and worthlessness apart from His. Since He humbled Himself by becoming obedient unto the death of the Cross, faith beholding such humility, builds the soul into its form and fashion. A true trust partakes of Him in all respects; and the soul then grows up in the fullness of His grace.

Receiving Redemption at the vast cost of divine sacrifice, one is infinitely obligated to Christ for all eternity. The humility of the Christian soul is therefore constitutional. Even in justification by faith, personality stands before God free because of the sufferings of the Son of God. There self-dependent faith has not even a speck of dust to stand on. The faith of Redemption is the fatal foe to pride.

Being justified by the justification that makes him just in the immeasurable righteousness of Christ's sacrifice for him, there can be no judgment on the one possessing faith in it; for he has passed out of death into life. He is "in Christ Jesus." He walks not after the flesh of selfishness but after the spirit of sacrifice.

By virtue of His sacrifice Christ is the Judge; and for Him to pass judgment on those in Him, *is really to pass judgment on Himself*. He possesses the soul as His own, in which He has ended self-realization in sin, and begun the self-realization in Him that will go on for ever.

"There is therefore now no condemnation to them who are in Christ Jesus." Faith in the infinitely faithworthy One is our escape from all condemnation unto all realization in God in Christ in Redemption. As Bishop Brooks once said: "The only way to escape from God is to run to Him."

" 'Tis vain to flee. . . . The further off we go
The swing of justice deals the mightier blow."

CHAPTER XXXIV

FAITH'S GENESIS AND EXODUS

THERE is an old German proverb which says: "All is unsteady where faith fails." But faith founds not only all stability but all ability. Where faith fails not, all good can succeed. And the highest success of faith is when the highest and best is believed in, to the end of meeting the greatest need and thus securing the greatest blessing. So the highest of its successes is when faith lays hold on Jesus Christ as Redeemer.

It is agreed today that intelligence is an essential element in all life. No life is found without it. Life, however, cannot use its intelligence without faith in it. So faith is as integral in life as intelligence. The higher the level of life and the greater its scope, the higher and greater the faith which is possible to it.

I. FAITH AS A FOUNDATION

Contrast is often drawn between salvation by faith and salvation by works. But salvation by works is also salvation by faith—faith in works. Faith was required by the Old Covenant as truly as by the New—faith in Jehovah as the true God, in His revelation of the law of man's well-being, in the law itself, and in all Jehovah would be to and do for His covenant-people. But the law had no provision for salvation; it made provision to do that which would avoid the need of salvation. So the law made nothing perfect that had fallen into imperfection.

Grace gave the law, but gave no grace in the law which said, "Do this and thou shalt live." This law brought no life when it was not kept. Not the law of God but the law of sin brought death. Then the higher law of grace was needed to give back life in place of that lost. If faith was required under the Old Covenant, so are works required under the New, but in a different way—as the manifestation of faith, not as its object. Luther found trouble in the teaching of James which seemed to be contradicting that of Paul. This was caused by Luther's failure to discern the fact that Paul was talking about the justification of the saved sinner, while James was demanding the justification of the faith that professed to save the sinner.

The Epistle to the Hebrews emphasizes the sacrifice of Christ as superior in every way to the sacrifices of the ceremonial law. Then faith in the former is better than faith in the latter. "By one offering hath He perfected for ever them that are sanctified," whereas the law was unable to perfect those who offered the sacrifices it called for.

This agrees with Paul's presentation of Christ's sacrificial death as the perfect object and finished foundation of faith. Faith in Christ brings peace because its object is absolutely acceptable to God. Other foundation of peace and acceptance can no man lay than the absolutely acceptable one in "Christ crucified and risen from the dead." On this the whole structure of life truly Christian must be reared.

Because as a missionary Paul found all his time taken up in making known the new foundation of salvation God had provided, he therefore did not once refer in his writings, as we have them, to the Sermon on the Mount. That sermon was delivered to disciples already established in Christ. It sets forth the ideal of the Christian life, not its foundation.

Well did Paul know that the fulfilment of perfection is at the end of the Christian course, not at its beginning. So he emphasized the new order of faith and its righteousness—righteousness by faith in the redeeming righteousness of Christ. All Christian experience is witness that every Christian grace is made possible, once there is established this genesis of faith in the Redemption of Christ. Faith in the Christ who for our sakes accomplished His exodus at Jerusalem, can accomplish finally its own exodus to the Promised Land, the Paradise of Perfection.

> ... "In such righteousness
> To them by faith imputed, they may find
> Justification towards God, and peace
> Of conscience."
> —Milton, *Paradise Lost*, Book XII.

II. SELECTION AND ASSIMILIATION BY FAITH

Faith is patently the pioneer power of the soul. It leads the way in every activity of personality. It originates and perpetuates the growth of the soul. Self-realization can only be by that believed in. Nothing is added to personality from that in which it has no trust. In the tree of life, faith is the tap-root. The soil yields up its substance only as the roots penetrate it and draw therefrom.

Faith does not receive indiscriminately, any more than the roots of various plants receive the same substance. The nature of the life in the roots discriminates and selects. So different faiths select and assimilate in keeping with their nature. The congruity in this correlativity has already been discussed. The selection of substance in keeping with its own nature is because of the innate faith of life in itself. This is the law of all life. It must believe in itself to continue its existence.

In personal growth the roots of faith may go down into the soil of the sacrifice of Christ; and the deeper and wider they go, the higher and larger the tree of personal life in Christ grows up and out and branches forth. And it bears the fruit of sacrifice; while its leaves are for the healing of the open sore of the world's selfishness.

As the roots of plants and trees are fitted to lay hold upon and transfer substance for the building up of their structure, so faith is fitted to lay hold on Christ, and from the grace and riches of His Person transfer to the needy soul the redemptive substance to purify and build up Christian personality. There is a twofold union of faith, even as there is first the union of the roots with the soil, and then the union of the substance conveyed into structure. So the rootlets of faith entwine themselves about and unite themselves to the Christ; and the substance conveyed to the soul is incorporated into its structure. "Faith is the substance of things hoped for, the evidence of things not seen." It translates into personality the substance of the unseen Christ, and from this God-given and God-giving Person brings to the believer His Redemption.

There is reciprocity and coöperation of our faith with Christ's. As soon as our faith in receiving from Him answers to His faith in giving to us, the process of self-impartation on His part, and of self-realization on our part, is inaugurated. All the power and virtue of His redemption is stored up in His Person; and its needed efficacy or merit is transferred by faith to each believing person. He Himself has faith in His vicarious Work in full proportion to its merit. There can be no deep, vital faith in Jesus Christ that is not correlate to what He believes about Himself, namely, in the sacrificial existence He has become by His death on our behalf. When our faith answers His faith, then may we realize in ourselves the transmission and transmutation by Redemption.

III. Faith and Repentance

In the process of self-realization the priority of faith marks its primal importance; and it explains the Gospel's insistence upon it at the very beginning. "This is the work of God that ye believe in Him whom the Father hath sent." Unless God Himself can work in the soul by faith in His Son, there is no foundation for salvation. Salvation of the power of self-realization means that it is given over to God to work in it as He wills to do. Through this faith He first leads the soul to repentance of sin and acceptance of Christ's attitude toward it. In one way we have no more faith in Christ crucified, then we have distrust in that which crucified Him.

In former days there was much debate as to which is first, faith or repentance. But repentance *is* faith. Every act of the soul expresses a faith of some kind. Repentance is the revulsion toward sin which comes from a reversal of faith. Unless the opposite to sin is believed in, the revulsion of repentance could never come. No act is ever wholly negative. True repentance is as positive in its faith in Christ as it is negative in faith toward sin. This ends sin's domination in self-realization.

We believe in the Christ who cared enough about us to be crucified for us. But the Crucifixion of Christ is as truly adapted to awaken repentance for sin as to awaken faith in Him who submitted to its death. Any regard for righteousness as it is in Christ must produce corresponding aversion and regret for the unrighteousness that crucified Him. When the Holy Spirit enlightens us to see that *our* sin is no different in trend and character from that which nailed Him to the Tree, we repent of that complicity as we discover ourselves sharers in its enormity.

The sense of right and wrong, of responsibility and guilt is mightily awakened by the reciprocity of faith in Christ. Repentance is a fruit of the Spirit, a proof that the human mind has become attuned to the mind of Christ, and thinks with it. In the full Christian sense, repentance is the sorrow and contrition which the Holy Spirit awakens in us, to the end of our forsaking that which slew the Lord of life and glory. It is the expression of the impartation of His feeling and thought about iniquity. The result is a repentance that needs not to be repented of.

IV. Christ's Adaptation to Sinners' Faith

Christ's sacrifice of Himself for man in his sin is adapted to awaken faith; and this adaptation is a double fitness. We have already noted that *He is not only the objective in faith, but also subjective in it through His Holy Spirit*. In considering the enablement of divine fulfilment in relation to sin, its adaptation of enablement to awaken the faith of sinners in it, was mentioned. Christ's redemptive work is so immeasurely rich in sacrificial love, and is so deep and many-sided in meaning, that it invites faith. In short, it is inherently fitted to be the object of saving faith for the sinner.

Because it is the utmost expression of redemptive love, Christ's sacrifice is adapted not only to awaken but also to satisfy faith. As previously said, even sinners believe in being loved. That God loves the whole world of sinners could not be more plainly or fully revealed than in the sacrifice of the Cross. It has the preëminent fitness to hold and enlarge the faith that looks to it for Redemption.

To a true faith, Christ and His Redemption from sin are inseparable. We cannot believe in the one without believing in the other. Faith in "the Christ of today" should be faith in what He became by His death for the sins of the world.

It is not faith, but unbelief, which attempts to look upon Jesus Christ apart from His sacrificial death. This unbelief can neither have Him nor see Him as He is. We are never moved toward Him to the same extent or with the same quality of devotion, when He is shorn of His sacrifice of Redemption. The response and devotion of faith is always greatest in those who delight to say, "He died for me to set me free."

Minus His Mediatorial Work, Christ is of much less value, if not wholly useless, as an object of faith. And the Father, also, is much less an object of faith when the great sacrifice in the vicarious death of His Son is disallowed. Now it takes a great faith to make a great soul. Emerson says, "All the great ages have been ages of belief." The history of the Christian centuries bears this out.

There is no faith on earth which goes down so deep, mounts up so high, reaches out so far, and accomplishes so much as that which trusts the great sacrifice of Christ in Redemption. It imparts its greatness to the persons and ages which believe in it; for it draws from the greatness of the Triune God in the most stupendous divine achievement, and it works the work of God in His mighty outreach of Redemption for the perishing world.

V. THE GREATNESS OF FAITH

We have been saying that faith is the foundation of salvation by and in self-realization when it lays hold upon the living Saviour. It is also the foundation of all greatness that is greatness to God. To this it leads the way by growing understanding and appreciation of Redemption. There, the greater things of God become visible.

> "The childlike faith that asks not sight,
> Waits not for wonder or for sign,
> Believes because it loves aright,
> Shall see things greater, things divine."

Human lives differ from each other at this point. They differ in outreach, resources, and vitality because their objects of faith differ in these matters. Of course, the greater faith's object is, the greater the grasp possible and the greater the importation by it.

The power of faith to build up greatness of personality depends on its own greatness and that of its object. When there is abundant response from the object, faith is enabled to take firmer and larger grasp of it, and faith enlarging itself the more, enlarges personality by transference through its own enlarged capacity. Christ's sacrificial nature is so great and responsive, it is impossible to place too much faith in it. All divine dependability is in it.

We are never greater than our faith. Nor are we ever less than it. Even God's greatness can be estimated in this way. He is the Infinitely Great Believer. His faith is as much greater than ours, as He is greater than us. He believes in Himself infinitely more than we believe in Him. There is no limit to the faith of Christ in the Father and in Himself as the Sacrificial Agent of the Father. But He is more: He is that self-sacrifice which the Father offered for the sin of the world. Why, then, should not His faith in what He has done and become, be absolute or unlimited?

Since our faith lays hold only in part on the riches of Christ in His Redemption, it has plenty of room to grow. A growing faith has growing power of union and of assimilation. As there is always a definite proportion between the size of a tree and its roots, so must there be a definite proportion between personality and its faith. As growing belief in truth makes for the larger mind to assimilate and hold it, so a growing faith in Christ develops a larger soul by and for Him. An expanding faith in persons increasingly enables them to impart themselves to be the content of life and the upbuilding of personality. There is a similar acceleration of faith in Christ. The more we draw from Him, the more we are able to draw.

VI. Saving Faith

There is a faith in Christ that gives of Him to others as well as receives from Him. The more of Him we have, the more of Him may we impart. In fact, the working principle of Christianity is receiving and imparting Jesus Christ. We are not preserve jars for bottling up Christianity: we are conduit pipes to pass the water of life on to a world dying of soul-thirst. Faith that gives as well as receives, has no stagnant waters of salvation.

There is another reciprocity of faith that makes for greatness of soul, and the best of all. Christ righteously believes in Himself. He knows Himself. On one occasion He refused to commit Himself to men because He knew what was in them. *Now it is just as necessary for Christ to believe in us as for us to believe in Him.* To believe in those refusing to believe in Him would be to believe in unbelief in Himself. He can believe in us only as we believe in Him.

And yet He believed in us before we believed in Him. He must have believed that we would believe in Him, or He could not have died for us. Evidently He had faith that we would believe in His death for us.

No doubt God believes in us far more than we believe in ourselves—and with much purer faith. Often half our faith in ourselves is mere conceit; and half our doubt of ourselves is really lack of faith in Christ. But the trust Christ reposes in us as His followers that we would make Him known to the world,—O God of Mercy! how poorly have we measured up to such a faith as that!

To grow in faith in God means that God's faith in us can grow too. The more we believe in Him and make His Redemption known to those who know it not, the more can He believe in us. Campbell Morgan says: "We miss the point of the opening verses of the Fourteenth of John by disconnecting them from Christ's announcement just preceding, that Peter and the rest would deny Him. He says He believes in them in spite of it. He knows the worst, their utmost weakness and failure, but "Let not your hearts be troubled . . . I go to prepare a place for you . . . I will come again and receive you unto myself, that where I am there ye may be also."

VII. FAITH'S ETERNAL GROWTH

It is faith in the Christ of eternally sacrificial spirit that makes possible the growth of life eternal. The faith we have in Him is as old as God. It has been eternally at work in God. By faith we become part of the eternal life of God, and share an identity of faith with Him, as well as a reciprocity in it. By this faith the Holy Spirit knits us into inseparable life in God. Illingworth quotes Athanasius (Contra Arian. iii. 25) as saying:

"We, apart from the Spirit, are strange and distant from God, and by the participation of the Spirit we are knit into the Godhead; so that our being in the Father is not ours, but the Spirit's, which is in us and abides in us."[1]

Faith always tends to beget faith. God's faith begets ours. And increase in faith of the one tends to

---
1. The Doctrine of the Trinity, p 95

an increase in the reciprocal faith of the other. One of the most glorious things in the destiny of the Christian is that His faith in God and God's faith in him shall go on in growth forever. To be included in the everlasting life of God's faith, this is something to be redeemed to! "He that believeth hath everlasting life."

Faith in God as revealed in Christ can go on forever, because it has no element of decay or of death in it. It is righteous clean through. On the other hand, we could never be right with a God of such sacrifice for us without believing in it and in Him. Judas did not more betray than the man who meets that infinite sacrifice on his behalf only to question its necessity, efficacy, and dependability.

If a righteous person has manifested his faith and interest in us by doing on our behalf some great work that we could not do for ourselves, the only way to be right with him is by believing in him and his work for us. "With the heart man believeth unto righteousness." We are made right with God in two ways, when believing in His redeeming righteousness. First, we meet His vicarious righteousness with the righteousness of faith; for faith in righteousness is itself a righteousness. Second, the greater righteousness is to be enfolded within the provisions, powers and holiness of His sacrifice for us. We cannot really believe in God and refuse to believe in the great offering which perfectly represents Him; and we cannot receive this sacrifice without having a righteousness infinitely beyond our own, thank God!

When faith grows, the righteousness which comes by faith grows also. Faith in Christ's vicarious sacrifice is a germinal righteousness that may develop without limit. And growth in righteousness helps growth in faith. If we should pray, "Lord increase our righteousness," we would find that His favorable answer had increased our faith also. He cannot do the one without doing the other.

CHAPTER XXXV

THE SONSHIP OF LOVE

WHILE faith may give and love receive, as a rule faith receives and love gives. As it is more blessed to give than to receive, the better love is that which gives. Faith makes love possible. Love was named as the spirit of Redemption; but faith is the source of love; and faith makes also the mediation of Redemption possible. Faith in sacrificial love makes propitiation for our sins; and faith in this redeeming love of Christ receives its reconciliation and redemption, and enables us to give ourselves to Him who loved us and gave Himself for us.

Since sacrificial faith makes sacrificial love possible, the two are really inseparable. There can be no love where faith in love has been lost. And where love has been lost, the faith that remains is a poor, barren thing, without life and satisfaction. Nowhere does sin more damage than in faith and love. When our faith and love had failed God, His faith in sacrificial love wrought that which reëstablished faith and love in human life. If by faith we stand fast, by love do we go forth as sons of God.

I. Love Not Static But Energetic

As holiness is the fundamental attribute of God in His Being or Nature, so love is the fundamental attribute of God in His relations. Holiness is the godliness of God, the absolute purity and unsullied integrity of His nature. Love is the godliness of His goings forth. In His relations He fills His place to the full with the fulness of His sacrificial spirit, the giving of Himself in the utmost possible.

When it is said that "God is Love," this is not an ontological but a theological statement. God is love not in substance but in manifestation. Love is not an essence of being; it is a form of activity. Emerson says: "Love is the essence of God." But love cannot be static or stored up as a substance of personal existence. It is a social relation; otherwise it is not love.

We may see this in our definition of love *as the highest form of self-expression, self-giving, and self-realization*. All these are personal activities. When a man says he has love in his heart, he mistakes emotion for love. Has he self-expression and self-giving stored up in his heart? Then he has motion that does not move. He gives his gold by keeping it in his purse. Love, to be love, must be like the Holy Spirit, the Proceeding Person of the Holy Trinity. While the Father is said to love the Son, He does not speak of His love for the Spirit, because the Spirit is His love, the God-Going-Forth Person.

II. LOVE AND FATHERHOOD

It is the genius of love to fulfil personal relations. Because of their perfect love for each other, the Father and the Son are able to fulfil their relations to each other. By redemption man is brought into the line of God's inter-triune activities of self-expression, self-giving, and self-fulfilment. When the mighty goings forth of God's love pass through man's nature, he is redeemed to go forth as God does. He is then caught up into the movement of divine love.

One of the many subjects of theological discussion is the divine Fatherhood. Is it universal or not? Are all men sons of God or only some of them? As the term "atonement" is a figure, originally a metaphor of covering, the endless ways possible to apply the metaphor has caused endless discussion as to what atonement means. So God's Fatherhood is a metaphor; and, because of the various ways in which it is applied, there arises misunderstandings and controversies about it.

The human father is not a metaphor. He and a mother beget a child. Son is a correlative term to father and mother. In the relations mentioned, the biological function is not the soul of it. Love is. Without love, fatherhood and motherhood is a crime, and sonship impossible. The relations of husband and wife, and parents and child exist to be filled by that which has no substitute, namely, love.

Because the relation which God fills as Father of our fathers and mothers, the metaphor is applied to Him. He is far more than a human father. The word is inadequate, as all terms must be which are derived from human relations and used to express the divine. He is the infinite Father, the source of all love. He gives us existence, the capacity for God—most of all in love. God is far more than One who is the Author of our existence. On His part there can be no doubt that He is the Transcendent Father to all men.

When we come to the correlative of the metaphor, we find men as much less than sons as God is more than Father. It is because men are not sons, that Redemption is needed. The redeeming love of God fulfilled itself in the sacrifice it made to redeem men unto sonship. The love of Christ possessing them enables men to fill their place as sons of God. This relation cannot be filled without love. And it cannot be savingly fulfilled except by the sacrificial love of God.

Fatherhood and sonship are meaningless except as they are counterpart to each other. As fatherhood is fulfilled in love to sons, so sonship is fulfilled in love to the Father. When the love of sonship dies out, Fatherhood is bereaved and its order of fulfilment altered. For as many as are led by the spirit of sonship, they are the sons of divine Fatherhood. The relation is left empty through sin. Rather it is filled by the wrong thing, by the opposite to love. Sonship without love to the Father is a relation without its spirit, a body without its soul, or possessed by an evil spirit. If marriage without love is misery, sonship without love is mockery. When fatherhood and sonship are reciprocal terms denoting mutual relation, kinship of spirit, life-including life, co-response, oneness of interest, inseparable destiny, one can hardly apply them to God and all men. What is the use of the name, if that which it means, is found wanting?

III. The Sons of His Love

It has been said that all the relations of God to the universe express in some way the relations between the Persons of the Holy Trinity. How God the Father and God the Son would term themselves to each other, we do not know. We should measure human relations by the divine, not the divine by the human. Yet the divine must be revealed to us in the terms of human relations, if they are to have meaning to us.

The universe is an expression of the inter-triune relation of the Godhead. The creation of man was a manifestation of the relation of the Father and the Son. We were made in the image and likeness of the Son. We were created in Him; and the love that the Father had for Him, He has for those in Him.

The failure of human sonship created a severe task for the faithful Sonship of the Son of God. As He was the Son of Obedience in love, the task of reconstruction called for His becoming the Son of Sacrifice by obedience. The love that had not broken down, in filling its own relation to the Father must also mend the broken relation of man. Having ceased as sons of Obedience, He must redeem by sacrifice to the sonship of sacrifice those who had failed the Father of Unfailing Love.

> "Can a woman's tender care
> Cease toward the child she bare?
> Yes, she may forgetful be,
> Yet will I remember thee.
>
> "Mine is an unchanging love,
> Higher than the heights above,
> Deeper than the depths beneath,
> True and faithful, strong as death."

Emerson said, "Every one is the son of his own works." The Master said, "If ye were the children of Abraham, ye would do the works of Abraham."

Men claimed to be the sons of God when they were doing the works of the devil. Jesus went on to say, "I know ye are the *seed* of Abraham . . . Ye are of your father, the devil. His works ye do." Here our Lord made a distinction between seed and sons. Later we find Paul making the same distinction (Cf. John 8:37-39 and Rom. 9:7). To Christ and His servant Paul, sonship is more than lineal descent; it is a thing of the Spirit; and the presence of the Spirit is shown by love and its works.

Scripture varies in the shades of significance with which it uses the same term. In the sense of source we have the expression, "The Father of all mercies." Perhaps a better rendering would be, the Father who is all merciful in nature, the Father from whom comes all mercies. He is "the Father of spirits," but not of the spirit of disobedience. The disobedient, sinful sons of men are in a way the seed of God, for the devil did not create them; he unmade them. He created in them the spirit of disobedience which dwells in them as "the children of disobedience." The spirit of sonship is identity with the spirit of the Father. Because of sin men are the dead or dying sons of God.

A son by natural descent, who has taken sick and died, is a son still. He died in body only, not to the father. When he dies in spirit, dies to all the father holds dear, will not love or own the father as his, then he is dead in the spiritual sense. In this deeper sense men are the dead sons of God. Their sonship being dead, they do not bear the resemblance of the spirit; they are the sons of the flesh.

"The works of the flesh are manifest, which are these: fornication, uncleanness, lasciviousness, idolatry, sorcery, enmities, strife, jealousies, wraths, factions, divisions, heresies, envyings, drunkenness, revellings, and such like."

It is plain that in all this catalogue of results, the flesh is far more than physical. Evidently it means the old, sinful, unregenerate nature, rebellious toward God, antagonistic to His spirit, and dead to His love.

> "He lives who lives to God alone,
> And all are dead beside;
> For other source than God is none,
> Whence life can be supplied."

IV. Restoration of Sonship

One of the great manward enablements of Redemption is the reconstruction of sonship in God. As already said, it was Christ's Sonship which made the necessary sacrifice to redeem man to the sonship of sacrifice. We may have theological theories about this; but this sonship is not a theory; it is a spirit, a love, a life, a living sacrifice.

The life which the Redeemer imparts has the spirit of sonship in it as a fundamental quality or element. It is inseparable from the Holy Spirit, for it is conveyed to us by Him, and ministered by His indwelling. Then the love of the Spirit "is shed abroad in our hearts." It is by His impartation and revivification that "we love him who first loved us."

We have said that life in a person is essentially inclusive of and being included by the lives of other persons. There is a right and a wrong way to include or to be included. To include with the spirit of God is to include by love. Love is the only answer to the problem of how the life-including life should include and be included.

The spirit of the life we include must affect the spirit of our love; and how we love determines the measure of our life. Hate lifted up the Christ on the Cross, but love made Him the central drawing power of the spiritual universe. Love is the supreme attraction; and the supreme love holds the attention of the world to God. Love fixes our gaze upon The Beloved; and beholding His likeness to the Father we are transfigured into the same likeness. Transformation by beholding the beauty of holy love is the way in which a higher and clearer image and likeness of God in man is brought out in unfading clearness.

Some one has said, "He only *half* dies who leaves

an image of himself in his sons." This also is true: he only half loves who does not become the image of that which he loves. There could be no half-love in Christ. He took on Himself the form and image of man that He might, by dying, have power to reproduce in man an image of His own Sonship in God,—that He might redeem us unto the sonship of love.

Faith in the Redeemer provides the instrumental means of His indwelling in us; and love enables Him as the ultimate means to reproduce Himself in us. The first word of the Gospel is faith; and the last is love. By His love He interprets Himself in us, gives Himself personally, and realizes Himself anew in multiplied incarnations. In a sense Christ re-incarnates Himself in every soul He fills with His love; for this enables the soul to love all He loves and in the way He loves.

Love not only redeems and reconstructs sonship; it fulfils the far-reaching relation it bears to all things in Christ. Moreover love subdues all things to Christ. Paul speaks of subjecting every thought to Christ. His love for us keeps us forefront in the mind of His love; and our love to Him makes Him our central thought. This proves itself when everything recalls the Christ and "minds us to His love."

> "There's not a strain to memory dear,
> Nor flower in classic grove,
> There's not a sweet note warbled here
> But minds us to thy love."

V. The Eyes Love Gives.

Love has wondrous powers of exploration and conquest. Every person is a vast world of undiscovered territory. How much more is this true of the pattern, Creator, and Redeemer of personality. Love has its own realms. It carries us and all our powers into its vast and various regions of richness incomparable. Traversing its territories and taking possession of them our powers are enlarged and ennobled thereby. And wisdom dwells in all the land of love. Whenever we are controlled by unrighteous hate, we are more or less fools in the thought that goes with it as part of it; but when we love, we are always far wiser than we know. The infinite wisdom of God is hidden in love.

Often has love been accused of blindness. Selfishness would thus justify itself; yet there is nothing in all the world so shortsighted as selfishness. When love appears blind, it is the blindness of concentration. Love looks upon only that which is of importance to it. It is blind to what selfishness and hate would see; and a blessed blindness is that! In gaining possession of and remaking personality it is at first handicapped by a blindness it did not cause, and which it seeks to remove. No, it is hate and not love that is really blind where blindness is weakness. The blindness of love is a strength; and it, alone, sees the things that are worth while, the values that are permanent.

Love illumines: hate darkens. Love enriches: hate impoverishes; for barren hearts make barren lives. Without love the soul can never be better than a pauper. No mind is really rich without the thoughts of love. Paul's mind mounted to the Empyrean Heights because his love lifted it to those regions. The mind of love can mount to the seventh heaven of cloudless altitudes. So heart helps head not less than head helps heart.

How marvellously clear, how patently transparent were the mental processes of the Son of God! No wonder that He could think as He did when He loved as He did. His redeeming love stirs our hearts with His wondrous, world-transcending thoughts, and quickens our minds to keep pace with our love for Him. It dispels the fogs without and chases away the mists which gather within the mind because of sin.

VI. Redeemed by and to the Love of Christ

The hallmark of sonship in God is love to Him. As love is the fulfilling of the law, so all that is good is summed up in love as in no other power of personality. "The great love wherewith He loved us," is the heavenly hallmark of the Son of God. To no one does love mean as much as to God. He, alone, knows the fulness of its meaning, the vastness of the place it fills in the relations in which He lives.

"They love indeed who quake to say they love." We may fail in love, but we call our love failure because we see its unscaled heights and unplumbed depths. We feel that our little love, to be called love, is almost sacrilege. How many-sided love's virtues are, we become aware as we summarize them from Paul's great poem on love, as recorded in the Thirteenth Chapter of First Corinthians: love is longsuffering, kind, magnanimous, meek, edifying, modest, self-denying, serene, unsuspicious, glorying in purity and truth, patient, trustful, and steadfast to the end.

The greatest hunger that man can know, is of the heart. The soul starved by sin has its heart-hunger satisfied in the love that daily redeems the days from lovelessness. Redemption sets the soul in the place where it belongs, enables it to love the right objects in the right way, the highest things in the highest way. The best thing we know about God is that He loves us; and this is also the most important fact concerning us. Love is the best thing we can do. It is the highest and fullest fruit of personality, the adaptation of soul to the consummating power of Christ's Redemption.

A loveless Redemption is as unthinkable as a loveless God. A soul cannot remain loveless and be in union with the Great Lover of souls. A loveless man is unhuman and unredeemed, no matter what other virtues he may have; for love is the soul of salvation. Love is the truth above all other truths, the reality above all other realities.

The redeeming love of God never rests till it gives rest to the sinful soul of man by bringing to pass the cleansing fulfilment of sonship in God. It labors unremittingly to perfect the image and likeness, the spirit and love of God in the soul of man. Redeeming love surges in his emotions, battles with his enemies, throbs in his struggles. It shoulders all our weaknesses, bears all our infirmities, heals all our diseases. It chastises and comforts, disciples and commissions, thrusts into the thick of the battle with evil, and even in the midst of the conflict gives us "the peace of God which passeth all understanding."

Because Christianity is fundamentally a religion of redeeming love, it possesses love's insight into the problem of human discord, and the adequate remedy for all disunity. It harmonizes man both with himself and with his fellow-man. Its final goal is to unify all things in Christ. Milton uses the expression, "Imparadised in each others' arms." By the Son's redeeming love human love is imparadised in the arms of the Fatherhood of God.

Love is a forestate of heaven. By it God is both enthroned in and enthrones the soul. It looks back to Calvary, forward to Christ's Return, and up to the Father's face as He sits upon the throne of God and of the Lamb. When the last sun fades from the skies, and the last star is tossed like a fleck of foam on the shores of eternity, love will still be reigning in its heaven as the life and soul of the whole united family of God. Then it will be, farewell old world of hate and deceit and doubt of God! Hail Kingdom of ever-biding faith and ever-abounding love! Than that, what better heaven could we wish?

"There are those who sigh that no fond heart is theirs,
  None loves them best; O vain and selfish sigh!
Out of the bosom of His love He spares—
  The Father spares the Son for thee to die.
For thee He died; for thee He lives again;
  O'er thee He watches in His boundless reign."

CHAPTER XXXVI

THE RICHES OF SACRIFICE

ONE of the richest lives ever lived was that of the Apostle Paul. It made him a multi-millionaire in spiritual wealth. He described himself as "poor yet making many rich." He became rich according to the law that all we give we have. No follower ever gave himself up more thoroughly to ministering the riches of Christ. Anent this he said: "Ye know the grace of our Lord Jesus Christ, that for your sakes he became poor, that ye through his poverty might become rich."

Enrichment by grace for sin-pauperized souls, is offered by the Gospel. The effect of the redeeming grace of God is bound to be manifest in spirit and personality. To receive it fully is to become in disposition what it is, even as we become forgiving when forgiven. To refuse to forgive is to deny forgiveness to one's self. To refuse to be gracious is to prove that grace is not in the soul. The richness of personality may be estimated by the measure of grace it manifests.

Christianity is nothing if not reciprocal. As already said, its working principle is receiving and imparting Jesus Christ. The more of Him we receive, the more we may and, in fact, must impart. And the more we impart, the more room is made to receive. This principle of enrichment depends for its working on union with Christ. Through faith and love we are so united to Him, that receiving from Him and imparting for Him is made possible. So receive we, and so give we, the riches of sacrifice.

I. Union With Christ

President A. H. Strong in reviewing his life-work said that he considered his thought on union with

Christ the most important in all his theological thinking. He saw this subject as strategic and vital in Christian thought. In this conclusion his devout soul and strong mind worked well together according to "the wisdom that cometh from above."

This union with Christ is set forth in Scripture under various figures: Adam and the human race, the firstborn and the rest of the family, a house and its owner dwelling in it, the human body and its members, a husband and his wife, a building and its foundation, a vine and its branches, and the union between the Persons in the Trinity.

To be united with Christ is one thing; to abide in this union is another. The stability of it is very important. "If a man abide not in me, he is cast forth as a branch and is withered." The fruit of his works also wither; and whatsoever he doeth shall not prosper. A pear tree was being picked when a large branch was accidentally broken off and laid beside the gathered pears. In a few days the fruit on the branch was shrunken, while the fruit in the heap was still fresh and luscious. The broken branch was sucking back the juice from its fruit. So his selfishness sucks the virtue out of whatever a man does, when he abides not in Christ. His leaf and fruit wither, because their substance is being used up to glorify him.

It is required that union with Christ be, not intermittent, but permanent; otherwise the process of receiving and giving cannot go on. Christ has far too much for us to be all received in a single act of appropriation. And the riches He would pass on to others, through us, are far too vast to be all given out in a day or two. It will take eternity for us to receive all He has for us and to give all He wishes to give through us.

Some times we may act as though we had received about all Christ has for us. This folly shows how little we have apprehended the riches of the resources of the sacrifice of Himself for us. The sacrifice is already made for our Redemption; and yet, in another way, it is going on and will go on—forever. The sacrifice is complete that answers for our sins; *but one sacrifice always calls for another.* Christ could save us unto Himself, only by giving Himself to us forever. He is still "the Lamb of God." "The throne of God and of the Lamb" in heaven means that the sacrifice of God in Christ is going on, and will continue to go on. Christ is no more exhausted or unneeded than God is exhausted or unneeded; for as sinners, all the God we can know and have is the God of Redemption, God in Christ, "the Lamb of God that taketh away the sin of the world."

The subject-object union with Christ in self-realization and self-dedication, being the foundation of the Christian life, its response to the Living Lord controls both growth and usefulness. Any interference with the closeness of this union, and retardation of its response to Him means that the source and scope of the Christian life is diminished. The development of Christian personality requires growing and deepening union and response to Him who alone can give life to sinners. By Him and by Him alone is it possible to reach full growth, increasing usefulness, and the perfection of the sacrificial self which is the consummation of Redemption.

II. The Sacrifice to Make Us Sacrificial

The Christian life, among other things, is a process of building up Christian personality by the one and only way in which it can be erected, that is, through union with Jesus Christ. We need to recognize in this connection that this personal upbuilding is as much a matter of impartation as of importation. Exercise is as necessary as food. Life is a reciprocity with environment, a correspondence with surroundings. Reciprocity would not be reciprocity, nor would correspondence be correspondence, if receiving were all that took place. Expenditure is, therefore, as vital to life as reception.

The growth of personality in its union with Christ

proceeds most rapidly when we are fully engaged in that to which we were redeemed, the Great Enterprise of God, i. e., the Extension of His Kingdom. All we do in building up Christ's Kingdom on earth builds us up in Him. It is in this way that His sacrificial spirit and nature may most thoroughly permeate our spirit and nature. Lives clogged with the debris of self-interest have really stopped their growth. It requires some self-expenditure for Christ-impartation. Self-denial in self-expenditure for Christ makes room for the enlarged self-impartation of Christ to us. The more we make the Lord Jesus Christ the object of our existence, and His Kingdom the end for which we live, the larger our self-realization by it.

The presence of the Holy Spirit in the soul is always fontal. He is not only the living means through which Christ imparts Himself to us, the Holy Spirit is also the living means through which Christ imparts by us as Christ-communicating personalities. He is equally necessary to both operations.

There is only One Mediator. There is also only one mediatorial method—the free process of the Mediator's spirit within the soul. And this process is untrammeled and unhindered when union with Him means union with His will and desire. His spirit cannot dwell in us, and His Word and Will be only on the outside.

Christ does not dwell in us as water in a pitcher, but as water in a conduit pipe. Too many turn the water of life into a stagnant pool; and then wonder why it has lost its refreshing taste. As Christ is as much for all others as for us, we can have Him only as belonging to others. To change our metaphor, short-circuiting the heavenly current instead of passing it on, brings damage to all concerned.

The essence of a life lies in its spirit. We cannot receive Christ's sacrificial spirit, and then change it to one of selfishness. The Holy Spirit cannot be holier, for He could not be better. If we have Him at all it will be at the price of obedience to the law and nature of the Spirit. No life can be received or given without its spirit. Since the life that redeems us is wholly sacrificial, as such it must be treated and imparted. A life that came to us at the cost of death, should not be put to death over again.

> "But whether on the scaffold
> Or in the battle's van,
> The fittest place for man to be
> Is where he dies for man."

Or where he lives for man sacrifically; and thus dies daily.

Jesus Christ did not make His great sacrifice for us that we might be saved from all sacrifice on our part. That would be a salvation to be saved from, a redemption to be redeemed from. He died to redeem us to the joy and riches of the sacrifice which He knows to be appointed of God from all eternity. Otherwise God would not have been eternally sacrificial in spirit.

It would be utter waste and misappropriation of sacrifice to suffer a sacrificial death for those who never come to share its spirit. It cannot be repeated with too much emphasis that the infallible insignia of union with Christ is His spirit of sacrifice reproduced and manifest in the life.

> "Though Christ a thousand times in Bethlehem be born,
> If He's not born in thee, thy soul is all forlorn . . .
> The Cross on Golgotha will never save thy soul;
> The Cross in thine own heart alone can make thee whole;
> Christ rose not from the dead; Christ still is in the grave,
> If thou for whom He died, art still of sin the slave."

III. THE FELLOWSHIP OF SACRIFICE

We must recognize that unless His same sacrificial spirit had been eternally in the heart of Christ, it never would have wrought its glorious work on Calvary. But the Eternal Spirit in the heart of God would have been of no use to us unless it made the sacrifice necessary to redeem us.

With this we must recognize that unless Christ on the Cross had made His sacrifice, there would not have been the cross in the human heart to save its soul. The Great Objective from which we draw the power and spirit and nature to be sacrificial is wholly indispensable. We have no part in that sacrifice, unless it becomes subjective in our spirit; and we have no power to become sacrificial in spirit apart from the transforming and communicating power of that Great Objective—"Christ crucified and risen from the dead." And let us not forget an important phase of this matter already mentioned—if the sacrificial spirit of Christ did not become subjective in us by the immanence of the Holy Spirit, we would not have that kindredship of the subjective able to draw from the Great Objective mentioned. Hence an objective redemption is after all but half. Jesus Christ without the Holy Spirit would be but half the means of our salvation.

The more we have of God the more we desire Him; and, unfortunately, the less we have of God the less we desire Him. So the greater our need of God, the less likely is that need to be supplied, as far as our subjective condition is concerned.

The riches of Christ's Redemption can meet the deepest need of man, abolish his poverty of soul. He needs God; but that is apt to be a trite saying. He needs God to become what God is in sacrificial nature. Then he can share God's experience with Him, can fill up what remains to be filled up in suffering sacrifice with Christ. Only in this way can there be real and deep fellowship with Him, namely, in interest, desire, effort, joy, and satisfaction.

We can never keep company with God by the stagnation of selfish existence. God is always moving on. To keep company with him, we must go with Him, and in the direction He is going, and how He is going. Mercifully He has left a large place in the Kingdom of God for human sacrifice, that we may be with Him in His eternal march of triumphant sacrifice. But there is no purely human sacrifice in the Kingdom of God; for it is divine sacrifice over again. There human lives have Christ so formed within them that He carries forward therein and thereby His Great Conquest of Sacrifice.

When we are enabled to enter into the sacrificial experience of God, then do we become rich indeed. The richest experience possible to man is that of the fullest fellowship with God in Christ; and fullest of all is "the fellowship of His sufferings."

There is really little or no depth of fellowship with Christ till we learn the art of sacrificially putting our feet into the suffering footsteps of "The Man of Sorrows," who was "acquainted with grief," and "smitten" for our sake. We never know Him as He is, till we are able to interpret His sacrificial soul by sharing its passion for the lost, His yearning over the perishing. It is salvation indeed to be saved to His passionate search for lost sheep.

> "Have ye looked for sheep in the desert,
>   For those who have missed the way?
> Have ye been in the wild waste places,
>   Where the lost and the wandering stray?
>
> "Have ye trodden the lonely highway,
>   The foul and darksome street?
> It may be ye'd see in the gloaming
>   The print of my wounded feet."

IV. THE SELF NOT FOR SELF BUT FOR GOD

Rich as God is in what He has, He is infinitely richer in what He is. Now the riches of Redemption lies in this—that it is the very substance of God Himself, what He is, which is brought to us.

Man's need of God is not a temporary stage of growth, for God is the goal of all development, all progress. Advance can never be beyond God. Christ is God leading us unto and into God. God in Christ redeems us to growing in God. There is plenty of room in God for the infinity of our possible progress. Led in God, gaining in God, living in God—these are true descriptions of what God in Redemption means.

Ultimately we grow tired and utterly soul-weary of mere thoughts about God. Apart from Him they cannot satisfy us. In fact, if we have nothing but them, they but add to our despair. We want nothing less than the very Lord God Himself. But He cannot be ours in Person, and dwell in our souls to make Himself our own, if selfishness is enthroned there. Either He excludes it; or it excludes Him. And lo! He hath put it within our power to say which shall be excluded.

Without God Himself coming into personality, by the very process of personal life, He would be unable to save us from the sickening staleness and stagnation of self-repetition and self-corruption in selfishness. And so sacrifice is not merely a step toward God, it is a step upward with God. Self-realization in sacrifice is rising above ourselves, above the self-for-self into the self-for-God.

"Unless above himself he can
Erect himself, how mean a thing is man!"

The old nature with its selfish lust is left to spur us on to final conquest and highest realization in battle with it. There is a divine discontent which is but the reverse side of our hunger for God. There is a holy dissatisfaction with present attainment and the imperfection of all we do. The greater our longing, the sweeter the secret of satisfaction by sacrifice. By the indwelling spirit of Christ we are able to reach out beyond ourselves and into God, and become the higher selves of the God-born hope of Redemption.

"And ah for a man to rise in me,
That the man I am may cease to be."

V. Enrichment By Sacrifice

In discussing "The Spirit" and "The Divine Enablement" of Redemption mention was made of "Possession by Sacrifice." What is true for God is also true for us in this respect, namely, that the sacrificial is the only spirit which ever really possesses anything good. The paradox of possession seems to be this: only what we have given into God's possession do we possess. Sacrifice is simply the most practical and fitting recognition of His ownership. Selfishness is a war with God to take things from Him which by every right belong to Him.

There is a unique joy in possessing; and Redemption gives this joy in at least four ways; in possessing God, persons, ourselves, and earthly things. Burns sadly says, "Man was made to mourn." Instead he was made to enjoy God and all that is in Him. It is sin which makes him mourn, because it is loss and soul-impoverishment and failure in the power of possession. Now self-realization by possession is a normal and necessary part of our self-fulfilment.

There is a righteous reason and a constitutional disability why a rich man, as such, can never enter the Kingdom of heaven. Continuing to believe himself the real owner of his wealth, he cannot enter the Kingdom where God owns all. To be saved he must become poor; he must acknowledge God to be the real owner of all he has. Only thus can he be saved from the illusion of independent possession.

> "Whate'er we fondly call our own
> Belongs to heaven's great Lord;
> His blessings lent us for a day
> Are soon to be restored."

Sacrifice has not only the power of true possession; It is also the eternal standard of value. It saves from over-valuing material things and under-valuing spiritual. When material riches are looked upon as higher in worth than the spiritual, "Property for use" is sure to be subjected to, or exploited by, "Property for power."[1]

When material wealth is given a fictitious and inflated value, its acquisition is pretty certain to be at the price of priceless moral character. Selfish possession fatally fools the poor tinsel-enamored souls who, coming to the end of life's journey, find themselves paupers forever. As the King of Poets puts this matter:

---
1. Property, Its Duties and Rights, p 10

"If thou art rich, thou art poor;
For, like an ass whose back with ingots bows,
Thou bear'st thy heavy riches but a journey,
And death unloads thee."[2]

VI. Laying Up Treasure in Heaven

As it is more to thank God for what He is than to thank Him for the things He sends, so it is more to rejoice in the riches of our personal being than in the riches of things we possess. It is here that the possession of God in Redemption so enriches, for it means enrichment of what we are. It is redemption to infinite possessions of personality and personal relations.

No man can really own anything at all till he owns it in God. Many a man has been fooled, thinking he owned something which really owned him. Redemption saves the heart of any man from being but a market-basket, and all his life a bad investment in bloated stocks, not only empty in dividends but levying their deficits upon him, all destined to be swept away in the panic of death.

It is in the spiritual values that ungodliness causes the greatest losses, and Redemption offers the greatest enrichment. Selfishness not only paralyzes the power of possession; it turns all things gained into barriers to life, into barricades between the soul and its God.

Sacrifice is the God-built highway into other lives to win the wealth of owning them and at the same time of enriching them. The greatest realm of possession by far is that we call personality. Selfishness is that poverty which makes the soul incapable of this great order of wealth. Unless destroyed it is the precursor of eternal pauperism. "So is he that layeth up treasure for himself, and is not rich toward God."

Christ's spirit of sacrifice redeems us from slavery to the spirit of selfish ungodliness. By it we gain possession of the power of possession. Then our ownership becomes a reality and not a seeming thing, not a delusion which death dispels. Acquiring wealth

---

2. Measure for Measure, Act III, Sc 1

is an art, and the higher the wealth and order of possession, the higher the art. Through the enrichment of soul that is in Christ's Redemption, we gain the art of forever growing richer in that imperishable wealth of the unchangeable values of the Kingdom of God.

The earthly goods of the Redeemed may be many or few, but "a man's life consisteth not in the abundance of the things which he possesseth." The gain of life eternal consists in ability to turn temporal possessions into everlasting treasure. It transfers its investments into eternal securities. They are "received into everlasting habitations." One could almost say they are securities on such.

As far as this world's wealth is concerned, many a redeemed soul's financial standing may be stated—"as having nothing, yet possessing all things." All the things we own being held for Jesus Christ and by Him, we thereby possess Him the more. He is our greatest possible possession, for we are joint-heirs with Him of all the Father's possessions. And the Father is far richer than in houses and lands, for he holdeth the wealth of the heavens and all eternity in His hands. How the Great Apostle to the Gentiles, because he was so rich in soul by outright, glad sacrifice, apprehended the art of spiritual enrichment:

"Howbeit what things were gain to me, these have I counted loss for Christ. Yea verily, and I count all things to be loss for the excellency of the knowledge of Christ Jesus my Lord; for whom I suffer the loss of all things, and do count them but refuse, that I may gain *Christ.*"

CHAPTER XXXVII

NEIGHBORLY CHRISTIANITY

WE HAVE been discussing in the previous chapter "the riches which add no sorrow therewith." Yet the world has ever preferred the wealth of earth. As Lyman Abbott says: "The world has always bowed at the shrine of wealth. To wealth Christ paid no deference. . . . He paid as little attention to the ecclesiastical aristocracy in the Church as to the aristocracy of wealth in society."[1] This mention of the Church is an anachronism. The Jewish state or religion was not the Church. No Jew so thought of it. The Church when it came into existence, through Christ, had anything but an aristocracy within it.

There are two extremes of attitude in theology as elsewhere. On the one hand truth may be held in an exclusive way. This is as unfortunate as unnecessary. To adopt a truth and fondle it as one would an only child, so that all other truths are ignored, is hurtful in every way.

On the other hand truth may be held as our Lord held it—in the inclusive way. For Him one truth always led to another; and the whole universe of truths was inseparably interrelated. Each truth has its own place, as Lowell has expressed:

> "Get but the truth once uttered, and 'tis like
> A new star born that drops into its place;
> And which, once circling in its placid round,
> Not all the tumult of the earth can shake."

Believing in the truth of individual redemption, we do not need to repudiate the truth of social betterment. Believing in a neighborly Christianity, we do not need to ignore or deny personal Christianity.

---
1. Christianity and the Social Problems, p 20

I. THE HORIZONTAL ASPECT OF CHRISTIANITY

Sociology is comparatively a modern study. In this it is not alone. Carrol D. Wright has pointed out that the word was first used by Auguste Comte in a work published in 1842. In this connection he remarks that: "Just how the organization of society first became conscious of itself is also a moot question."[2] It is more than that; for an organization possesses no more a consciousness, than a corporation a soul.

Looking at this matter from the theological point of view, there are three aspects of the work of Christ: the social presents the reconstruction of human society, the educational the instruction in the way of life, and the redemptive the freeing of the individual from sin.

These three estimates of Christ's Work arise from three corresponding estimates of sin. The first views it as a social defect, the second as an intellectual defect, and the third as a religious or Godward defect. The last view when adequately stated presents and includes the other two, for the Godward involves all other directions. Robert Browning suggests this when he says:

"Religion's all or nothing; it is no mere smile
O' contentment, sigh of asperation, Sir—
Rather, stuff
O' the very stuff, life of life, and self of self."

There can be little doubt that the method of the Master was the articulation of the social and all other problems in that of personal salvation. He made plain that redemption to right relation to God is foundational to all good. He made equally plain that a man cannot be redeemed unto God without his life becoming a channel of blessing to his fellow-men. In other words a redemption from on high naturally has its horizontal outworkings.

In one way Jesus Christ was not a social reformer; but in another He was incomparable as such. Mere reform, however, was never His aim. While He made

---
2. Outline of Practical Sociology, p 3.

no attempt to reconstruct social or political institutions, yet from His ministry has come the greatest social betterment the world has seen.

In this world many things are most surely attained by indirection. Happiness, for example, is to be found only in this way. So all social reform that goes deeper than the surface, is accomplished by seeking something more, something else first—even the foundation of the individual's right relation to God. There we must begin, for

"God is in all that liberates and lifts,
In all that humbles, sweetens, and consoles."

There is no evidence whatever that Christ accepted as His mission, the adjustment of financial ills, political problems, or other social difficulties. Manifestly His plan was to found a relation and impart a spirit that would solve all of life's difficulties. For them there are no separate solutions. He Himself is the solution of them all. He saw that all social or horizontal lines of cleavage were due to lack of right vertical relation.

In such a world as this, one is sure to be misunderstood in exact proportion to the greatness of the task he undertakes. For this reason Christ was and is most misunderstood of all. When one reads the life of Abraham Lincoln, naturally he wonders what was the matter with all the folk who so misunderstood him. Was it not because very many were living on a plane so far below his, they could not measure up to him in soul-aim, in goal-spirit?

II. The Depth of the Problem

Jesus Christ saw the depth of the problem of human life as no one else did. Inequality in the amount of this world's goods is a long, long way from the bottom of this problem. Not long ago an imported socialist said, "There is just one thing I have against Jesus Christ: He did not attack the rich." The level of this solution Shakespeare reveals in,

"Well, whiles I am a beggar, I will rail,
And say,—there is no sin but to be rich;
And being rich, my virtue then shall be,
To say,—there is no vice but beggary,
The logic of this sad cynicism leads to the resolve:—
'Gain, be my Lord, for I will worship thee.' "[3]

So it comes to pass that the socialist is as much and sometimes more a worshiper of Mammon than the plutocrat he despises. In this connection, Chancellor Day quotes a German socialist, who, discussing the endowment of libraries, said, "Why did not Mr. Carnegie give the money to the poor?"[4] So it was money, not intelligence, the socialist was after! Mr. Carnegie did give the money to the poor; but his fault lay, according to the socialist view, in not handing out the cash to them. In his own book discussing this very matter on page thirty-eight, he shows the impossibility of equal financial possessions. His own attitude is expressed in these words:

"It is a low and vulgar ambition to amass money, which should always be the slave, never the master, of man."[5]

In the previous page he has expressed himself in a line one can hardly ever forget: "Millionaires who laugh are rare." Once millionaires themselves were rare. Surely "the deceitfulness of riches" makes money a treacherous god to worship, and covetousness of it a dangerous idolatry.

The problem of human life does not center in the variance of the amount of worldly goods possessed. In the Gospel story we see how selfishness would use the Christ for its own ends. When He miraculously fed the multitude, how it fired the enthusiasm of the bread-basket followers!

Christ disappointed them in His birth; and here He disappoints them again. He refused political kingship.

"They all were looking for a king
    To slay their foes and lift them up on high;

---
3. King John, Act II, Sc 2
4. My Neighbor, the Working Man, p. 47.
5. Problems of Today, p 36

> Thou cam'st a little baby thing
> That made a woman cry."

To the utter bewilderment of most of His followers, Jesus told them He had come to meet the needs that are deeper than those of the body; and He offered Himself to them as the Bread of Life. He warned them against making the things that perish the aim of life. He announced that He was the way to permanent satisfaction of soul, and that in Him are the imperishable riches.

The answer of the multitude to this teaching was to melt away. One wonders with what expression on His countenance the Master said to the small remnant left, "Will ye also go away?" Perhaps the same look is in His eyes today as He beholds those who are giving themselves to the gospel of scrub brushes and bath tubs, who should be pointing men to the redemption of soul, the cleansing of man from the defilement of sin. Often disappointed but never discouraged or turning back, the Redeemer continues His task; for God in Christ is still the fount and fulfilment of all social life, as necessary to bind human society together as to create and redeem those who form it.

The interpretation of the famous image in the book of Daniel seems to have some application to the disintegration of today. The iron and the clay do not hold together. Only in Christ do all things hold together. The restless world will never find rest anywhere but in Him who said, "Come unto me . . . and ye shall find rest unto your souls." Twenty years ago Professor Henderson felt this uneasiness:

> "Our age is restless and uneasy. Multitudes are looking forward with anxiety or hope, with fear or joy, with anger or yearning. All will confess to a division, a conflict, a want of understanding." [6]

III. Social and Individual Redemption

If this were possible, Christ is more needed today than ever before. We should be searching His Word

---
6. Social Elements, p 12

and seeking Him to find the way out. We need sane interpretation of His teaching and faithful presentation of His Gospel.

Christian socialists usually present "the Kingdom of God" as the teaching of Christ, embodying the social order He would have. They quote, "Seek first the Kingdom of God." But the Master never meant by this that we should seek first the social order of the Kingdom; but rather that we should seek God first in His Kingdom. We cannot find His Kingdom without first finding Him. Then having found Him, His rule over us will secure all the good things in a social as well as in any other way; for, not a single social ill exists, but the lack of God's rule is the cause of it. To quote again from Robert Browning:

> "Man is not God, but hath God's end to serve,
> A master to obey, a course to take,
> Somewhat to cast off, somewhat to become."

It is the folly of a first rate fallacy to attempt to minister the blessings of the rule of God in His Kingdom to those outside that Kingdom. As long as men repudiate the Kingdom of the Christ, they cannot be saved from the ills due to the lack of this rule. To attempt to provide for those who will not accept the provisions of God's Kingdom, will get exactly the same response that Christ did when He fed the multitude near Bethsaida.

Only when God comes to His own in men, can men come to their own in each other. We cannot do more than God or take precedence over Him. Only as men come to their own in God, and lead others to do the same, are they following the social program of God. It has pleased God so to frame the social order that all righteousness and blessing in it must be rooted and founded in right personal relation to Him. This order no man has power to change, any more than he can change the order of the heavens.

It is impossible for Godless lives to be right toward each other in social relations. God in Christ is the one thing needful in the social as in the individual world. Our social salvation can be worked out only by God working within us personally His good pleasure. What a man will not be to God, he cannot be to his fellowman. So the Kingdom of God cannot be among us without being first within us; and it cannot be within us without being among us.

It is biological law that internal state and external manifestation correspond with each other. That, too, is the social law and in fact the law of the Kingdom of God. This being so, we cannot Christianize the social or external order faster than we Christianize the persons within it.

Two things are true in complementary fashion: the social life needs to be restored to God by the redemption of man's social nature; and personal redemption needs the social life to give it full expression. No person can be fully redeemed to God as long as the social channel of his redemption is choked, or pours itself out in maintaining social swamps.

As men become conformed to a world of unredeemed social order and life, they tend to miss their personal redemption. Its benefits are attained and maintained by striving to make Christian all that is un-Christian. This is one-half of the matter.

The other half is: any social service that does not manifest to men the fact that we have faith in Jesus Christ as Redeemer, and our conviction that they, too, need the same, we had better leave to those who would not be misrepresented by such service. Let us not try to force the redemptive blood of Christ through veins and arteries not belonging to His body.

IV. THE TASK OF THE CHURCH

This brings us to the point where it may be remarked that since Christ has left us here in a world alien to His spirit, there is bound to be difficulty of adjustment. Whatever we do, should come from having our eyes fixed on our Leader. As Rauschenbusch has said:

"Let us work out for ourselves the social meaning of the personality and thought of Jesus Christ; and be prepared to face His challenge to the present social and economic order of which we are a part."[7]

Christians are bidden to do good to all men, specially to those who are fellow-followers. There is no real helpfulness that the Christian man should not be interested in, and help forward as far as possible. The Church with the word and spirit of Christ teaches this neighborliness.

That the Church, as an organization, should lend itself to function in every form of social service, is a very different matter. Some are bitter in denunciation of the Church because it will not take the social program they have for it. For example, Professor Vedder says:

"The Gospel of Jesus is mainly believed, preached, and lived by those outside the churches. Within the churches there is a vast quantity of piety, but very little of the religion that Jesus taught. A Gospel is believed and proclaimed by the churches, and passably lived, but it is not the Gospel of Jesus."[8]

Let us remember that merely doing good is not a distinctive mark of Christianity. Moreover, every institution has its distinctive work; and giving itself up to indistinctive endeavor tends to destroy it. As some theorists outline the program for the Church, one would not have to be a disciple of Jesus Christ at all to follow it.

It is the follower's business to follow Christ, not to outline programs for Him and His Church. No one is competent to set the task for the Church, except He who founded and maintains it. He has not neglected to attend to this matter. HE HAS MADE THE ONE BUSINESS OF THE CHURCH, FIRST, LAST, AND ALL THE TIME THAT OF MAKING HIM KNOWN. To that end He called it into existence. For that purpose and mission everything else must stand aside or be subservient.

---
7. The Social Principles of Jesus, p 1.
8. The Gospel of Jesus and the Problems of Democracy, p 30

The greatest good the Church can render for society is to catch men for Christ. That is a greater service than has been recognized. In any case Christ never intended the Church to feed the world on the bait of social kindness taken off the hooks of the Gospel. It is not the business of the Church to be making the unsaved a bit more comfortable on their way to perdition.

It would be well that we recognize that the Church is an organization wholly for Christ's purposes and aims. To insist on having the Church good for everything, is to make it good for nothing. If any man wants an organization to do the things he would like to see done, let him found his own church by being crucified, and the third day rise from the dead and then so commission those believing in him.

The most neighborly act in the world is to bring men into right relation to God through Jesus Christ. To be setting men right socially with God is the foundation of all truly Christian socialism.

Christ commissioned His followers to be fishers of men. Simply doing good is not catching men for Christ. Christ sent the Church, not merely to do good, but to do THE BEST. Then it is failing Him to allow the doing of ordinary good to take up all our time from our one task of doing the best. Christ ever went about doing good, but never in a way that did not contribute to His great aim of the *GREATEST GOOD,* i. e., that of making known the Father in His redeeming love.

Members of the Church as citizens of the state should be faithful to their political duties. That the Church, as an organization, should be in politics, is no more fitting than that the home as an organization should be in politics. The Church in politics means politics in the Church. This means that the Christocracy of the Church is done for. And with that gone, the Church descends to the level of a human organization.

That old temptation of the devil offering to hand over the world at a price, would soon submerge the Church in utter worldliness. Christ did not mean to have the Church "of this world," any more than His

Kingdom. To be in the world and yet not of it, is indispensable to the Church in belonging to Christ and being like Him.

V. THE TEMPTATION OF THE CHURCH

The supernatural functioning of the Church depends upon maintaining its submission to the supernatural rule of Christ. To this Benjamin Kidd seemed to assent when he said:

"No form of belief is capable of functioning as a religion in the evolution of society, which does not provide an ultrarational sanction for social conduct in the individual."[9]

Dr. George Lorimer, however, took this for what it is worth. He said in discussion of Kidd's position:

"His tribute to religion was so genuine and glowing that his volume on 'Social Evolution' was received at first with unbounded satisfaction by Christian people, the echoes of which have not yet died away. It was thought that at last a writer on economics had appeared who was ready to do ample justice to the influence exerted by revealed truth and the church on the development of society. But a more careful scrutiny of his brilliant treatise has somewhat dispelled this impression."[10]

The danger of the Church is the loss of supernatural direction. With her paramount task before her, to be busy here and there at the call of a multitude of human needs, her efficiency in winning men to Christ is bound to be impaired. Midst the clamor of a world always ready to exploit anything that will permit it, the Church must keep her ear open to the One who has commissioned and sent her forth.

Our Lord refused to act as "a judge or a divider," not because this was not a good work, but because it was not the work He came to do. And if Christ was thus self-limited, how much more His Church! When everything needing to be done cannot be done, the Church must choose that which she was commissioned to do.

---
9. Social Evolution, p 108
10. Christianity and the Social State, p 116.

There can be no good comparable to that of the redeeming sacrifice of Christ. The Church's testimony to its primacy, necessity and the urgency of having the world know of it, should be unwavering. This brings to mind the words of Sir William Robertson Nicoll in an editorial in the *British Weekly:*

"Christ has not set His Church on earth primarily to do things, but to bear witness that He has done everything, and that the burden of humanity lies on the Rock of Ages."

CHAPTER XXXVIII

EDUCATION

PERHAPS the greatest problem of Christian life, from the practical point of view, is the adjustment of personal relations. Almost as great is the problem within—how to impart without increasing the wrong things, selfishness most of all. Here intelligence and care is greatly needed. Education is, therefore, part of our social problem.

While it is a social task, it must, nevertheless, be done individually. We cannot educate the public except by educating the persons who form its community. All progress is rooted in personal soil. Emerson has said:

"There is no prosperity, trade, art, city, or great material wealth of any kind, but, if you trace it home, you will find it rooted in a thought of some individual man."

Many are still enamored of mass movements; but human lives are lived singly, and all advance depends upon individual progress. This is suggested by Browning also in the lines:

" 'Tis in the advance of individual minds
That the slow crowd should ground their expectations
Eventually to follow—as the sea
Waits ages in its bed, 'til some one wave
Out of the multitude aspires, extends
The empire of the whole, some feet perhaps,
Over the strip of sand which could confine
Its fellows so long a time; thenceforth the rest
Even to the meanest, hurry in at once,
And so much is clear gain."

This reminds one of Shakespeare's Sixty-Fourth Sonnet:

"What I have seen the hungry ocean gain
Advantage of the kingdom of the shore,
And the firm soil win of the watery main,
Increasing store with loss, and loss with store."

I. Salvation and Education

Sin is the great divisive, disconnecting, and separating factor that dogs the steps of Christianity everywhere. Cast out by divine redemption it is ever seeking reinstatement by means of deception. The need of discernment, and the education of the moral and religious sense to recognize it and refuse it in all its subtle forms, is apparent.

We see how the sin-plagued mind separates things God meant to go together, sets at odds things that are counterpart. For example, social service instead of being a by-product is made the main business of the Church. Education displaces evangelism. Liberty is turned into license.

"Make disciples of all nations . . . teaching them to observe all things I have commanded," said our Lord in His marching orders to the little company left to conquer the world. The old arch enemy is still at the trick of dividing our forces. The over-enthusiast in evangelism would leave out teaching; and the over-enthusiast in teaching would leave out the making of disciples by conversion and regeneration.

Education is good in its place, but its place is not the whole place. The problem of sin cannot be adequately met by education alone. Sinners cannot be educated out of sin. Education is not regeneration. Disease of the heart is not cured by expansion of the head. Knowledge, alone, does not keep men from sinning; and knowledge, alone, does not restore them after iniquity has been committed. To quote Browning again:

> " 'Tis one thing to know and another to practice,
> And hence I conceive the real God-function
> Is to furnish a motive and injunction
> For practicing what we know already."

Man is more than mind, and Redemption is for the whole man. When a man is lost, all of him is lost; and when he is saved, all of him is saved. There are few more elastic terms in the New Testament than *salva-*

tion. There are so many ills and losses and dangers to be saved from. Salvation is in all tenses. "By hope were we saved." "Those who are being saved." "Now is the day of salvation." "Now is our salvation nearer than when we believed." "Eternal salvation."

Primarily we do not need to know more about God, but to be rid of the sin which makes the knowledge of God impossible. It is possible to be "ever learning yet never able to come to the full knowledge of the truth."

Everything depends upon what we have to educate. Is it a nature born of God, a soul redeemed in which the process of personal realization is at work? Betts tells us that, "Personality is not born, it is made."[1] This superficiality blinks the fact that life cannot be made. Education does not make personality: it helps to develop the person.

One must begin with that which has the requisite capacity. "Except a man be born from above, he cannot see the Kingdom of God." And one is not regenerated by example. We do need the example of Jesus Christ's life; but a mere exemplar is a long way from being a Saviour. But for His Redemption, the spotless example of the Redeemer would have but added to our despair.

The revelation of Christ must not only be *to* us but *in* us. We must have the adequacy to receive the revelation Christ made, as certainly as He had the adequacy to make it. A mineral could not be the revelation of a flower; a flower could not be the revelation of an animal; an animal could not be the revelation of a man; and a man could not be the revelation of God. The mineral may reveal something about the flower, the flower something about the animal, the animal something about the man, and the man something about God. To hear something about God is not, however, to hear HIM.

There is as much need of the divine in capacity to

---

1. How to Teach Religion, p. 16.

receive as in power to reveal. Regeneration is as necessary as Incarnation. If Christ were not God the Son, His revelation would be about God rather than of God. And to an unregenerate mind His revelation of God would be an objective without correlativity to the subjective, an incongruity creating an enigma instead of a revelation.

The revelation Christ made was in proportion to His Person. For this reason we need the expansion of constant growth to develop into that which He has to reveal to us. He has many things yet to reveal unto us, as fast as we are educated to receive them. There is little use of calculus or trigonometry before the preparatory mathematics and geometry are learned. Christ has heights of revelation as yet undreamed of by us.

Education is the subject-object process of self-realization in the revelation of Christ. His mind is objective to us and His Spirit subjective in us in this process of Redemption. Because He is God in Person and at the same time a human person, His Redemption enabled Him to express the full meaning and revelation it bears to us as to God, sin, and ourselves. For one thing it revealed by the poured-out blood on Calvary, that the poured-out life is the genius of Christianity.

II. The Stamp of the Teacher

Much of what passes today as "religious education" is a misnomer. There is no religious arithmetic different from the ordinary sort. Algebra is no more religious when taught in one school than in another. Pedagogy is just pedagogy. The turkey eaten after grace is said, is not a religious diet therefor. It is not any the less turkey without the blessing asked, and it is not any the more turkey when it is asked.

On the other hand the pure paganism in many of our schools and colleges is not education at all. It is the propagation of heathenism. An agnostic has just as much right to teach as has a "typhoid-carrier." Every teacher infects the pupil with what he is. While education must be considered as education, the teacher always passes into the realm of faith, and under guise of education may proceed to make or destroy religious faith.

What a teacher is in faith is infinitely more important than what he is in intellect. It is a fearful price to pay for a bit of mental discipline to have the graduate come out an educated infidel. Far better never to have seen a college or university than to lose one's faith in God and His Word. Instead of being fitted for life, he has incorporated death, when his training has put to death his faith in life by Jesus Christ our Lord.

The cry "Have the Bible in the schools and colleges," is wholly futile. In Christian colleges men have systematically taught unbelief and with the Bible as textbook. Unless we have the Bible in the teacher and the faith of Jesus Christ in his heart, he can and will use the Bible just as the devil does—to his own ends. Religious education is not so much the subject taught, as the teacher taught to be religious in all his teaching. Religious education is more than teaching how to teach religion. That is pedagogy; and pedagogy is just pedagogy. Religious pedagogy is one thing: religious education is another, and vastly broader: it is the growth of religious intelligence.

Why cannot a school, college, or seminary be dedicated to the proposition that Jesus Christ is absolutely sufficient to meet the world's need of God? He who teaches otherwise is unfitting and damaging. And the day of God's judgment shall declare it, when adaptation to Christ shall be the measure of every soul and life and school.

A pagan teacher cannot teach pagan mathematics, because there is no such thing; but he will teach and impart his paganism, because it is a person not a subject he teaches, and it is a person not a subject who teaches. A Christian teacher cannot teach Christian classics, because there is no such thing; but no one ever sat in the class of Latin or Greek taught by Professor Jones in Acadia University without looking into the face of Jesus Christ. It is the self-realization of soul going on in the teacher which really teaches. The rest is incidental. We may soon forget the professor's words; the impact of his spirit we can never forget. That went into the education of the soul, which is infinitely more than education of the mind. When Christ is great enough to a man and great enough in him, he could teach Choctaw in such a way that his students would come to know and love Jesus Christ unforgetably, ineffaceably, and with abandon of passion and devotion for ever. Senator Upshaw, of Georgia, tells of a father who said he preferred to have his son go without education rather than get it at the cost of loss of Christian faith. "Better for him to have to learn his A B Cs in heaven, than be able to read Greek in hell."

Martin G. Brumbaugh with experience as Professor of Pedagogy in the University of Pennsylvania, Superintendent of the schools of Philadelphia, and once Governor of the State of Pennsylvania has said:

> Education is more than a transforming process, it is a creative process. By it we become a new creature. . . . Teaching is always prophetic. . . . A wise teacher concerns himself primarily with the task of equipping human souls for life's service. It lays the emphasis of its concern, not upon the scraps of knowledge which it gives from day to day, but upon the fiber of character which it builds for all the years to come. The Sunday school is not an organization primarily to acquaint children with Biblical facts, but to set the currents of the soul in the channels of truth, that they may flow out into wider and wider reaches of power and steadier and steadier sweeps of influence."[2]

III. Education Not Redemption

Preaching is not necessarily a substitute for Christianity, though it may offer such a substitute; it is an appointed method of Christian work. So education is not necessarily a substitute for Christianity, though it

---
2. The Making of a Teacher, p. 6.

may educate in such a way to become a substitute; it, too, is an appointed method of Christian work. Education and evangelism are complementary to each other. In either case the truth and the theme is Christ the Saviour.

The Gospels set forth Christ as both Teacher and Redeemer. He teaches the way of life; and He is the way. He reveals the truth; and He is the truth. But His revelation was more in deed than in word, and more in Person than in deed, though His words are such as man never spake, and His deeds, the finest part of the whole world's history.

In His redeeming death the Son of God made a deathless revelation of Himself. There God expressed Himself in the highest form of utterance—that of the shed blood of life divine. In the incarnate Person of the Son, God's revelation to man reached its highest and fullest; and in Jesus Christ, this revelation reached its highest and fullest when He offered Himself in sacrifice on the Cross for our sins.

Christian teaching, alone, cannot be sufficient, for such teaching reveals the sufficiency of Christ alone. If Christ had offered nothing more than information to "the man that was born blind," he would have died in his blindness. If the Revealer had brought nothing more than revelation to those blinded and benighted by the curse of sin, they would have died in their sins. As truly as only the finger of God can open blind eyes, so only the regenerating Spirit of God Himself can awaken sinners to life in Himself. Having had this experience they may see and learn the things God has to teach to those who love Him.

The love of God is revealed not only in telling its story, but also in Him of whom the story tells. Christ did not die by education, though much of that called by this name, crucifies Him afresh. How much less would be the great message of John three-sixteen, if it read: God so thought of the world that He sent His greatest teacher, that whosoever receives His instruction should not be led astray in thought but have everlasting truth.

IV. EDUCATION AND EVANGELIZATION

What is an education? This depends on who is to be educated, what condition prevails, and what end is desired. It is, of course, human persons who are educated. And the outstanding condition is sinfulness, and the end fully realized personality through the Redeemer. Prof. Coe, in discussing education as development of living beings, says:

"Our definition of education says that it is an effort to assist development. It consists in exercising influence upon a living being. Now, the effort of any influence depends not merely upon the source, direction, and intent of it, but also upon the kind of object upon which it is directed. . . . In education we have to do with life, not with mere things. . . . Further, it is not only vital but personal. To be a person is not merely to act from a law that is within, and to impose this law upon external material; it is also to take possession of the law, to be a law-giver to one's self, and so to have self-knowledge and exercise self-control. A mere thing has no self; a plant or animal has no self; for they never take possession of themselves, and their acts are never their own in this deep sense, but rather processes wrought upon or through rather than by them. Now education seeks to influence action that is already self-action, or in process of becoming such. It is a relation between persons."[3]

All education that loses sight of the fact that man is a sinner and that Redemption from sin is found in Jesus Christ, has ceased to be, in reality, for the service of Christianity. It may have merit in a worldly way, but it is not a form of self-realization in Christ. Any education that ignores the redemption of self-realization by the Son of God, is under other auspices than Christian.

Because sin is more than mental hurt, more than intellectual ignorance and blindness, the Redeemer met the full necessity. Sin has not only destroyed the soul's vision of God, it has destroyed its life in Him. "The wages of sin is death," death of soul, not of mind alone.

A blind eye may be taken as an illustration of the

---

[3]. Education in Religion and Morals, pp. 98, 99

living death that sin causes. The blind eye is both dead and alive at the same time. It is dead to the light and use for which it is made, but alive as part of the body. Its blindness does not come from lack of light, and no manifestation of light, however great, can cure it.

In a similar way a soul can be at the same time both dead and alive, dead to God and His love, but alive to sin and self. Its state of death is not due to any lack of love on God's part, and no amount of the mere teaching of God's love can make the dead soul live. Life itself must be imparted. As blind eyes were restored to sight by the touch of the Creator-Redeemer, so dead and loveless souls are redeemed to life and love by the touch of Him who alone has this power.

The love of God revealed itself in sacrifice adequate to redeem us. Those who would substitute teaching for evangelism, usually believe in redemption by love's exhibition. On this Alexander Maclaren says:

"It seems to me that those who in the name of the highest paternal love, reject the thought of Christ's sacrificial death, are kicking away the ladder by which they have climbed, and are better than their creeds, and happily illogical."

CHAPTER XXXIX

FREEDOM

WE HAVE just been considering education. In it two opposite tendencies appear to be making headway today, one toward bondage, the other toward liberty. At present our high school courses cover more subjects than college courses used to cover. Study after study has been added to each curriculum like frill upon frill, ruffle upon ruffle, flounce upon flounce, and train upon train, till the skirts of American education are mostly outskirts,—and this is an age of shortened skirts!

Some one has defined an expert as one who knows more and more about less and less. Today education is mostly by experts; and it is becoming slavery to superficiality, teaching the everywhereness of the nowhere. The multiplicity of subjects has thrown upon young students the overstrain of unnecessary burden that unfits rather than prepares for life, and has made for superficiality rather than depth of erudition.

On the other hand there are two signs of a movement in the direction of freedom. Electives have greatly multiplied, and far too enormously. The Dalton plan surely offers real liberty both to acquire and to help in student life. American schools should be leading in the use of it, inasmuch as this system originated in this country. To compensate they have instead run away with a multiplicity of studies.

I. Education in the Use of Liberty

The greater the liberty human life enjoys, the greater should be the education to go with it, to preserve it, and to use it, rather than to abuse it. When liberty outruns education it becomes license. By education is here meant, the education that teaches how to use freedom religiously. Intellectual education, alone, is no safeguard to liberty. Today, we have thousands upon thousands of educated criminals.

On the other hand the less liberty human life has, the more the need of that education which will bring to pass the required liberation. People usually think of political freedom first of all, yet it is far from being the most important liberty needed.

If freedom of the polls were denied in the United States, there would be war in consequence; yet half the eligible voters in the last national election refused the duty of exercising this franchise. In other words it is the freedom to make no use of freedom, the freedom to flout the responsibilities of citizenship, which half the nation would fight for, and imagine themselves heroes therefor.

It is only when freedom is interpreted by the higher realm of religion that its sanctions are secured. Ignorance of the nature and implications of liberty as set forth in the Christian interpretation thereof menaces today state, home and Church. Corruption of freedom and of religion naturally go together.

Freedom is a great subject—politically, socially, and theologically. Life and freedom are correlate everywhere. The larger and higher the life, the larger and higher the liberty which naturally accompanies it. Genetic freedom gives life its beginning; and the genesis of growth lies in the liberty that makes it possible.

II. The Love of Liberty

President Mullins discussing this subject of Freedom says:

"Our age, beyond all others, is the age of freedom. Freedom is the winged word which, since the Reformation, has led human progress in all realms of endeavor. The revolt has been complete against all kinds of tyranny, and one might almost say against all forms of authority. . . . Freedom of belief in religion, of research in science, of opportunity and effort in the industrial world, absolute freedom in all spheres is the ideal."[1]

---
1. Freedom and Authority in Religion, p 11.

Two years after these lines went to press the World War broke loose. For a time it looked as though it were only the powers of evil that had found "absolute liberty." Since then false ideas of freedom have been promulgated in many directions. Expressionism and Behaviorism in psychology, Bolshevism and Indifferentism in politics, Voluntaryism and Modernism in theology are much in evidence. The world, after its debauch of war, is slowly wakening to the truth that abuse of freedom is as dangerous as repression of liberty. If the world is delivered from all such false ideas of freedom, it will be by learning at the feet of the Great Teacher the lesson of true liberty.

On this subject the New Testament is the divine textbook. Jesus said, "I am the truth. The truth shall make you free. If the Son make you free, ye shall be free indeed." The Gospels and the Epistles alike proclaim "the liberty wherewith Christ makes us free." "through the redemption that is in Christ Jesus" by which we obtain "the liberty of the sons of God."

Freedom is one of the sacred words of our language. More sacred still is freedom itself. The world has yet to learn, however, that freedom is sacred only when used sacredly, that is, for sacred ends. Liberty when demanded by evil, interpreted by false notions, and used to unholy purposes, ceases to be true liberty, and is but slavery in disguise.

In every human breast there is a native love for freedom. Every Christian feels he has a God-given right to liberty; but God has given no one the right to abuse it. Unfortunately all do not preserve their right to liberty. A man must reap what he sows. He who uses his freedom to sow seeds of bondage, must reap bondage.

Life may be used to destroy life, strength to destroy strength, and liberty to destroy liberty. Jesus said, "He that committeth sin is the bond-slave of sin." It it unreasonable to expect any legislation to give freedom to those who enslave themselves. Cowper said:

> "He is the freeman whom the truth makes free,
> And all are slaves besides."

Liberty given to badness and withheld from goodness would soon destroy us. Freedom to evil cannot be other than injury and lead to enslavement. Men have made loud claims to liberty without a thought as to what kind of liberty or to what purpose. Freedom to commit crime means that civilization's liberty is assailed. Men have no right to liberty except to do right; otherwise right ceases to have meaning.

Weeds may take the liberty of growing in one's garden; but the gardener must not only deny their right but remove them. Otherwise his garden has less liberty to be a garden.

> " 'Tis liberty alone that gives the flower
> Of fleeting life its lustre and perfume;
> And we are weeds without it."

Thus Cowper thought. As no man can have the right to do wrong, so no man has the right to liberty to wrong others. That is the way civilization thinks.

III. THE LIMITATION OF LIBERTY

Too much liberty cannot be given to righteousness, nor too little to unrighteousness. Liberty like any other good thing needs to be guarded from misuse, from prostitution to evil ends. The best use of it is to enlarge the freedom of righteousness. The highest use of liberty is to give Christ liberty within our lives.

Freedom used against itself leaves us but "free to fall," to use a phrase of Milton. Evil, to be such, must misuse and assail goodness. Goodness must then be militant in defense of its liberty to its own righteous ends. In one of his great speeches Daniel Webster said:

> "God grants liberty only to those who love it, and are always ready to guard and defend it"

Unlimited liberty is possible only to unlimited existence. For created things there cannot be more than a limited liberty. A limited life cannot make use of more. Finite life cannot have freedom to go beyond its finite limits. Every created life has its own range of existence, and an equal range of liberty within it. In Shakespeare's Comedy of Errors he says:

> "Why, headstrong liberty is lash'd with woe,
> There's nothing situate under heaven's eye,
> But hath his bound, in earth, in sea, in sky." [2]

In all our dreams of freedom we are apt to forget our limitations. Fishes, swimming in a bowl, have as much liberty as the bowl is big—wide and deep. Even in the sea their liberty would end with the shore, unless they belonged to the strange order of fishes in India that can climb trees. Schiller discussing the limits of freedom said, "Freedom is only in the land of dreams." But the dreams of some men come true have increased liberty. The reverse of this is also true.

Jesus Christ is first in freedom, first in freedom's cause, and first by sacrificing most to restore it. The liberty of His life He used in but one way, that is in manifesting God to restore to man his lost liberty. The more one lives to manifest God in any direction, the more of that found there shall he have. When liberty means to us, filling the place which God has assigned to us, then the greater range of liberty therein is destined to become ours. And then we shall be less likely to barter away our freedom for a masked bondage.

IV. LIBERTY AND DIVINE SOVEREIGNTY

Liberty may be measured by life, and life itself by liberty. There can be no liberty apart from life, and life cannot be less important than liberty. Dryden overstated the truth when he said:

> "The love of liberty with life is given,
> And life itself the inferior gift of heaven."

There are the two views of life, the personal and the mechanistic or necessitarian. In the latter even the illusion of freedom is fated, produced by fixed, unalter-

---

2. Act II, Sc 1.

able causes and processes. The personal view is not so much a philosophic theory as an interpretation of life and personality as we find them and know them to be. If this interpretation itself is held to be necessitated illusion, the reply is that then it must be an illusion which so regards this as illusion. On its own interpretation its foundation is the illusion that we have an illusion. If it is illusion that we have the illusion of liberty, then liberty is no illusion, even as not nothing must be something.

There have been mechanistic interpretations of freedom due to mechanistic interpretations of personality. The parts of personality have been looked upon as acting independently, more independently even than the parts of a machine. The old psychology that put abstractions in place of attractions and coöperations, was much at fault in this matter.

One of the great questions of abstract theology was, "How can absolute divine sovereignty possibly leave any room for human free-will, or any free-will other than God's? Bergson has pointed out that it is the fallacy of abstract will which is responsible for this question. Will in a person is inseparable in operation from other powers of activity. And as already remarked in an earlier chapter, it is not will that wills, but personality. An act of pure will is impossible to personality. So this problem of absolute sovereignty is an artificial one, created by false and untrustworthy psychology.

Will always acts as part of and in conjunction with the other parts of personality. When God wills, it is the will of a Person of infinite intelligence, immeasurable love, unselfish desire, perfect sacrificial spirit and incorruptible righteousness acting along with it, through it, and in it.

That personal will ever acts independently of, or unaffected by, or not expressive of, the rest of personality, is pure fiction. So it is impossible that absolute divine will and human free-will are contradictory existences, for this resolves itself into asserting that God's existence and ours are contradictory of each other.

The real question must be: Does infinite divine Personality make impossible by its liberty the liberty of finite human personality? The answer is, the former is that which makes the latter possible. Personality would be neither divine nor perfect if it did otherwise. God Himself is free. But He could not be free if engaged in withholding freedom. As Booker T. Washington said: "The slave-owner was not free himself. You cannot hold a man down in the ditch without being in the ditch yourself."

God is not without freedom, because He exists to give freedom; but He would not be free if He were not the source of freedom. His liberty is the assurance of ours. It is not God but sin that interferes with our freedom. Sin is slavery always and everywhere. We have liberty in God's liberty. Sin detaches us from that liberty. And God loses liberty in the loss of ours. Were it not for sin He would be at liberty to enter and move and manifest himself in human life as He cannot because of it. When we lose our liberty, it is really out of God's. Sin cannot interfere with our liberty without interfering with God's. That which binds man, also binds God. And that which frees man, gives proportionate freedom to God.

God interferes, not with our liberty, but with our abuse of it. He interferes with our interference with Him. Our license, lust and selfishness interferes with God in such a way that He is compelled to interfere with us. So we lose liberty, not at the hand of God, but by refusing and opposing His hand. We may therefore say, all interference with our freedom is because of its interference with the freedom of God, even as all freedom is because of the freedom of God.

V. The God-Given Empowerment of Liberty

This brings us to the point where it may be freely asserted that *human freedom is really a divine empowerment.* When we deny liberty to God, we cannot but deny it to ourselves, for then we prevent the empowerment that comes through God being free to empower us. Thus we are bound in two ways—bound in binding Him, and bound because of the loss of His empowerment of us.

We cannot reasonably expect God to empower our preventing His empowerment of us. And our freedom thus lost can be regained only in the way it was lost. To refer to Shakespeare again:

> "Every bondman in his own hand bears
> The power to cancel his captivity."[3]

So the veriest slave of sin is still free to stop withholding freedom from God. His prison is locked from the inside. By letting God do for us as He wishes to do in Redemption, our lost liberty is restored.

This divine empowerment is for all our powers. It is a poor psychology that makes liberty something peculiar to the will alone. Our wills could not be free unless the rest of our powers were free. There is no more reason to discuss free-will than free mind, free desire, free affection, or free personality as a whole. The empowerment of personality with the freedom of the life given relates every part to it and in it. Freedom to include the empowering life of God secures to self-realization the largest and most important operation of liberty—the free impartation and reception of Redemption.

Freedom is necessary to self-realization in God. Sin is the enslavement of this power. It prevents our working with God in building up personality in Him in His freedom. The emancipation from sin must enter by the same doorway that sin did. Redemption must capture the entrenchment of sin in self-realization and entrench itself there, to work within us our Redemption.

The subjective of this process must be free to relate itself to the objective in Redemption. It is the subjective evil that subjects us. But for this internal evil

---
3. Julius Cæsar, Act I, Sc 3

the external would have no power to enslave us. It is the slavery within that is strategic to sin. In freeing us from the thraldom of iniquity Redemption unseats its control of the subjective by the alliance with the subjective and the regenerating change and empowerment which the Holy Spirit brings.

VI. How Christ Emancipates

As to the process of liberation, Christ emancipates and empowers all our powers. He becomes the liberating spirit within our spirits, the freeing will within our wills, the delivering desire within our desires, the releasing, righteous purpose within our purposes, the emancipating love within our loves.

"Abhor that which is evil," says the Word of God. This abhorrence is an impartation and realization that blocks the doorway to sin. Such detestation of evil is necessary for our preservation in a world of evil. Such hate of sin is but the love of God facing the enemy in battle. It is fighting the good fight of faith in divine Redemption; for sin is always seductive, militant, and struggling to enslave.

The self-realization which comes by battling with sin produces an aversion to it all the stronger, a righteousness all the deeper, a character all the hardier and more dependable. Self-realization without any contest with evil is soft and unstable. Faith and love with no difficulties to battle with, no enemies to fight, are the weaker and not the stronger therefor.

A hate which is not the battle of a righteous love, is a weakness. The stronger a love, the stronger must be its hate of its enemy that would destroy it. Jesus said, "Love your enemies." But He did not say, love the enemy of love,—love sin. In one way there is as much liberating power in hating sin as there is in loving righteousness. "Cleave to that which is good." Love of the bad is a bondage the same as hatred of that which is good. Hate of evil is as truly a part of freedom as love for that which is good.

As long as we have love for any sin, we are in danger of being enslaved by it. As long as there is any part of us that does not detest iniquity, but in some measure desires it or what it brings, the soul's freedom is in jeopardy. Liberty and iniquity are mutually incompatible.

One important part of Christ's redeeming work comes from His power or ability to impart His own hate of sin and love of God. The interpenetrating and communicating presence of His spirit in us imparts to us His feelings, transfuses us with His aversions and attractions.

Having suffered and passed through the death-throes of Calvary and having there experienced the utmost enmity of sin, Christ became in personality fully adapted to communicate to all in union with Him His instinctive dread of, His unconquerable aversion to, iniquity. Having died at the hands of sin He gained added ability to kill faith in sin, and destroy the false hope of any profit by it.

When our Redeemer brings us to hate sin as He does, distrust it as He ever has, and to love Him sufficiently to refuse to help it crucify Him afresh, a long way has been traversed toward the ultimate liberation from it. Full freedom given His life in us gives us complete mastery over sin.

VII. GIVING CHRIST FULL LIBERTY IN THE SOUL

There is something stronger than aversion to sin: there is the passion for purity which is the direct product of the positive love of God as revealed in Jesus Christ His Son. Redemption means liberation; and all liberation is not only *from* but *to*. And what one is liberated to determines the permanence and power of the emancipation from.

The measure or range of liberty possible is determined by the extent and height of the plane on which it moves. The highest possible plane on which human life that has sinned, can move, is where personality is realizing itself in Christ. This is the plane of belonging to God and growing Godward. Here is where true liberty in God is found, and the largest measure thereof that is possible will be realized.

Since liberty in God is really God at liberty in us, we find, in growing Godward, the plane of the purest and largest liberty, because there the greatest forces of divine liberation are at work, and there the largest freedom naturally belongs. There, the greatest room for God is made, and there is created the greatest room for His liberty and the liberty He gives. His growing presence within the growing soul measures the constantly enlarging scope of the soul's liberty in Him.

Christ, by means of His indwelling is us, gives to us of His own freedom as the Son of God. He enables us to become, not only sin-hating, sin-resisting, but also God-loving persons. Our part in securing this great freedom in Him is by giving Him unhampered freedom in life and soul. Increasing our faith in Him, in His liberating and overcoming power, and enlarging our love by obedience to the law of life in Him, first passes into consciousness of mastery over sin, and then into sense of complete fellowship with Him. Both of these gives the Redeemer the free hand needed in shaping, adapting, and equipping the soul for the enterprises to which it is redeemed in God.

The Redeemer-Artist of our souls needs a freedom in proportion to His ability to fashion, mould, and designate human personality to the fulfilment of the purposes of God in it and by it. This prepares for both freedom and fellowship in the undertakings of God.

A bird released from its cage, mounts up joyously into native air. Each upward glide is a pulsating joy in the freedom of the open sky. So joy unspeakable and full of glory thrills the souls of the redeemed when in the glad liberty of the sons of God they enter into full fellowship with the Father in Heaven.

Who can measure the delight of the freedom when our desires are no longer for that which brings slavery, when love is no longer for that which binds the heart in chains, when the mind no longer thinks enslaving thoughts, when personality delights no longer to will the selfishness which deludes and degrades? The measure of Christ's own eternal freedom as the Son of God becomes the measure of the freedom of the life He fills. And its liberty and its joy will be equal.

Because God is eternally sacrificial in nature and spirit, the redemption of self to become the self-not-for-self, or the self-for-God, gives it the whole freedom of the unlimited sacrificial life of God. The Christ is not only the secret of freedom, but also the security of it. The highest liberty is to the highest usefulness, for without usefulness the highest satisfaction would be wanting. And where secure satisfaction is found, the security of joy eternal is assured. The words of Josiah Quincy in His Centennial Address in Boston in 1830 may be appropriately quoted here:

"Human happiness has no perfect security but freedom:— freedom none other but virtue; virtue none other but knowledge; and neither freedom, nor virtue, nor knowledge has any vigor, or immortal hope except in the principles of the Christian faith, and in the sanctions of the Christian religion."

CHAPTER XL

AUTHORITY

LIBERTY and authority are terms used in many senses and in many shades of meaning. There is good liberty and bad, liberty within and without, liberty in every realm, in every direction and institution. There is mechanical freedom and that which is vital; and the vital has as many shades of meaning as there are grades of life. The freedom of Redemption we have just been considering. This we found closely related to the freedom of God. "For freedom did Christ set us free; stand fast therefore, and be not entangled again in a yoke of bondage."

Authority is also as varied in meaning as there are spheres and orders of it. Many are the kinds of authority. Every study and every pursuit has its own authority or authorities. Authorities in religion vary with the orders and their departments; but over all is that of God.

Authority and liberty are not contradictory but complementary. The redemptive Work of Christ establishes both. The circulatory system of the blood may be taken as a partial illustration of the counterpart relation of freedom and authority. The blood is free to flow through arteries and veins; but it is restrained from going elsewhere by the walls of these bloodvessels. If either this freedom or this restraint ended, death would result. Even so the Christian life needs freedom to flow in the proper channels; and it also needs to be restrained from flowing forth or pouring itself out in wrong directions.

This illustration falls short in setting forth one important thing: authority is not only restrictive, it is directive. It not only restrains from the undesired, it directs to what is willed. Christ's authority not only would restrict from evil, it would direct our lives into that which is good—even the fulfilment of the purposes of God.

Naturally the life upon which we depend, is an authority to us. And the life to which we are infinitely indebted, must rule in our regard. It is both the place and the right of infinite wisdom, love, and righteousness to direct the finite of the same and belonging to it by Redemption. In one way, authority in religion is the right adjustment of the finite to the infinite in related plans and purposes. Faith in the Lord and Master gladly accepts His authority, for love loves to obey Him because of "His great love wherewith He loved us." So faith in Him in its very genesis obediently confesses "with the mouth Jesus as Lord."

> "Faith is the subtle chain
> Which binds us to the Infinite; the voice
> Of a deep life within, that will remain
> Until we crowd it thence."

I. THE DIRECT RULE OF CHRIST

In these days of revolt against law and authority, it is often assumed that rule is sufficient cause for revolt; and that between the ruler and the ruled must go on the contest of the one against the other. But obedience to authority is after all, just as the Scripture puts it, not primarily a matter of will, but of love. "If ye love me, keep my commandments." A husband and wife find that love solves this and many other problems of the home.

> "He ruled because she would obey;
> And she by obeying ruled as well as he;
> There ne'er was known between them a dispute,
> Save which the other's will should execute."

The authority of Christ is grounded in who He is, what He is, and in the relation which we bear to Him as Redeemer. His perfect knowledge of the mind and will of the Father, and His sacrifice of Himself to the end of establishing the same in human life, together establish His place as Lord and Master.

There is the special need of Christ's authority arising from the immaturity and need of training which the childhood of Christianity on earth necessitates. We are the children of God; and Christianity is as yet but in its childhood in us.

Christ is the one and only Mediator between God and man. His authority is an essential part of His Mediatorship. It cannot be deputed. Since Christ's mediation is by the direct, personal relation of each soul to Him, then His authority must of necessity be also direct, immediate, and personal. His authority is but the governmental phase of His Mediatorship. There is therefore no need that any one intervene between the soul and its Saviour, for such interference must be from that which is infinitesimal in its competence. How can the human efficiently rule over the divine in life? Man may rule over man, but the divine is not divine which he can rule over. Either the divine life is not in the church, or God alone can direct it.

There is the constitutional right of Christ and the personal privilege of His follower to have no one interrupt or supplant His rule over His follower. Nothing in Christianity has been more exploited than the rule of Christ in His Church. Instead of being a Christocracy, it persists in being an anthropocracy. James and John have had many successors, but some instead of wishing to be next to Christ in authority, have really taken His place. Even in the congregational form of church government where the boast is democracy, human love of authority asserts itself just the same. In every group, political, commercial, religious, or otherwise, the strong man is bound to take up the reins of authority. The people never rule. They may choose their rulers, but they themselves do not rule. Every church has its boss or bosses as truly as does every political group. Democracy is just as really a foe to Christocracy as any of the episcopal or hierarchical forms. The foe is not so much the form of church government as the spirit in humanity that is bound to rule at the cost of Christ displaced; and it cannot rule and He be not displaced. Better the wrong form and a spirit of subjection to Christ, than the right form and the hypocrisy of human rule while pretending to be ruled by the Lord.

II. THE USURPATION OF CHRIST'S AUTHORITY

If no one is needed to rule in Christ's place in the Church, no one can so rule. And if no one can, then all forms of church government that lend countenance to any other rule than Christ's are dead wrong. Alike, they are Jacobean—supplanters. When Christ comes to "put down all rule and authority," He will begin with the Church.

How can the Church do without the rule of men? By putting away the things which make it necessary. The human schemes and exploitations, the earth-born programs and substitutions always need the *homo* who originated them to "put them across." Homocracy has brought hell on earth instead of heaven. It is the source of all division and heresy. If there were but Christ's spirit and one consuming ambition to make the rule of Christ a reality, then the form of Church organization would adapt itself accordingly. And the best form would be that most fitted to realize the actuality of Christ's reign in His Church, which can never be truly *His* till He alone has the rule in it and over it.

The greatest religious robbery in the history of the world has been that of the authority of Christ over His Church which cost Him his agony and death on Golgotha. No one else has so sacrificed for man. No one else so perfectly understands the human soul and the plans and purposes of God. No man is bigger than an atom in the throne of Christ. Some day Christ will spoil the smirk on the face of the officials who say to the pastor, "Do thus and so, or we'll do you." And pastors will be past who have bolstered up the authority of man in place of that of the Son of Man, and then reaped what they have sown.

All organization that assumes that Christ is not here ready and waiting to rule over His blood-bought body, is sheer impertinence. It is not that He cannot rule, but that men do not *want* His rule. The assumption that He cannot, is but announcement of the intention of exploitation.

The Lordship of Christ can be no more deputed than His Deity, and it is just as indispensable. His right it is to rule. Those who, in His name, claim His right do not seem to realize that the spirit of their claim proclaims their unfitness to represent the Christ. Nor do they realize that Christ's authority would be undoing itself by deputing to church officials the right to rule over the Christian lives of others who stand in precisely the same relation to Him that these officials do, and who, in fact, have just the same access to Him and immediate relation to His authority that any man-appointed official can have. Two orders of devils seem to be working overtime—the demons of disintegration and those of usurpation. Milton's lines on this matter here come to mind:

> "O execrable son! so to aspire
> Above his brethren, to himself assuming
> Authority usurp'd, from God not given,
> He gave us only over beast, fish, fowl,
> Dominion absolute; that right we hold
> By his donation; but man over men
> He made not lord; such title to himself
> Reserving, human left from human free."

III. Unity By Authority

In the Church man's assumption of Christ's authority is as unwarranted as it is unnecessary, as injurious as it is divisive. The Christian Church should be dedicated to the truth that Christ is competent as the Head of His Body. How better can the Church be dedicated to Him? If we believe He is competent as Mediator, why do we then refuse His direct mediation of the rule of God by attempting the re-mediation of His mediation in authority? As no one else was competent to offer

Redemption's sacrifice, equally so, no one else is competent to exercise the authority growing out of it.

Anything which comes between the soul and its Saviour and which does away with the direct, immediate rule of the Lord Jesus Christ cannot do other than injure, impoverish and misdirect it, and prove a foe to the progress of Christ in the soul and in the world.

In the Christian Church assumed authority is as bad as unregulated liberty. Either one cheats the soul out of a rich personal fellowship with Christ. He is as much opposed to the one as to the other. The rule of the Lord is wholly feasible, for no people ever sought in vain to know His will.

To hold that centralized, ecclesiastical government is necessary to secure unity among the followers of Christ is due to a misunderstanding of unity and a misreading of church history. Nothing can really unify which blocks the way to the direct control of the ONE AND ONLY UNIFIER. The only thing that ever brings men together in Christ is that which puts them personally and directly under His sway.

Unity is a matter of spirit, not of identity of form; and the spirit of loyalty giving to Christ the place of authority He desires to fill is the real unifying power from the human viewpoint. As all abnormal liberty turns out to be but slavery in disguise, so all abnormal authority turns out to be but masked tyranny. When it has sufficiently entrenched itself, the mask is thrown away and absolute authority declared. Then the ecclesiastical office rather than the spiritual excellence of the man is the seat of official power.

> "Thou hast seen a farmer's dog bark at a beggar.
> And the creature ran from the cur: There,
> There, thou might'st behold the image of authority;
> A dog's obeyed in office."

Any other than the freedom which Christ gives (to return to our metaphor), breaks down the walls of the blood-vessels in the Body of Christ; and any constraint other than that which Christ Himself imposes, constricts its arteries and veins, and by its unwarranted interference impedes the flow of the blood of life divine. Varicose veins and clotted arteries is the penalty which results from submitting to any ecclesiastical power usurping the authority of the throne of God the Son. Selfishness rules to sacrifice the ruled; sacrifice rules to give itself to the ruled. The rule and its result must correspond.

IV. Subjective Authority

If ecclesiasticism has sought to fill the place of religious authority, subjectivism has wrought to empty it. If all love must be self-love, all consciousness self-consciousness, all faith faith in self, and all will self-will, then subjectivism would have its way. One can hug himself; but if he insists that self-embrace is the only kind possible, a good wrestler could teach him better. Kipling says of one " 'E don't obey no orders unless they is 'is own." So our subjectivist would have autonomous authority to be all that religion has. One could quote many authorities (?) to illustrate this. Let Prof. Coe represent them:

"But deeper still lies an opposition between two conceptions of God's relation to the world—God as existing in only external relations to creation, and God as imminent in the whole of it. . . . The Christian thought of our time has already made choice between these alternative views. The immanent God, whose authority is internal and identical with the laws of self-realization, and with whom we come into relations not primarily through belief but rather through the whole circle of impulses and aspirations that make us men—this is the standpoint that we have won."[1]

If the professor had been a politician, he would not have needed to learn the art of claiming everything. That this is "the Christian thought of our time" which has come to the subjectivist view, is surely claiming so much that nothing more could be claimed.

In the first place, it is very poor psychology that

---
1. Education in Morals and Religion, p. 390.

puts God outside the universe in order to be objective authority. Has Prof. Coe to leave the world to be an authority? And it is equally bad to make the subjective and objective of authority identical. That the laws of self-realization are shut up to subjectivity is utter misinterpretation of these laws.

The cardinal misapprehension in all such misinterpretation is the failure to distinguish between the various realms in which authority moves and has its being. In the subjective realm of self, in matters that concern the ego only, subjective authority fits. In the realm of the home, more is concerned than self, and here subjective authority will not work. In the state the circle is wider still, and the authority of the self, or of the home will not do. In the religious realm the sphere is the widest of all, and in it neither subjective, home, nor state authority is fit or commensurate. In other words authority is coëxtensive and in keeping with the realm in which it works. Christ's authority alone is coëxtensive with His realm.

V. Christ's Rule Indispensable

As personality does not consist of a combination of separate, "water-tight compartment" powers, we cannot have relation to one part or power of Christ's Person without relation to them all. Authority is the relation of His whole Person to us where His will is foremost in its expression; but in another sense all His powers are authority to us. His love is an authority to ours, His faith to ours, His desire to ours, and His devotion to ours. Submissive relation to the Person of Christ makes Him an authority in every way and in everything. In the mediation of His Redemption, His rule covers everything that concerns the moulding and making of personality and its fulfilment in Him.

While we cannot bear relation to the will of Christ alone, we cannot bear relation to the rest of His Person and not bear relation to His will. For example, we cannot relate ourselves to His love apart from His will. "If ye love me, keep my commandments."

Creating the fiction of abstract will, some discuss the authority of God as though it were the god of authority. On the basis of this artificiality and misconstruction, reasons are then conjured up for rejecting all religious authority.

The more faith in and love for Christ the more welcome His authority. He cannot too much have the rule over us. There cannot be faith in Him and no faith in His will, even as there cannot be love for Him without love of His rule. How can it really be faith, love, or devotion that has attempted to dissolve His authority and evaporate it in the mists of subjectivities?

Jesus plainly taught that His authority cannot be dispensed with, if we are to enter His Kingdom and enjoy its blessings. "Ye call me Master and Lord, and ye say well; for so I am." "Not every one that saith unto me, Lord, Lord, shall enter into the kingdom of heaven; but he that doeth the will of my Father who is in heaven."

Christ's Kingdom, without any real rule, empties its meaning. As our King He has issued His new commandment. It might be called His renewing commandment, for obedience to it ever renews life in Him: "Love one another." In one way His greatest commandment is the Great Commission. It might have been called the Great Omission. "Go into all the world, preach the Gospel to every creature, disciple all nations, teach them to observe all things whatsoever I have commanded you."

It might be expected that Christ's authority would rise to the highest in the highest enterprise. God help us to see that loyalty to the highest is to be our salvation from slavery to the lowest! All the highest in consecration comes from unreserved acceptance of our Leader as Ruler. David Garrick, says, "Corrupted freemen are the worst of slaves." Then, for us, it is either consecration or corruption! What does any consecration mean with the will of God left out? And what corruption of soul is worse than that which breeds disruption and rejection of the Rule of the Redeemer of men?

VI. FRUITS OF THE RULE OF CHRIST

The blessings and benefits of the rule of the Redeemer are so many that eternity alone will be sufficient to enumerate them. Nothing is more closely connected with our everlasting destiny than His authority. In obeying His will we achieve a greater wisdom than we realize at the time, we fulfil vaster purposes than we comprehend, we attain a development of personality far beyond the highest of earth's dreams, and we gain a permanent power of achievement, a stability on a foundation that never can be swept away. "He that doeth the will of God, shall abide for ever."

The final test of Christ's authority is achievement for God and the riches of personality it accumulates thereby. The soul shaped to the will and plans of God, redeemed to the fulfilment of the mighty purposes of the Almighty and All-loving, finds therein the consummation of its existence. Man's self-fulfilment brought to pass under the control of the Christ is the summit of redemptive result from the achievement of Mount Calvary. "Blessings abound where'er He reigns." And the last blessing is the fullest, the most comprehensive. It is the fitting of personality to be the instrument of everlasting usefulness and satisfaction to God through the rule of His Son Jesus Christ.

Our Redeemer is "King of kings, and Lord of lords." This has an inner and an outer meaning. His authority is above and over all. But it also means that those He rules in Redemption become thereby rulers themselves. In His Kingdom, Christ reigns only over Kings. His reign imparts His kingliness to us, makes us kings. Then we may reign with Him. Then, too, He is our Great High Priest, and through Him we become "a kingdom of priests unto God." Raised to be co-kings with Him we do not then rule over one another. There is enough else to rule over; and so His sovereignty saves us from the pernicious evil of attempting to "lord it over God's heritage."

Another benefit of the redeeming rule of Christ is the power of self-control it develops. Within the realm of self the authority in keeping with the extent and character of its realm is brought into being. The self-not-for-self has its own self-control. Nothing so gives a man the grip of full mastery over himself as the full mastery of Christ over him. The human will, like all the rest of the redeemed powers, is strengthened when it functions as the will of the self-for-God. This self-mastery is part of the symmetry of redeemed personality.

Autonomous authority is all right in the autonomous realm, and all wrong beyond it. The rule of Christ is not opposed to self-rule, unless the latter is pushed beyond where it belongs and into the realm of the Kingdom of God. There, it is as much out of place as self-love would be in replacing the love of Christ.

Self-will in place of the will of the King is really rebellion. Christ's authority over us can no more be reduced to a subjectivity than faith in Him can be reduced to faith in ourselves. Autonomous authority is like autonomous courtship. It is somewhat lonely. The soul married to self-love by self-will must dwell in a barren loneliness. This is the old attempt of the soul to fulfil itself in itself.

VII. No Outgrowing Christ's Authority

The question has been raised by religious psychology, "Is not religious authority a hindrance, an intrusion, something to be outgrown or transformed into autonomous authority?" Even as good a writer as George Steven says:

"The child comes before the man and authority comes before freedom. But authority is of value only until manhood is reached. . . . There is no government worth the name but self-government, and all other government should lead to it. This is manhood and we are children until we reach it." [2]

---

2. The Psychology of the Christian Soul, pp. 47, 53

Logically this means that our whole relation to God in Christ is to be outgrown, for our relation to the will of God cannot cease without the cessation of the relation of all the rest of God's Person. God cannot cease to will concerning us; and, further, we cannot realize ourselves in Him who has no will concerning us.

The analogy of children outgrowing the will and authority of parents is beside the mark. We grow up to the stage of parent level and become parents ourselves. We do not grow up to the level of God and become gods ourselves. The will and authority of God can be outgrown only when He is outgrown. God must forever continue to be infinitely greater than we can ever be, and have plans and purposes for our lives greater than our finite understanding can comprehend. The finite can never outgrow its subordinate relation to the infinite, the created cannot outgrow the Uncreated. We have seen that freedom and unity come only by obedience to the central authority of the divine rule. Then to outgrow religious authority would be to outgrow freedom and unity.

Considering what our Redemption has cost Christ, there can be but one appropriate attitude to His will, that of unquestioning obedience. This, however, remains to be said, that the more our characters become rounded out into symmetry by self-realization in Christ, the less shall His will seem to stand out in unwelcome prominence among His other powers in relation to us. The more we "grow into Him" the less strain and struggle shall there be in subjecting ourselves to His authority.

It was the Perfect One who said, "I delight to do thy will, O God!" The more like Him we become, the more shall we, too, rejoice in doing the will of God. Bacon says:

"There never was law, or sect, or opinion did so much magnify goodness, as the Christian religion doth."

One reason for this is, it magnifies from first to last the Will of God.

The picture of heaven is not that of the authority of God passed away. The Hallelujah Chorus rings out there: "The Lord God Omnipotent reigneth." Christ is not "drest in a little brief authority." His own everlasting perfection is the everlasting acceptance of the Father's will. If He never outgrows the Father's authority, *how shall we?* The very last glimpse of "things to come" as set forth in Holy Writ is a picture of the permanence of divine authority. The depths of meaning in this mysterious passage we may be unable to plumb TILL THAT DAY.

"And when all things have been subjected unto him,
Then shall the Son also be subjected unto him,
That did subject all things unto him,
That God may be all in all."

CHAPTER XLI

THE BLOOD-BOUGHT CHURCH

TO PREPARE for the rule of the King throughout the earth the Church was called into being by Him. It can function, in this respect, only as it is a Redeemer-ruled body. It is, properly, a Christ-crowning organization. While the Church may "crown Him with many crowns," this and all else in service depends upon its being the sacrificial body that must give Him in the eyes of the world His crown of Redemption. As such He is the eternal King:

> "Awake my soul and sing
> Of Him who died for thee;
> And hail Him as thy matchless King
> Through all eternity."

As truly as Christ's Redemption is sacrificial, so truly must be sacrificial the organization growing out of, and expressing His Redemption. What Christ redeems the individual to, the Church was organized for. The body of Christ must be as sacrificial as His Spirit, without whose indwelling it cannot be His body.

The Church is the social or organizational counterpart of Christ's Redemption. As there is necessarily the union of Christ with those who are redeemed by Him, there is also necessarily the union of the redeemed with each other in Him and for Him. There is the individual self-realization in social relation as part of the organization of Christ's Redemption. Part of the saved soul's fulfilment is attained as a member of the sacrificial body of Christ—the Church.

I. The Blood Sacrosanct

Paul once used (Acts 20:28) a striking form of expression to interpret to a ministers' conference the nature of the Church—"The church of God which he hath purchased with his own blood." This mention of the blood of God reminds one of the old Patripassian heresy, which was an offshoot of early Christian belief. According to this teaching the Father Himself came to earth, suffered and died for us. Paul never taught this interpretation of Redemption. When he used this expression, he was in too much of a hurry in his farewell words to explain all that he meant. The pastors were doubtless familiar with this truth. Elsewhere he taught that "God was in Christ reconciling the world unto himself." "Christ loved the church and gave himself for it." For this reason Paul speaks of "the church of God which he (God in Christ) hath purchased with his own blood." If God, the Word, made flesh, can have a body, surely He can have blood in it.

There are some Christians who dislike all mention of the blood of Redemption. Because they know not the depth as well as the delicacy of its meaning, the beauty of its sacrificial nature, they object to all mention of the blood of Redemption as crass, coarse, and unrefined in form of expression.

The Holy Spirit is the Author of all refinement that is redeemed, all delicacy that is devout, and all beauty and felicity of expression born of the beauty of holiness. It was no accident of training or environment which caused the Scripture writers to use the language of the blood. Christ Himself also used it. Once the depths of its sacredness is understood, blood cannot be reasonably objected to as a form of Christian expression in Redemption. It is not materialistic, for "the blood is the life," and life is spiritual. Of all physical existences, nothing surpasses the sacrificial character of blood.

Of course, experience and training has much to do with awakening or hindering appreciation of the sacredness and sacrificial nature of blood. A lady who, in other ways as well, was somewhat fastidious, always objected to both Scripture lessons and hymns mentioning "the blood." When such a hymn as "There is a fountain filled with blood," was sung, she was so disturbed that she would leave the service of worship.

This went on for some time, until she contracted an anemic condition. The time came when but one thing could save her life—the transfusion of blood. While several, including her husband, volunteered to give their blood, that of her husband proved best adapted. After the transfusion which restored her health, her attitude was completely changed. Having her life at the cost of this blood-transfusion, this sacrifice on her husband's part, blood became to her a saving, a sacred, a divine thing. From the analogy of her experience she could understand how Christ's saving life had entered into her own, how His sacrificial life had redeemed her. After this she could not hear too much about the redeeming blood of Christ. Hymns telling of the "sacrifice of nobler name and richer blood," than "all the blood of beasts on Jewish altars slain," now sounded as heavenly melody in her ears. Experience had lifted her up to the language of the blood.

II. BLOOD AN APT SACRIFICIAL SYMBOL

We were not redeemed by ordinary blood. It was the blood of One who was infinitely more than man, that redeemed us. We are told that our Lord "came by water and blood." He did not come merely as a spirit dwelling in a human life. The Incarnation and its sacrifice were both realities. As a rule it is those denying the miraculous Incarnation by the Virgin Birth, who dislike all mention of the blood of Christ. Some try to prove their refinement by calling it "Slaughterhouse salvation." If similarly a doctor's blood-transfusion operation were called slaughter-house surgery, something would be likely to happen to the man so depicting it. Is our characteristic acquaintance with blood to be linked to places where animals are killed? Why do not those who think blood so coarse and gruesome, try filling their veins and arteries instead with ice-water?

Let us not be too severe with those who live in the

cold clime of frozen devotion to Christ's redemption. Byron says:

> "The cold in clime are cold in blood,
> Their love can scarce deserve the name."

Why should not a man "whose blood is warm within," leap at the thought of the precious blood that redeemed him? Longfellow in Hiawatha thinks as much appropriate in human relations:

> "Does not all the blood within me
> Leap to meet thee, leap to meet thine
> As the springs to meet the sunshine."

It was no cold-water devotion of Christ that fulfilled the sacrificial nature of God. He counted not His life too great a price to pay for our Redemption. His sacrifice in death is the great center of all His sacrifice for us. So He counted not His blood too good to shed on behalf of sinful men.

Blood is the most apt physical figure of sacrifice, and the shed blood the best physical symbol of Redemption. The Roman Catholic Church materializes the spiritual, while Jesus spiritualized the material. Transubstantiation professes to turn the wafer into the very body and blood of God. Jesus used His blood as the fit, poetic symbol of His sacrificial and imparted life. His followers so understood it when they spoke of "the blood of redemption." Because blood is literally a combined physical and spiritual sacrifice, it is an appropriate symbol of Christ's sacrifice as Son of God and Son of Man.

There are the two great directions in which Redemption works—the vertical and the horizontal, the Godward and the manward. By it we are redeemed not only unto God, but also to each other. The blood of Christ cleanses from all sin—from the sin of separation from God and from the sin of separation from each other. Redemption not only makes God our life, it makes the life of each Christian a vital part of the life of his fellow Christians.

Whose blood we share, we share his life. With

whom we share our blood, they share our life. It is the bond of divine sacrifice which binds us together religiously and socially. As the blood of the body needs veins and arteries through which it may flow, so the blood of divine redemption needs veins and arteries through which it may flow. It needs a social body, the Church, in which it may pulsate. The Church may well be called, then, a blood-bought body.

III. THE LIFE-BLOOD OF THE CHURCH

The blood of divine Redemption is the secret of the Church's existence. The sacrificial spirit imparted by Christ called into being the Lord's body. Every living body has its own blood; and as the body differs, so does its blood. There is one blood of birds, another of beasts, and another of men. The Church being a divine institution, has fittingly the divine life-blood to animate it. Its blood-life is a most important aspect.

As well might we try to have a living body without living blood in it, as to have a true body of Christ without His blood in it. The true Church is more than any formal organization could call into being. The common possession of the sacrificial life of Christ relates together the members so banded together. When the Father possesses persons in common, they are drawn together like a family. The Church-life is then a home-life.

Not organization but organism is that through which divine life-blood flows. Men and money can make an organization, but only God can create an organism. Of course, the Church must have organization, but it should be more than it. If organization originates the Church, it cannot be an organism. All too many churches act as organizations of men rather than organisms of God. The Church is not a club, not the organization of a natural affinity. A fortuituous concourse of individuals may be drawn together by some earthly interest, but it is of the earth and worldly. The divine interest, the social coherence of the divine life, marks the genuine Church. Its organization and cohesiveness are from above. The Church is one body, one blood, one life, one spirit in Christ.

As the Church is primarily the organization of Divine Redemption, only redeemed persons are qualified to be members of it. Unregenerate members become clots in the life-blood of the Church, and if allowed to move in the circulation of its life, they cause paralysis and death. The membership of an Ananias and a Sapphira in the infant Church at Jerusalem threatened to end the spread of Christianity, and called for drastic measures to preserve its existence and integrity. Persons not born of the Holy Spirit, nor under His control, could bring only disaster to the first Church, or to any Church for that matter. Such unredeemed members clogging the flow of the blood of life eternal have no place there. It is no injustice to them to remove them in the way that serves to prevent recurrence of the trouble. Better that the clot be destroyed than the body of the blood of Redemption, the Church itself.

Churches might be saved from many an agony and much ill health by insistence on regenerate membership. Otherwise they pierce themselves through with many sorrows. Some are added to the Church in much the same way that a splinter of wood is added to a human body. If more care and discrimination were exercised at the door of the Church, there would not be so much poisoning to the body ecclesiastical from festering splinters within it. It is far easier to take into the Church those who have mistaken impression for regeneration, than to undo afterwards the mischief their membership causes.

IV. The Ministry of the Blood

But even a regenerate member may become a menace to the Church. Usually some of the elect are derelict. They may be disease-carriers, or in some other way hinderers. The general principle may be laid down that the free flow of the blood of Redemption in the veins and arteries of the Church is the secret of ecclesiastical health. This is a very important matter, for the health of the Church affects this body of God in manifesting His Son to the world and in fulfilling the mission for which it was called into existence.

Weakness may come from loss of blood, and this may be due to various causes. Clashes of members, in which they wound each other, means bleeding the Church to death. Much depends upon whether it is veins or arteries which are severed. Sometimes hemorrhages are caused by unwise operations of discipline. When the ecclesiastical surgeon is but a tyro, he may sever artery or important nerve because he is really ignorant of ecclesiastical anatomy.

A medical doctor from Australia, after undergoing thirty-eight major operations, claims that he is an example of results of inefficient experimental surgery. He had the spines of three vertebræ removed. A mistake was made while intending to sever a neuritic nerve at its origin in a plexus, resulting in severing instead a cervical sympathetic nerve. The loss of his arm finally resulted after several operations. The right side of his body lost power of sensation and perspiration. The right side of his face was expressionless, while the other side was perpetually smiling. Is not this a picture of some churches after the surgery of amputating a pastor?

It is the business of the Church to see to it that all bleeding veins and arteries are tied up, all wounds of a serious nature healed, and all mortified portions removed. When the life-blood is in good condition, wounds soon close up and heal over. If the wounds are left open, infection is likely to set in, and bloodpoisoning may result. Either through ignorance or accident the body may wound itself, or it may be wounded in the conflict with the world which is ever seeking to make its rapier-like thrusts at the body of Christ. But the more serious matter is when members of the same church gash each other in internal warfare. Then the whole body is injured and Christ Himself is wounded, and His work greatly hindered.

Decidedly, the more dangerous wounds are the internal ones. In the address of Paul in which he used this expression of the blood of God, he speaks of his burden of heart and mind about the future welfare of the Church. "I know that after my departing grevious wolves shall enter in among you, not sparing the flock; and from among your own selves shall men arise speaking perverse things, to draw away the disciples after them." Prophetic insight enabled Paul to see the dangers both within and without, and that the gravest dangers are always from within. No church ever dies except by suicide.

After all, the greatest problem of the Church is not in relation to the world without, but the relation of the Church within. The higher the type of life, the higher and more insidious its enemies and the more difficult harmony of adjustment within. Lack of forgiveness in the Church, repression of compassion, and poverty of love cause constricted veins and hardened arteries.

Anything which restricts the flow of the divine blood to the various parts of this divine body affects its temperature and growth. Normal temperature is as necessary to the Lord's body as to a human body. Some churches have evangelistic fever and some anti-missionary chills. A revival may be like a fire of shavings, which, quickly dying down, leaves the ashes to blow about in the faces and eyes of those abiding after the crowd has scattered. True evangelism is not a fever but a fervor that lasts as long as there are yet souls to be saved. Usually the anti-revival church is united—frozen together like a row of icicles under a leaky, perforated eave-gutter. Why should the devil disturb that kind of church?

V. The Health of the Church

A sanguine, healthy church is made so by the richness and warmth of the blood of Redemption in normal circulation to every part. For this reason it is the secret also of the unity of the Church. The one blood means one spirit and that the spirit of sacrifice. There is no unity that stands the test except that obtained at the price of divine sacrifice. And sacrifice is the health of the life of God. Health is always the best safeguard against disease and disintegration. By the health manifest in the free flow of the life divine the Church quickly "finds herself." Ecclesiastical self-realization by any other spirit than that of Christ in sacrificial redemption, is like an existence which does not know what to do with itself. When the new ship "finds herself," the creaking and groaning of unadjusted parts ends. By the life-blood of Christ the Church discovers herself and her place, and internal adjustment follows.

Through the vitalization by the divine blood, a working unity comes to the Church. Internal friction always takes far more out of the Church than any church work does. When the life of the Son of God is animating the Church, the members are enabled to regard each other in God. Social and business distinctions are sloughed off. A homogeneity born of heaven fills the Church. This is the heart and soul of all true church fellowship.

This divine regard for each other, native to sacrificial nature, is constitutionally the strongest of any form of fellowship. This is true in married life, friendship, and all social relations. The life-blood of Christ carries His nature and spirit with it, and communicates His compassion, interest, and goodwill. It reproduces the regard, care and devotion of His love. To the great Head of the Church there are no obscure or unimportant members. There are no cold corners in the Church heated by the warmth of the sacrificial love of God.

When Christ's redemptive blood flows unrestrictedly throughout the body of the Church, all the rich qualities of His life and spirit manifest themselves. Then real progress throbs in the pulses of the Church. Then no member lives in his disgusts instead of his admirations, in his repulsions rather than in his attractions. When the black blood of hate rather than the red blood of love courses through the blood-vessels of the Church, disunity, disintegration, and unhappiness cannot fail to result. When instead of living the love of Christ in its humility and unselfishness, the Church adopts the proud selfishness of the world's social distinctions, standards of value, pursuits, and superficialities, she cannot find either joy or satisfaction. The effect upon the members is always in keeping with the spirit and life within the church. So is it determined, whether her forces are an army of conquest or patients in an ecclesiastical hospital, whether members prefer conventions to crusades, and excursions in the world rather than incursions into the ranks of evil. After all happiness is attendant upon unity and fulfilment of existence; and happiness of the deepest measure goes with the finest achievement of the purposes of Christ. Church realization by the blood of sacrifice secures many unities, unity of source of satisfaction, unity of service, unity of joy, and unity with Christ Himself. This is the living unity of one blood, one body, one Head, one family, one fellowship, one love and life in God.

VI. Overcoming Disease

Another great service through the ministry of the blood is that of nourishing, rebuilding and protecting. In its circulation the blood not only takes away worn out particles of the body, it brings the new elements to replace them. Even the worn-out blood corpuscles are utilized by transformation to bile by the liver. The different orders of blood corpuscles have different duties. As is well known, the white ones are the policemen or soldiers on guard against all enemy bacteria. Some are wandering or roving guards (phagocytes). The many-nucleated leucocytes multiply rapidly in the presence of invading organisms, thus indicating the seriousness of an infection. The one-cell leucocytes ingest and absorb bacteria and usually sacrifice themselves in the process. The lymphocytes are mainly the reserves. In man the lymphatic system to function depends upon the circulation of the blood. Lymph lubricates the joints, eliminates fatigue toxins from the body, and provides nourishment for the nervous system. The more numerous red corpuscles absorb oxygen and convey it to the tissues, and bring back to the lungs carbon-dioxide, whence it is expelled. As the circulation of the blood is controlled by the nervous system, so the Spirit of Christ controls and directs the imparted life of Christ. As the brain heads up the nervous system controlling the ministry of the blood, so Christ Himself as Head of the Church governs all the impartation and mission of Redemption.

There are many wonders in the nature and ministry of the blood which cannot be here mentioned, let alone described. We see, however, enough to increase our appreciation of the blood of Redemption. It keeps life in the body of the Church. When the local churches are organized, as though each separate department had a circulatory system of its own, there is more or less dismemberment. And then there is no common source of nourishment, movement, and direction. Members are interested not in the church as a whole, but in some finger or toe of the body where their fragmentary interest is located. Some make a church out of the Sunday School, the Young People's Society, or some club or committee or board. The church is a congregation in two senses in this situation, a congregation of people and also of organizations more or less loosely affiliated together. Over-organization and under-vitalization cause serious constitutional impairment in the Church of the Living God.

The sacrifice of worship which should be offered by the whole church, is not seriously considered by most Protestants. They should be Attestants to the need of this. We hear frequently of the increasing lack of attendance at worship. ' What else can there be when entertainment is replacing worship and selfishness displacing sacrifice. Pope says:

> "As some to church repair,
> Not for the doctrine, but the music there."

There is no cause without effect, nor effect without its cause. This at least can be said that the Roman Catholic Church has taken adequate means to hold her people to her services. Nothing has happened in Protestant churches but what we have prepared for and brought to pass. If we give worship-emptying and worship-ending doctrine and training, what else must we expect but lumberyards of empty pews?

Protestantism should begin at home with its reformation. But we need more. We need a great Protestant Regeneration, an awakening to the sacrificial nature of the Church and of Christian Worship. The Protestant pulpit has attempted everything but the one thing that could succeed in holding the Church together, *adequately interpreting the Redeeming Blood of Jesus Christ.* Unless Protestantism wakens to the Redemptive genius of Christianity and the sacrificial soul of the Church necessary to spread it, its constitutional, functional, and contagious diseases will put it beyond the help of even the Great Physician.

VII. The Sanguiferous Church

Lastly, the mission of the Church is in the blood of Redemption. The Church is a sanguiferous body. HER MISSION IS TO BEAR THE BLOOD OF GOD TO A LOST WORLD. Her task is to bring the redeeming life of God to life-lost men. Every body has its mission and every organ its function. For the Church to attempt other missions and functions is to perpetrate the deed of Judas Iscariot raised to the nth power.

The spiritual condition of the Church, the health of this body, cannot but determine how her mission will be carried out. Much depends upon the attitude of the Church to her appointed mission. Health comes as much from proper work as from proper food. The work of the body must be that which it was designed to do.

Much also depends upon that prayerful and devout contact with the Great Head of the Church which is able to create the atmosphere of hopefulness and success. Prayer is breathing the atmosphere of heaven. The breath of Jesus Christ is the Holy Spirit. "He breathed on them and said, "Receive ye the Holy Spirit." Along with giving His blood, Christ can breathe the breath of Redeeming Life into the Church. By communion with Christ the blood of the Church is oxygenated, so to speak, with the oxygen of heaven. Christ feeds the Church on His presence; and such food is as much better than angels' food, as He is better than they. Thus invigorated and strengthened the Church can face her task and do her work in "the joy of the Lord which is her strength."

The great mission of the Church is to bring the very life of God to the unsaved, and so bring the unsaved to Christ. The Church is not only veins and arteries to provide for her own needs; His body is hands and feet for the Master to work and run for Him, mouth to speak for Him, brain to think for Him, and heart to love for Him. What the Church has not for herself, she cannot give to others. Only an overflowing vitality is sufficient to be efficient in her ministry. Sacrificial love always overflows. "By this shall all men know that ye are my disciples." The love we cannot show to fellow-members, no one will believe we have for Christ.

Redeeming love alone can teach how to love. Condemning the world has never yet reached it. We are sent with blood, not with a blister. Members who think a moral censorship is the mission of the Church to the world, have yet to come intelligently in touch with the redeeming love of Christ within them.

For the Church as for the Saviour Himself, the Cross of sacrifice alone leads to the crown and the crowning. We hear everywhere, "The Church is at the crossroads." In the busy marts of human life, every block has its own crossroads. At any such as these the sanguiferous Church need never pause, "With the Cross of Jesus going on before."

The redeemed Church never renders stagnant the water of life, nor stops the flow of the blood of the world's redemption. The true Church of Christ cannot loll at ease while all the world lies a-dying of sin's disease. The Great Physician has opened his veins for the transfusion of His sufficient blood to the whole race. His wounds alone can heal the wounds of humanity which sin has made. The wounds of the Crucified One are for the healing of the nations. Bringing the life of Redemption flowing from those wounds to the open sore of the world, the Church can never fail, and will be secure in the only security that means anything to a sacrificial body. As Charles Wesley sang:

"See the Gospel Church secure,
   And founded on a Rock!
All her promises are sure,
   Her bulwarks who can shock?
Count her every precious shrine;
   Tell, to after ages tell,
Fortified by power divine,
   The Church can never fail"

O blood-bearing body, haste with the healing and imparting the whole world needs! Thy need of this redeeming blood of Christ for life, health, and efficiency is Christ's own appeal! And as long as the unsaved world needs the blood of divine Redemption, the appeal of Christ Crucified and pouring out His Risen Life must be made. So may we hasten the King's Personal Return. "Even so come, Lord Jesus!

"Dear dying Lamb, thy precious blood
   Shall never lose its power,
Till all the ransomed Church of God
   Be saved to sin no more.

"E'er since by faith I saw the stream
   Thy flowing wounds supply,
Redeeming love has been my theme,
   And shall be till I die."

CHAPTER XLII

THE SUCCESS OF THE CROSS

THE note sounded at the beginning of this book was the centrality of the Cross. It is the source of Church success and the starting point of all Christian theology. With the same note this chapter shall close the book.

Bethlehem is the birthplace of Christ; but Calvary is the birthplace of Christianity. It is a spiritual eminence unrivaled. Its Cross-crowned height is the highest on earth, for there heaven and earth meet.

In a time of theological fog this preëminence of Calvary may not be apparent to all. Deep and many have been the mists that have gathered about it since the Saviour died. Yet through all times and seasons of fog, through all the conflicts of centuries raging around it, the Cross of Calvary has stood "Tow'ring o'er the wrecks of time." In truth it towers not only over the wrecked, but also over the unwrecked works of time, yea, over all the rest of the works of God Himself.

The centrality of the Cross is because of the primacy of Redemption; and the primacy of Redemption is because it represents God's greatest possible sacrifice. It is also paramount in importance because it meets man's primal need.

This paramount position of the doctrine of Redemption may be discerned only by the saved sense of proportion. Full salvation means, for one thing, salvation of the sense of proportion or value. When sin has deranged this sense, it attributes value to the worthless and injurious, and depreciates the ultimate and infinite values.

Jesus referred to the unbalanced sense of proportion when He said that some tithed little garden herbs and neglected the great matters of the law of God. Whenever we behold as small and low, that which God sees as great and high, we need to be saved to seeing as He does. Human lives are all unbalanced and misdirected as long as they are guided by a deranged sense of proportion or value, and are blind to the heaven-towering height of the Cross of Calvary.

I. AT THE FOOT OF THE CROSS IS THE SPRING OF CHRISTIAN THEOLOGY

So to speak, the Cross of Christ is the cradle of Christianity. The birth of every truly God-born soul takes place at the foot of the Cross. Not the Cross itself, but the Christ of the Cross is able to save. It is "Christ crucified" and not Christ apart from His death for us, who makes the sin-smitten soul well. The death of Christ is the life of him who trusts in it. The sacrifice of Redemption is the substance of salvation.

As no one can find life except through the life given on the Cross, so no theology worthy of the name of Christian has ever been born at any other place than at Calvary. All theology beginning its existence elsewhere is blind and without sense of spiritual proportion. And theology is purest when flowing forth fresh from the very fount of life in Christ. The nearer we come to the source of life in the Saviour, the better will be the theology of the life so endeavoring to account for itself and the life that gave it birth.

The foot of the Cross being the birthplace of Christian theology, Calvary is its native air. Such theology is never ashamed of its origin nor of the place thereof. Its characteristic cry is, "God forbid that I should glory save in the Cross of Christ." No theology which has been under the drip of the blood of the Cross, counts it other than a privilege to proclaim the blood of Redemption.

Theology with Calvary as its birthplace always proves true to the primacy of Redemption. Theology born on the Arctic ice-cakes of naturalism is naturally cold to the Cross; but the theology born of the passion of Redemption and with the divine warmth of the blood of Christ pulsing through it, can never freeze in the soul's veins.

Calvary-created theology is marked by the place it gives to what Christ wrought out for us in His death. With apologies to Scott—Breathes there a theology with soul so dead, that never to itself has said, this is my soul's own native land, the place where died the Son of God, that it might live in God and God in it.

Greatest of all the facts we know about God is this— that He gave His only begotten Son to save us to what He is. It is the very sanity of God that inspires this great estimate put upon the divine sacrifice for sin. By putting first His greatest gift, we come into deepest harmony with Him. Thereby, too, our sense of proportion and standard of value come to agree with that of God in other matters also.

On the plains of human life there is no more tragic failure of vision than the blindness of men to the supreme height of the love of God on Calvary. Its Cross is the holiest symbol of the highest sacrifice of divinest love. Heaven help us to see its heaven-reaching height! "Thy lovingkindness, O Jehovah, is in the heavens; thy faithfulness reaches unto the skies. Thy righteousness is like the mountains of God."

II. THE WORTH OF A THEOLOGY CONSECRATED AT CALVARY

Many consequences follow when the primal place is assigned to the redeeming sacrifice of Christ. They are more than we are able to enumerate. Here we shall look at but three of them—the worth of theology, the helpfulness of the pulpit, and the success of the Church. These all depend upon recognizing the primacy of the propitiation Christ became for our sins.

To begin with these in order, a theology which assumes that it is more Christian in spirit than the Scriptures which set forth the propitiation of Christ, loses worth at the start. The appointed and appropriate satisfaction to God should not be denied. All our satisfactions have to be reflections of those of God to be true. It is not a pagan idea that God is dissatisfied to the point of vexation with sin, and that Christ is God putting away this dissatisfaction by the sacrifice of Himself.[1] Rather it is paganism to deny this propitiation. But such terminology is unfair to heathenism, for it had no revelation of how God feels about sin and the propitiation which the Bible reveals.

There is more satisfaction than that of propitiation in Christ's sacrifice of Himself; there is the satisfaction of salvation, that God is saved unto us when we are saved unto Him. "Salvation unto God" sings one of the songs of Revelation. This wakens us to the wonder of what man is to God, to the marvel of the value man is to God. This wonder is genetic to worship as well as to theology. We worship in wonder, for wonder means appreciation; and by an appreciation of the greatest wonder of all—God's grace in Redemption—we are able to enter into right relation with Him. "With the heart man believeth unto righteousness," the righteousness of being made right with Him. We could be right with a man who had sacrificed his utmost for us, only by due recognition of that sacrifice. So failure to give Christ His place of preëminence in sacrifice for us would seriously interfere with all our relations with Him.

No matter what a man thinks about other things, a true estimate of this great work of God in Christ is essential to the health of his spiritual life and the wealth of his influence in the Church. Noting the distinction between the imitational and the evangelical types of faith, W. Mackintosh Mackay points out that each of the two great Christian classics presents one of these two contrastive but not necessarily contradictory views of the Christian life.

He says, John Bunyan in "Pilgrim's Progress" "begins in a resting and ends in a following," while Thomas á Kempis in "The Imitation of Christ" "be-

---

[1]. Edward Grubb, "The Meaning of the Cross," p 36 says: "That is to say it (atonement) is not used in the heathen sense of propitiating Him or trying to gain His favour When the expression 'to make atonement' is used, it is not in the sense of appeasing God Sacrifice, then, was not thought of by the Hebrew teachers and writers (whatever the popular conceptions about it may have been) as intended to propitiate God This is the vital distinction between the Hebrew and the pagan ideas . . And it would seem that the pagan idea tended continually to recur"

gins in a following and ends in a resting." The Roman Catholic conception of salvation by obeying the Church could never begin with "the rest of faith" in the finished Work of Christ. The Roman system puts a value on human sacrifice which Protestantism does not; and Protestantism puts a value on the sacrifice of Christ which the Roman system does not. So Mackay remarks that both John Bunyan and Thomas á Kempis agree that "Christ was lifted up, not as merely an example to follow, but as an atonement to believe in, as sacrifice and substitute."[2]

Not only does the feeling of Christian devotion take its rise at the Cross, but the Christian thinking which expresses it, comes from the same source. This is not merely a matter of arrangement of doctrines; it is a matter of seeing things as they are, and where such seeing is the power that transforms personality. The soul is "transformed by beholding" Christ as He is—the Crucified One—which means seeing Him in the character and proportions of the sacrifice He has made on our behalf.

Redemption from sin being the cardinal doctrine of Christianity, so regarding it helps mightily in understanding all the other doctrines of the Christian faith. Speaking on "Christ Crucified, the Central Thought of Christianity and of all Truth," Prof. Edwards A. Park, when preaching the dedication sermon of Broadway Tabernacle, New York City, said:

"The Atonement is a great theme—its greatness lies, in part, in its reducing all other doctrines to a unity, its arranging them around itself in an order which makes them all easily understood. We know in other things the power of unity amid variety. We know how simple the geography of a land becomes by remembering that its rivers although meandering in unnumbered circuits around the hills and through the vales, yet pursue one main direction from one mountain to the sea.

"Now all the truths of God flow into the Atonement. They are understood by means of it, because their tendencies are toward it; and it is understood by means of them, because it

---

2. The Disease and Remedy of Sin, pp. 125, 128

receives and comprehends them. . . . It gives to them all a unity by illustrating them all. Other truths are not so much independent themes, as they are branches growing upward or sidewise out of this one root; and they need this single theme in order that their relations may be rightly understood. . . . The Atonement crystallizes all other truths around itself, and reduces them into a system, not only because it explains them, but also because it makes them explain it."

III. REDEMPTION THE ORGANIZING DOCTRINE OF CHRISTIANITY

Without controversy great is the doctrine of the Death of Christ. It is the depth of this doctrine which leads to deeps of experience through believing in it. Denial of it has never tended to deepen theological thinking. Candid objectors to it have admitted that "the Old Faith" in divine Redemption has power and passion which opposing faiths never have. One reason for this is, the Old Faith draws from the deep things of God. Better have the Old Faith and new power than new faith and no power.

The Scriptures have not hesitated to present the deepest mysteries of the very processes of God in relation to man's sin. This is well illustrated in the revelation these processes make of the saving sacrifice of Christ. Here "deep calleth unto deep." The infinite deep of the divine movement in Redemption answers the call of the infinite deep of man's need of it.

Normally, the Christian has an open ear to the Word of God, for faith in God comes by hearing the Word of God. Now, all the rays of Scripture are focussed on the Crucified and Risen Christ. Holy Writ pictures and places Him as the center of Christianity and the source of it because His vicarious sacrifice is central in it. What He accomplished for us by His sacrificial death, He thereby became to us; and this must ever be foundational to our faith in Him. Our relation to Him is built on the significance of His work for us; and its significance is built on its efficacy; and this in turn secures our standing before God, and defines our spiritual situation for all time.

Before Christ's death, the outstanding fact of the situation of man was man's sinfulness. Ever since the central fact is Christ's Redemption from sin. If we had not been sinners and the Son of God had not died for us, the central fact of our situation would have been very different. Of necessity, then, the Cross of Christ stands in the center of the whole field of the facts of Christianity. It is from Calvary, therefore, we must ever take our theological bearings.

"Great is the mystery of godliness,"—the godliness of "God manifest in the flesh," revealing His love, and dying to redeem us. This is the mystery of all mysteries now made known, the gleaming revelation that lights up the whole field of Christian truth. Leave it out, and nothing remains to help us. Begin with any other truth as primary and an impenetrable maze of conflict, an inextricable tangle of contradictions confronts us.

The meaning and place of all the other Christian doctrines come into view in the light of Calvary. Speaking of this W. M. Clow says:

"I have long been convinced that the reason why there is so much which seems incredible and irrational in Christian thinking, is that it is incredible and irrational apart from the Atonement. All the realities which the Christian faith asserts—sin, guilt, judgment here and judgment to come, the love of God, the Virgin Birth, the stainlessness of Jesus, the assurance of peace with God—are ghostly and fleeting shadows unless in the light of the Atonement. . . .

"Apart from the Atonement that Christ rose from the dead is of no more consequence than that Lazarus came forth from his tomb. Even the Trinity is irrational, and never is accepted unless in the light of the Atonement. In the day when men empty the death of Christ of its sacrificial meaning, the coherence, the unity, the credibility of the other great doctrines of the Christian life, to which men so pathetically cling, are imperilled."[3]

IV. THE THEOLOGY OF A PULPIT OF POWER

The redeeming sacrifice of Christ is not only the organizing doctrine of Christian theology, it is also

---
3. The Cross in Christian Experience, p 316.

the power-giving truth of the pulpit. Giving the Cross its place of primacy has been the open secret of many a great ministry. Great preachers have come and gone; but the Great Theme of all truly great preaching goes on for ever.

It is held that gentlemen prefer to be faked by a fair female. The attractive fake fools many. Surely no preacher prefers brainless beauty in theology! The pulpit has had its mental as well as its moral tragedies. The most subtle and seductive spirit that has ever tempted the pulpit, is working overtime today. "Samson wist not that the Lord was departed from him." Men seem unaware that preaching Christ apart from His Cross, or preaching the Cross apart from its Godward efficacy, is deserting the Gospel, depleting the power of the pulpit, and devitalizing the grace of God.

Some one has said that in modern times Charles Haddon Spurgeon proved to be the greatest preacher, and could have been the greatest orator; and that Henry Ward Beecher was the greatest orator, and could have been the greatest preacher. Hearing Beecher men said, "What a preacher!" Hearing Spurgeon they said, "What a Christ!" Be that as it may, both of these great men of God gave the Cross of Christ its supreme place and rightful glory. Speaking in 1881 on the text "Without me ye can do nothing," Spurgeon uttered this striking sentence: "A sermon without Christ as its beginning, middle, and end, is a mistake in conception, a crime in execution."[4] And this peerless preacher knew no other than the Christ of vicarious sacrifice.

Some men take their handicaps and turn them into advantages; and others take their advantages and turn them into handicaps. On a recent Easter a preacher with a long ancestry of faithful ministers of the Word, and with a degree of doctor of philosophy from a leading university, said in his sermon on that occasion, "We no longer believe in Christ's physical resurrection, His Virgin Birth, His miraculous Gospel

---

4. The Metropolitan Tabernacle Pulpit, Vol XXVII, p 598

of salvation. Evolution precludes all that, and in time will give us a better gospel, a better Sermon on the Mount, a better Christ." Alas! What faith in the froth of a wave of thought refused to the Rock of Ages. "False teachers shall bring in destructive heresies, denying even the Master that bought them."

All faiths have their roots as well as their fruits; and it is their roots that determine their fruits. Faith rooted in the Incomparable Christ is bound to have the fruits of God in Redemption. On the other hand, faith in the chimera of an unproved hypothesis of agnostic philosophy, disguised as scientific theory, has the usual result of blindness to the fact that science is never hypothesis, and that scientific theory, in that sense, is a flat contradiction in terms.

The Spirit of the Master can never lead us to forsake the Master Himself, can never take the crown from His brow to put it on that of naturalistic unbelief. Preachers there be who, after all their efforts to prove evolution, are really illustrating devolution. Where could there be more downright devolution than that of the pulpit which displaces salvation by Christ with the slime-struggle of naturalism?

Vainly preachers keep on trying one experiment after another in the pulpit, though there but one thing, the pure Gospel of Jesus Christ, has ever succeeded,— in that which God accounts success. One of the outstanding ministries of this country was that of Theodore L. Cuyler. We may well heed his witness to a theology of pulpit power, for the testimony of one successful preacher is worth all the guesses of those who have failed. Dr. Cuyler said:

"Into that fact (of Redemption) are pressed three great and glorious ideas—Substitution, Sacrifice, and Salvation. The apostle's keynote struck amidst the idolatries of Corinth and, in defiance of Cæsar's lictors at Rome, has been the secret of converting power everywhere. Luther preached this Gospel of blood to slumbering Europe and it awoke from the dead. Amid all his emphasizings and defense of the divine sovereignty, Calvin never ignored or belittled the Atonement. Cowper sang of it in sweet strains. Bunyan made the Cross the starting-point for the Celestial City. John Wesley proclaimed it to the colliers of Kingswood, the swarthy miners of Cornwall. Spurgeon thundered his doctrine of vicarious Atonement into the ear of peer and peasant with a voice like the sound of many waters. The heart of God's Church has in all the ages held to this as the heart of all Christian theology. 'Christ died for our sins.' This sublime central truth is no more obsolete today than yonder sun in the firmament."

V. THE PREACHER'S APPOINTED TASK

The Christ-appointed business of the preacher is to preach Christ. Absolutely indispensable in a minister of the Gospel is this—that he be found faithful to the sacrifice of Christ as the cure of the world's curse.

If instead of presenting the divine ethic of himself as Redeemer, Christ had turned aside to preach mere morality, there would never have been any Christianity to preach. How could He have righted the world's social conditions while it remained rotten to the core with the social disintegration through the selfishness of sin? What can be cured and sin be left rampant? Is it not the health of faith in Christ that puts heart and life in ethics and social service?

The depersonalization of God makes true religion impossible. Even so, a devitalized Gospel makes true Christianity impossible. It is useless to seek eternal life in the casket of a dead theology laid out in the shroud of modern philosophy. The dead are but burying their dead when preaching fails to present Christ as "the resurrection and the life." No one more needs resurrection in Christ than the preacher who has ceased to see the world's need of Redemption.

As a master sermon-builder, true to His Master's message, and as the preacher of presentations as transparent as true, Alexander Maclaren of Manchester remains unsurpassed. Near the close of his life he gave an address to ministers entitled, "An Old Preacher On Preaching." The following is an excerpt from it:

"A Christ without a cross is a king without a throne. If our ministry is to have power, it must all center in the death for the world's sins. Otherwise, it will be like a lighthouse without a lamp. It will have no grip, no impulse, no regenerating power. 'I, if I be lifted up, will draw all men unto me.' There are preachers who demagnetize the Gospel, because they falter in the proclamation of the 'lifting up.'

"To keep fast by the Cross and passion of the Lord while he is following out the issues of his work to their remotest consequences, is the task of the Christian preacher in his capacity as teacher. . . .

"The wider the teacher sweeps his circle, the stronger must be its center. The more he lengthens his cords, the more he must strengthen his stakes—and the middle prop that holds up the tent is the Cross with Christ upon it. 'Him first, Him last, Him midst and without end!' All that the teacher has to teach is summed up in one word—Christ. His whole theme is 'the truth as it is in Jesus.'"

VI. THE THEOLOGY FOR CHURCH SUCCESS

The redeeming sacrifice of Christ is not only the dominant doctrine of Christianity, and the master-message of the pulpit; it is also the sovereign source of the success of the Church. Rejoicing recognition of its primacy is the sacred secret of faithful service to the mission of Christ to the world.

The old truism that, "Nothing succeeds like success," does not say what success is. That which is success to one, is failure to another. And some successes are but failures in disguise, even as some failures are in appearance only. How true this was of the failure of Jesus when challenged to come down from the Cross! What an infinite success was the defeat of His death! Has not His Cross become the criterion of the highest success—that of love and sacrifice? Surely then the church that succeeds in any other way, fails all the more therefor.

"Love never fails." Love abides for ever and its success with it, when all else has passed away. In the death of Christ love and sacrifice won a success consistent with the character of Christ and commensurate with the great-heartedness of God. Some one has said, "There are none so low but they have their triumphs; small successes suffice for small souls." Surely the obverse of this is also true. What a success it took to suffice for the sacrificial soul of the Son of God!

The early history of the Christian Church abundantly and unmistakably bears witness that all its evangelists and preachers emphasize the primacy of the Redemption of the Risen Christ. That which was fundamental then must still be so regarded, if Christianity is to remain Christian.

The accounts of the Four Gospels alike converge all their divine data about the death on Calvary. The New Testament never argues about the preëminence of the Cross of Christ; it simply proclaims it. This was not accidental on the part of these pioneers of the pulpit of Christ. Well did all these men of supernatural power know whence it came. Evidently they expected their successors would have the same appreciation of the supreme thing in human history.

The two great ordinances of the Christian Church appointed by Christ Himself bear witness to the paramount importance of His sacrificial death. "Baptized into His death." "Ye do show forth the Lord's death till He come." These most solemn observances of Baptism and the Lord's Supper have ever since published the primacy and centrality of the Cross.

The great missionary apostle, writing to one of the Churches which under God he had founded, said:

"I determined not to know anything among you, save Jesus Christ and him crucified. . . . I delivered unto you first of all that which I also received; how that Christ died for our sins according to the Scriptures; and that he was buried; and that he hath been raised on the third day according to the Scriptures."

VII. The Infallible Law of Success

The pulpit is a strategic place. Success or failure there means the success or the failure of the whole church. The pastor, as the appointed interpreter of Christ and Christianity, has the power to make or unmake the church. When the pulpit is faithful in fully magnifying Jesus Christ, the church will do one of two things: either it will silence such a pulpit or succeed along with it in faithfulness to Christ.

The law of Church success is as definite and unalterable as any law of nature or of the supernatural, whence the laws of nature have come. This is simply the law of adequate means. The Church succeeds only when it functions for Christ. Back of its efforts there is then the divine sufficiency. We live in a day when church methods are supposed to solve every problem and insure every success. While method has its importance, an adequate message and sufficient spiritual power will usually take care that the method be adequate. What is the use of the most up-to-date methods in a church whose message to the lost is gone? The best method without the presence of the Holy Spirit is worthless. The Adequate Advocate is rendered inadequate when Christ is presented apart from His redemptive death; and the sufficiency of the Holy Spirit is then disconnected from the Church. The law of Church success by the efficiency of the Holy Spirit no man can change. It is either of these alternates:— recognize this law or wither without its operation. The adequate Gospel preached by adequately equipped men is necessary to the adequate Church.

There is also the law of efficient contact. The contact-power of the Cross is essential to save the lost and to edify the saints. The unsaved know instinctively that a Crossless gospel or a Christless Christianity has nothing for them. While empty pews do not indicate great success, neither are crowds a sure proof of it. For a time the preacher may hold the crowd with natural ability and sheer hard work; but real success depends upon teaching them to crowd around the Christ, so that they will not scatter when he is gone, as a crowd does when the railway train pulls out. Too much preaching tries to capture eagles with decorated canary cages. He who called himself "the prisoner of the Lord," preached to all the Gospel of liberty in the one thing worth while, by becoming bond-slaves to the redeeming love of Christ.

To a church in living contact with Christ, His saving power can never be out of date. While the powers of enslavement are legion, He alone can liberate into life in God and its work of saving the lost. But one thing absolutely insures success to the Church, this is to give Jesus Christ full liberty in it to do with it as He pleases. He can give the keys to the Church, only as the Church gives Him the master-key to every room in its activities.

Christ's great purpose in the Church is to universalize His success in saving the lost. He must be the beating heart of the Church, if the throbs of success are to beat in all her arteries. We may well give Doctor Cuyler the closing word:

"This is the core and marrow of the Gospel. The Atonement is the cardinal doctrine of the New Testament. All its paths converge on Calvary. The Gospel does not underrate ethics or the beauty of human brotherhood or the spotless example of Jesus; but the Atonement is the sublimest display of divine love, and it transcends all other truths in saving power.

"If I could deliver but one discourse to all the nations of the globe, this would be my text, 'Christ Jesus died for our sins.' This is the touchstone for every pulpit. Whenever the highest power has been attained, there has been the most faithful preaching of the guilt of sin and of salvation through the redemptive work of Christ Jesus on the Cross of Calvary."

THE END

INDEX

Abbot, Lyman, 383
Absolute, 279
Adaptation, 172, 239, 242, 356
Appeasement, 52
Assurance, 37
Athanasius, 360
Atonement, 49, 50, 53, 55, 57, 62, 66, 71, 75, 78
Attitude, 217
Attraction, 227
Authority, 415

Balance, Law of, 192
Baldwin, J. M., 31
Bergson, Henri, 408
Betts, G. H., 396
Bible, 19, 31, 41, 60
Blindness and Vision, 86
Blood, 74, 76, 240, 242, 243, 428
Body, the Resurrection, 154
Boswell's Life of Johnson, 260
Bowne, Borden P., 17, 328
Brooks, Phillips, 152, 312, 341, 351
Brumbaugh, Martin G., 399
Bushnell, Horace, 34, 76, 199

Campbell, McLeod, 345
Carnegie, Andrew, 386
Cave, Alfred, 55, 65, 66, 69
Christ, 25, 26, 76, 86, 112, 147, 151, 167, 191, 197, 210, 212, 238, 240, 244, 296, 357, 411, 416
Christian, 35, 45, 46
Christianity, 20, 28, 30, 78
Church, 348, 389, 417, 428, 452
Clarke, W. N., 328, 333
Clow, W. M., 102, 448
Consciousness, 331
Correlativity, 337
Coe, G. A., 390, 401, 421
Covenant of Works, 71
Covenant of Grace, 72
Crawford, Dan, 299
Creation, 14, 79, 246
Cross of Christ, 164, 169, 175, 177, 187, 189, 227, 244
Cuyler, Theodore, 450, 455

Dale, R. W., 49, 113
Davidson, A. B., 15, 55, 56, 62, 64, 65, 280
Day, J. R., 386
Death of Christ, 19, 35, 36, 45, 94, 115, 155, 182, 184, 185, 187, 209, 229, 235, 240, 246, 301, 451.
Denney, James, 54, 94, 299, 309
Devil, Demons, 178, 232, 234, 265
Devotion, 21
Discernment, 42, 253, 258
Disease of Sin, 293
Disraeli, Benjamin, 136
Drummond, Henry, 294

Education, 394, 403
Effect, Godward, 202, 208, 274
Elect, 238
Enablement, 214-249
Eternal Atonement, 190, 207
Eternal Punishment, 311
Ethical Theory of Atonement, 53
Etymology as a Guide, 55
Evangelism, 24, 31, 401
Evolution, 29, 264
Experience, 27, 32, 35, 36, 155, 166, 173, 174, 259, 289, 291
Extent of Redemption, 190

Fairbairn, A. M., 268
Fairbairn, Patrick, 68, 69
Faith, 30, 36, 243, 257, 259, 321, 338, 350, 352
Fatalism, 264
Fatherhood of God, 208, 226, 363
Fellowship, 376, 378
Forgiveness, 107
Forsaking on the Cross, 181
Freedom, 403, 415
Froude, James A., 120
Fulfilment, 78, 79, 83, 87, 90, 93, 97, 106, 102, 139, 176, 190, 196, 208, 214, 216, 329

Genesis of Theology, 21, 28, 29, 32, 242
Genetic and Generic, 37, 45
Genetic Truth, 25, 34, 46

INDEX

Glory of God, 162, 163
God in Person, 18, 80, 89, 90, 106, 115, 143, 190, 274, 203, 218, 220, 362, 290, 409
Grace, 122, 135, 218, 220
Grubb, Edward, 445
Guilt, 342

Haering, Theodore, 57, 271
Hall, Charles C., 173
Heartbreak of Christ, 179, 185, 210, 211
Heart and Spirit, 43
Heaven, 236, 310
Hell, 307, 310
Henderson, Chas. R., 387
Holiness, 100, 116, 133, 280, 343
Holy Spirit, 27, 35, 40, 42, 44, 45, 58, 59, 98, 120, 147, 204, 275, 345, 360, 375, 377
Howard, John, 100
Humility, 229, 231

Identification, 141, 150
Illingworth, J. R., 326, 328, 340, 360
Immanence, 186, 282, 286, 375, 377
Imputation, 113
Incarnation, 20, 82, 115, 144, 147, 152, 156, 186, 210, 312, 324
Including Nature of Life, 323, 330
Institution, 145, 146, 194
Isaiah, 85

James, William, 293
Jehovah, 15
Jesus, the Name, 15
Johnson, Franklin, 5
Jones, Prof. R. V, 339
Judgment of Christ, 215
Justification, 346, 350

Kenosis, 93, 115, 181, 230, 237
Kidd, Benjamin, 392
King, Henry Churchill, 29
Kurtz, J. H., 69

Ladd, George T., 320, 330
Laplace, Pierre Simon, 278
Law, the Moral, 71
Life, Personal, 323, 325
Light of God, 87
Limitation of Christ's Knowledge, 181, 210
Lorimer, George E., 392

Lotze, Hermann, 328
Love, 121, 124, 126-139, 214, 216, 362

Mackintosh, H. R., 11, 333
Maclaren, Alexander, 24, 52, 402, 451
Mackay, W. Mackintosh, 293, 315, 445
Matter, 15
McCormack, R., 77
Method of Redemption, 141
Milton John, 49, 82, 249, 307
Miracle, 29
Moberly, R. C., 107, 326, 337
Modalism, 204, 333
Modernism, 27, 28, 41, 42
Morality, 91
Morgan, G. Campbell, 60
Morrison, G. H., 282, 283
Moral Judgment, 257
Moses, 85
Muller, Julius, 267, 306
Mullins, E. Y., 29, 287, 404

Name, Significance of, 14, 159
Naturalism, 42, 263
Nature, 32
Necessity of the Cross, 199, 239
Nevius, John L, 232
Newton, John, 266
Nicoll, Sir W. R., 114, 232, 313, 393

Omnipresence, 285
Other-consciousness, 90, 104, 335
Optimism, 315

Park, Edwards A., 446
Parker, Joseph, 163, 301, 308
Passover, 69
Paul, 84, 140, 146, 353, 382, 453
Pentecost, 25
Penal Theory, 107, 133, 145, 149, 176, 183, 191, 210, 213
Penalty, 127, 184, 308
Personality, 18, 77, 110, 130, 165, 166, 213, 238, 242, 274, 306, 319, 323, 327, 329, 339, 409
Philosophy, 23, 24
Physical Phase of Experience, 154
Piepenbring, Ch., 56
Possessing, 119, 372, 379, 381, 386
Prayer, 340
Preaching, 24, 25

INDEX 459

Priesthood of Christ, 73
Process of Fulfilment, 151
Propitiation, 52, 55, 92, 117, 151, 223
Psychological Interpretation, 278

Quincy, Josiah, 414

Ransom, 52, 54
Rauschenbusch, Walter, 275, 389
Reality of Redemption, 31
Reason, Place of, 23
Reconciliation, 54
Re-creation, 245
Redemption, 19, 50, 52, 59, 61, 78, 82, 91, 105, 108, 137, 175, 213, 226, 239, 241, 369, 411, 447
Religious Education, 398
Releasement by Death, 236
Repentance, 107, 191, 355
Responsibility, 275
Revelation, 396
Riddle of the Universe, 314
Righteousness, 71, 111, 132, 133, 171, 219, 361
Ritschl, Albrecht, 54, 213

Sacrifice, 61, 70, 73, 76, 89, 91-106, 110-118, 121, 163-173, 215, 220, 223, 226, 235, 246, 335, 348, 372
Salvation, 16, 17, 18, 50, 358, 395
Saphir, Adolph, 70, 72, 73, 74
Sawyer, A. W., 278
Satisfaction, 223
Schleiermacher, F. E. D., 271
Science and Theology, 11, 28
Selbie, W. B., 59
Self-conscious, 77, 90, 135, 151, 303, 304, 332
Self-denial, 101
Self-expression, 130
Self-giving, 134, 225
Self-realization, 135, 151, 165, 168, 174, 178, 277, 298, 303, 305, 319, 335, 410
Self-sacrifice, 101, 160, 161, 173, 178, 180, 210, 221
Septuagint, 54
Serum, Cure by, 240
Seth, James, 328
Sin, 19, 36, 51, 65, 77, 83, 94, 95, 168, 172, 187, 214, 223, 240, 253, 256, 298, 305, 309, 316

Snowden, James H., 18, 327
Social Christianity, 142, 383
Sons of God, 197, 226, 362, 367
Source of Redemption, 99, 110
Spinoza, 279
Spirit of Christ, 26
Spirit and Thought, 34, 38, 43
Spirit and Place, 42
Spirit Fulfilled, 79, 98, 121
Spiritual Death not that of Christ, 182
Spring, Gardiner, 229
Steven, George, 425
Stevens, G. B., 54
Strong, A H., 161, 372
Struggle of Christ, 154, 158, 170, 180
Spurgeon, C. H., 256, 449
Substitution, 145, 194
Substance of Christ's Work, 78, 89, 99
Subjectivism, 334
Supernatural, 16, 17, 157
Symbol, 70

Temptation of Christ, 157
Theologian, 11, 16, 27, 30
Theology, 11, 14, 27, 28, 33, 34, 41, 44, 58, 442, 451
Thought and Spirit, 38, 39, 42, 45
Theories of Atonement, 81, 191
Transcendent, 286
Trinity, 89, 90, 93, 103, 143, 165, 202, 213, 224, 247, 333, 358, 365
Truth, 34, 39
Type and Symbol, 70

Unchangeable Past, 192
Unity, 247, 419
Union with Christ, 372
Upshaw, Senator, 399

Vedder, Henry C., 390
Vicarious, 145, 193, 195, 198
Virgin Birth, 152, 153, 156, 324

Ward, James, 278, 331
Wescott, B. F., 198
Will, the Human, 320
Word in Creation, 14
Worship, 99, 438
Wounds of Christ, 212, 213, 295
Wright, Caroll D., 384